The Autobiography of
W. E. B. DU BOIS

The Autobiography of
W.E.B. DuBOIS

A Soliloquy
on Viewing My Life
from the Last Decade
of Its First Century

International Publishers

Dedicated to
My Great Grandfather: JAMES DU BOIS
My Grandfather: ALEXANDER DU BOIS
My Parents: ALFRED DU BOIS and MARY BURGHARDT
My Children: BURGHARDT GOMER DU BOIS
YOLANDE DU BOIS
DAVID GRAHAM DU BOIS
My Granddaughter: DU BOIS MCFARLANE

SBN (cloth) 7178-0235-3; (paperback) 7178-0234-5

Library of Congress Catalog Card Number: 68-14103

Manufactured in the United States of America

EDITOR'S PREFACE

Relatively rare are those whose autobiographies are published; very rare are those who live so long and so consequentially that two autobiographies see the printed page. But surely a rarity of rarities—if not quite unique in literature—is one to whom it is given to produce three autobiographies and have all three published.

It is this rarity that the reader now holds. In his 50th year —1918-1919—Dr. Du Bois wrote *Darkwater: Voices from within the Veil*, copyrighted in 1920 and published in 1921 by Harcourt, Brace; in his 70th year—1938-1939—he wrote *Dusk of Dawn: An Essay toward an Autobiography of a Race Concept*, issued in 1940 by the same publisher. And in his 90th year—1958-1959—he wrote the basic draft (somewhat revised by him in 1960) of this present book. The manuscript was carried by the Doctor to Ghana late in 1961 and published, in somewhat shortened versions, in 1964 and 1965, in China, the USSR, and the German Democratic Republic. Rescued from Accra, after the military coup of early 1966, the manuscript is now published for the first time in the language of its composition and in full. It is published as Dr. Du Bois wrote it; changes have been few and only of a technical nature—correcting a date, completing a name, and the like.

In the "Apology," introducing his *Dusk of Dawn*, Dr. Du Bois wrote, "in my own experience, autobiographies have had little lure"; hence, that book was, as its subtitle indicated, not so much a conventional autobiography as an essay on the concept of race as illuminated by his own life. And his earlier *Darkwater* tried, through impressionistic essays and impassioned poetry, to lift the veil and illuminate life within and without from that vantage point.

The present volume is quite different from the other two not only because of its additional two-decade span, and the significantly altered outlook of its author, but also because in it—unlike the others—he seeks, as he writes, "to review my life as frankly and fully as I can." Of course, with the directness and honesty which so decisively characterized him, he reminds the reader of this book of the intense subjectivity that inevitably permeates autobiography; hence, he writes, he offers this account of his life as he understood it and as he "would like others to believe" it to have been.

Certainly, while Dr. Du Bois was deep in his ninth decade when he died, longevity was the least remarkable feature of this Promethean life. As editor, author, lecturer, scholar, organizer, inspirer, and fighter, he was among the most consequential figures of the century. Necessarily, therefore, the full and final accounting of that life and his times—by the man who lived it and experienced them—becomes an indispensable volume for all to whom Life itself has any meaning.

The editor provided occasional translations in square brackets in the text, as well as the reference notes, selected bibliography, and biographical calendar to be found in the appendices of the book.

October, 1967   HERBERT APTHEKER

CONTENTS

PART THREE

APPENDICES

ILLUSTRATIONS

Follow page 192 of text

PART ONE

CHAPTER I

MY 15TH TRIP ABROAD

August 8 was a day of warm and beautiful sunshine, and many friends with flowers and wine were at the dock to bid me and my wife goodbye. For the 15th time I was going abroad. I felt like a released prisoner, because since 1951, I had been refused a passport by my government, on the excuse that it was not considered to be "to the best interests of the United States" that I go abroad. It assumed that if I did, I would probably criticize the United States for its attitude toward American Negroes. This was certainly true.

Later the State Department changed its reasons, and refused to issue a passport unless I declared in writing that I was not a member of the Communist Party. As a matter of fact, I was not a member of that party. Yet I refused to make any statement on the ground that the government had no legal right to question me concerning my political beliefs.

Then unexpectedly the Supreme Court of the United States handed down a decision in 1958 which said that "Congress had never given the Department of State any authority to demand a political affidavit as prerequisite to issuing a passport." The Department of State in July issued passports to several persons who previously had been denied the right to travel, including Paul Robeson and his wife, and me and my wife, Shirley Graham. Paul and his wife went abroad immediately, and we prepared to follow in September, but since the President of the United States rushed a special message to Congress asking for new legislation, we hurried and sailed early in August.

The sea was calm throughout the trip. The ship was well arranged; although the air conditioning on our inside cabin did not function well. The passengers were rather more courteous that I expect Americans to be, and we had pleasant social relationships with the Rumanian ambassador to the United Nations and his family.

On arriving in London, our luggage was subjected to more careful examination than we have ever been used to, but finally we were courteously released, and with our good friend Cedric Belfrage drove from Southampton to London, through New Forest, and near Bedales, where my daughter attended high school. We stopped three weeks in Paul Robeson's apartment while he was singing in Moscow.

During August and September, I saw something of Britain, Holland and France; then in the Fall and early Winter, I lived in the Soviet Union, resting a part of the time in a sanatorium. In the Winter and Spring I was three months in China, and then returned to Moscow for May Day. I visited the tenth session of the World Council of Peace in Stockholm, and finally stayed a month in England. On July 1, 1959, I came home.

I mention this trip in some detail because it was one of the most important trips that I had ever taken, and had wide influence on my thought. To explain this influence, my Soliloquy becomes an autobiography. Autobiographies do not form indisputable authorities. They are always incomplete, and often unreliable. Eager as I am to put down the truth, there are difficulties; memory fails especially in small details, so that it becomes finally but a theory of my life, with much forgotten and misconceived, with valuable testimony but often less than absolutely true, despite my intention to be frank and fair.

Who and what is this I, which in the last year looked on a torn world and tried to judge it? Prejudiced I certainly am by my twisted life; by the way in which I have been treated by my fellows; by what I myself have thought and done. I have passed through changes by reason of my growth and willing; by my surroundings without; by knowledge and ignorance. What I think of myself, now and in the past, furnishes no certain document proving what I really am. Mostly my life today is a mass of memories with vast omissions, matters which are forgotten accidentally or by deep design.

Forty years ago when at the age of 50, I first essayed a

brief autobiography, my memories furnished many details and conclusions which now disappear or return as quite strange. There are of course some fixed documents, like that memorandum on my 25th birthday, some letters to my mother, and that priceless letter to former President Hayes. In *Dusk of Dawn* I wrote much about my life as I saw it at the age of 70, which differs much from what I think at the age of 91. One must then see these varying views as contradictions to truth, and not as final and complete authority. This book then is the Soliloquy of an old man on what he dreams his life has been as he sees it slowly drifting away; and what he would like others to believe.

The century in which was mine to live is now in its last decade. In all probability I shall not finish it, since life seldom goes by logical completeness, but I shall be near enough its end to speak with a certain sense of unity. In all my plans and dreaming, I do not remember ever thinking of a long life. The people of my family on both sides usually reached the 70's, but I know none of 90; and my immediate parents died in their 50's.

I remember writing a sort of semi-biography on my 50th birthday in my book called *Darkwater*. I was not thinking of immediate death, but I was sure that by far the largest part of my life had passed. Indeed, it characterized my day that most men thought their work would be about done at 60 and they would be dead or practically dead at 70.

Yet, I had no thought of dying. At 65 I had accepted a life-time job at Atlanta University without a moment's pause to ask what was to happen when I was judged too old to work. That neglect to worry about my old age was peculiar and contradicted my complete surroundings. In my own family old folk found a home with relatives; but in the surrounding community the first worry of the average citizen was for provision for his old age. Personally this problem never bothered me until suddenly at 75 I was retired from work with practically no savings, and no pension in view sufficient to support me. Failure to give attention to this part of my future was due to no laziness or neglect. I was eager to work and work continuously.

CHAPTER II

WESTERN EUROPE

I know Western Europe through a repeated series of visits covering the years 1892 until the present. I knew Germany as a student and traveler before the world wars, and as a traveler since. I had lived at times in various places in England and Scotland, in France, and in Holland and Belgium. I have been more briefly in Switzerland, Italy, Spain and Portugal; in Greece, Turkey and in the old Austro-Hungarian empire. During my earlier visits, Europe seemed very much like America, but older, with a longer history, and with inspiring memories of the past, in buildings and monuments, and in cultural differences.

This time I noticed more because here was a group of countries which had been through the terrible experiences of world war. Revolution had shaken the world, and now mankind in this center of Western civilization was trying to rebuild itself into something new. I, on the other hand, represented something old which had projected itself into a new America, and clothed in slavery and poverty had begun a modern race problem. I looked therefore upon this world, as I had looked before, as a member of the darker race, which had suffered from the oppression of the white European world.

As a student, I had learned of the struggle between races; of the way in which the slave trade had been stopped, slavery abolished, colonial imperialism begun, until finally in the 20th century the nations of Europe had fallen to fighting each other over the problem as to who should dominate Asia and Africa. I came to Europe to learn if now European imperialism was about to disappear, and what hope we had of a future. Was a world of peace and racial equality about to emerge?

I was disappointed. London was a clean and comfortable city, with parks, trees and flowers. England was still a leading nation. Holland was clean and respectable; yet both these nations frightened me. I knew the restraint and correct manners of the British; their excellent newspapers, studious magazines and thoughtful books. But today, in streets and gatherings, in shops and factories, there lurked a great fear. The British empire was falling. The domination which Englishmen had so long exercised over the world was approaching an end, and nothing could stop it; and this the British knew. They were leaning with increased dependence on the wealth and technique of the United States, which could be seen in the vast American investment in buildings and business, and in the increasing, even if sullen, respect for American manners and opinion.

I knew that in the past, to put the matter bluntly and simply, the British empire had built its prosperity on cheap labor, which the colored peoples of the world were forced to do, and on lands and materials which had been seized without just compensation by the British throughout the world. Granted that in the past the British had been morally no worse in their exploitation of labor and wealth than other peoples, and had even worked more efficiently and scientifically than most, and thus had become more wealthy and powerful; nevertheless, the terrible result of all this had been world war, universal murder and destruction, maiming and disease to an extent that made many men despair of the future.

I came therefore to Europe in 1958, to try to learn if possible how far the lessons of the past were guiding the future, and what the hope of that future was. I came to the conclusion that the people of Britain were determined to proceed on the whole along the same paths which they had followed in the past—that they were determined to maintain their comforts and civilization by using cheap labor and raw materials, seized without rightful compensation, and to change their treatment of other people only if this required no essential yielding of comfort or even luxury.

This system had been in use during the last half of the 19th century. It worked so well that in the 20th century

Britain and France, Germany, Italy, Russia, the Netherlands and Belgium fought each other in terrible wars for a redivision of the spoils of colonial exploitation. This fighting complicated the situation by increasing the demands of home labor for higher wages and by arousing the consciousness of the colonial peoples who were brought in to assist in the fighting, and who began to demand increased income for work, larger use of land, and even political power. The second half of the century faced a free India and China; a struggling Indonesia; growing demand for autonomy all over the rest of Asia and Africa; with repercussions in South and Central America, and the islands of the sea.

Leading and encouraging this revolt and unrest, is Russia, transformed into the Union of Soviet Socialist Republics, which denies the right of private ownership of capital, the profit motive in industry, and colonial imperialism.

Girding itself against this is the United States of America, which arose 200 years ago as a free-thinking democracy, with limitless land and resources; but which sank into dependence on slave labor, transformed itself into a vast center of capital monopolized by closed corporations, and now seeks to replace the British empire by stopping socialism with force, and ruling the world by private capital and newly invented technique.

Western Europe views this duel with frightened amazement. I see in Britain, France, the Netherlands and Belgium, the utter and desperately-held belief of the ruling classes in these lands that their culture and comfort depend absolutely on cheap labor, seized land and materials belonging to defenseless peoples; some of these workers are their own "lower classes," most of whom are the "lesser breeds without the law." Western Europe hopes that without essential alteration in its way of life an accommodation can be made between their demands and the upsurging of the lower classes and peoples.

They see this chance in four ways: home labor appeased by elementary education and some political power; with higher wages paid out of profit from investment in foreign lands, which the home labor makes sure by fighting in world wars. They hope to make the alteration in their way of life minor, by the rise of a small class among the backward peoples who will join them in exploiting their own people for the profit of both themselves and the imperialists. Their home labor may through trade union activity win increasing wages out of the large profit of the employers; their taxes and military service abroad will make such grants agreeable to investors. If the colonial peoples grow impatient revolt may ensue and war start; this imperialists with atom bombs can win unless the communist countries join in fighting, and if neutrals like India and Egypt stand aside.

On the other hand, what seemed to me absolutely certain was that if the majority of the world's people who are unsheltered, with starvation and poverty, can in reasonable time obtain a minimum supply of food, clothing and shelter, and the beginning of modern culture, imperialism cannot maintain itself unless Western acquisitive society pays for it with less comfort, less luxury, and goods and privileges more equally divided. This price, as it seems to me, Britain, France, Holland and Belgium, refuse to pay, and here lies the problem of the modern world. No country of Western Europe is ready for such sacrifice. No labor party will risk lower wages in order to improve the condition of colonial labor.

I realized this most startlingly in Holland. It was a Dutchman who in the early 18th century kidnapped my great grandfather on the coast of West Africa, and sold him into slavery in the valley of the Hudson. This was the century in which the Dutch began to take part in that stealing of labor in Africa, started by Portugal and Spain. The British in the 18th century succeeded in displacing them as the world's greatest slave traders, and established slavery in their American colonies. This commercial rivalry between the Dutch and British resulted finally in a system of Dutch colonies which covered Southeast Asia.

The center of this colonial empire was Indonesia, whose land, materials and cheap labor made the Dutch people rich and comfortable, and their land became famous for cleanliness and beautiful flowers. Then the Indonesians revolted, and I visited Holland just at the time when the full realization of the meaning of this blow was being felt. Colored people of mixed Dutch and Indonesian blood had begun to pour into Holland, bringing problems of race and class. Incomes of the well-to-do were being reduced. The impact of the Second World War was now being realized. I made the mistake of speaking on peace at a Hague cultural club, composed of teachers and professional men—social workers and the white collar class. They did not want to hear about peace, and least of all about peace between America and the Soviet Union, because it was the Soviet Union that kept Holland from regaining Indonesia, and it was America which was the Soviet Union's great rival for domination of the world.

Therefore in a Europe which had suffered grievously from war and destruction, a prosperous and intelligent people did not want to hear about peace. To me this was a surprise and disappointment; to those who listened to me the occasion was a disappointment and an insult. They wanted comfort and civilization even if that involved the same imperial control of land and labor on which the civilization of the Dutch had long been based.

I turned from Holland and went swiftly to France, passing by Belgium and its current exposition. I had a feeling that what I might say in Brussels concerning the Belgian Congo would not be pleasant for the Belgians to hear. I came to France at the time when De Gaulle was making his great bid for domination. I had seen France first in 1892, and last in 1950. I sensed the crucifixion through which the French people had lived. All my life, France had been close to me. My name was French, my blood was part French. I knew Paris better than any city in the world outside America. I spoke a little of "the most beautiful language in the world." I had experienced on French soil less prejudice of color and race than anywhere else in the world. I would have gladly made France my home, if that had seemed consonant with my duty to American Negroes.

Here, in 1949, I had seen the greatest demonstration for peace, for the total abolition of war that I had ever imagined possible. Now ten years later all this was being overthrown. France again was at war and preparing for war. France under a great but strangely mistaken idealist was searching for a glory that could never be regained. There was death in her eyes, in her speech, in her gestures. The gates of my most loved of public parks, the Luxembourg Gardens, were guarded by police armed with machine guns. I saw Algerian boys searched on the public streets. Fear, hate and despair rode the streets of Paris.

I have looked upon this quivering of France; the dark death which shadows its life today. I have seen the sting of new grim poverty, and the concentrated power of its great wealth. Here loom French genius and taste along with ruthless will and drunken beauty. The beautiful wine of France has in its way been its undoing. I remember my friend [John] Hope,[1] somewhat naive and unsophisticated in the ways of the wicked world, once said to me in France, as he was working for the Young Mens' Christian Association, "Du Bois, the French do not get drunk, they stay drunk!" When the French went to Algeria and the blight came to French vineyards, the colonies stopped planting the wheat which fed the Algerian people, and planted grapes instead. Cheap Algerian wine poured into France and undersold French wines, while the people of Algeria starved. Then came more drunkenness, revolt and war. There is the eternal struggle and endless contradiction within a people who can never die, so long as men remember Roland, the kings called Louis, Napoleon and Alexander Dumas.

Sweden was a sort of last glimpse of Western Europe before I returned home. I had long known of the Scandinavian nations. Socialists called them the "middle way" between private capitalism and communism. They saw the increase of social control of the welfare state over the anarchy of individual profit. The new housing intrigued me; the pension system, the schools. This was the way Socialists hoped to ward off revolution and save rugged individualism. My recent visit was symbolic. Ten years ago in 1949, I had sat in on the formation of the World Council of Peace after that marvelous Paris meeting. Then for nine years I missed the meetings for lack of a passport. I could not attend that meeting which adopted the great "Stockholm Appeal," which America called a "Communist trick" to disarm the West. The meetings continued, and most of the world joined, but I was not present. Then came 1959, and I could attend. I gave up visits to Hungary and the Balkans, which I would have loved to make. I saw Sweden, that beautiful Northern light nesting on its 14 islands. I saw what is perhaps the finest popular housing in the world.

Sweden had avoided war, but she was not welcoming world peace. I was amazed as I realized this. She did not want this World Council of Peace to meet in Stockholm. She would not repulse it, but she gave it no welcome. Her press and pulpit ignored it. Her homes, with a few exceptions, closed their doors in the face of many men and women of world leadership, because they met to promote world peace, and because they met together with nations who did not believe in private capitalism, but did hate war. It was astonishing. Was Sweden afraid, and if so, of what? Did peace encourage communism, and if so, what an admission! Was Sweden frightened of America and Britain? If so, what an accusation! I saw an Indian author whose books, never printed in the United States, I was just reading. He looked a bit upset; he said, "My Swedish publisher asks me not to call on him until this Council meeting is over." Only a few citizens of Stockholm attended the service in honor of Frederic Joliot-Curie. Few met Eugenie Cotton, the white-haired leader of the women of France, and Madame Isabelle Blume of Belgium, who helped keep me out of an American jail.[2]

Today, to my mind, Western Europe is not prepared to surrender colonial imperialism. It clings desperately to the wealth and power which comes from cheap colonial labor, held in serfdom by modern technique. There is no European labor party ready to help emancipate the workers of Asia and Africa. On the contrary, all are willing to take higher wages based on colonial profits; and to fight wars waged to defend those profits. Back of this attitude of Western Europe is the United States: ready with funds to help Europe; ready to assist any European power to keep control of colonial peoples, or to supplant it as colonial ruler.

CHAPTER III

THE PAWNED PEOPLES

In the center of Europe lies Germany, long a pawn of France, then a plaything of Napoleon; but under the Hohenzollerns, a mighty empire seeking European leadership. Overreaching itself, it was overthrown in the First World War, groveled in bankruptcy and distress until Hitler roused it to frenzy and drove it to attempt world domination on a scale that frightened humanity. The Soviet Union and the allies overthrew him but, refusing further alliance after the war, the allies tore Germany in two. The United States led. France eagerly cooperated and Britain could not hesitate for fear of offending the United States.

But center and spark of the whole scheme was big business: the German cartels, the great French manufacturing and mining corporations and the interlocked banks of Britain and America were united in imperial enterprise and determined to make a new Germany which would restore the plan to dominate the world under Western control. To these great corporations were added the trade unions of Britain and the United States who believed that their high wage depended on the profits of big business from exploitation of labor and seizure of materials in colonies. They tried to take control of the new colonial unions at the Paris meeting of trade unions in 1945, but failed. Eventually, however, they split the unions into two groups of capitalistic and communistic organizations, while the African unions called a fifth Pan-African Congress in England. This meeting I attended and presided over.

The British unions and the American Federation of Labor united to divide Germany and to restore the Nazis to power in West Germany. Naturally, the military joined the movement led by General Clay, who was the head of corporations making immense profits in North and South Africa, and collecting money in America for a "Crusade for

Freedom" to overthrow communism. A former president of Harvard became High Commissioner of West Germany, representing not only American intellectuals but also the corporate wealth which was supporting the great universities of the United States. The Marshall Plan furnished new capital to West Europe, dominated by America, and strengthened the fight against labor. Thus the same forces which at one time sought to overthrow the Soviet Union, now were united to build a great capitalist state in West Germany and, bypassing the United Nations, formed NATO with military might led by the officers who once followed Hitler. The mass of the West German people were the Social Democrats who once fought the Hohenzollern monarchy.

East Germany, known as the German Democratic Republic, was led by the heirs of social democracy and manned by socialist workers. It is developing the faith of Karl Liebknecht and Rosa Luxemburg and becoming a socialist state, after the pattern of the Soviet Union. This was the Germany where I attended the University in 1892, and here I went in 1959. It looked familiar. It had dropped its old name "Friederich Wilhelm" and was now the Humboldt University of Berlin, named after the great scholar. I walked down Unter den Linden to the Brandenburger Thor. There I stopped. I could not visit again my old lodging on the Schöneberger Ufer. That lay in "West" Berlin, and if I had entered, American soldiers might arrest me on any pretext they invented. I turned back and traversed a city with new buildings and enterprises, along with ghosts of war and destruction. In the great hall of the University, with women students now common but in 1892 never admitted, I sat in the office where in my day Rudolph Virchow had presided as Rector Magnificus. A group played the soft music of Sebastian Bach, and the faculty of economics bestowed on me the honorary degree of Doctor of Economics. I had coveted this degree 65 years before, but then the University of Berlin would not recognize my graduate study at Harvard, and I was not allowed to take the examination.

Between Western Europe and the Union of Soviet Socialist Republics, lie a number of nations: the Baltic states; Poland, Czechoslovakia and Hungary; and to the Southwest, the Balkan states of Albania, Bulgaria and Rumania. These peoples differ in race and composition, but have had a history with many resemblances. Most of their territory has long been ruled by a hereditary aristocracy of conquerors, invaders and great landholders. They have been annexed by neighbors, and have fought each other. During the world wars, most of this territory came to be looked upon as a *Cordon Sanitaire;* nations which would be used eventually by the West to reconquer Russia, or at least to recover lost investments; and by the new Soviet Union, it was looked on as territory which it must neutralize in sheer self-defense against expanding Western capitalism.

These are the folk whom the Americans call, "The Captive Peoples," and they include the Baltic states of Esthonia, Latvia and Lithuania; Poland, which for centuries has been raped and torn by Europe; Bohemia and Slovakia, long a part of the Austro-Hungarian empire; and the Hungarian part of that alliance. Many of these lands have been the center of the political ambitions of the Roman Catholic church. Beyond these lie the Balkans, including today Bulgaria and Rumania, and portions of what once belonged to Turkey and Greece.

I have seen some of these countries on this trip and during former journeys. I was in Poland in 1893 and 1950. I was in Czechoslovakia in 1893, 1950, and 1951. Save my sojourn in Germany, these trips were not long enough for intensive study and observation, but taken together they tell an interesting story. For one thing, there is no doubt in my mind but that the people in these lands are far better off in 1959 than in 1893 or in 1950. They are better fed and better dressed, and they look more content. I shall never forget the abject groveling of the Polish church worshippers in 1893; and how that year my Berlin classmate, Stanislaus Ritter von Estreicher, begged me to visit him in Krakow, so as to show me how much more Poles were oppressed than

Negroes in the United States. His father, librarian of the University, opened my doubting eyes. In 1950, Poland showed the horrible crucifixion which she had suffered under Hitler, but she showed also the beginnings of mighty resurrection.

Czechoslovakia is a prosperous nation. The people are busy and decidedly more hopeful than when I had previously seen the nation. Prague has spilled over into the neighboring valleys, and is grov ing. Socialism is making a normal growth; even Slovakia, which when I had spoken there in 1950 seemed sullen if not discontented, is now humming with new hope and housing. I remember my lovely girl guide and interpreter of 1951, and her enthusiasm for socialism.

In Prague I had one surprise which lifted my spirits. Charles University was founded 100 years before Columbus discovered America. It was a great center of learning in the Middle Ages, and after the First World War many persons in the West hoped that Charles University would lead the resistance against communism. It did not. It accepted communism, and now in addition it honored me in the face of the known attitude of the United States toward Negroes. No American university (except Negro institutions in understandable self-defense) has ever recognized that I had any claim to scholarship. I had no reason to think that Charles University even knew my name. But I was summoned to the restored beauty of the old Caroleum, and amid the fanfare of medieval trumpets, marched in procession with rector and faculties of the University to the high rostrum. I was given the degree of Doctor of the Science of History, *honoris causa,* while the "Star-Spangled Banner" was played in honor of my American citizenship. This gesture of a communist nation doubtless prejudiced me in favor of socialism. But I do not think it was alone decisive.

In neighboring Hungary I sensed the age-old strife between the Roman Catholic church and landholding aristocracy in one group; the rising bourgeoisie supported by Western enterprise and capital in another group; and the great mass of degraded peasants who, as I saw them in 1893, were distinctly below the level of American Negro serfs. I was not surprised when the pushing businessmen and artisans, calling themselves "Commons" and despising laborers and serfs, rebelled against communism in 1956. I was glad when the Soviet Union intervened and thus served notice on all reactionaries that the Russian revolution was still unwilling to yield its gains before a show of force. The Hungarian Academy made me a corresponding member.

I did not see the Balkans in 1959, but I met many of their folk. I knew what their petty aristocrats, joined with American money, had made their masses endure in the last century. I cannot imagine that the people of the Balkans are worse off today than they were in the 19th century. I think they are much better off. The University of Sofia gave me a degree, before I left America.

Today the majority of intelligent people who work for a living in the Baltic states, Poland, Czechoslovakia and the Balkans seem to me quite evidently to want communism. It was quite true a generation ago that most of the landholders, capitalists and aristocracy in these lands opposed communism, and being the only ones with political power could truly say that their countries, as they represented them, did not want to be socialized. But these classes did not represent the mass of people, and when this mass obtained political power, they built and held communist states.

Between the First and Second World Wars, Western capitalism and Soviet socialism sought to increase their influence in these states. The First World War broke up the anomalous Austro-Hungarian empire with the vast political backing of the Roman Catholic church. Germany seized Austria. Poland became independent, with the landlords in control and a dictatorship under Pilsudski from 1926 to 1935. In Czechoslovakia, land was distributed widely among the peasants, and a bourgeoisie under Masaryk and Benes took control, helped by Western investors. The First World War left the rich Ukraine independent, but it was later fought over by the Soviets, then Germans and by the bandit

Denikin, backed by the West. By 1920 the Soviets were in control.

To call these peoples "captive" is misleading. The great mass of them were the pawns of privilege and exploitation. They reeled helplessly under the blows and beckonings of their masters. Their upper classes represented the rich and privileged among them who called the nation their property, and sought to dominate it for their own personal advantage, assuming that what was good for the ruling classes was best for all. On the other hand, there was the doctrine of communism being tried out under great difficulties in the Soviet Union. This system would be in continual danger and attack, partly because they believed that the masses of people in the Baltic states, Poland, Czechoslovakia and the Balkans needed for their own good, just the system which the Soviet Union was trying with much success to install.

Then came the rise of Mussolini and Hitler, threatening war in order to redistribute not only the colonies of Asia, Africa, South and Central America, but to add to this exploited area Eastern Europe, which their rivals had hitherto monopolized. A series of political moves ensued. Hitler threatened the Soviet Union. Stalin sought alliance with the West against Hitler, and was repulsed. The West, ignoring the Soviet Union, joined with Hitler at Munich in opposition to the Soviet Union. The Soviet Union in countermovement accepted a non-aggression pact with Hitler. Dropping his mask suddenly, Hitler now attacked the Soviet Union, and the West, certain that the vast German war power would wipe out communism, stood aside. Let Nazis and Communists kill each other off, said Truman. Help either when the other weakens.

The world watched with bated breath. The United States and Britain helped the struggling Soviet Union as it tottered; but the help was slow, and at no time did it form a decisive part of what this sorely beset nation needed. Finally, to the surprise of mankind, David overpowered Goliath, and the Soviet Union won the war over Germany at Stalingrad. Western capitalism instead of seeing communism destroyed, found itself in 1945 allied with triumphant communism.

The Pawned People whose future depended so absolutely on the outcome of this war were in a curious situation. Poland was at various times on both sides; now fighting the Soviet Union; now fighting the Germans; but to the very end refusing to treat the Soviets as trusted allies. When at last the Poles led a premature attack on Warsaw, the Soviet army suspicious of where the Poles stood, refused to take part. The end of the war left Poland in doubt between the Soviet Union and Germany, which was backed by Britain, France and America. The political power of Roman Catholicism tried to compel a decision, but communism held. It was the Soviet armies in the end that rescued Poland from their cruel captors. Hungary fought against the allies and was punished by the wretched treaty of 1947. Frustrated land reforms, false democracy, foreign investors and anti-communist revolt led to the effort to overthrow communism which was stopped by the intervention of the Soviet Union. Czechoslovakia fought with the Allies, but her bourgeois leaders bitterly opposed communism, until the rising political power of the workers proved that further opposition was useless.

Thus, these states, whose former rulers wished to ally themselves with the West, were opposed by the mass of their people who had long suffered from exploitation and disfranchisement. To the disgust of the ruling classes the working classes and peasants gradually gained control and introduced socialism on the Soviet model. The Baltic, Polish and Slav immigrants to the United States had left for the most part before the success of socialism in the Soviet Union and were led by American propaganda to oppose socialism in their native countries. They used their political power against the socialist regimes and gave money and refuge to counter-revolutionists. There is no doubt that the present condition of the peoples of these countries is improving and is far better than 50 years ago. They have the support of the overwhelming mass of their inhabitants.

CHAPTER IV

THE SOVIET UNION

I have in a sense seen the Union of Soviet Socialist Republics grow, not as a casual visitor, nor hurried tourist. In 1926, I saw a Russia just emerging from war with the world. The people were poor and ill-clothed; food was scarce, and long lines stood hours to get their share. Orphan children, ragged and dirty, crawled in and out of sewers. The nation faced foreign force, and Russian traitors. Yet, despite this, I saw a land of hope and hard work. Schools were multiplying; books were being printed and widely read; workers were being protected with a living wage, nurseries for children, night schools, trade unions and wide discussion.

Indeed this wide discussion and criticism intrigued me. Never had I seen such public interest in social matters on the part of men, women and children. Here was a people seeking a new way of life through learning the truth, and cooperating with each other and by willing sacrifice. Not everybody was happy, but most Russians saw a bitter past being succeeded by a great future, not swiftly, but surely. I visited Kronstadt, Leningrad, Moscow, Nizhni Novgorod, Kiev and Odessa. There were no signs of prostitution or unusual crime. There was some drunkenness, but little gambling. Priests were plentiful, and tarnished gold-domed churches abounded, but dogma was being driven from the schools. Above all, the spirit of the people was high, the officials were working desperately hard and with efficiency.

I had known that Tsarist Russia naturally resisted the revolution. But of the extent of that counter-revolution and of the active help in manpower, material and arms supplied by the civilized world; of the spying and intrigue from all Europe which had accompanied and inspired this war of reaction, I had but the vaguest information. Indeed I did not learn the whole story until Michael Sayers and Albert Kahn published their *Great Conspiracy* in 1946.

What amazed and uplifted me in 1926, was to see a nation stoutly facing a problem which most other modern nations did not dare even to admit was real: the abolition of poverty. Taking inspiration directly out of the mouths and dreams of the world's savants and prophets, who had inveighed against modern industrial methods and against the co-existence of progress and poverty, this new Russia founded by Lenin and inspired by Marx and Engels, proposed to build a socialist state with production for use and not for private profit; with ownership of land and capital goods by the state, and with state control of public services, including education and health. It was enough for me to see this mighty attempt. It might fail, I knew, but the effort in itself was social progress and neither foolishness nor crime.

Russia was handicapped by 90 per cent illiteracy among her peasants, and nearly as much among her working classes; by a religion led by a largely immoral priesthood, dealing in superstition and deception, and rich with the loot of groveling followers. Most of her industrial capital was owned by foreigners, whose only interest was the 50 or 75 per cent profit which they reaped from merciless exploitation. Her government had long been shot through with dishonesty and graft under dissolute nobles and fawning lackeys. Her punishment of crime and independent thought had long affronted the civilized world. Yet the best people of Europe and America seldom raised a finger of protest, but fawned on Russian royalty and aristocracy, receiving them with open arms and expressing loud sympathy when they were repudiated.

There is no question but that governments can carry on business. Every government does. Whether governmental industry compares in efficiency with private industry depends entirely upon what we call efficiency. And here it is, not elsewhere, that the Russian experiment is astonishing and new, and of fateful importance to the future of civilization. What we call efficiency in America is judged primarily by the resultant profit to the rich and only secondarily by the results to the workers. The face of industrial

I was on Red Square at the great Seventh of November celebration with a half-million spectators. A uniformed major escorted me to the hotel, and on the way we stopped and saluted Khrushchev and the government, and Khrushchev raised his hat.

Next I went to a sanitarium. I was weary from travel. It is a great solemn place with tall pines and snow. We had servants for every wish, and all were as kind as can be. I was there a month, and had every probe and test possible. My heart was measured a dozen times, my blood tested, my blood pressure taken, and I was poked inside and out.

I was granted an interview with Prime Minister Khrushchev at my request. For about two hours, I and my wife, Shirley Graham, discussed with him the peace movement in the United States and the Pan-African movement.

I told him of my indictment and acquittal in 1951 of the charge of not registering as a foreign agent, because I secured signers for the Stockholm Appeal. We discussed the tenth anniversary of the World Peace Council. I talked about African independence and unity, and of establishing in Moscow an institute under the Academy of Sciences to study African history and culture.

I said Africa has just taken a decisive step at the conference at Accra toward independence, union and free cultural development. The first effort of Africans will be in political lines and then for industrial progress and economic organization; I said education will receive attention, but resources will be limited, and teachers scarce. I said that here the Soviet Union can be of great assistance to new Africa. The scientific study of Africans and their continent was necessary for the guidance of their education and the organization of their culture. This was one of the ways in which the progressive world could help its lagging parts and one in which there were fewest causes for friction and diversity of interest.

I suggested, therefore, that the Soviet Academy of Sciences establish an institute for the study of Pan-African history, sociology, ethnography, anthropology and all cognate studies.

This institute of the Academy would aim at promotion of scientific research into all the activities, past and present, of the peoples of Africa, together with a study of their physical and biological environment. This series of studies would be carried on with the central idea of the unity of the whole subject and the conviction that history is not separate from sociology, or culture from biology, but that all research in such related fields seek the one end of unified scientific knowledge. While this enterprise would start and center in the Soviet Union, its object would be the welfare and progress of Africa, and from the first, it should seek cooperation wherever it could be found, and especially among Africans.

The institute should try, by offer of scholarships to Africans, and by cooperation with African students and institutions of learning, eventually to build within Africa a center of scientific study, which would lead in world study and in the promotion of world peace.

Realizing how in modern history the exploitation and almost universal underestimation of Africans have led to wide denial of the very existence of their history and culture, it would be a first duty of this institute to make known the history of the African peoples and to distribute knowledge of this in libraries and museums, in textbooks and university studies, and as common knowledge. No greater work for world peace can be conceived, no quicker way to convince mankind that no part of it must exist for the exploitation and comfort of the rest at the cost of suffering black folk. Already this institute has been established, with my friend Ivan Potekhin at its head.

The Soviets are making a new people, a disciplined people. This is not a matter of police; few police are in evidence, and there is little giving of orders. Secret dread? I sense none. But let me illustrate: Out from my hotel window I look on two great squares; the furthest is Red Square with the towers of the Kremlin walls and the brown tomb where Lenin sleeps his last long sleep. Across these squares yesterday a half-million people marched, walked, and danced; they ate and sang, they laughed and cheered. This morning when I arose and looked out, there was not a scrap of paper or sign of dirt. That meant work in the night I'm sure, but it meant much more than this: it meant that most of this half-million people dropped no dirt and threw away no paper, and they did this not under orders, but because they felt these squares were theirs, and they must not soil their own. These people feel a vested interest in this nation such as few Americans feel for the United States.

Why? I do not know, and yet it may be because they are consulted about it. They are asked, continually asked; they sit and sit and talk and talk, and vote and vote; if this is all a mirage, it is a perfect one. They believe it as I used to believe in the Spring Town Meeting in my village. There is power rivalry and personal jealousy; all things in the Soviet Union are not perfect. Mails miscarry, cables come a day late, styles are often queer; the world problem of domestic service has not been settled. The question of life careers and the decision between what one wants to do and what one is fitted to do, and what efforts are needed—these matters have not yet found final answers; but they are being frankly faced, and experiments are making.

The Soviet Union is great and growing greater, and, as it seems to believe, it belongs to this two hundred million folk about me. I am strongly inclined to agree with them.

Nowhere are public questions so thoroughly and exhaustively discussed. Russians sit and listen long to talks, lectures, expositions; they read books, magazines and newspapers, not just picture books. Each problem of existence is discussed in village and factory. Comments, spoken and written, are welcomed, until every aspect, every opinion has been expressed and listened to, and the matter rises to higher echelons, and is discussed again. Gradually agreement is approached, until when the thrashed-out result reaches the All-Soviet height, there is usually but one opinion and decision.

This is not unexpected. How many right answers to each of our problems are there? This is a sifting of democracy which the West has lost. In America there is little real political discussion. It is discouraged in every way; by stopping meetings, refusing use of halls, closing columns of newspapers, refusing radio time, and even by police interference and jail. In Britain there is freer discussion, but it is limited by convention and prestige; by aristocratic influence and the money and leisure of the dominant class. In France, parliamentary debate is directed by the powerful interests who work the puppets and pull the strings. In Italy, the church stands always in the shadow, keeping watch above its own. The church represents wealth, and wealth rules.

In the Soviet Union the overwhelming power of the working class as representing the nation is always decisive. Above this and rising out of it and expressing its thoughts and ideals, rises the real aristocracy of the Soviet Union, the writers and scientists. They get the highest wage, they enjoy such privileges as the law and public opinion allow. How free are they? Science is free from religious dogma and vested interests. The writer has a wide leeway and rich applause, but he is limited by the aims of socialism to serve all and not a few, and by the fear of foreign attack which in the past has nearly ruined the Soviet Union. The recalcitrant writer, the idealists and dreamers disagree, but variety of opinion is becoming reassuringly common and open. As the Soviet Union becomes stronger and more self-confident, and less sensitive to that Western opinion which has so long ruled the world with a rod of gold, it will become freer. Never, I hope, so free as to betray the ideals of the land as French writers have betrayed France, and as American writers distort truth today.

For years most American leaders regarded the figures on Russian progress as exaggerations or lies. The Teachers' Union once begged me not to say in answer to a citation that the schools of Moscow were better than those of New York. Ex-President Conant of Harvard declared that the Communist party would not allow promotion to higher schools by examination; presumably only by favor. Then came Sputnik. Then followed unanswerable proof of Soviet su-

periority in science. There were revealed the startling figures
as to education in schools and colleges.

What I saw in the Soviet Union was more than triumph
in physics; it was the growth of a nation's soul, the confidence
of a great people in its plan and future. And beyond that the
realization around the world that the Seven Year Plan was
not boasting, but knowledge shared by 200 million people.
Around these millions were gathered even greater millions
in China, Vietnam and Korea, who believed in socialism,
and sought communism.

Is it possible to conduct a great modern government without autocratic leadership of the rich? The answer is: this is
exactly what the Soviet Union is doing today. But can she
continue to do this? This is not a question of ethics or economics; it is a question of psychology. Can Russia continue to
think of the state in terms of the workers? This can happen
only if the Russian people believe and idealize the workingman as the chief citizen. In America we do not. The ideal of
every American is the millionaire—or at least the man of
"independent" means of income. We regard the laborers as
the unfortunate part of the community, and even liberal
thought is directed toward "emancipating" the workingman
by relieving him in part, if not entirely, of the necessity for
work. The Soviet Union, on the contrary, is seeking to make
a nation believe that work, and work that is hard and in
some respects even disagreeable, and to a large extent physical, is a necessity of human life at present and likely to be
in any conceivable future world; that the people who do this
work are the ones who should determine how the national
income from their combined efforts should be distributed;
in fine, that the workingman is the state; that he makes
civilization possible and should determine what civilization
is to be.

For this purpose he must be a workingman of skill and
intelligence, and to this, Russian education is being organized. This is what the dictatorship of the proletariat means.
This dictatorship does not stop there. As the workingman is
today neither skilled nor intelligent to any such extent as

his responsibilities demand, there is within his ranks the Communist party directing the proletariat toward their future duties. This is nothing new. In the governments "of the people," we have elaborate and many-sided arrangements for guiding the rulers. The test is, are we and Russia really preparing future rulers? Insofar as I could see in the Soviet Union, in shop and school, in the press and on the radio, in books and lectures, in trade unions and national congresses, the Soviet Union is; we are not.

It is the organized private capital of America, England, France and Germany which is chiefly instrumental in preventing the realization of the Russian workingman's psychology. It has used every modern weapon to crush Russia. It sent against Russia every scoundrel who could lead a mob, and has given him money, guns and praise; and when Russia nearly committed suicide in crushing this civil war, modern industry began the industrial boycott, the refusal of capital and credit, which is being carried on today just as far as international jealousy and greed will allow. And can we wonder? If modern capital is owned by the rich and handled for their power and benefit, can the rich be expected to hand it over to their avowed and actual enemies? On the contrary, if modern industry is really for the benefit of the people, and if there is an effort to make the people the chief beneficiaries of industry, why is it that this same people is powerless today to help this experiment, or at least give it a clear way? On the other hand, so long as the most powerful nations in the world are determined that the Soviet Union must fall, there can be but a minimum of free discussion and democratic difference of opinion in the Soviet Union.

There is world struggle then in and about Russia; but it is not simply an ethical problem, as to whether or not Russia can conduct industry on a national scale. She is doing it today and in so doing she differs only in quantity, not in quality, from every other modern country. It is not a question merely of "dictatorship." We are all subject to this form of government.

There is under communism a use of women for more than

pleasure and physical reproduction; but primarily for their talent in work and thought. This has made possible the increase of medical facilities, since 60 per cent of the Soviet physicians today are women. With this goes a socialization of the family group. It is no longer customary to regard babies as playthings or nursery jobs; or as means of prolonging the father's cultural patterns, or to inherit his wealth or privileges. The child is becoming a recognized ward of the state to be raised and educated for the welfare of the people of the state and not merely for the privilege of a family group or of a special class. For this purpose nurseries, kindergartens and schools are provided; cooperative kitchens and dining rooms. The masses of communist women are being released from household drudgery, and the state has a tremendously widened reservoir of ability to serve its needs.

The Soviet Union which I see in 1959 is power and faith and not simply hope. When the Seven Year Plan was announced, not only Soviet citizens but the world knew that this nation could do what it planned, and barring no unexpected difficulties would reach these enormous goals. It is only a matter of time and a comparatively short time when the Soviet Union will lead the world in industry.

The Russian question is: Can you make the worker and not the millionaire the center of modern power and culture? If you can, the Russian Revolution will sweep the world. One can stand on the streets of Moscow and Kiev and see clearly that Russia has struck at the citadels of power that rule modern countries. Not manhood suffrage, women's suffrage, state regulation of industry, social reforms, nor religious and moral teaching in any modern country have shorn organized wealth of its power, as the Bolshevik Revolution has done in Russia. The Soviet Union seems to me the only European country where people are not more or less taught and encouraged to despise and look down on some class, group or race. I know countries where race and color prejudice show only slight manifestations, but no white country where race and color prejudice seems so absolutely absent. In Paris, I attract some attention; in London I meet elaborate blankness; anywhere in America I get anything from complete ignoring to curiosity, and often insult. In Moscow, I pass unheeded. Russians quite naturally ask me information; women sit beside me quite confidently and unconsciously. Children are uniformly courteous.

We had just finished our trip through Western Europe, when a cable came inviting us to a conference of Asiatic and African writers at Tashkent. I had heard nothing of this meeting, but had wanted very much to attend the conference at Bandung in 1955. Again my government had prevented me, and the message which I had sent by an American Negro reporter reached nobody. Further correspondence made our attendance upon this Congress at Tashkent seem of real importance. It was 2,000 miles southeast of Moscow, with five hours difference in time. The passage branched from my trip in 1936, veering toward the South. We heard the blood of Stalingrad far to the West, where Stalin conquered Hitler and saved Europe. After leaving Kazan, we crossed Kazakhistan and entered Uzbekistan. We were near the storied Samarkand; where:

> *In Xanadu did Kublai Khan,*
> *A stately pleasure dome decree*
> *Where Alph the sacred river ran*
> *Through caverns measureless to man*
> *Down to a sunless sea.*

But today there is sunshine over the 150,000 square miles of the Uzbek Soviet Socialist Republic. Over seven million brunette and curly-haired folk of Asiatic descent live here speaking a language differing from the Russian, and inheriting an old culture. Tashkent, a city of over 600,000, founded in the seventh century on the trade route between Samarkand and Peking, welcomed its guests with banners and applause. They filled the festooned streets. Their fields were growing tall, long-staple cotton, which an American Negro from Tuskegee first planted. New housing was replacing the old compounds, and schools were spreading.

The huge square with its fountain had a new modern

hotel on one side, and on the other a great conference hall with facilities for translating into Russian, Arabic, Chinese and English. This choice of languages was significant. The city was adorned, and the square filled with people greeting the visitors, and besieging the stalls, where books were on sale, and not chewing gum and hot dogs. One stall sold in a day ten thousand rubles worth of books in the Tartar language alone.

One hundred and forty writers from 36 countries and 45 writers from the Soviet Republics were present. We saw and heard of men whose works are read by millions, and yet whose names most of us Westerners had never heard. I was surprised to find my work known to many of the delegates, and the Congress gave me a standing ovation when I entered. I was shown to the platform, where I sat as a member of the directing committee. The discussion and the papers were mainly on cultural matters, although politics, and especially colonialism continually forced themselves to the front. The interrelation of all cultures was stressed, and the contribution of the West, despite its aggression against Asia and Africa. As one poet from the mountains of Daghestan said, "We must not confuse colonialism with culture, nor Dreiser with Dulles." Efua Sutherland, a black woman from Ghana, called the conference "A step toward unification of the disrupted soul of man." A permanent Afro-Asian writers' bureau was set up, with headquarters in Ceylon, to publish books, a journal, and an encyclopedia, and to promote translations.

I leave one subject to the last, as I leave the Soviet Union —religion. I lived two months opposite the inscription on the Second House of the Soviets, written by Marx: "Religion is the opium of the people!" Whatever was true of other lands, this was certainly true in Russia in 1926 and before. Symbols of religion ruled Moscow, the vast five domes of the Cathedral of Christ and the 350 other churches of the city dominated the landscape, as they loomed and glowed. There were gems of beautiful bejewelled churches; hordes of priests intoning litanies, begging alms, forgiving sins. There were thousands of shrines. Only one who has heard the chant of a Russian service, seen its color and genuflections; only those who know the gorgeous litany and the beauty of Russian churches can realize what Lenin, agreeing with Marx, meant when he called the Russian religion "opium."

But is was worse than opium. It was a Russian priest, Father Petrov,[3] who said of Russia in 1908, "There is no Christian Tsar and no Christian government. Conditions of life are not Christian. The upper classes rule the lower classes. A little group keeps the rest of the population enslaved. This little group has robbed the working people of wealth, power, science, art and religion, which they have also subjected; they have left them only ignorance and misery. In the place of pleasure they have given the people drunkenness; in the place of religion, gross superstition; and beside the work of a convict, a work without rest or reward. The ruling clergy with its cold, heartless bony fingers, has stifled the Russian church, killed its creative spirit, chained the Gospel itself, and 'sold' the church to the government. There is not an outrage, no crime, no perfidy of the state authorities, which the monks who rule the church would not cover with the mantle of the church, would not bless, would not seal with their own hands."

The British Trade Union report of 1925 said: "A very strong propaganda in the Press, the schools, colleges and Trade Union clubs is, however, carried on against religion generally, and especially as practised by the old Orthodox Church. The former Government-controlled licensed houses of prostitution where girls were exposed for hire at recognized fee, have been closed. In Tsarist days these houses were a recognized government institution; the opening ceremony was undertaken by a police officer and the premises blessed by Russian Orthodox Priests."[4]

All this has gone and none regrets that the Russian Orthodox religion has been dethroned. But the Russian church remains and other churches still carry on in the Soviet Union. However, the Soviet Union does not allow any church of any kind to interfere with education, and religion is not taught in the public schools. It seems to me that this is the greatest gift of the Russian Revolution to the modern world. Most educated modern men no longer believe in religious dogma. If questioned they will usually resort to double-talk before admitting the fact. But who today actually believes that this world is ruled and directed by a benevolent person of great power who, on humble appeal, will change the course of events at our request? Who believes in miracles? Many folk follow religious ceremonies and services; and allow their children to learn fairy tales and so-called religious truth, which in time the children come to recognize as conventional lies told by their parents and teachers for the children's good. One can hardly exaggerate the moral disaster of this custom. We have to thank the Soviet Union for the courage to stop it.

The United States has moved from the hysteria of calling all Soviet women prostitutes, all Russian workers slaves and the whole Russian people ready for revolt, of regarding all Soviet rulers as criminals conspiring to conquer the United States and rule the world; of breaking every treaty they made. From this false and utterly ridiculous position, we have begun to recognize the Soviet Socialist Republic as giving its people the best education of any in the world, of excelling in science, and organizing industry to its highest levels. Our increasing number of visitors to Russia see a contented people who do not hate the United States, but fear its war-making, and are eager to cooperate with us. From such a nation we can learn.

CHAPTER V

CHINA

I saw China first in 1936, on my trip from the Soviet Union to Japan. I was struck by its myriads of people. This amorphous mass of men, with age-old monuments of human power, beauty and glory; with its helpless, undefended welter of misery and toil, has an organization of life and impenetrable will to survive that neither imperial tyranny, nor industrial exploitation, nor famine, starvation and pestilence can kill—it is eternal life, facing disaster and triumphing imperturbably.

There passed a glory from the earth when Imperial China fell. Built as it was on skulls, it was bravely built and the remains are magnificent. In all essential respects they surpass the Stones of Europe. Where Europe counts its years in hundreds, Asia counts its in thousands. There is absent that all too apparent European effort to dramatize and exaggerate the past; to emphasize war and personal glory. China shows a finer effort to let the past stand silent, frank and unadorned; to tell the truth simply about men and fully; and to record the triumphs of education, family life and literature far more than murder.

I write this now as things were in 1936. I am standing on the Great Wall of China, with 23 centuries beneath my feet. The purple crags of Manchuria lie beyond the valley, while behind are the yellow and brown mountains of China. For 70 cents I have been carried up on the shoulders of four men and down again. And here I stand on what has been called the only work of man visible from Mars. It is no mud fence or pile of cobbles. It surpasses that mighty bastion of Constantinople, which for so many centuries saved Mediterranean civilization from German barbarism. This is a wall of carefully cut stone, fitted and laid with perfect matching and eternal mortar, from 20 to 50 feet high and 2,500 miles long; built by a million men, castellated with perfect brick, and

44

standing mute and immutable for more than 2,000 years. Such is China.

Shanghai was an epitome of the racial strife, the economic struggle, the human paradox of modern life. Here was the greatest city of the most populous nation on earth, with the large part of it owned, governed and policed by foreign nations. With Europe largely controlling its capital, commerce, mines, rivers and manufactures; with a vast welter of the greatest working class in the world, paid less than an average of 25 cents a day; with a glittering modern life of skyscrapers, majestic hotels, theatres and night clubs. In this city of nations were 19,000 Japanese, 11,000 British, 10,000 Russians, 4,000 Americans, and 10,000 foreigners of other nationalities living in the midst of 3,000,000 Chinese. The city was divided openly by nations; black-bearded Sikhs under British orders policed its streets, foreign warships sat calmly at her wharfs; foreigners told this city what it may and may not do.

Even at that, matters were not as bad as they once had been. In 1936, foreigners acknowledged that Chinese had some rights in China. Chinese who could afford it might even visit the city race track from which they and dogs were long excluded. It was no longer common to kick a coolie or throw a rickshaw's driver on the ground. Yet, the afternoon before I saw a little English boy of perhaps four years order three Chinese children out of his imperial way on the sidewalk of the Bund; and they meekly obeyed and walked in the gutter. It looked quite like Mississippi. And, too, I met a "missionary" from Mississippi, teaching in the Baptist University of Shanghai!

I went by invitation to the American-supported University of Shanghai and I said to the president that I should like to talk to a group of Chinese and discuss frankly racial and social matters. He arranged a luncheon at the Chinese Banker's Club. There were present one of the editors of the China press, the secretary-general of the Bank of China, the general manager of the China Publishing Company, the director of the Chinese Schools for Shanghai, and the executive secretary of the China Institute of International Relations.

We talked nearly three hours. I plunged in recklessly. I told them of my slave ancestors, of my education and travels; of the Negro problem. Then I turned on them and said, "How far do you think Europe can continue to dominate the world, or how far do you envisage a world whose spiritual center is Asia and the colored races? You have escaped from the domination of Europe politically since the World War— at least in part; but how do you propose to escape from the domination of European capital? How are your working classes progressing? Why is it that you hate Japan more than Europe when you have suffered more from England, France, and Germany than from Japan?"

There ensued a considerable silence, in which I joined. Then we talked. They said, "Asia is still under the spell of Europe, although not as completely as a while back. It is not our ideal simply to ape Europe. We know little of India or Africa, or Africa in America. We see the danger of European capital and are slowly extricating ourselves, by seeking to establish control of capital by the political power of taxation and regulation. We have stabilized our currency—no longer do English Hong Kong notes form our chief circulating medium. Our wages are too low but slowly rising; labor legislation is appearing; we have 16 million children in school with short terms and inadequate equipment, but a beginning of the fight against our 90 per cent illiteracy."

We talked three hours but it was nearly a quarter of a century before I realized how much we did not say. The Soviet Union was scarcely mentioned, although I knew how the Soviet Union was teaching the Chinese. Nothing was said of the Long March which had just ended its 6,000 miles from Kiangsi to Yenan, led by Mao Tse-tung and Chu Teh. We mentioned America only for its benefactions and scarcely for its exploitation. Of the Kuomintang and Chiang Kai-shek, almost nothing was said, but hatred of Japan for its betrayal of Asia was amply pointed out.

In 1959 I came again to China. I wanted to re-visit China

because it is a land of colored people; and again because in 1956 China had officially invited me to visit and lecture, but the United States had refused to permit me. My passport stated that it was "not good for travel to China." It was a fair conclusion that if I did not use this passport to secure entrance to China and made no claim on the United States for protection, the State Department had no legal right to forbid me to visit China. Certainly the United States could give me no less protection in China than it could in Mississippi. On the other hand by legal fiction, the United States was still "at war" with China, since the Korean War had never been legally finished. It was possible then if I went to China, to jail me for "trading with the enemy." This risk I thought it my duty to take, since my invitation to visit had been renewed by the cultural minister, Kuo Mo-jo and by Madame Soong Ching-ling.

I left Moscow February 9 and returned April 6. It was the most fascinating eight weeks of travel and sight-seeing I have ever experienced. We remember Peking; a city of six million; its hard workers, its building and re-building; that great avenue which passes the former forbidden city, and is as wide as Central Park; the bicycles and pedicycles, the carts and barrows. There was the university where I lectured on Africa, and a college of the 50 or more races of China. We looked out from our hotel window at the workers. They all wore raincoats beneath the drizzle. We saw the planning of a nation and a system of work rising over the entrails of dead empire.

I have traveled widely on this earth since my first trip to Europe 67 years ago. Save South America and India, I have seen most of the civilized world and much of its backward regions. Many leading nations I have visited repeatedly. But I have never seen a nation which so amazed and touched me as China in 1959.

I traveled 5,000 miles, by railway, boat, plane and auto. I saw all the great cities: Peking, Shanghai, Hankow and its sisters; Canton, Chungking, Chengtu, Junming and Nanking. I rode its vast rivers, passed through its villages and sat in its communes. I visited its schools and colleges, lectured and broadcast to the world. I visited its minority groups. I spent four hours with Mao Tse-tung and dined twice with Chou En-lai, the tireless Prime Minister of this nation of 680 million souls.

We come to Chengtu. We ride about this farthest Western stopping place, close to the crowds and the workers and the homes, old and new. We visit a commune of 60,000 members. We climb the mountain to see irrigation being widened today, yet started 2,200 years ago. There is a glorious temple on its summit, and below a wide lake between winding roads. Four rivers roll down from the Himalayas, out of Tibet into the Yangtze.

Then we fly to Kunmin, the end of the American Burma Road. It is warm and quiet, and at the state school the minorities dance and sing welcome, and among them are Tibetans. There are more Tibetans in China than in Tibet. In Tibet while we were on its border in Szechuan, the landholders and slave drivers and the religious fanatics revolted against the Chinese, and failed as they deserved to. Tibet has belonged to China for centuries. The Communists linked the two by roads and began reforms in landholding, schools and trade, which now move quickly. At Kunmin we were at the end of the Burma Road and near the Great Mekong River. Below lay Vietnam, Laos, Cambodia and Thailand. The nest of grafters, whoremongers and gamblers at Saigon, helped by Americans, have broken the Geneva treaty which closed the French Indo-Chinese War, and are attacking the Communists. That is called "communist aggression." It is the attempt of American business and the American Navy to supplant France as colonial ruler in Southeast Asia.

There is at Canton a marble commercial building where the import and export exposition was recently opened. There are five floors of exhibits. I am convinced that America cannot make anything which is not today being made by China, or which cannot be made cheaper, and for the most part made quite as well; for out of the things that China makes come no profits for private exploiters. Most nations of the world are beginning to buy **China's** goods, except the United States. China sells increasingly to Europe, to Asia and South America; to India, Burma, Ceylon, Indonesia, and Malaya; to Africa and the West Indies; to Australia and New Zealand. And such goods: silk and woolen clothing, watches, clocks, radios and television sets; looms, machinery and lamps, shoes and hats, pottery and dishes. All Chinese seem to be at work, and not afraid of unemployment, and welcoming every suggestion that displaces muscle with machinery.

In every town and city we went to the opera, and can never forget the assault of the Monkey King on the hosts of Heaven, facing God and the angels. A night sleeping train took us over the 30-hour trip from Peking to Wuhan. There I saw the bridge that had been miraculously thrown across the Yangtze. We rested in a little hotel adorned with flowering cabbages. We visited the great steel mills and shook hands with welcoming workers. The colored American prisoner of war who stayed in China rather than return to America and is happy with his wife and baby, came to visit us.

My birthday was given national notice in China, and celebrated as never before; and we who all our lives have been liable to insult and discrimination on account of our race and color, in China have met universal goodwill and love, such as we never expected. As we leave may we thank them humbly for all they have done for us, and for teaching us what communism means.

The people of the land I saw: the workers, the factory hands, the farmers and laborers, scrubwomen and servants. I went to parks and restaurants, sat in the homes of the high and the low; and always I saw a happy people; people with faith that needs no church or priest, and who laugh gaily when the Monkey King overthrows the angels. In all my wandering, I never felt the touch or breath of insult or even dislike—I who for 90 years in Amerca scarcely ever saw a day without some expression of hate for "niggers."

What is the secret of China in the second half of the 20th century? It is that the vast majority of a billion human beings have been convinced that human nature in some of its darkest recesses can be changed, if change is necessary. China knows, as no other people know, to what depths human meanness can go. I used to weep for American Negroes, as I saw what indignities and repressions and cruelties they had passed; but as I read Chinese history in these last months and had it explained to me stripped of Anglo-Saxon lies, I know that no depths of Negro slavery in America have plumbed such abysses as the Chinese have seen for 2,000 years and more. They have seen starvation and murder; rape and prostitution; sale and slavery of children; and religion cloaked in opium and gin, for converting the "heathen." This oppression and contempt came not only from Tartars, Mongolians, British, French, Germans and Americans, but from the Chinese themselves: Mandarins and warlords, capitalists and murdering thieves like Chiang Kai-shek; Kuomintang socialists and intellectuals educated abroad.

Despite all this, China lives, and has been transformed and marches on. She is not ignored by the United States. She ignores the United States and leaps forward. What did it? What furnished the motive power and how was it applied? First it was the belief in himself and in his people by a man like Sun Yat-sen. He plunged on blind and unaided, repulsed by Britain and America, but welcomed by Russia. Then efforts toward socialism, which wobbled forward, erred and lost, and at last was bribed by America and Britain and betrayed by Chiang Kai-shek, with its leaders murdered and its aims misunderstood, when not deliberately lied about.

Then came the Long March from feudalism, past capitalism and socialism to communism in our day. Mao Tse-tung, Chou En-lai, Chu Teh and a half dozen others undertook to lead a nation by example, by starving and fighting; by infinite patience and above all by making a nation believe that the people and not merely the elite—that on the contrary the workers in factory, street and field—composed the real nation. Others have said this often, but no nation has tried it like the Soviet Union and China. And on the staggering and bitter effort of the Soviets, beleaguered by all Western civilization, and yet far-seeing enough to help weaker

China even before a still weak Russia was safe—on this vast pyramid has arisen the saving nation of this stumbling, murdering, hating world.

In China the people—the laboring people, the people who in most lands are the doormats on which the reigning thieves and murdering rulers walk, leading their painted and jeweled prostitutes—the people walk and boast. These people of the slums and gutters and kitchens are the Chinese nation today. This the Chinese believe and on this belief they toil and sweat and cheer.

They believe this and for the last ten years their belief has been strengthened until today they follow their leaders because these leaders have never deceived them. Their officials are incorruptible, their merchants are honest, their artisans are reliable, their workers who dig and haul and lift do an honest day's work and even work overtime if their state asks it, for they are the state; they are China.

A kindergarten, meeting in the once Forbidden City, was shown the magnificence of this palace and told: "Your fathers built this, but did not enjoy it; but now it is yours; preserve it." And then, pointing across the Tien an Men Square to the vast building of the new Halls of Assembly, the speaker added: "Your fathers are building new palaces for you; enjoy them and guard them for yourselves and your children. They belong to you!"

China has no rank or classes; her universities grant no degrees; her government awards no medals. She has no blue book of "society." But she has leaders of learning and genius, scientists of renown, artisans of skill and millions who know and believe this and follow where these men lead. This is the joy of this nation, its high belief and its unfaltering hope.

China is no utopia. Fifth Avenue has better shops where the rich can buy and the whores parade. Detroit has more and better cars. The best American housing outstrips the Chinese, and Chinese women are not nearly as well-dressed as the guests of the Waldorf-Astoria. But the Chinese worker is happy. He has exorcised the Great Fear that haunts the West; the fear of losing his job; the fear of falling sick; the fear of accident; the fear of inability to educate his children; the fear of daring to take a vacation. To guard against such catastrophe Americans skimp and save, cheat and steal, gamble and arm for murder. The Soviet citizen, the Czech, the Pole, the Hungarian have kicked out the stooges of America and the hoodlums set to exploit the peasants. They and the East Germans no longer fear these disasters; and above all the Chinese sit high above these fears and laugh with joy. They will not be rich in old age, but they will eat. They will not enjoy sickness but they will be given care. They will not starve as thousands of Chinese did only a generation ago. They fear neither flood nor epidemic. They do not even fear war; as Mao Tse-tung told me, war for China is a "paper tiger." China can defend itself and back of China stands the unassailable might of the Soviet Union.

Envy and class hate are disappearing in China. Does your neighbor have better pay and higher position than you? He has this because of greater ability or better education, and more education is open to you and compulsory for your children. The young married couple do not fear children. The mother has pre-natal care. Her wage and job are safe. Nursery and kindergarten take care of the child and it is welcome, not to pampered luxury but to good food, constant medical care and education for his highest ability. All this is not yet perfect. Here and there it fails, falls short and falters; but it is so often and so widely true, that China believes, lives on realized hope, follows its leaders and sings: "O, Mourner, get up off your knees."

The women of China are becoming free. They wear pants so that they can walk, climb and dig; and climb and dig they do. They are not dressed simply for sex indulgence or beauty parades. They occupy positions from ministers of state to locomotive engineers, lawyers, doctors, clerks and laborers. They are escaping "household drudgery"; they are strong and healthy and beautiful not simply of leg and false bosom, but of brain, brawn, and rich emotion. In Wuhan I stood in one of the greatest steelworks of the world. A crane which moved a hundred tons loomed above. I said, "My God, Shirley, look up there!" Alone in the engine-room sat a girl with ribboned braids, running the vast machine.

You won't believe this, because you never saw anything like it; and if the State Department has its way, you never will. Let *Life* lie about communes; and the State Department shed crocodile tears over ancestral tombs. Let Hong Kong wire its lies abroad. Let "Divine Slavery" persist in Tibet until China kills it. The truth is there and I saw it.

Fifteen times I have crossed the Atlantic and once the Pacific. I have seen the world. But never so vast and glorious a miracle as China. This monster is a nation with a dark-tinted billion born at the beginning of time, and facing its end; this struggle from starved degradation and murder and suffering to the triumph of that Long March to world leadership. Oh beautiful, patient, self-sacrificing China, despised and unforgettable, victorious and forgiving, crucified and risen from the dead.

Interlude:

COMMUNISM

COMMUNISM

I have studied socialism and communism long and care-fully in lands where they are practiced and in conversation with their adherents, and with wide reading. I now state my conclusion frankly and clearly: I believe in communism. I mean by communism, a planned way of life in the production of wealth and work designed for building a state whose object is the highest welfare of its people and not merely the profit of a part. I believe that all men should be employed according to their ability and that wealth and services should be distributed according to need. Once I thought that these ends could be attained under capitalism, means of production privately owned, and used in accord with free individual initiative. After earnest observation I now believe that private ownership of capital and free enterprise are leading the world to disaster. I do not believe that so-called "people's capitalism" has in the United States or anywhere replaced the ills of private capitalism and shown an answer to socialism. The corporation is but the legal mask behind which the individual owner of wealth hides. Democratic government in the United States has almost ceased to function. A fourth of the adults are disfranchised, half the legal voters do not go to the polls. We are ruled by those who control wealth and who by that power buy or coerce public opinion.

I resent the charge that communism is a conspiracy: Communists often conspire as do capitalists. But it is false that all Communists are criminals and that communism speaks and exists mainly by means of force and fraud. I shall there-fore hereafter help the triumph of communism in every honest way that I can: without deceit or hurt; and in any way possible, without war; and with goodwill to all men of all colors, classes and creeds. If, because of this belief and such action, I become the victim of attack and calumny, I will react in the way that seems to me best for the world in which

I live and which I have tried earnestly to serve. I know well that the triumph of communism will be a slow and difficult task, involving mistakes of every sort. It will call for progressive change in human nature and a better type of manhood than is common today. I believe this possible, or otherwise we will continue to lie, steal and kill as we are doing today.

Who now am I to have come to these conclusions? And of what if any significance are my deductions? What has been my life and work and of what meaning to mankind? The final answer to these questions, time and posterity must make. But perhaps it is my duty to contribute whatever enlightenment I can. This is the excuse for this writing which I call a Soliloquy.

PART TWO

CHAPTER VI

MY BIRTH AND FAMILY

I was born by a golden river and in the shadow of two great hills, five years after the Emancipation Proclamation, which began the freeing of American Negro slaves. The valley was wreathed in grass and trees and crowned to the eastward by the huge bulk of East Mountain, with crag and cave and dark forests. Westward the hill was gentler, rolling up to gorgeous sunsets and cloud-swept storms. The town of Great Barrington, which lay between these mountains in Berkshire County, Western Massachusetts, had a broad Main Street, lined with maples and elms, with white picket fences before the homes. The climate was to our thought quite perfect.

In 1868 on the day after the birth of George Washington was celebrated, I was born on Church Street, which branched east from Main in midtown. The year of my birth was the year that the freedmen of the South were enfranchised, and for the first time as a mass took part in government. Conventions with black delegates voted new constitutions all over the South, and two groups of laborers—freed slaves and poor whites—dominated the former slave states. It was an extraordinary experiment in democracy. Thaddeus Stevens, the clearest-headed leader of this attempt at industrial democracy, made his last speech, impeaching Andrew Johnson on February 16, and on February 23 I was born.

The house of my birth was quaint, with clapboards running up and down, neatly trimmed; there were five rooms, a tiny porch, a rosy front yard, and unbelievably delicious strawberries in the rear. A South Carolinian, lately come to the Berkshire Hills, owned all this—tall, thin and black, with golden earrings, and given to religious trances. Here my mother, Mary Burghardt, and my father, Alfred Du Bois, came to live temporarily after their marriage ceremony in the village of Housatonic, which adjoined Great

61

Barrington on the north. Then after a few years my father went east into Connecticut to build a life and home for mother and me. We meantime went to live on the lands of my mother's clan on South Egremont Plain in the southern part of our town.

The black Burghardts were a group of African Negroes descended from Tom, who was born in West Africa about 1730. He was stolen by Dutch slave traders and brought to the valley of the Hudson as a small child. Legally, Tom was not a slave, but practically, by the custom of the day, he grew up as either slave or serf, and in the service of the Burghardts, a white family of Dutch descent. Early in the 18th century, "Coonraet Borghardt" and Tom came east from the Hudson Valley and settled in Berkshire County, Massachusetts, which was described as a "howling wilderness." When the Revolutionary War broke out, Tom Burghardt "appears with the rank of private on the muster and payroll of Captain John Spoors company, Colonel John Ashley's Berkshire county regiment."

Tom "was reported a Negr." He enlisted to serve for three years; but how long or where he served the records do not show. At any rate this war service definitely freed him and his family from slavery; and later the Bill of Rights of 1780 declared all slaves in Massachusetts free.

Tom's mother or wife was a little black Bantu woman, who never became reconciled to this strange land; she clasped her knees and rocked and crooned:

> *Do bana coba—gene me, gene me,*
> *Ben d' nuli, ben d' le—*

The song came down the years and I heard it sung at my grandfather's fireside. Tom died about 1787, but of him came many sons; one Jack, who took part in Shays' rebellion; and a daughter named Nancy Pratt. Jack is said to have married the celebrated Mom Bett as his first wife. Violet was Jack's second wife, and from these two were born a mighty family, splendidly named: Harlow and Ira, Chloe, Lucinda, Maria and Othello!

These Burghardts lived on South Egremont Plain for near 200 years. The last piece of their land was bought from a cousin of mine and given to me in 1930 by a group of friends. Among them were Jane Addams, Clarence Darrow, Mrs. Jacob Schiff and Moorfield Storey. I planned eventually to make it my country home, but the old home was dilapidated; the boundaries of the land had been encroached upon by neighbors, and the cost of restoration was beyond my means. I sold it in 1955.

Here in the late 18th and early 19th centuries the black Burghardts lived. I remember three of those houses and a small pond. These were homes of Harlow and Ira; and of my own grandfather, Othello, which he had inherited from his sister Lucinda. There were 21 persons in these three families by the Census of 1830. Here as farmers they long earned a comfortable living, consorting usually with each other, but also with some of their white neighbors.

The living to be earned on the farms gradually became less satisfying, and the group began to disintegrate; some went to the Connecticut Valley; some went West; many moved to town and city and found work as laborers and servants. Usually their children went to school long enough to learn to read and write, but few went further. I was the first of the clan to finish high school.

Work for black folk which would lead to a more prosperous future was not easy to come by. Just why this was so it is difficult to say; it was not solely race prejudice, although this played its part; it was lack of training and understanding, reluctance to venture into unknown surroundings, and fear of a land still strange to family mores which pictured travel as disaster. In my family, I remember farmers, barbers, waiters, cooks, housemaids and laborers. In these callings a few prospered. My cousins, the Crispels of West Stockbridge, owned one of the best homes in town, and had the only barber shop; my Uncle Jim long had a paying barber business in Amherst; several hotel cooks and waiters were in charge of dining rooms, did well and were held in esteem; a cousin in Lenox was a sexton in the most prominent church, and his wife and four daughters ran an exclusive laundry; the family was well-to-do, but they worked hard and unceasingly. Few of my folk entered the trades or went into mercantile business or the professions. My cousin Ned Gardner, a nice-looking and well-bred man, worked his whole life at the Berkshire Hotel; honest, prompt, courteous; but he died a waiter. One uncle became the lifelong servant of the Kellogg family, and the legend was that his unpaid wages kept that family from suffering until one daughter married the Hopkins who helped build the Pacific Railroad. She was left a rich widow and returned to Great Barrington in 1880. This circumstance helped me enter the profession of teaching.

My mother's ancestral home on Egremont Plain, the house of my grandfather, Othello, one of three farming brothers, was sturdy, small and old-fashioned. There was a great fireplace, whose wrought-iron tongs stand now before my fireplace as I write. My immediate family, which I remember as a young child, included a very dark grandfather, Othello Burghardt. I dimly remember him, "Uncle Tallow," strongvoiced and redolent with tobacco, who sat stiffly in a great high chair beside the open fire, because his hip was broken. He was good-natured but not energetic. The energy was in my grandmother, Sally, a thin, tall, yellow and hawk-faced woman, certainly beautiful in her youth, and efficient and managing in her age. She had Dutch and perhaps Indian blood, but the rest of the family were black.

Othello and Sally had ten or more children. Many of these had moved away before I was old enough to know them; but I remember my Aunt Lucinda, who married a Gardner, and after his death a Jackson; then my Aunt Minerva, whose married name was Newport. The youngest children were my Uncle Jim and my mother, Mary Silvina. She was born in 1831, and died in 1885, at the age of 54 years. Mother was dark shining bronze, with smooth skin and lovely eyes; there was a tiny ripple in her black hair, and she had a heavy, kind face. She gave one the impression of infinite patience, but a curious determination was concealed in her softness.

As a young woman she had a son, Idelbert, born of a love affair between her and her first cousin, John Burghardt. The circumstances of this romance I never knew. No one talked of it in the family. Probably the mating was broken up on account of the consanguinity of the cousins. My mother became a silent, repressed woman, working at household duties at home, helping now and then in the neighbors' homes, and finally going into town where her married sisters lived and where she worked as a housemaid. When she was 35, Alfred Du Bois came to town.

In the early 17th century, two French Huguenots, sons of Crétian Du Bois, migrated from Flanders to America. Perhaps a third son who spelled his name Du Bose went South. Louis and Jacques Du Bois settled in Ulster County, New York State. They were in all probability artisans descended from peasants; but the white American family declares they were aristocrats, and has found a coat of arms which they say belongs to them.

From Jacques in the fifth generation was descended James Du Bois, born about 1750, who became a physician in Poughkeepsie, New York, and migrated to the Bahamas. Lord Dunmore, Governor of New York and later of Virginia and the Bahamas, had given grants of land to various members of the Du Bois family, who were loyalists, and young Dr. James Du Bois went to the Bahamas soon after the Revolution and took over several plantations and one lake of salt which still bears his name. He prospered after some vicissitudes, and founded a family.

Whether, as is probable, he took a slave as a concubine, or married a free Negro woman—in either case two sons were born, my grandfather Alexander in 1803 and a younger brother, John. After their mother's death, Dr. James Du Bois brought both boys to New York in 1810. Both were white enough to "pass," and their father entered them in the private Cheshire School in Connecticut. He visited them regularly, but on one visit, about 1820, he suddenly fell dead.

The white New York family removed the boys from school and took charge of their father's property. My grandfather was apprenticed to a shoemaker. Just what happened to John, I do not know. Probably he continued as white, and his descendants, if any, know nothing of their colored ancestry. Alexander was of stern character. His movements between 1820 and 1840 are not clear. As the son of a "gentleman," with the beginnings of a gentleman's education, he refused to become a shoemaker and went to Haiti at the age of perhaps 18. Boyer had become President just after the suicide of Christophe, and held power until 1843, bringing the whole island under his control and making a costly peace with France.

Of grandfather's life in Haiti from about 1821 to 1830, I know few details. From his 18th to his 27th year he formed acquaintanceships, earned a living, married and had a son, my father, Alfred, born in 1825. I do not know what work grandfather did, but probably he ran a plantation and engaged in the growing shipping trade to the United States. Who he married I do not know, nor her relatives. He may have married into the family of Elie Du Bois, the great Haitian educator. Also why he left Haiti in 1830 is not clear. It may have been because of the threat of war with France during the Revolution of 1830 and the fall of Charles X.

England soon recognized the independence of Haiti; but the United States while recognizing South American republics which Haiti had helped to free, refused to recognize a Negro nation. Because of this turmoil, grandfather may have lost faith in the possibility of real independence for Haiti. Again trade with the United States was at this period exceeding the trade of England or France and amounting to more than a million dollars a year. This trade was carried on with Northern cities like New Haven, but it was also demanded by the rapidly growing Cotton Kingdom in the South. Also, perhaps domestic difficulties with his wife's family and over family property may have arisen. For any or all of these reasons my grandfather left Haiti and settled with his son, now five years of age, in New Haven.

He arrived from the West Indies at a critical time: David

Walker had published his bitter *Appeal* to Negroes against submission to slavery, in 1829; Nat Turner led his bloody Virginia slave revolt in 1831; slavery was abolished in the British West Indies in 1833; the rebelling slaves of the ship *Amistad* landed in Connecticut in 1839, and their trial took place in New Haven. Riots against Negroes occurred in New England cities, in New York and Philadelphia in this decade, and Negroes held conventions in Philadelphia. Among other things these Negroes determined to build an industrial college in New Haven, and later Prudence Crandall tried there to let Negro girls enter her seminary, to the disgust of the whites. In New Haven, the abolitionists Simeon Jocelyn and Arthur Tappan worked, and here Garrison visited.

In New Haven my grandfather settled. He opened a grocery store at 43 Washington Street. The color line was sharp in New Haven and abolitionists were stirring up dissension. In Trinity parish of the Episcopal church were a few colored communicants, including my grandfather. But the rector, Harry Croswell, was reactionary and openly condemned the abolition movement. Soon the colored communicants of Trinity were given to understand that they would be happier in their own racial church. Alexander Crummell, the great Negro minister, encouraged this move, and the example of Amos Beman who was building the Temple Street Negro Congregational Church, made the move inevitable.

This must have infuriated my grandfather, and yet his very pride drove him into joining this segregated church. He was made treasurer probably because he owned property; eventually he became the first senior warden of St. Luke's, as this "jim-crow" church was called. It still exists. Also, he and certain other Negroes with property were permitted to buy lots at the rear of the new Grove Street Cemetery, opposite the Yale campus. Years later when this cemetery was enlarged, those Negro lots lay on the center path. Here my grandfather lies buried and here I shall one day lie.[5]

Alexander, in addition to his grocery, now became steward

on the passenger boat which ran between New Haven and New York. Here he reformed the treatment of the servants, kept the boats in first-class order, and achieved a degree of independence. He was in charge of repairing and hiring. He had charge of the workers and saw to it that the Negro servants were served their meals regularly at a table. But race segregation in New Haven and New York was growing, and grandfather, after a time, determined that Springfield, Massachusetts, offered a better place for him and his family to live. In 1856 he removed to Springfield. He bought a farm not far from the city, down the Connecticut River, and established his family in the city of Springfield. He spent the winters there, but in Spring and Summer kept his stewardship of the New York-New Haven boats. He lived well: "bought a silk vest at Laws Clothing Store for $6.75. . . . Had a few invited guests at supper, one-half past six o'clock, champagne, a rather poor quality from Webster's . . . dedication ball at city hall." He joined the white Episcopal church and notes attendance at lectures. "Finished reading Shakespear's *Othello*," he writes one day.

Suddenly, in late May 1861, my grandfather took a trip to Haiti. This may have been caused by the outbreak of the Civil War. Perhaps he had just lost an American wife. In March, 11 American slave states had seceded and formed the Confederacy. In April, Southern ports were blockaded, and on May 14, Lee became Brigadier-General. The relation of colored folk to the war was uncertain, and my father, Alfred, was eligible for drafting. The future of colored folks in the United States was a problem; then, too, the rector of St. Luke's was Theodore Holly, who early in 1861 had led a migration of Negroes to Haiti, and painted a future for them there. It is possible also that grandfather was seeking property either of his father, Dr. James Du Bois, in the Bahamas, which was but a few hundred miles north from Haiti; or, perhaps, especially in Long Key, his birthplace; or from the family of his former Haitian wife. But he was a reticent man, and even his diary is silent on the most important points.

"*Thursday, May 9*. Have thoughts of leaving the vessel, but want resolution to do so. Wrote to friends we should sail on Friday the 10th. Feel ashamed to back out, will wait a day or two longer but feel like one rushing on his fate. If God forsakes me, I am undone forever. 'There is a divinity that shapes our ends, rough hew as we will.'

"*May 15*. Sun rose clear, wind west. Hove anchor, got under way 20 minutes past six o'clock. God speed the ship, and grant me deliverance from my enemy that I may conquer before I die." (Who was this enemy? The white Du Boises? The colored Haitians?)

On his lonely trip grandfather writes poetry, not very good, but indicating deep emotion. On May 19:

> *A single soul, One! Only one!*
> *Of all I know or ever knew*
> *My star by night, by day the sun*
> *Now guide my bark, now bound my view.*
>
> *It may be right, perchance tis wrong*
> *To love without the priestly ken,*
> *Such things are often known among*
> *The disappointed Sons of Men.*
>
> *Bodies may be joined together*
> *By priestly craft and laws, so strong*
> *In vain you try the bonds to sever*
> *Yet love in laughter breaks the thong.*

(Was grandfather confessing desertion of a Haitian wife whom he had not married and excusing his marriages in the United States?)

"*Monday, June 3:* Landed in Port Au Prince, took board at Mr. Fredd's, Rue Caserne; rain clearing; mosquitoes, jackasses, Negroes, mud water, soldiers, universal filth.

"Saw emigrants at the emigrant house in a condition that if not changed soon will send many to the grave. Poor men and women, I am sorry, heart sorry for them. They put on an air of cheerfulness, which I am satisfied there is not one of them, but would give all they had in the world if they could stand where I did a few weeks ago."

Boyer had ruled Haiti. He had united the whole island under Haitian rule and had finally made peace with France, albeit on almost fatal terms. Four Presidents succeeded in the next four years; and then for ten years came the Emperor Faustin, who had been the slave Soulouque. The regime had an impressive magnificence, but was an economic failure.

The empire was overthrown in 1859 and Geffrard, a progressive and hard-working man, became President, from 1859 to 1867. He promoted education and industry and tried to cooperate with American abolitionists and colored leaders like Holly in encouraging the immigration of American Negroes. It was under Geffrard that my grandfather arrived. He "saw the President, Baron Dennis, August Elie; invited me to take passage in government steamer to St. Mark." It was in the vicinity of St. Mark that he had resided when he formerly lived in Haiti, and here his son Alfred had been born. Perhaps here were his strongest ties to Haiti. He stayed from June 4 to June 9. He says no word of what he did or whom he saw. We only know that on June 10 he was bound home on a British steamer "just eight days after I went ashore; I felt happy to arrive. I am more than happy to leave."

The ship loaded 6,000 tons of salt, the commodity which was the basis of Alexander's father's wealth, but Alexander does not mention the fact; nor apparently does he stop at Long Key where he himself was born. He is silent until Monday, June 24, when he lands in the United States. It is possible that in Haiti he received funds which gave him greater independence, or again it may be that he had left Alfred in Haiti, when he left in 1830; that his wife had died and that in 1861 he returned to get his son and bring him to America. This is conjecture.

Soon after returning he seems to have given up his New Haven work and connections and taken up a new career in Springfield, Massachusetts, where he had been living for some time. On July 12, 1861, "Du Bois and Thomas rented a shop on Main Street of W. W. Parsons at $150 a year."

I saw grandfather but once, when I was 15 and he 77. Always he held his head high, took no insults, made few friends. He was not a "Negro"; he was a man! Yet the current was too strong even for him. Then even more than now a colored man had colored friends or none at all, lived in a colored world or lived alone. A few fine, strong, black men gained the heart of this silent, bitter man in New York and New Haven. If he had scant sympathy with their social clannishness, he was with them fighting discrimination.

Beneath his sternness was a very human man. Slyly he wrote poetry—stilted, pleading things from a soul astray. He loved women in his masterful way, marrying after his Haitian experience three beautiful wives in succession, in the United States, clinging to each with a certain desperate, even if unsympathetic affection. As a father he was naturally a failure —hard, domineering, unyielding. His four children reacted characteristically: one was until past middle life a thin spinster, the mental image of her father; one died; one passed over into the white world, and her children's children are now white, with no knowledge of their Negro blood; the fourth, my father, bent before grandfather, but did not break —better if he had. He yielded and flared back, asked forgiveness and forgot why, became the harshly-bold favorite, who ran away and rioted and roamed, and loved and married my brown mother.

He arrived in Great Barrington in 1867. He was small and beautiful of face and feature, just tinted with the sun, his wavy hair chiefly revealing his kinship to Africa. In nature, I think, he was a dreamer—romantic, indolent, kind, unreliable. He had in him the making of a poet, an adventurer, or a Beloved Vagabond, according to the life that closed round him; and that life gave him all too little.

I really know very little of my father. He had been brought from Haiti by his father. How he was schooled, I do not know. New Haven then had separate schools and all public schools were poor. Perhaps he was put into one of the better private Negro schools, which existed in New Haven at times. What he did between the ages of 15 and 35, I do not know. He probably worked and wandered here and there. There is no hint of his marrying during this time. But his picture which he gave mother showed him in the uniform of a Civil War private. How long he served or where, I do not know, nor whether he enlisted as colored or white. Connecticut raised two Negro regiments.

When my father came to Great Barrington in 1867, the black Burghardts did not like him. He was too good-looking, too white. He had apparently no property and no job, so far as they knew; and they had never heard of the Du Bois family in New York. Then suddenly in a runaway marriage, but one duly attested and published in the *Berkshire Courier,* Alfred married Mary Burghardt and they went to live in the house of Jefferson McKinley. Here they lived for a year or two and against them the black Burghardt family carried on a more or less open feud, until my birth.

I was of great interest to the whole town. The whites waited to see "when my hair was going to curl," and all my Burghardt relatives admired me extravagantly. They still looked askance at my father and he was not attracted by them. There loomed the question as to where we were going to live and what my father was going to do for a living. He must have had some money on hand when he came, and he recoiled from grandfather Burghardt's home where Mary and her baby were expected eventually to live. After a year or more of hesitation, father went away to establish a home for his family. He would write for mother to come. Mother and I went to live on Egremont Plain with the Burghardts. In a few months father wrote from New Milford, a small town in Connecticut about 40 miles south of Great Barrington on the Housatonic River. Mother hesitated. She had seldom been out of her hometown. Once as a girl she had taken an excursion to New York. The family objected to her leaving and expressed more and more doubt as to father. The result was in the end that mother never went and my father never came back to Great Barrington. If he wrote, the letters were not delivered. I never saw him, and know not where or when he died.

My mother worried and sank into depression. The family closed about her as a protecting guardian. The town folk who knew the Burghardts took her and me into a sort of overseeing custody. We lived in simple comfort, and living was cheap. And yet as I look back I cannot see how mother accomplished what she did. Her brother and sisters, her cousins and relatives always stood by. My silent older half-brother early went to work as a waiter and was seldom home, but always he was ready to help.

My mother seldom mentioned my father. She was silent before family criticism. She uttered no word of criticism or blame. I do not remember asking much about him. Why, I am not sure; but I think that I knew instinctively that this was a subject which hurt my mother too much even to mention.

As I look back now, I can see that the little family of my mother and myself must often have been near the edge of poverty. Yet I was not hungry or in lack of suitable clothing and shoes, or made to feel unfortunate in company with my fellow students. That was partly because most village folk were poor or middle class. There were but few rich families. Most of my schoolmates belonged to families of small farmers, artisans, or shopkeepers. When special expenditures were called for, new shoes or school books, the money often came from gifts from my uncle or aunts or less frequently from white families, long closely connected with the Burghardts. There may have been other gifts but they were never conspicuous. I never wore cast-off clothes. I never asked folk outside the family for money. Our landlord, Mrs. Cass, received no rent, I am sure, for long intervals. I think the rent was four dollars a month, and finally it was accounted for by settlement as a gift when I went to college.

We continued to live with grandfather Burghardt until I was about five, and grandfather died. The family then moved into town. We lived on the Sumner estate on south Main

Street, where we had rooms over what was once the stables. There was a nice wide yard and a running brook which afforded me infinite pleasure. Right opposite the front gate was the long lane leading down to the public school grounds. I suspect this nearness to school induced mother to choose this home. Then after grandmother died, we moved up to Railroad Street, right next to the station. We lived with a poor white family, kindly, but the wife was near insanity.

Soon after, my worrying mother had a paralytic stroke from which she never entirely recovered. As I remember her, she was always lame in her left leg, with a withered left hand. We always walked arm in arm. The misfortune never seemed to me to hurt us. I continued in school and had plenty to eat. Aunts and cousins did our mending and neighbors were always ready to help out. Sometimes mother went out for a day's work and people seemed to like to have her. I always went to bring her home at night and was never left alone.

We soon moved to the Cass home which mother and I occupied during my high school days. It was on Church Street and stood back of the Cass residence and next to the horsesheds of the Congregational church, which was empty except on Sunday. We occupied two rooms and a pantry on the ground floor and two bedrooms on the second half-story.

None of these successive homes had modern conveniences: the "back house" and running water were outdoors; our heat came from stoves. Usually the houses were weatherproof and we had furniture enough for health and comfort. We had no gardens, but sometimes a border bit of land. Always after I was 12, I had a bedchamber to myself, a luxury which I never dreamed was so rare until I was much older.

In the public schools of this town, I was trained from the age of six to 16, and in the town schools, churches, and general social life, I learned my patterns of living. I had, as a child, almost no experience of segregation or color discrimination. My schoolmates were invariably white; I joined quite naturally all games, excursions, church festivals; recreations like coasting, swimming, hiking and games. I was in and out of the homes of nearly all my mates, and ate and played with them. I was as a boy long unconscious of color discrimination in any obvious and specific way.

I knew nevertheless that I was exceptional in appearance and that this riveted attention upon me. Less clearly, I early realized that most of the colored persons I saw, including my own folk, were poorer than the well-to-do whites; lived in humbler houses, and did not own stores. None of the colored folk I knew were so poor, drunken and sloven as some of the lower class Americans and Irish. I did not then associate poverty or ignorance with color, but rather with lack of opportunity; or more often with lack of thrift, which was in strict accord with the philosophy of New England and of the 19th century.

On the other hand, much of my philosophy of the color line must have come from my family group and their friends' experience. My immediate family eventually consisted of my mother and her brother. Near to us in space and intimacy were two married aunts with older children; and a number of cousins, in various degrees removed, lived scattered through the town and county. Most of these had been small farmers, artisans, laborers and servants. With few exceptions all could read and write, but few had training beyond this. These talked of their work and experiences, of hindrances which colored people especially encountered, of better chances in other towns and cities. In this way I must have gotten indirectly a pretty clear outline of color bars which I myself did not experience. Moreover, I couldn't rationalize my own case, because I found it easy to excel most of my classmates in studies, if not in games. The secret of life and the loosing of the color bar, then, lay in excellence, in accomplishment. If others of my family, of my colored kin, had stayed in school instead of quitting early for small jobs, they could have risen to equal whites. On this my mother quietly insisted. There was no real discrimination on account of color —it was all a matter of ability and hard work.

This philosophy saved me from conceit and vainglory by rigorous self-testing, which doubtless cloaked some half-conscious misgivings on my part. If visitors to school saw and remarked on my brown face, I waited in quiet confidence. When my turn came, I recited glibly and usually correctly because I studied hard. Some of my mates did not care, some were stupid, some excelled, but at any rate I gave the best a hard run, and then sat back complacently.

I entered public school at the age of about five or six. For ten years I went regularly to school, from nine o'clock until noon, and one o'clock until four each day, five days a week, ten months a year. The teachers were mature women, most of them trained in State Normal Schools and invariably white American Protestants. Miss Cross, my first primary teacher, was stern and inflexible, but with an inward kindliness and sense of fairness which made her a favorite of mine; and since I was a bright boy who got his lessons, I became a favorite of hers.

The school grounds were not particularly attractive or large, and yet they were ample for the play of children at recess. A great choke-cherry tree with bared roots gave shade in the summer, and fences hemmed us in from the private homes at the side and the low meadows beyond. The primary schoolhouse was wooden, with wooden hand-made furniture, and usually pretty well crowded. The grammar and high school building was brick. We had short devotions and singing each morning and there my clear young voice brought some initial distinction.

Gradually I became conscious that in most of the school work my natural gifts and regular attendance made me rank among the best, so that my promotions were regular and expected. I look back upon my classmates with interest and sharpened memory. They were boys and girls of town and country, with a few Irish and never but once another colored child. My rapid advancement made me usually younger than my classmates, and this fact remained true in high school and at college and even when I began my life work it influenced my attitudes in many ways. I was often too young to lead in enterprises even when I was fitted to do so, but I was always advising and correcting older folk.

Of course, I was too honest with myself not to see things

which desert and even hard work did not explain or solve. I recognized ingrained difference in gift. Art Benham could draw pictures better than I; but I could express meaning in words better than he; Mike Gibbons was a perfect marble player, but dumb in Latin. I came to see and admit all this, but I hugged my own gifts and put them to test.

As playmate of the children I saw the homes of nearly everyone. The homes I saw impressed me, but did not overwhelm me. Many were bigger than mine, with newer and shinier things, but they did not seem to differ in kind. One class of rich folk with whom I came in contact were summer boarders who made yearly incursions from New York. I think I was mostly impressed by their clothes. Outside of that there was little reason so far as I could see to envy them. The children were not very strong and rather too well dressed to have a good time playing. I think I probably surprised them more than they me, for I was easily at home with them and happy. They looked to me just like ordinary people, while my brown face and frizzled hair must have seemed strange to them.

The schools of Great Barrington were simple but good, well-taught; and truant laws were enforced. I started on one school ground, and continued there until I was graduated from high school. I was seldom absent or tardy. The curriculum was simple: reading, writing, spelling and arithmetic; grammar, geography and history. We learned the alphabet; we were drilled vigorously on the multiplication tables and we drew accurate maps. We could spell correctly and read with understanding.

CHAPTER VII

BOYHOOD IN
GREAT BARRINGTON

Great Barrington was a town of middle-class people, mostly native white Americans of English and Dutch descent. There were differences of property and income and yet all the men worked and seemed at least to be earning their living. Naturally the income was not proportioned to the effort; some men worked three hours a day and earned several thousand dollars a year; carpenters worked 12 hours a day for a dollar, and servants toiled day and night for two dollars a week. But we did not dream of a day when a man doing nothing could be a millionaire at 35, while his fellow broke back and heart and starved.

The women were housekeepers, with a few exceptions, like teachers, the postmistress, and a clerk now and then in stores like Fassett's shop for women's apparel. The ownership of property, of homes and stores, of a few mills of various sorts, was fundamental, and the basis of social prestige. Most families owned their homes. There was some inherited wealth but not in very large amounts. There were no idle rich and no outstanding "society." I dimly remember one rich old man who was apparently retired and did no work. He rode about town now and then in a carriage with a liveried coachman. I recall my astonishment when I learned that the splendid gentleman on the high front seat, with beaver hat, shining boots and gold braid, was not the owner. The owner was the little fat man crouched in the rear seat.

This, however, was exceptional. The Russell brothers, middle-aged men whom I knew quite well, went to work every day, superintending the Berkshire Woolen Mills in the upper part of town. The Whitings, an old well-to-do family, ran a drugstore, and a white Burghardt who spelled his name Burgett had the leading grocery store. The Girlings had a clothing store, and the Brewers dealt in hardware and fuel. There were two hotels; the Berkshire catered to summer visitors, chiefly from New York; the Miller House depended on local trade. There was for a time a steam bakery which turned out delicious food until the National Biscuit Company swallowed it up and it disappeared. There was a bank, the Mahaiwe National.

Of course there was also the usual contradiction: while property and income were the main bases of social status, at the same time the facts concerning them were a carefully guarded secret. No one knew exactly how rich the Russells were or just what was the financial status of the Coffins and Churches. There were, of course, rumors and general estimates which were in all probability not far from the truth, but few knew with any exactitude the economic status of the important persons of the town.

There was no great exhibition of wealth. The homes of the Russells, the Churches and Dr. Collins were comparatively large with perhaps eight or ten rooms and built of wood or, more rarely, of stone. There was an abundance of cheap blue granite in the neighboring mountains. Most of the houses were of wood, four to six rooms, and all of them were furnished according to a common pattern: horse-hair sofas and chairs in the "parlors," with old-fashioned wooden furniture and corner "what-nots." They were usually heated by coal stove; one in each room, anthracite coal and wood from the vicinity were used. Bathrooms and indoor toilets were rare; each home had its outdoor privy, often nicely arranged.

In general living, the contrast between the well-to-do and the poor was not great. Living was cheap and there was little real poverty. Some food like local fruit was almost common property; vegetables like potatoes, navy beans and cabbage were grown in small home gardens; corned beef and chickens fetched low prices and eggs could often be raised at home; "greens" and rhubarb grew in back yards and in the Fall canning and preserving cost only the sugar. There were no flashy carriages and the social life was quite private. When the *Berkshire Courier,* our local weekly newspaper, made social announcements it was usually marriages, births, and deaths, visiting relatives from out of town, and trips to New York or the West by local residents.

I grew up in the midst of definite ideas as to wealth and poverty, work and charity. Wealth was the result of work and saving and the rich rightly inherited the earth. The poor, on the whole, were themselves to be blamed. They were unfortunate and if so their fortunes could easily be mended with care. But chiefly, they were "shiftless," and "shiftlessness" was unforgivable.

The chief criterion of local social standing was property and ancestry; but the ancestors were never magnates like the patroons of the manors along the Hudson to the west; nor were they persons of great prestige and learning with aristocratic connections like the residents of Boston and eastern Massachusetts. They were usually ordinary folk of solid respectability, farm owners, or artisans merging into industry. Standing did not depend on what the ancestor did, or who he was, but rather that he existed, lived decently and thus linked the individual to the community. Physically and socially our community belonged to the Dutch valley of the Hudson rather than to Puritan New England, and travel went south to New York more often and more easily than east to Boston.

The stores dealt chiefly in staples for ordinary living— food, clothes, medicines, and so forth. Most of them originally catered to a large farmer trade between country and town. The surrounding farmers brought in their produce and traded it for manufactured goods and certain luxuries. But this type of trading in my boyhood was being gradually reduced in extent. Western farm produce was underselling local efforts except in the case of milk, butter and fresh vegetables. There were one or two good jewelry and watch-repairing stores, a confectionery store and a number of tropical fruit stands.

One of our citizens impressed me greatly. C. C. Taylor was a little white-haired man who was writing a history of the town: he was an official of the bank and, what was of closer interest to me, he lived on a beautiful hill on lower Main Street. He kept a herd of cattle. They gave so much milk that he told my mother that anytime she wanted skimmed milk, to send me down and get all we wanted. I remember those morning walks up to the great elm on our corner; down the vast expanse of Main Street; past the Town Hall and the watering trough opposite; then by the Kellogg meadow and home and Mike Gibbons' cottage and up to the Taylor home and the delicious fresh milk.

There were one or two liquor saloons, which the town did not like to recognize, but had to. George Briggs, a native American, used to run such a saloon, but got out of the business when I was quite small and went into the more respectable business of selling meat; but the townspeople never forgot his former calling. The most prosperous saloon in my boyhood was on Railroad Street, which led from Main Street to the railroad station. It was run by a man of foreign descent named Brazie. Here was a center of drinking and carousing and perhaps some gambling. My mother laid down here one of her few strict commands; she was not talkative, but listened well. She gave few commands; but she said firmly that I was never to go into a liquor saloon or even near it. I never did, and indeed, so strong was the expression of her wishes that never in my life since have I felt at ease drinking at a bar.

The reason for my mother's attitude was clear. Great Barrington had few places of amusement or means for recreation. Community social life centered in entertainments in Town Hall; the "Bohemian glass blowers," or, as I vividly remember, the Sam Lucas singers; but for the ordinary man, including both hard-working merchant and busy artisan, not to mention laborers and visitors passing through, the liquor saloon was recreation and drunkenness was escapism. Numbers of the most respectable townsfolk were sometimes openly seen the worse for overindulgence in liquor. My own Uncle Jim, a reputable and hard-working barber, came home now and then walking very straight because of liquor. When the Murphy crusade for total abstinence swept the valley, I as a boy was one of the first to don the blue ribbon. I kept the pledge until I went as a student to Germany.

Over against this general basic community of white Americans were two groups. One was composed of a mass of Irish peasants who began to reach this town in the early 50's after the well-known famine. They were Catholics and came in increasing numbers as house servants and workers in the local woolen mills. The older Irish families became laborers on the railroads and artisans of various sorts. They formed a group of the respectable poor. They were followed by poorer and more ignorant peasants, ill-trained and ragged and given to drink. They became herded in slum areas in the upper part of the town surrounding the mills. They received low wages and were exploited in the usual ways, not as much as in the cities, but more than was necessary in a town like Great Barrington. As a boy, I was afraid of the Irish and kept away from their part of town as much as possible. Sometimes they called me "nigger" or tried to attack me. On the other hand, the older and better class of them had children in school whom I knew quite well.

The mass of the Irish, however, were separated from the townfolk by their religion and their monopoly of house service. The Catholic church was perched across the river beyond the mills, and thither the girl servants trudged faithfully early mornings to mass. This and other traits of the Irish became the basis of jokes and ridicule in town and throughout New England. Indeed, I was struck in later years when I came back from the South to New England, to find that the "nigger" jokes of Tennessee were replaced at Harvard by tales of the "two Irishmen" and songs like "mush-mush-mush turaliady."

My own attitude toward this hard-working Irish minority was naturally complicated. They did not belong to my traditional community and consequently I felt no comradeship with them. I think I rather assumed, along with most of the townfolk, that the dirty, stinking Irish slums were something that the Irish themselves preferred and made. Certainly in school and church and on the street, I got no idea that the town was responsible for the slums. My Housatonic River, for instance, was "golden" because of the waste which the paper and woolen mills poured into it and because more and more the river became a public sewer into which town and slum poured their filth.

The other minority in my town were my own colored people, but they were few in number. In Great Barrington there were perhaps 25, certainly not more than 50, colored folk in a population of 5,000. My family was among the oldest inhabitants of the valley. The family had spread slowly through the county intermarrying among cousins and other black folk, with some, but limited, infiltration of white blood. Other dark families had come in and there was some intermingling with local Indians. In one or two cases there were groups of apparently later black immigrants from Africa, near Sheffield for instance. Surviving also was an isolated group of black folk whose origin was obscure. We knew little of them but felt above them because of our education and economic status.

The colored population of the town had been increased a little by "contrabands," freed Negroes from the South, who on the whole were well received by the colored group; although the older group held some of its social distinctions and the newcomers astonished us by forming a little Negro Methodist Zion church, which we sometimes attended. There were the Masons, a family of six, a little uncouth and very religious; but good-hearted, hard workers and so jolly. I came to like them very much. There were visitors from neighboring towns. I remember a lovely little plump, brown girl who appeared out of nowhere, and smiled at me demurely; and there were always strange cousins. The colored folk were not set aside in the sense that the Irish were, but were a part of the community of long-standing; and in my case as a child, I felt no sense of difference or separation from the main mass of townspeople.

After I entered high school, I began to feel the pressure of the "veil of color"; in little matters at first and then in larger. There were always certain compensations. For in-

stance, George Beebe was a handsome classmate in high
school, two or three years older than I, and extravagantly
dressed. My own clothes were never ragged, but seldom new
and certainly not in current style. Yet George and I were
excellent friends because with all his clothes he was rather
dumb in class and knew it, while I was bright and just this
side of shabby, so that we balanced each other. The Sabins,
Clarence and Ralph, lived near me on the opposite street.
Clarence was serious and studious, and Ralph a little devil.
We were friends and playmates. Art Benham, whose father
was a railroad engineer, was a pixie, red-haired, ugly and
gifted. He and I were joint editors of the only paper that
was ever published during my day. It was the high school
Howler, gotten out by hand, and lasting only for two or
three issues.

The boy who lived nearest me was Jim Parker, son of a
watchmaker. He and Fred Sanford used to go hunting with
firearms in the forest. This repelled me a little, as I did not
like killing things, but they were all good pals whom I could
easily outdistance in class. Other boys of my group were
Boardman Tobey, son of a jeweler, who came to school once
with shoes said to have cost four dollars. We did not believe
such a price possible. George Phelps, the tinner's son, lived
next door and we met daily. Ned Hollister's father had his
large grocery store near the watering-trough for horses; his
stock of tropical fruit introduced me to dozens of oranges
which Ned forced on me when accidentally his stone hit me
instead of the "duck on the rock" at which he was aiming.
He attained fame by bringing the first high-wheeled bicycle
to town.

One girl, Mary Dewey, eldest daughter of our most distinguished lawyer, surpassed me in arithmetic. She could
add up columns of figures with astonishing rapidity, but my
grasp of history and ability to write were better than hers.
The other girls in my classes were not to me notable. Edith
Pixley and Lottie Doolittle were pretty but did not know
much. Sabra Taylor and Minnie Crissy were sober country
girls and good students whom I liked. Agnes O'Neil was a

newcomer to town whose ancestors nobody knew. She dressed quite gorgeously and George Beebe escorted her about. But otherwise she was negligible.

In our day and school, because we were younger and less sophisticated, our chief business was studying or playing. I can remember when the new school principal, Frank Hosmer of Amherst, tried to introduce a uniform cap with gilt lettering, G.B.H.S. on the front, to indicate the "Great Barrington High School." We were almost unanimously against it, and called it "The Great Big Hosmer Speculation." As a matter of fact, we students for the most part and particularly myself, did not have the money to pay for this unnecessary expense. On the other hand, we did have some interesting group activities. Hosmer and young Frank Wright, who was reading law in Judge Dewey's office, put on a play at Town Hall, Scott's *Lady of the Lake,* and most high school students took some part. There was a folk play, *Old John Brown Had a Little Indian,* in which I was one of the participants. For recreation we played games: "marbles," "hi-spy," "duck on a rock," and "Indians." We went mountain climbing and explored caves. We swam, and coasted the long hill from far up Castle Street, across the railroad tracks down to Main Street. Most of the children used to skate; but not I for two reasons: skates cost too much, and mother was afraid of the water.

Our chief holidays were Fourth of July, Cattle-show and Christmas. Fourth of July was a romp for children, with a few but not many casualties. Once in a while we had fireworks as a treat from some philanthropist. Usually we only set off our individual packs of small crackers. Christmas was a festival of church and home, and there was no public illumination, and no frantic buying of presents. We played baseball but it had not yet become a national game and consisted of "one old cat" or at most two chosen sides. We tried football sometimes. I was not particularly good at these games but joined gaily in the fun.

Of other schoolmates, there were two Irish boys whom I liked—Mike Gibbons had marvelous facility at playing "marbles," and Ned Kelly who was fat and jolly. Later he became town clerk. An older fellow student of long English ancestry, Walter Sanford, became local judge. Will Beckwith lived on a farm near town, where sometimes my mother went as temporary "help." I always came out over week-ends, played with Will, and ate with the family. Mother always had a rich cake ready for me. Later, Will was one of the few Great Barrington boys who went to college.

Three other boys I knew quite well, but they did not go to the public school. Charles and John Church went to Edward Van Lennep's private school, where numbers of rich young people from out of town were taught. Our own opinion in the high school was that these students did not have brains enough to go to public school. We were probably prejudiced. Mr. Van Lennep tried to have good relations between the town boys and his pupils. The Church family had considerable inherited wealth from their ancestors, the Coffins. The Coffins had taken advantage of the war tariffs and manufactured paper. The young Churches were educated to become a part of the idle rich, but Charles did not take to this role kindly. He and I were quite good friends. The younger, John, on the other hand, was a little exclusive. I remember him especially because he married May Loop, an orphaned hoyden of an old but poor family. She lived next door to me, and was one of the group with which I played on Church Street, where I lived. Later, when I had left town and gone South to school, she had married John. She wrote me and asked if I could find her a colored servant. I couldn't.

There was one little boy to whom I was closely drawn. He was Louis Russell, the son of Farley Russell, the mill owner, who had married a second wife. This Mrs. Russell, whom I knew and who was well acquainted with my family, was a lovely lady who tried to rear young Louis. He was frail, good-hearted, but slow-witted, and did not go to public school. Mostly he was kept at home, and Mrs. Russell made special effort to find companions for him, and she especially chose me. So that quite often I went across the railroad tracks and up the wide and flowered meadow which led to the Russell home. It was one of the most imposing in the village, isolated, and surrounded with grass, flower, and fruit. There were stables in the rear, and outhouses for farming.

I always had a good time when I went to play with Louis. We were welcomed in the house; we ate bread and milk together in the big kitchen; and the Irish servants were kind. Once or twice Mrs. Russell insisted on my taking home certain of Louis' toys. The one which gave me most pleasure was an old wooden bicycle. It was Mrs. Russell to whom my high school principal turned when he wanted me to take up Greek, and my mother and I hesitated because of the cost of the books. She bought all my Greek books.

Of the other town folk outside my schoolmates, I remember especially Johnny Morgan. He was a small man, I think of Welsh descent, and ran a bookstore in the front part of the little shop where the village post office occupied the rear. I went to the post office daily, not because I was expecting mail or often got any, but because of the intriguing exhibition of periodicals and books in Johnny Morgan's store. He became interested in me and very sympathetic. He did not repel me by asking too many questions or trying to find out my plans and ideas. But he made little suggestions and did not object to my looking at the illustrations in *Puck* and *Judge*. I looked them over each week.

I remember one momentous transaction. From early days I had been intrigued by books as books. In our living room I took possession of an old "secretary" which had come down in the family and gathered together in it a number of stray volumes which I found about the house. One I distinctly remember, *Opie on Lying*. There were a few others. I did not read them, but they formed my library. Then one Fall —it was in 1882 and I was in my second year in high school—I saw in Johnny Morgan's window a gorgeous edition of Macaulay's *History of England,* in five volumes, and I wanted it fiercely. Its price was, of course, far beyond my ability to pay, but Johnny Morgan suggested that I buy it on installments. This was not a usual method at that time in Great Barrington. It was our rule to "pay as you go." But I seized on Morgan's suggestion and for several months paid installments of, I think, 25 cents a week. At Christmas time I took my precious purchase home and it still stands in my library.

The first glimpse in the outer and wider world was through Johnny Morgan's store. There I remember very early seeing pictures of U. S. Grant and Tweed, who was beginning his extraordinary career in New York; and later of Hayes and the smooth and rather cruel face of Tilden. Johnny Morgan made other suggestions to me. He arranged while I was in high school that I become the local Great Barrington correspondent of the *Springfield Republican,* which was the most influential and widely circulated paper in western Massachusetts. I sent it from time to time some items of interest, but not many, as I was soon graduated from high school.

Outside my school, my chief communication with the people of the town was through the church. In Great Barrington there were three leading Protestant churches, and later a fourth. The most important church was the Congregational. It had the largest attendance of all the churches, including merchants and farmers, and professional men of the town. My own family on both sides had been Episcopalians, but because we lived near the Congregational church, and because my mother had many acquaintances there, and because the minister, Scudder, was especially friendly, my mother early joined this church. I think we were the only colored communicants. But I grew up in this church and its Sunday School, and it was there that one of the lady members, looking down on a chubby little brown child walking beside his mother, saw me take off my hat. My rather stiff long curls were revealed, and with considerate kindness she said sweetly: "Little girls keep their hats on in church." This of course precipitated at home a wild fight on my part to have my curls cut off, and of course in time, and to my mother's grief, off they came.

In the festivities of the whole year, when strawberries became ripe, when harvest brought in fruit and vegetables, and at Christmas time, there were celebrations in Sunday School, and I was always there. I felt absolutely no discrimination, and I do not think there was any, or any thought of it. When the great church was burned down, I was a sensitive mourner and oversaw at every period its pretentious rebuilding. I remember the altar, whose Greek inscription I was proudly able to read: *"He ilethia eleutherosi humas."* (The truth shall make you free.) I heard the dedicatory sermon: "For thus said the High and Mighty One, who inhabiteth eternity, Whose Name is Holy. I dwell in the high and lofty place. With him also that is of a contrite and humble spirit to revive the spirit of the humble, to revive the heart of the contrite ones."

The new Sunday School building was my chief pride and joy. It had climbed out of the basement and had broad and beautiful rooms with sunlit windows looking out on lawn and flowers. The carpet, the chairs, the tables, were all new, and the teachers were inspired to new efforts with their growing classes. I was quite in my element and led in discussions, with embarrassing questions, and long disquisitions. I learned much of the Hebrew scriptures. I think I must have been both popular and a little dreaded, but I was very happy.

The other leading church was the Episcopalian, a little more heavy in architecture and aristocratic in concept. The older families and the more well-to-do attended. I remember one incident which characterized the religious situation in town. Our leading lawyer had been made a county judge. Judge Dewey lived on the corner of my street, and in a house with which I was very familiar. As a little boy there lived in one of the upper chambers there, overlooking both Main and Church Streets, a young lady who was sick. My mother used to take me there once in a while and I would spend an hour or so in this chamber talking to the lady. Of what we talked, I have not now the faintest idea, but apparently we both were much interested. My mother explained that the lady had cancer, which was the first I had heard of this dread disease. Then visits ceased.

In this house, Judge Dewey and his family lived, his eldest daughter Mary, who had the phenomenal mathematical ability which I have mentioned, a second daughter Sarah, and little Margaret. In the Congregational church, of which Judge Dewey was a high official, the governing board decided to use at Communions individual wine cups instead of the one great silver beaker. Judge Dewey was outraged. He declared that the decision was against the Bible, and he led his flock from Church Street down to the Episcopal church, where thereafter he became a communicant. It was a town sensation.

In the upper part of the town, toward the mill, was a small white wooden Methodist church. It had a small congregation of the less well-known inhabitants of the town. They met quietly and regularly. Then of course across the river, and uncounted by the mass of town folk, was the Catholic church, with a large attendance of Irish working people, and a cemetery nearby. Later, and while I was in high school, the colored folk of the town, mostly newcomers, and not old families like the Burghardts, organized a small branch of the A.M.E. Zion church, which had been formed in New York late in the 18th century. The colored people had long owned a small plot of land in the lower part of the town on Main Street. They were induced to sell this for a small plot on a side street, and there they built a little chapel. The older Negroes were not at all happy about this segregated institution, but now and then we used to attend the services, which became an inconspicuous part of the religious organization of the community.

There was little crime or misdemeanor in our town. We had a single policeman, a little old man named Abe who wore a badge and carried a club. We boys used to make sly fun of him. But there was a little one-roomed "lock-up" and once in a while it had an occupant for a night. In school there were the usual youthful disputes and arguments; but seldom were there fights, and never gangs or feuds. I remember being principal of one fight when I was in grammar school. It was with a strong country boy, but what it was about I have quite forgotten; it had no racial cause I am sure. We left school at noon and instead of going home to lunch, we went up back of the railway station. There before cheering schoolmates we slugged it out manfully. I was pretty thoroughly trounced, but we were both able to report to class at one o'clock looking fairly presentable with our "honor" vindicated. It was as I learned in later life, quite a usual human culture pattern.

Once while I was in high school, a number of us students stole some grapes from a tempting arbor. Now, taking fruit had never been regarded by us as more than the right of town boys and we knew all the best orchards. But in this case we filched some choice and carefully tended grapes from a prominent citizen. There was considerable indignation and Judge Dewey suggested that I and the others might be better off in Reform School. We had a very good one in the eastern part of the State with which the judge was connected. The victim of the theft, however, refused to press any charge and nothing more was heard of Judge Dewey's proposal. But I was considerably disturbed. During my ten years of boyhood life there was in the county one murder; once the bank was robbed of a small sum; there were minor cases of stealing and trespass and some drunkenness which called for arrest.

In government, Great Barrington was in theory and largely in practice a democracy of the New England type. In general politics we were nearly all Republicans. Indeed, it was not respectable to be anything else; one of our prominent lawyers, Joyner, a thin, tall swarthy man, was a Democrat and we suspected him of low origin and questionable designs.

From early years, I attended the town meeting every Spring and in the upper room in that little red brick Town Hall, fronted by a Roman "victory" commemorating the Civil War, I listened to the citizens discuss things about which I knew and had opinions: streets and bridges and schools, and particularly the high school, an institution comparatively new. We had in the town several picturesque hermits, usually retrograde Americans of old families. There was Crosby, the gunsmith, who lived in a lovely dale with brook, waterfall and water wheel. He was a frightful apparition but we boys often ventured to visit him. Particularly there was Baretown Beebe, who came from forest fastnesses which I never penetrated. He was a particularly dirty, ragged, fat old man, who used to come down regularly from his rocks and woods and denounce high school education and expense.

I was 13 or 14 years of age and a student in the small high school with two teachers and perhaps 25 pupils. The high school was not too popular in this rural part of New England and received from the town a much too small appropriation. But the thing that exasperated me was that every Spring at Town Meeting, which I religiously attended, this huge, ragged old man came down from the hills and for an hour or more reviled the high school and demanded its discontinuance.

I remember distinctly how furious I used to get at the stolid town folk, who sat and listened to him. He was nothing and nobody. Yet the town heard him gravely because he was a citizen and property-holder on a small scale and when he was through, they calmly voted the usual funds for the high school. Gradually as I grew up, I began to see that this was the essence of democracy: listening to the other man's opinion and then voting your own, honestly and intelligently.

While without conscious socialist tendencies the town owned its own water supply which poured into the homes from a dark and secret lake hidden in the hills; our charity looked after the few paupers who were "on the town" and we cared for our streets and sewers. On the other hand, our fire department was volunteer and we had no public park save the square around the Town Hall. Indeed what with our meadows and mountains, we needed none.

We made no social arrangements for sickness. That was mainly a matter of friendly charity among relatives and neighbors. There was but one hospital in the county, and that was at Pittsfield and called the "House of Mercy." We had a few physicians in town and they in attending my family were very considerate in their charges. I was seldom sick: whooping cough and measles I remember, but little else. Fortunately I have never broken a bone.

In general thought and conduct I became quite thoroughly New England. It was not good form in Great Barrington to express one's thoughts volubly, or to give way to excessive emotion. We were even sparing in our daily greetings. There was on the street only a curt "good morning" to those whom you knew well and no greetings at all from others. I am quite sure that in a less restrained and conventional atmosphere I should have easily learned to express my emotions with far greater and more unrestrained intensity; but as it was I had the social heritage not only of a New England clan but Dutch taciturnity. This was later reinforced and strengthened by inner withdrawals in the face of real and imagined discriminations. The result was that I was early thrown in upon myself. I found it difficult and even unnecessary to approach other people and by that same token my own inner life perhaps grew the richer; but the habit of repression often returned to plague me in after years, for so early a habit could not easily be unlearned. The Negroes in the South, when I came to know them, could never understand why I did not naturally greet everyone I passed on the street or slap my friends on the back.

Of course our democracy was not full and free. Certain well-known and well-to-do citizens were always elected to office—not the richest or most noted but just as surely not the poorest or the Irish Catholics.

The town and its surroundings were a boy's paradise: there were mountains to climb and rivers to wade and swim; lakes to freeze and hills for coasting. There were orchards and caves and wide green fields; and all of it was apparently property of the children of the town. My earlier contacts with playmates and other human beings were normal and pleasant. Sometimes there was a dearth of available play-mates but that was peculiar to the conventions of the town where families were small and children must go to bed early and not loaf on the streets or congregate in miscellaneous crowds. Later, in the high school, there came some rather puzzling distinctions which I can see now were social and racial; but the racial angle was more clearly defined against the Irish than against me. It was a matter of income and ancestry more than color. I have written elsewhere of the case of our exchanging visiting cards when one girl, a new-comer, did not seem to want mine, to my vast surprise.

I presume I was saved evidences of a good deal of actual discrimination by my own keen sensitiveness. My compan-ions did not have a chance to refuse me invitations; they must seek me out and urge me to come as indeed they often did. When my presence was not wanted they had only to refrain from asking. But in the ordinary social affairs of the village—the Sunday School with its picnics and festivals; the temporary skating rink in the Town Hall; the coasting in crowds on all the hills—in all of these, I took part with no thought of discrimination on the part of my fellows, for that I would have been the first to notice.

Indeed, even in high school it was not regarded as good form for the boys to pair about with the girls. They did not walk together on the streets. They did not talk with each other too often on the grounds. I suppose that this fact ex-plains much that bothers us today. Today, high schools with their higher age level, and retarded pupils, have become social centers and even matrimonial agencies, particularly in the South. It is this concept of the high school which par-tially explains the fanatical resistance to desegregation as at Little Rock.

Later, I was protected in part by the fact that there was little social activity in the high school; there were no fra-ternities; there were no school dances; there were no honor societies. Whatever of racial feeling gradually crept into my life, its effect upon me in these earlier days was rather one of exaltation and high disdain. They were the losers who did not ardently court me, and not I, which seemed to be proven by the fact that I had no difficulty in outdoing them in nearly all competition, especially intellectual. In athletics I was not outstanding. I was only moderately good at baseball and football; but at running, exploring, story-telling and planning of intricate games, I was often if not always the leader.

After I entered the high school, economic problems and questions of the future began to loom. They were partly settled by my own activities. My mother's limited sources of income were helped through boarding the barber, my uncle, supplemented infrequently by her own day's work, and by some kindly unobtrusive charity. But I was keen and eager to eke out this income by various jobs; splitting kindling, mowing lawns, doing chores. I early came to understand that to be "on the town," the recipient of public charity, was the depth not only of misfortune but of a certain guilt. I presume some of my folk sank to that, but not to my knowledge. We earned our way. I have a little postcard dated in 1883 in which Miss Smith on September 19 writes, "We would like to have you come certainly next Saturday as you did last week to do some splitting for us." This was a matter of splitting up kindling for two maiden ladies and this was one of the first of my economic enterprises.

My first regular wage began as I entered the high school: I went early of mornings and filled with coal one or two of the new so-called "base burning" stoves in the millinery shop of Madame L'Hommedieu. From then on, all through my high school course, I worked after school and on Saturdays.

For some time too I sent weekly letters to a colored weekly *New York Age* and sold copies, and before the A&P stores dealt in groceries and simply were selling tea, I was one of their local agents. Thus in all sorts of little ways I managed to earn some money and never asked or thought of gifts.

Of the great things happening in the United States at that time we were touched only by the Panic of 1873, when my uncle in 1876 came home from the little town east of us where he was a leading barber. He brought me, I remember, a silver dollar, which was an extraordinary thing. Up to that time I had seen nothing but paper money.

The United States in the decades 1870-1890 was an extraordinary country. Grant, Hayes, Garfield, Arthur and Grover Cleveland were presidents. James G. Blaine was an aspirant who barely missed the highest office, and the country was reckless and prosperous; squandering its seemingly endless resources; tying East and West with railways; exploiting iron and coal and oil and making fortunes for a new and ruthless caste of businessmen who were cashing in on the cost of the Civil War. Many results of this I could see in my town.

On the other hand, the inner social group of my own relatives and colored friends always had furnished me as a boy most interesting and satisfying company. The color line was manifest and yet not absolutely drawn. I remember a cousin of mine who brought home a white wife. The chief objection was that he was not able to support her and nobody knew her family; and knowledge of family history was counted as highly important. Many of the colored people had some white blood from unions several generations past. That colored folk congregated together in their own social life was natural because that was the rule in the town. There were little social knots of people, but not much that today would be called social life, save that which centered about the churches; and there the colored folk often took part.

The fate of my various relatives among the black Burghardts I do not know very well. One cousin, Jimmie Burghardt, lived near Williams College and always wanted to enter. But he never did. He lacked both money and Greek and worked as college janitor. But his granddaughter is stenographer in a large New York corporation. Others have prospered as western farmers, one became a singer and teacher of music and another was head of the home economics department in the colored school system of a large border state city. Of course it is probably true that there are hundreds of black Burghardt descendants working as ordinary citizens—teachers and a few others in the professions, civil servants, artisans and skilled laborers; and plain hard workers on street and in home. I greet them all.

Now and then I made little trips to neighboring towns: to my cousins, the Pipers in Sheffield, five miles south, to play with John and his sisters; to Pittsfield, two long miles north, where my cousins Mary and Lizzie Potter lived and where I saw the lovely Rita Tredwell. Once I stayed with my uncle in Amherst who lived with a niece and owned a barber shop. He bought me a new suit of beautiful "navy-blue" cloth.

But my greatest boyhood trip came in 1883, when I was 15 and in third-year high school. In 1874 my grandfather having lost his third wife was proposing to marry a widow, Mrs. Green, and assured her of a home in New Bedford whither he had moved from Springfield. He writes: "I have bought of the Petomska Mills Corporation the house and lot southwest corner of Landby and Third streets. The lot is the whole width of what the corporation owns on Landby and runs south far enough to comprise 20 roods for $2,000 —one half to be paid in cash—and the rest either over a year or with 7% interest and secured by mortgage on the premises."

Grandfather then adds: "Entreat me not to leave thee or to return from following after thee, for whither thou goest, I will go, where thou lodgest will I lodge, thy people shall by my people, and thy God my God. Where thou diest will I die, and there will I be buried."

"I like you better as our acquaintance extends, my dear Anna. Come to my house as soon as it shall please you so to do, there shall be but one home, one purse, one affection, one God."

They were eventually married, and in 1883 my grandfather's last wife wrote my mother. She had known and liked my father and understood his difficulties with his father. When he had left us and was presumably dead, she heard of me and wanted me to come and let my grandfather see and know me. My mother was excited and determined that I should make the trip. How she managed to raise the money, I do not know. But always, Mother, in her resourceful way, got for me whatever she thought I needed. She got together money for my trip, hoping that grandfather might eventually help in my education. So off I went to my first great excursion into the world.

I went down the Housatonic railroad to Bridgeport and missed my train to New Haven because of the contradiction of clocks with the new standard time. I traded my ticket for another route by way of Hartford. There I saw the capitol building and wrote about signing the register for "distinguished guests!"—was late in reaching Providence and a bit put out because my grandmother's friend was not promptly on hand to meet me.

One incident during my stay was unforgettable. One afternoon the center table in the parlor was decorated with a festive cloth, cut-glass decanter of wine and two wineglasses. Grandfather expected a visitor, and so I hovered in the background.

The visitor proved to be a large black man, with pleasant countenance, and well-dressed. My grandfather in long black coat, received Mr. Freedom with grave courtesy. They sat down and talked seriously; finally my grandfather arose, filled the wineglasses and raised his glass and touched the glass of his friend, murmuring a toast. I had never before seen such ceremony: I had read about it in books, but in Great Barrington both white and black avoided ceremony. To them it smacked of pretense. We went to the other extreme of casual greetings, sprawling posture and curt rejoinder. The black Burghardts indulged in jokes and back-slapping. I suddenly sensed in my grandfather's parlor what manners meant and how people of breeding behaved and were able to express what we in Great Barrington were loath to give act to, or unable. I never forgot that toast.

The house in New Bedford was sold after grandfather's

death in 1887 for $2,110. He is buried in Oak Grove Cemetery near the Yale Campus, New Haven, in a lot which he owned, and which is next to that of Jehudi Ashmun of Liberian fame. His eldest daughter married a light mulatto and their descendants are now passing for white and probably quite unaware of their colored blood. My Aunt Henrietta married a man named Bates, of Cumberland, Allegheny County, Maryland.

On my return from New Bedford I had another stirring experience. I stopped again with grandmother's friend in Providence and he took me to the annual picnic at Rocky Point on Narragansett Bay where the colored people of three states were wont to assemble. I viewed with astonishment ten thousand Negroes of every hue and bearing, saw in open-mouthed astonishment the whole gorgeous gamut of the American Negro world; the swaggering men, the beautiful girls, the laughter and gaiety, the unhampered self-expression. I was astonished and inspired. I apparently noted nothing of poverty or degradation, but only extraordinary beauty of skin-color and utter equality of mien, with absence so far as I could see of even the shadow of the line of race. I came home by way of Springfield and Albany where I was a guest of my elder half-brother and saw my first electric street light blink and sputter.

I was graduated from high school in 1884 and was of course the only colored student. Once during my course another dark boy had attended the school for a short time, but I was very much ashamed of him because he did not excel the whites as I was quite used to doing. All 13 of us graduates had orations, and mine was on Wendell Phillips. The great anti-slavery agitator had just died in February and I presume that some of my teachers must have suggested the subject, although it is quite possible that I chose it myself. But I was fascinated by his life and his work and took a long step toward a wider conception of what I was going to do.

Most of the short speeches were fairly conventional essays; but I thought the talk of Minnie Crissey on reading was especially good and I envied her knowledge of books. My own essay brought loud applause from the audience because of my race and subject. I was born in a community which conceived itself as having helped put down a wicked rebellion for the purpose of freeing four million slaves. They deeply admired Phillips despite the fact that recently he had adopted socialism. My mother was in the audience and was filled with pride.

Meanwhile, elsewhere in the world there were stirring and change which were to mean so much in my life: In Japan the Meiji Emperors rose to power the year I was born; in China the intrepid Empress Dowager was fighting strangulation by England and France; Prussia had fought with Austria and France, and the German Empire arose in 1871. In England, Victoria opened her eighth parliament and the duel of Disraeli and Gladstone began; while in Africa came the Abyssinian expedition and opening of the Suez Canal, so fateful for all my people.

CHAPTER VIII

I GO SOUTH

In the Summer of 1884, after my graduation from high school, there loomed the problem as to where I was to go to college. The fact that I was going had been settled in my own mind from the time that my school principal, Frank Hosmer, had recommended my high school course. Hosmer was a graduate of Amherst and later in life he became president of Oahu College, Hawaii. He suggested, quite as a matter of course, that I ought to take the college preparatory course which involved algebra, geometry, Latin and Greek. If Hosmer had been another sort of man, with definite ideas as to a Negro's "place," and had recommended agriculture or domestic economy, I would doubtless have followed his advice, had such "courses" been available. I did not then realize that Hosmer was quietly opening college doors to me, for in those days they were barred with ancient tongues.

This meant a considerable expenditure for books which were not free in those days, and were more costly than my own folk could afford; but Mrs. Russell, the wife of one of the mill owners, or rather I ought to describe her as the mother of one of my playmates, after some hesitation offered to furnish all the necessary books. I accepted the offer as something normal and right; only after many years did I realize how critical this gift was for my career. I am not yet sure how she came to do it; perhaps my wise principal suggested it. Comparatively few of my white classmates planned or cared to plan for college—perhaps two or three in my class of 13. I became therefore a high school student preparing for college and thus occupied an unusual position among whites in the town.

I collected catalogues of colleges and over the claims of Williams and Amherst, nearest my home, or of Yale not much further, I blithely picked Harvard, because it was oldest and largest and most widely known. But a question arose in my case, a young and ambitious colored man. What were the possibilities of employment or of any career after such training? I imagine this matter was discussed considerably among my friends, white and black.

However in my mind there was no doubt but that I was going to college. The whole matter was subtly taken out of my hands and a sort of guardianship of family and white friends was quietly established. I was advised that after all I was rather young to go directly to college; and also our high school was below the standard of Harvard entrance requirements. It might then be wise for me to work and study a year and then enter college in the Fall of '85. There followed an unexpected change when in the Fall of 1884 my mother died.

I felt a certain gladness to see her at peace at last, for she had worried all her life. Of my own loss I had then little realization. That came only in after years. Now it was the choking gladness and solemn feel of wings! At last, I was going beyond the hills and into the world that beckoned steadily. There followed the half-guilty feeling that now I could begin life without forsaking my mother. I had realized all along that even college would not have induced me to leave my mother in want. I somehow argued that the family would support mother in my absence, yet I must have known this was impossible; that what she would always need was for me to be near. Now I was free and unencumbered and at the same time more alone than I had ever dreamed of being. This very grief was a challenge. Now especially I must succeed as my mother so desperately wanted me to.

I was, however, an orphan, without a cent of property, and with no relative who could for a moment think of undertaking the burden of my further education. My grandfather was growing old, and had little. But the family at home could and did help out; and the town in its quiet and unemotional way was satisfied with my record and silently began to plan. There were three white men in Great Barrington who seemed to have clear ideas as to my future. The first was the high school principal, whom I have mentioned. The second was Edward Van Lennep, principal of the only local private school, and very active in the Congregational church, where he was superintendent of the Sunday School, which I attended. Whether or not he consulted with Mr. Hosmer, I do not know, but he probably did. At any rate he was satisfied that I ought to go to college and that the fact that my skin was colored was of no importance. When, then, a suggestion was made which involved the raising of a scholarship for me, Mr. Lennep and his pastor, Mr. Scudder, were eager to cooperate.

The third man was the Rev. C. C. Painter, whose son Charles was a schoolmate of mine during the high school course. Mr. Painter was a Congregational minister and for a time served in the Federal Indian Bureau. There and elsewhere he saw the problem of the reconstructed South, and conceived the idea that this was the place for me to be educated and that in the South lay my future field of work.

Meantime my family contributed an unexpected piece of good fortune. There had been a great-uncle of mine, Tom Burghardt, son of Jack, whose tombstone I had often seen in the town graveyard. My family used to say in undertones that the unpaid wage of Tom Burghardt helped to build the Pacific Railroad. Nearly all his life Tom Burghardt had been a servant in the Kellog family, only the family usually forgot to pay him any wage. Finally when he died they did give him a handsome burial and a white tombstone. Then Mark Hopkins, a son or relative of the great Mark, appeared on the scene and married a daughter of the Kellogs. He became one of the Huntington-Stanford-Crocker Pacific Associates who built, manipulated and cornered the Pacific railroads and with the help of the Kellog nest-egg, Hopkins made 19 million dollars in the West by methods not to be too strictly inquired into.

His widow came back to Great Barrington in the 80's and took up residence in the old family mansion on Main Street, overlooking the wide meadows and great East Mountain beyond, with its wealth of blue granite. I know the old white house well and its picket fence. I passed it almost daily when as a little boy I went to get milk from the Taylor home on the opposite hill. Mrs. Hopkins brought with her to Great Barrington from San Francisco a young man named Dennis who became my friend. He was a well educated young mulatto, quick, competent and in complete charge of Mrs. Hopkins' local business affairs. I used to meet him almost daily on my way to school and we had most interesting conversations. He was perhaps the first to tell me of his employer's plan to build a new mansion of blue granite, between the old home and the school yard and rising above the lovely stretch of meadows. I think it was Dennis in consultation with my family who saw to it that I was offered a place as timekeeper on the new project, at what seemed to me the fabulous wage of a dollar a day. I had never before earned more than a dollar a week.

Norcross Brothers of Worcester were the contractors; stonecutter, masons and carpenters came to town. I was duly installed in one of the temporary work sheds, with desk and high chair, fronting a window, by which passed all the yardfull of workers each day. My superior was a pleasant Frenchman, who liked my French name and whose home I visited now and then.

It was a most interesting experience and had new and intriguing bits of reality and romance. As timekeeper and the obviously young and inexperienced agent of superiors, I was the one who handed the discharged workers their last wage envelopes. I talked with contractors and saw the problems of employers. I poured over the plans and specifications and even came in some contact with the distinguished English architect, Searles, who finally came to direct the work after the American architect failed to meet the expanding ideas of Mrs. Hopkins. Searles had the glamour and the clothes of an English gentleman and soon the whole direction and control of the Hopkins fortune passed into his hands. Dennis, the steward, was gradually pushed aside and down into "his place." The architect eventually married the widow and her wealth, and the steward killed himself.

So the Hopkins millions passed strangely into foreign hands, and after the death of Mrs. Hopkins and Searles himself, went to his nephew, an utter stranger to the town and its people. This posed for me my first problem of inheritance. Meantime the fabrication and growth of this marvelous palace, beautiful beyond anything that Great Barrington had seen, went slowly and majestically on, and always I could sit and watch it grow. Eventually its grounds occupied my old school site; the school buildings were torn down and new grounds were found across the river.

Here I worked through the Summer of 1885. I boarded with my Aunt Minerva at a nominal charge. I bought a new wardrobe, visited my cousins now and then in the county, and then in September came the plan which Mr. Painter had evolved for a scholarship. He induced my mother's Congregational church and three other churches which he had once pastored in Connecticut, each to furnish me $25 a year for the length of my college course. This would be enough to support me at Fisk University, a college for Negroes in Nashville, Tennessee, which was said to do excellent work.

Disappointed though I was at not being able to go immediately to Harvard, I regarded this merely as a temporary change of plan; I would of course go to Harvard in the end. But here and now was adventure. I was going into the South; the South of slavery, rebellion and black folk; above all, I was going to meet colored people of my own age and education, of my own ambitions.

My family and colored friends rather resented the idea. Their Northern free Negro prejudice naturally revolted at the idea of sending me to the former land of slavery, either for education or for living. I am rather proud of myself that I did not agree with them. Whether or not I should always live and work in the South, I did not then stop to decide; that I would give up the idea of graduating from Harvard, did not occur to me. But I wanted to go to Fisk, not simply because it was at least a beginning of my dream of college, but also, I suspect, because I was beginning to feel lonesome in New England. Unconsciously, I realized that as I grew

older, and especially now that I had finished the public
school, the close cordial intermingling with my white fellows
would grow more restricted. There would be meetings,
parties, clubs, to which I would not be invited. Especially in
the case of strangers, visitors, newcomers to the town would
my presence and friendship become a matter of explanation
or even embarrassment to my schoolmates. I became aware,
once a chance to go to a group of young people of my own
race was opened up for me, of the spiritual isolation in which
I was living.

I heard too in these days for the first time the Negro folk
songs. A Hampton Quartet had sung them in the Congregational church. I was thrilled and moved to tears and seemed
to recognize something inherently and deeply my own. I was
glad to go to Fisk. On the other hand, my people had clung
to a more unromantic view of the situation. They said frankly
that it was a shame to send me South. I was Northern born
and bred and instead of preparing me for work and giving
me an opportunity right there in my own town and state,
they were bundling me off to the South. This was undoubtedly true. The educated young white folk of Great Barrington became clerks in stores, bookkeepers and teachers, and
a few went into professions. Others went to the cities or the
West where they were welcome. Great Barrington was not
able to conceive of me in such local positions. It was not so
much that they were opposed to it, but it did not occur to
them as a possibility.

On the other hand, there was the call of the black South;
teachers were needed. The crusade of the New England
schoolmarm had done a fine work. The freed slaves, if properly led, had a great future. Temporarily they were deprived
of their full voting privileges, but this was but a passing set-
back. Black folk were bound in time to play a large role in
the South. They needed trained leadership. I was sent to help
furnish it.

Meantime I was learning something of industry. I began
to see the workers as human beings and to know how hard a
task stonecutting by hand was; I began to realize what dis-

charge from a job meant when there was no union and no funds for supporting the unemployed; but all this was vague in my mind.

I went into Tennessee at the age of 17 to enter Fisk University. I collected all my personal property which I could take with me: my books; my grandfather's wrought iron tongs and shovel; I kept a few pieces of the blue china which all my life had graced the Thanksgiving and Christmas table. I longed for the great brass kettle in which Grandmother Burghardt had washed and made soap, but I was dissuaded. Nor could I carry the family Bible which went to cousin Ines. Mrs. Cass remitted the rent due so as to cover my railway fare. I left no other debts.

Then came the fascinating railroad ride to New York; the ferry ride up the Hudson past the great city, and transfer to Grand Central. Next day as I was riding through Kentucky, a brown boy from Bowling Green sat down beside me. He was Otho Porter and was also going to Fisk University. I liked his frank face and very neat appearance and when he proposed that we be roommates I eagerly consented. Roommates we were for all my college course. He became the leading colored physician in Kentucky, whom I often visited in after years. Ah! the wonder of that journey, with its faint spice of adventure, as I entered the land of slaves.

I was thrilled to be for the first time among so many people of my own color or rather of such various and such extraordinary colors, which I had only glimpsed before, but who it seemed were bound to me by new and exciting and eternal ties. Never before had I seen young men so self-assured and who gave themselves such airs, and colored men at that; and above all for the first time I saw beautiful girls. At my home among my white schoolmates there were a few pretty girls; but either they were not entrancing or because I had known them all my life, I did not notice them; but at Fisk the never-to-be-forgotten marvel of that first supper came with me opposite two of the most beautiful beings God ever revealed to the eyes of 17. I promptly lost my appetite, but I was deliriously happy! Of one of these girls I have often said, no human being could possibly have been as beautiful as she seemed to my young eyes in that far-off September night of 1885. She was the great-aunt of Lena Horne and fair as Lena Horne is, Lena Calhoun was far more beautiful.

So I came to a region where the world was split into white and black halves, and where the darker half was held back by race prejudice and legal bonds, as well as by deep ignorance and dire poverty. But facing this was not a lost group, but at Fisk a microcosm of a world and a civilization in potentiality. Into this world I leapt with enthusiasm. A new loyalty and allegiance replaced my Americanism: henceforward I was a Negro.

To support this was the teaching and culture background of Fisk of the latter 19th century. All of its teachers but one were white, from New England or from the New Englandized Middle West. My own culture background thus suffered no change or hiatus. Its application only was new. This *point d'appui* was not simply Tennessee, which was never a typical slave state, but Georgia, Alabama, Mississippi, Louisiana and Texas, whence our students came; and who as mature men and women, could paint from their own experience a wide and vivid picture of the postwar South and of its black millions. There were men and women who had faced mobs and seen lynchings; who knew every phase of insult and repression; and too there were sons, daughters and clients of every class of white Southerner. A relative of a future president of the nation had his dark son driven to school each day.

I arrived on the Fisk campus in September and in October was struck down by a severe attack of typhoid fever which was too prevalent in Nashville. This was a campus crisis. First I was from New England, a rare phenomenon at Fisk. Second my excellent public school training landed me in the sophomore class, an unheard of thing, especially for a lad of 17 when my college mates averaged five to ten years older. I was a campus curiosity even for the teachers. As I lay deathly sick, an orphan in a strange land, the whole school hung on the bulletins. When I at last crept out, thin and pale, I was the school favorite.

Then in a few weeks came the annual school-wide English examination, which induced poorly trained students to review reading, writing and arithmetic. I stood second with only Mary Bennett, the white German teacher's daughter, outranking me. I could not quite forgive her as a girl and a white one at that. I also knew that the test was unfair to most of the students who had never had decent elementary school training in the colored public schools of the South. Nevertheless my popularity rather went to my head. I was bright, but sharp-tongued and given to joking hard with my fellows. Some resented this and I remember C. O. Hunter, a big, black, earnest boy near twice my size who resented some quip of mine. He took me so firmly by the arm that I winced. He said, "Don't you do that again!" I didn't.

Proctor was a tall, rail-like lad in the class below me. We were rivals in debate, and 20 years later, I met him again in Atlanta, swollen physically to huge proportions and pastor of the leading Negro church for intelligent social work. We worked together after the Atlanta riot [of 1906]. G. D. Field was a little black man, serious, who knew and hated the white South. He always carried a pistol. "No," he answered as I expressed surprise, "You don't need it often, but when you do, it comes in handy!" L. B. Moore was tall and dark, with a scintillating mind. He was always a leader in jokes and study. He married a Methodist bishop's daughter and eventually became head of a department at Howard University.

One man whom we called "Pop" Miller, I grew cordially to dislike. He was much older than most of the students and had been retarded by poverty in his education. His wife was taking in washing to keep him in school. He was a fat, black man, and exceedingly pious. When I recovered from the fever, quite naturally on the rebound, I joined the college Congregational church. I was not "religious" but I was honest and believed, in our placid New England way, most of the church creed. I wrote of this to the pastor of my church in February 1886:

"You have no doubt expected to hear of my welfare before this, but nevertheless you must know I am very grateful to

you and the Sunday School for what you have done. In the
first place I am glad to tell you that I have united with the
Church here and hope that the prayers of my Sunday School
may help guide me in the path of Christian duty. During the
revival we had nearly forty conversions. The day of prayer
for colleges was observed here with two prayer meetings. The
Rev. Mr. Aitkin, the Scotch revivalist, spoke to us a short
time ago, and tomorrow Mr. Moody will be present at our
chapel exercises.

"Our University is very nicely situated, overlooking the
city, and the family life is very pleasant indeed. Some mornings as I look about upon the two or three hundred of my
companions assembled for morning prayers I can hardly realize they are all my people; that this great assembly of youth
and intelligence are the representatives of a race which
twenty years ago was in bondage. Although this sunny land is
very pleasant, notwithstanding its squalor, misery and ignorance spread broadcast; and although it is a bracing thought
to know that I stand among those who do not despise me for
my color, yet I have not forgotten to love my New England
hills, and I often wish I could join some of your pleasant
meetings in person as I do in spirit."

But "Pop" Miller did not allow my church membership
to progress as placidly as I planned. He was an official of the
church and a fundamentalist in religion. He soon had me
and others accused before the church for dancing. I was astonished. I had danced all my life quite as naturally as I sang
and ran. In Great Barrington there was little chance to dance
on the part of anyone but in the small group of colored folk
there was always some dancing along with playing games at
homes. When I came South and was among my own young
folk who not only danced but danced beautifully and with
effortless joy, I joined and learned eagerly. I never attended
public dance halls, but at the homes of colored friends in the
city, we nearly always danced and a more innocent pastime I
could not imagine. But Miller was outraged. What kind of
dancing he was acquainted with I do not know, but at any
rate in his mind dancing figured as a particularly heinous

form of sin. I resented this and said so in very plain terms.
The teachers intervened and tried to reconcile matters in a
way which for years afterward made me resentful and led to
my eventual refusal to join a religious organization. They
admitted that my dancing might well be quite innocent, but
said that my example might lead others astray. They quoted
Paul: "If meat maketh my brother to offend, I will eat no
meat while the world standeth." I tried to accept this for
years, and for years I wrestled with this problem. Then I resented this kind of sophistry. I began again to dance and I
have never since had much respect for Paul.

I remember quite vividly many others of those schoolmates of long ago. Ransom Edmondson was a handsome man,
tall and thin, olive-skinned with a mass of brown hair, wear-
ing spectacles and curiously dignified. He was five or six
years older than I and acted as assistant librarian under Professor Morgan who taught Latin. He and a younger brother
were sons of a rich white planter. Frank Smith of the class
ahead of me was a yellow dandy, faultlessly dressed and a
squire of dames. He later married Lena Calhoun with whom
I was hopelessly in love; but Smith was over 25 years of age
and ready for a wife. I had yet ten years to work and wait.
Tom Talley had one of the great bass voices of all time. But
he gave his life and strength to teaching and singing for the
college and never had sufficient time for the study which his
magnificent voice required. Little Sissie Dorsey, a golden
fairy with the voice of an angel, sang at all our concerts.
Mattie Nichol was a dark cream and gorgeous little person
with a fiery temper. John Barber was a handsome smiling
playboy, spoiled by his mother. After graduation he married
Mattie but two years later he laid his head on the railroad
tracks and let a locomotive run over it.

All my schoolmates were not handsome and rich. There
was black, coarse-looking Sherrod, poor and slow, who worked
his way painfully through college, studied medicine at neighboring Meharry Medical School and became one of the best
physicians in Mississippi.

Two girls were rivals of mine and resented my superior

attitude toward girls; but we did not dislike each other. Maggie Murray crowed over me when I forgot my lines at rhetorical exercises. Later she became the third wife of Booker Washington and survived him. Mamie Steward came from Western New York and was my classmate. We were keen but appreciative rivals. Emma Terry was black, smooth-skinned and kindly, and a favorite with all. Tom Calloway was a pal of mine and remained so for 40 years. He was the executive go-getter, strong and tireless. I was the planner. Together we collected funds for the first Fisk gymnasium. I edited the school paper, the *Fisk Herald,* and Calloway was business manager. We made it self-supporting during our time.

Other Fiskites who impressed me were William Morris who was the first colored member of our faculty and to my pride as good as any of the whites. The colored Crosthwaite family as students and graduates greatly influenced me. George McClennan was an old graduate, very religious but not dogmatic, who wrote poetry which had merit. He talked earnestly to us about life. Alice Vassar was another of our beautiful voices to whom we listened with joy.

The college curriculum was limited but excellent. Adam Spence was a great Greek scholar by any comparison. Thomas Chase with his ridiculously small laboratory nevertheless taught us not only chemistry and physics but something of science and life. In after years I used Bennett's German in Germany, and with the philosophy and ethics of President Cravath, I later sat under William James and George Palmer at Harvard. The excellent and earnest teaching, the small college classes, the absence of distractions, either in athletics or society, enabled me to arrange and build my program for freedom and progress among Negroes. I replaced my hitherto egocentric world by a world centering and whirling about my race in America.

For this group I built my plan of study and accomplishment. Through the leadership of men like myself and my fellows, we were going to have these enslaved Israelites out of the still enduring bondage in short order. It was a battle

which might conceivably call for force, but I could think of
it mainly as a battle of wits; of knowledge and deed, which
by sheer reason and desert, must eventually overwhelm the
forces of hate, ignorance and reaction. Consider for a moment our president, Erastus Cravath, whose son became head
of one of the nation's leading corporation law firms. When
he died in 1901, I said at his memorial exercises in Atlanta:

"He was cast in body and mind of large mold—one never
expected little actions in any work from him either of hand
or soul. There was none of that quick nervous energy or
hasty action or brilliant deed that have so often seared and
marred the world. His was rather a slow well-balanced mind.
He knew how to pause in his work and in his speed and
gather strength for slow but irrepressible advance. But if
his mind worked slowly and calmly it also worked with a
logical persistency and far-reaching grasp of thought that was
bound to bring results in the long run. I remember that as
students it was a standing joke among us that no matter how
long President Cravath's sentences might be or how intricate
and involved, they were sure at some time to come to a logical and grammatical conclusion—their construction was never
changed—there were no rhetorical dashes but they moved
ponderously and doggedly to the end and the end was usually worth hearing. He was a man of broad sympathies. He
appreciated a joke although he was not quick to see one.
There was once in school a very small and terribly mischievous boy named Cummings, but I doubt if the grave president ever knew why the school persisted in smiling when he
prayed, 'Oh Lord forgive us for our shortcomings.'

"Erastus Cravath was a man who formed his life ideal
when he was yet young; who early came to believe in the
possibilities of the Negro race and the reality of the broader
humanity taught by the Christian religion. He did not hold
this merely as a theory, as an intellectual belief, but as a
thing worth living and fighting for—and for it he lived and
fought."

Always in my dreaming, a certain redeeming modicum of
common sense has usually come to my rescue and brought

fantasy down to the light of common day. I was not content to take the South entirely by hearsay; and while I had no funds to travel widely, I did, somewhat to the consternation of both my teachers and fellow-students, determine to go out into the country and teach summer school. I was only 18 and knew nothing of the South at first hand, save what little I had seen in Nashville from the protected vantage ground of a college campus. I had not seen anything of the small Southern town and the countryside, which are the real South. If I could not explore Darkest Mississippi, at least I could see East Tennessee, which was not more than 50 miles from the college. I determined to know something of the Negro in the country districts; to go out and teach during the summer vacation. I was not compelled to do this, for my scholarship was sufficient to support me, but that was not the point. I had heard about the country in the South as the real seat of slavery. I wanted to know it.

Needless to say the experience was invaluable. I travelled not only in space but in time. I touched the very shadow of slavery. I lived and taught school in log cabins built before the Civil War. My first school was the second held in the district since Emancipation. I touched intimately the lives of the commonest of mankind—people who ranged from barefooted dwellers on dirt floors, with patched rags for clothes, to rough, hard-working farmers, with plain, clean plenty.

First, there was a Teachers' Institute at the county seat; and there distinguished guests of the superintendent taught the teachers fractions and spelling and other mysteries— white teachers in the morning, Negroes at night. This was to supplement the wretched elementary training of the prospective teachers. A picnic now and then, and a supper, and the rough world of the colored folk was softened by laughter and song.

There came a fine day when all the teachers left the Institute and began the hunt for schools. I learned from hearsay (for my mother was mortally afraid of fire-arms) that the hunting of ducks and bears and men is wonderfully interesting, but I am sure that the man who has never hunted a country school in the South has something to learn of the pleasures of the chase. I see now the white, hot roads lazily rise and wind and fall before me under the burning July sun; I feel the deep weariness of heart and limb as ten, eight, six miles stretch relentlessly ahead; I feel my heart sink heavily as I hear again and again "Got a teacher? Yes." So I walked on and on—horses were too expensive—until I had wandered beyond railways, beyond stage lines, to a land of "varmints" and rattlesnakes, where the coming of a stranger was an event, and men lived and died in the shadow of one blue hill.

Sprinkled over hill and dale lay cabins and farmhouses, shut out from the world by the forests and the rolling hills toward the east. There I found at last a little school. Josie told me of it; she was a thin, homely girl of 20, with a dark-brown face and thick, hard hair. I had crossed the stream at Watertown, and rested under the great willows; then I had gone to the little cabin in the lot, where Josie was resting on her way to town. The gaunt black farmer made me welcome and Josie, hearing my errand, told me anxiously that they wanted a school over the hill; that but once since the Civil War had a teacher been there; that she herself longed to learn—and thus she ran on, talking fast and loud, with much earnestness and energy.

Next morning I crossed the tall round hill, lingered to look at the blue and yellow mountains stretching toward the Carolinas, then plunged into the wood, and came out at Josie's home. It was a dull frame cottage with four rooms, perched just below the brow of the hill, amid peach trees. The father was a quiet, simple soul, calmly ignorant, with no touch of vulgarity. The mother was different—strong, bustling, and energetic, with a quick, restless tongue, and an ambition to live "like folks." There was a crowd of children. Two boys had gone away. There remained two growing girls; a shy midget of eight; John, tall, awkward and 18; Jim, younger, quicker and better looking; and two babies of indefinite age.

Then there was Josie herself. She seemed to be the center

of the family; always busy at service, or at home, or berry-picking; a little nervous and inclined to scold, like her mother, yet faithful, too, like her father. She had about her a certain fineness, the shadow of an unconscious moral heroism that would willingly give all of life to make life broader, deeper and fuller for her and hers. I saw much of this family afterwards, and grew to love them for their honest efforts to be decent and comfortable, and for their knowledge of their own ignorance. There was with them no affectation. The mother would scold the father for being so "easy"; Josie would roundly berate the boys for careless-ness; and all knew that it was a hard thing to dig a living out of a rocky side-hill. I found a place where there had been a Negro public school only once since the Civil War; and there for two successive terms during the summer I taught at 28 and 30 dollars a month.

It was an enthralling experience. I remember the day I rode horseback out to the commissioner's house with a pleasant young white fellow who wanted the white school. The road ran down the bed of a stream; the sun laughed and the water jingled, and we rode on. "Come in," said the commissioner, "come in. Have a seat. Yes, that certificate will do." I was pleasantly surprised when the superintendent in-vited me to stay for dinner; and he would have been astonished if he had dreamed that I expected to eat at the table with him and not after he was through.

The schoolhouse was a log hut, where Colonel Wheeler used to store his corn. It sat in a lot behind a rail fence and thorn bushes, near the sweetest of springs. There was an entrance where a door once was, and within, a massive rickety fireplace; great chinks between the logs served as windows. Furniture was scarce. My desk was made of three boards reinforced at critical points, and my chair, borrowed from my landlady, had to be returned every night. Seats for the children—these puzzled me much. I was haunted by a New England vision of neat little desks and chairs, but, alas the reality was rough plank benches without backs, and at times without legs. They had the one virtue of making naps dangerous, possibly fatal, for the floor was not to be trusted. All the appointments of my school were primitive: a windowless log cabin; hastily manufactured benches; no blackboards; almost no books, long, long distances to walk. On the other hand, I heard the sorrow songs sung with primitive beauty and grandeur. I saw the hard, ugly drudgery of country life and the writhing of landless, ignorant peasants. I saw the race problem at nearly its lowest terms.

It was a hot morning late in July when the school opened. I trembled when I heard the patter of little feet down the dusty road, and saw the growing row of dark solemn faces and bright eager eyes facing me. First came Josie and her brothers and sisters. The longing to know, to be a student in the great school at Nashville, hovered like a star above this child-woman amid her work and worry, and she studied doggedly. There were the Dowells from their farm toward Alexandria—Fanny, with her smooth black face and wondering eyes; Martha, brown and dull; the pretty girl-wife of a brother, and the younger brood.

There were the Burkes—two brown and yellow lads, and a tiny haughty-eyed girl. Fat Reuben's little chubby girl came, with golden face and old-gold hair, faithful and solemn. 'Thonie was on hand early—a jolly, ugly, good-hearted girl, who slyly dipped snuff and looked after her little bow-legged brother. When her mother could spare her, 'Tildy came— a midnight beauty, with starry eyes and tapering limbs; and her brother, correspondingly homely. And the big boys— the hulking Lawrences; the lazy Neills, unfathered sons of mother and daughter; Hickman, with a stoop in his shoulders, and the rest.

There they sat, nearly 30 of them, on the rough benches, their faces shading from a pale cream to a deep brown, the little feet bare and swinging, the eyes full of expectation, with here and there a twinkle of mischief, and the hands grasping Webster's blue-back spelling book. I loved my school, and the fine faith the children had in the wisdom of their teacher was truly marvellous. We read and spelled together, wrote a little, picked flowers, sang, and listened to stories of the world beyond the hill.

At times the school would dwindle away, and I would start out. I would visit Mun Eddings, who lived in two very dirty rooms, and ask why little Lugene, whose flaming face seemed ever ablaze with the dark-red hair uncombed, was absent all last week, or why I missed so often the inimitable rags of Mack and Ed. Then the father, who worked Colonel Wheeler's farm on shares, would tell me how the crops needed the boys; and the thin slovenly mother, whose face was pretty when washed, assured me that Lugene must mind the baby. "But we'll start them again next week." When the Lawrences stopped, I knew that the doubts of the old folks about book learning had conquered again, and so, toiling up the hill, and getting as far into the cabin as possible, I put Cicero's [oration] *pro Archia Poeta* [In Defense of the Poet Archia] into the simplest English with local applications, and usually convinced them—for a week or so.

On Friday nights I often went home with some of the children—sometimes to Doc Burke's farm. He was a great, loud, thin black, ever working, and trying to buy the 75 acres of hill and dale where he lived; but people said that he would surely fail, and the "white folks would get it all." His wife was a magnificent Amazon, with saffron face and shining hair, uncorseted and barefooted, and the children were strong and beautiful. They lived in a one-and-a-half-room cabin in the hollow of the farm, near the spring. The front room was full of great fat white beds, scrupulously neat; and there were bad chromos on the walls, and a tired center-table. In the tiny back kitchen I was often invited to "take out and help" myself to fried chicken and wheat biscuits, "meat" and corn pone, string-beans and berries.

On this visit, at first I was a little alarmed at the approach of bedtime in the one lone bedroom, but embarrassment was very deftly avoided. First, all the children nodded and slept, and were stowed away in one great pile of goose feathers; next, the mother and the father discreetly slipped away to the kitchen while I went to bed; then, blowing out the dim light, they retired in the dark. In the morning all were up and away before I thought of waking. Across the road, where fat Reuben lived, they all went outdoors while the teacher retired, because they did not boast the luxury of a kitchen.

I liked to stay with the Dowells, for they had four rooms and plenty of good country fare. Uncle Bird had a small, rough farm, all woods and hills, miles from the big road; but he was full of tales—he preached now and then—and with his children, berries, horses, and wheat he was happy and prosperous.

Often, to keep the peace, I must go where life was less lovely; for instance, 'Tildy's mother was incorrigibly dirty, Reuben's larder was limited seriously, and herds of untamed insects wandered over the Eddingsos' beds. Best of all I loved to go to Josie's, and sit on the porch, eating peaches, while the mother bustled and talked: how Josie had bought the sewing machine; how Josie worked at house service in winter, but that four dollars a month was "mighty little" wages; how Josie longed to go away to school, but that it "looked like" they never could get far enough ahead to let her; how the crops failed and the well was yet unfinished; and, finally, how "mean" some of the white folks were.

For two summers I lived in this little world; it was dull and humdrum. The girls looked at the hill in wistful longing, and the boys fretted and haunted Alexandria. Alexandria was "town"—a straggling, lazy village of houses, churches and shops, and an aristocracy of white Toms, Dicks and Captains. Cuddled on the hill to the north was the village of the colored folks, who lived in three- or four-room unpainted cottages, some neat and homelike, and some dirty. The dwellings were scattered rather aimlessly, but they centered about the twin temples of the hamlet, the Methodist and the Hard-Shell Baptist churches. These, in turn, leaned gingerly on a sad-colored schoolhouse. Hither my little world wended its crooked way on Sunday to meet other worlds, and gossip, and wonder, and make the weekly sacrifice with frenzied priest at the altar of the "old-time religion." Then the soft melody and mighty cadences of Negro song fluttered and thundered.

I heard the Negro folksong first in Great Barrington, sung by the Hampton Singers. But that was second-hand, sung by youth who never knew slavery. I now heard the Negro songs by those who made them and in the land of their American birth. It was in the village into which my country school district filtered of Saturdays and Sundays. The road wandered from our rambling log-house up the stony bed of a creek, past wheat and corn, until we could hear dimly across the fields a rhythmic cadence of song—soft, thrilling, powerful, that swelled and died sorrowfully in our ears. I had never seen a Southern Negro revival. To be sure, we in Berkshire were not perhaps as stiff and formal as they in Suffolk of olden time; yet we were very quiet and subdued, and I know not what would have happened those clear Sabbath mornings had someone punctuated the sermon with a scream, or interrupted the long prayer with a loud Amen!

And so most striking to me, as I approached the village and the little plain church perched aloft, was the air of intense excitement that possessed that mass of black folk. A sort of suppressed terror hung in the air and seemed to seize them—a pythian madness, a demoniac possession, that lent terrible reality to song and word. The black and massive form of the preacher swayed and quivered as the words crowded to his lips and flew at us in singular eloquence. The people moaned and fluttered, and then the gaunt-cheeked brown woman beside me suddenly leaped straight into the air and shrieked like a lost soul, while round about came wail and groan and outcry, and a scene of human passion such as I had never conceived before.

I have called my community a world, and so its isolation made it. There was among us but a half-awakened common consciousness, sprung from common joy and grief, at burial, birth or wedding; from a common hardship in poverty, poor land and low wages; and, above all, from the sight of the Veil that hung between us and Opportunity.

All this caused us to think some thoughts together; but

these, when ripe for speech, were spoken in various languages. Those whose eyes 25 and more years before had seen "the glory of the coming of the Lord," saw in every present hindrance or help a dark fatalism bound to bring all things right in His own good time.

The mass of those to whom slavery was a dim recollection of childhood found the world a puzzling thing: it asked little of them, and they answered with little, and yet it ridiculed their offering. Such a paradox they could not understand, and therefore sank into listless indifference, or shiftlessness, or reckless bravado. There were, however, some—such as Josie, Jim, and Ben—to whom War, Hell and Slavery were but childhood tales, whose young appetites had been whetted to an edge by school and story and half-awakened thought. Ill could they be content, born without and beyond the World. And their weak wings beat against their barriers—barriers of caste, of youth, of life; at last, in dangerous moments, against everything that opposed even a whim.

No one but a Negro going into the South without previous experience of color caste can have any conception of its barbarism. It is not a matter of law or ordinance; it is a question of instinctive feeling; of inherited and inborn knowledge. On a Nashville street, 71 years ago, I quite accidently jostled a white woman as I passed. She was not hurt in the slightest, nor even particularly inconvenienced. Immediately in accord with my New England training, I raised my hat and begged her pardon. I acted quite instinctively and with genuine regret for a little mistake. The woman was furious; why I never knew; somehow, I cannot say how, I had transgressed the interracial mores of the South. Was it because I showed no submissiveness? Did I fail to debase myself utterly and eat spiritual dirt? Did I act as equal among equals? I do not know. I only sensed scorn and hate; the kind of despising which a dog might incur. Thereafter for at least half a century I avoided the necessity of showing them courtesy of any sort. If I did them any courtesy which sometimes I must in sheer deference to my own standards of decency, I contrived to act as if totally unaware that I saw them or had them in mind.

Murder, killing and maiming Negroes, raping Negro women—in the 80's and in the southern South, this was not even news; it got no publicity; it caused no arrests; and punishment for such transgression was so unusual that the fact was telegraphed North.

Lynching was a continuing and recurrent horror during my college days: from 1885 through 1894, 1,700 Negroes were lynched in America. Each death was a scar upon my soul, and led me on to conceive the plight of other minority groups; for in my college days Italians were lynched in New Orleans, forcing the Federal government to pay $25,000 in "indemnity," and the anti-Chinese riots in the West culminated in the Chinese Exclusion Act of 1892. Some echoes of Jewish segregation and pogroms in Russia came through the magazines; I followed the Dreyfus case; and I began to see something of the struggle between East and West. Yet at this time the full force of legal caste in the South had not yet fallen on Negroes. Streetcars were not yet separate and there was still some Negro voting.

One unforgettable thing Fisk University did for me and that was to guide and enlarge my appreciation of music. In Great Barrington the only music we had was that of the old English hymns, some of them set to German music. The music was often fine, but the words usually illogical or silly. I grew up, therefore, singing lustily bits of real music and paying little or no attention to the words. Then there were the so-called Gospel Hymns, with the rhythm of the Negro spirituals and words of no account at all. Yet I warbled blithely "Hold the Fort, for I am coming!"

At Fisk, little Professor Spence, the great Greek scholar, had a rare appreciation of music and took it upon himself to guide the school. Already Fisk had the tradition of her Jubilee Singers, who once hid in a Brooklyn organ loft, lest pious Congregationalists see their black faces before they heard their heavenly voices. Henry Ward Beecher took them to Plymouth church where the newspaper called them

"Beecher's Nigger Minstrels"; then the nation listened and the world opened its arms and the Fisk Jubilee Singers literally sang before Kings. They brought back to Nashville enough money to build Jubilee Hall. There I met some of these singers and heard their music.

When I came to Fisk, Spence had organized the Mozart Society and gathered in it all the good voices of the school, some of which were of phenomenal excellence. He trained them in the rendition of the great religious oratorios. They sang *The Messiah*, the *Elijah*, and Mozart's *Twelfth Mass*. I became a member of the Mozart Society and it did great things for my education.

Every year we sang at commencement the *Hallelujah Chorus*. I can see now the banked mass of faces of every color and hue with no orchestra save the piano; and the little long-coated, white-haired Spence waving his hands in front. And there Ed Bailey stood, a slight black boy whom the average American would have completely ignored, or said that he ought to be plowing instead of singing. His clear tenor voice rose with singular beauty; and we who listened were always near to tears, feeling what he was saying: "Comfort ye, comfort ye, my people!" We there then were the People to whom Jehovah spoke. No student ever left Fisk without a deep and abiding appreciation of real music.

The net result of the Fisk interlude was to broaden the scope of my program of life, not essentially to change it; to center it in a group of educated Negroes, who from their knowledge and experience would lead the mass. I never for a moment dreamed that such leadership could ever be for the sake of the educated group itself, but always for the mass. Nor did I pause to enquire in just what ways and with what technique we would work—first, broad, exhaustive knowledge of the world; all other wisdom, all method and application would be added unto us.

In essence I combined a social program for a depressed group with the natural demand of youth for "Light, more light." Fisk was a good college; I liked it; but it was small, it was limited in equipment, in laboratories, in books; it was not a university. I wanted the largest and best in organized learning. Nothing could be too big and thorough for training the leadership of the American Negro. There must remain no suspicion of part-knowledge, cheap equipment, for this mighty task. The necessity of earning a living scarcely occurred to me. I had no need for or desire for money.

I turned with increased determination to the idea of going to Harvard. There I was going to study the science of sciences—Philosophy. Vainly did Chase point out, as William James did later, that the world was not in the habit of paying philosophers. In vain did the president offer me a scholarship at Hartford Theological Seminary. I believed too little in Christian dogma to become a minister. I was not without faith: I never stole material nor spiritual things; I not only never lied, but blurted out my conception of truth on the most untoward occasions; I drank no alcohol and knew nothing of women, physically or psychically, to the incredulous amusement of most of my more experienced fellows. I above all believed in work, systematic and tireless.

My early political knowledge came largely from newspapers which I read outside my curriculum. I read of the contests of the Democratic and Republican parties, from the first seating of Hayes, through the administrations of Garfield and Arthur, Cleveland, Harrison and Cleveland again. All this complied with the conventional theory of party government, and while the issues were not as clear-cut and the motives as unmixed as they ought to have been, nevertheless the increasing triumph of democratic government was in my mind unquestioned. The Populists as a third party movement, beginning during this time, did not impress me, since I did not know its significance.

The year before I entered college, England killed the arbitrary power of the Justice of the Peace and the County Squire, doubled the number of its voters and was forced into a struggle to yield Ireland home rule; eventually Japan attempted a constitution with elective representatives; Brazil was struggling to become a republic and France fought to curtail the political power of the Catholic church.

My problem then was how, into the inevitable and logical democracy which was spreading over the world, could black folk in America be openly and effectively admitted; and the colored people of the world allowed their own self-government? I therefore watched, outside my textbooks and without reference to my teachers, the race developments throughout the world. The difficulty here, however, was securing any real and exhaustive knowledge of facts. I could not get any clear picture of the current change in Africa and Asia.

At Fisk I began my writing and public speaking. I edited the *Fisk Herald*. I became an impassioned orator and developed a belligerent attitude toward the color bar. I was determined to make a scientific conquest of my environment, which would render the emancipation of the Negro race easier and quicker. The persistence which I had learned in New England stood me now in good stead. Because my first college choice had been Harvard, to Harvard I was still resolved to go.

It was a piece of unusual luck, much more than my own determination, that admitted me to Harvard. There had been arising in Harvard at that time a feeling that the institution was becoming too ingrown, too satisfied with a sense of its New England sufficiency. A determined effort was made in 1884 and later to make Harvard a more national institution, with good students from the South and West. I saw advertisements of scholarships which were to be offered and I made application. In my favor were my New England elementary education, and the fact that I was studying in the South and that I was colored. There had been hitherto very few colored students at Harvard.

I was immediately accepted on condition that I enter as a Junior, even after receiving my Fisk A.B. This was not altogether unfair, since my own high school in New England was somewhat behind Harvard's requirements and Fisk, because of the wretched Southern common school system, still further behind. However, all this made little difference to me. I wanted to go to Harvard because of what it offered in opportunity for wide learning. I received the promise of

$250 Price Greenleaf Aid to cover my expenses for the year 1885-1886.

My class was graduated from Fisk in June 1888. There were five of us—from Texas, Tennessee, New York, Massachusetts and Mississippi. Edmondson had to leave school before graduation, but we later restored him to the class roll. We all had spoken Commencement orations; others talked of "Anglo-Saxon Influence"; "Women in Public Life"; "Feudalism"; "Thought as the Prime Condition of Progress." I took as my subject "Bismarck." This choice in itself showed the abyss between my education and the truth in the world. Bismarck was my hero. He had made a nation out of a mass of bickering peoples. He had dominated the whole development with his strength until he crowned an emperor at Versailles.

This foreshadowed in my mind the kind of thing that American Negroes must do, marching forth with strength and determination under trained leadership. On the other hand, I did not understand at all, nor had my history course led me to understand, anything of current European intrigue, of the expansion of European power into Africa, of the industrial revolution built on slave trade and now turning into colonial imperialism; of the fierce rivalry among white nations for controlling the profits from colonial raw material and labor; of all this I had no clear conception. I was blithely European and imperialist in outlook; democratic as democracy was conceived in America.

So far my formal education had touched politics and religion, but on the whole had avoided economics. It was the moral aspects of slavery which we stressed, not the economic. I saw serfdom when I taught a rural school, but in class I do not remember ever hearing Karl Marx mentioned nor socialism discussed. We talked about wages and poverty, but little was said of trade unions and that little was unfavorable. The parents of the students almost never belonged to unions, because of the opposition of white workers. Most of us looked forward to the learned professions as a life career. We knew something of land and farming, but nothing of transport and manufacturing. Manual labor and house service was the first step of our masses toward income.

At Fisk a very definite attempt was made to see that we did not lose or question our Christian orthodoxy. At first the effort seemed to me entirely superfluous, since I had never questioned my religious upbringing. Its theory had presented no particular difficulties: God ruled the world, Christ loved it, and men did right, or tried to; otherwise they were rightly punished. But the book on "Christian Evidences" which we were compelled to read, affronted my logic. It was to my mind, then and since, a cheap piece of special pleading. Our course in general philosophy under the serious and entirely lovable president was different. It opened vistas. It made me determine to go further in this probing for truth. Eventually it landed me squarely in the arms of William James of Harvard, for which God be praised.

After graduation I must start for Harvard. In order to supplement my scholarship, I had something of the small wage which I earned by teaching at country schools during vacation. This needed to be added to and a scheme to this end was planned by Fortson, a student in the high school department of Fisk. Fortson was a very earnest and austerely religious young man, who had for some time earned money to go to school by serving as waiter in a summer hotel at Lake Minnetonka near Minneapolis. He had risen to the position of second waiter and knowing the demand for music he proposed to several of us that we form a Glee Club and spend the summer at Minnetonka. He selected four boys who had been singing as a Glee Club. They were Calloway, Talley, McClellan and Anthony. They had all had some experience, but not much, at working at hotels.

Finally, I was selected as business manager—with the idea that I could accompany the group, work with them during the summer, and then toward the end of the season go on ahead to make a series of engagements for them in Minnesota, Wisconsin and Chicago. From there they would return to Fisk and I would go east to Harvard. During college I had developed rather as the executive planner, the natural secretary of affairs rather than ornamental president and chairman. The only difficulty about the Minnesota excursion was that I had never worked in a hotel in my life.

In this way I received an impression of American civilization in the Middle West at the age of 20. I knew New England by my birth and elementary education. I had spent three years in the South and now I was having a chance to see the West. The experience was extraordinary. I had never seen a hotel of the type of that at Lake Minnetonka. The Berkshire House in Great Barrington catered to rich people from New York. They were on the whole a quiet and rather stodgy set. They sat on the front porch, took drives into the country, and sometimes played cards.

The crowds at Lake Minnetonka were larger and noisier. They were not as well-bred. They spent a great deal of money and drank a good deal of liquor. Usually during the daytime at least they were fairly respectable in behavior, and had among them a majority of conventional people of good repute. But I began to realize that at night, especially on weekends, their behavior approached an orgy. Husbands arrived with other men's wives and gay women without husbands were in evidence. Poor Fortson was greatly distressed and got us to draw up a protest and revelation for the hotel management. I am sure they did not thank him for it. The head waiter, his superior, was a large, dark man of middle age with impeccable manners, who without doubt knew what to expect at this hotel and was not at all disturbed by it.

Our group of Fisk students were rather carefully guarded and had our own dormitory, where we knew but little of the goings on. Not being experienced waiters, we acted as bus boys, standing around the edge of the dining room and carrying out from time to time the loads of dirty dishes. Those who were alert and watchful could often pick up tips. I never received a cent in this way because I was always looking with astonished curiosity at the actions of the guests and the antics of the waiters. I remember one time overhearing a group of cooks and stewards staggering in bleary eyed in the morning. One of them remarked as he passed: "The sporting life's hell!" I was curious to know of just what the sporting life consisted. Then there came the difficulty of getting food. We were supposed to have our meals served before the dining room opened, but I noticed with astonishment that none of the waiters bothered to come to such meals, and I was facing the prospect of starving, when I learned that practically all the help got their food by deftly stealing it. Orders of the choicest viands never reached the guests in numbers of cases, while the waiters were well fed. Thereafter I didn't steal food, but I ate much that others stole.

It was on the whole a rather disillusioning experience. But the concerts which we gave were fairly successful, and early in September I sorrowfully left my comrades and started South and East. On my success in securing engagements depended the real fate of this summer venture. Here then came another series of adventures. I stopped at Minneapolis and St. Paul, at Madison and Milwaukee, and at Chicago. It was a hot summer and particularly in Chicago I suffered more from the heat than I had in Nashville. It was a hard two weeks' work, and I met all sorts of people. Some were not interested in Negro singers even if they came from Fisk. Others were interested in me and the school. On the whole, my reception was pleasant and courteous. I met some very sympathetic and understanding persons—ministers, heads of Christian associations, and literary groups. My technique was to present what few letters of introduction I had; to tell them of the work of Fisk University and of the object of this group of singers. Despite rebuffs and disappointments, I succeeded in getting enough engagements so that the group netted about $100 apiece outside of expenses for this part of their summer's work.

Then I started East, and here again in a couple of days' trip, I met a phase of American civilization that I had read about but never before experienced. I had a very small amount of pocket money, which would be supplemented later by remittances from the Glee Club and my Harvard scholarship. I think I had less than $50 in my pocket. Naturally I could not afford a Pullman and so sat up in the coach all night. It was, I think, upon the second night when the train made a short stop in Rochester, New York. I was awakened by a young man who was in a great hurry and who asked me if I could possibly do him a favor. He wanted to send a remittance of ten dollars and mail it on this train before it started. He had, however, only small bills. Could I possibly let him have a ten-dollar bill in exchange for them? I aroused myself and said yes. He handed me the bills and asked me to count them. Instead of ten dollars, there were only nine. He apologized profusely and counting the bills again immediately handed me the extra dollar bill, thanked me, hurried to mail his letter and disappeared. By that time I was thoroughly awake and getting a little suspicious. When I counted my bills again I found I had five dollars, not ten dollars. This was almost a catastrophe, which was increased when the college demanded as I registered that my tuition of $150 must be paid in December. I reminded them that I had Price Greenleaf Aid of $250, but was told that that was not payable till later in the year. I had to protest pretty strongly before they agreed to advance enough to cover my tuition. These experiences gave me a new idea of culture in the United States.

For several decades after I was graduated from Fisk, alumni called on me to criticize publicly changes in Fisk University policy which in their opinion threatened the established ideals of the institution. In 1898 Booker Washington was made a member of the Fisk board of trustees following the advice of my schoolmate, Maggie Murray, who had just married him. It was thought that Washington's influence might bring contributions to the dwindling income of this leading Negro college. Industrial courses were substituted for regular studies. At the urging of George Haynes, I spoke at the 1898 Commencement on "Galileo Galilei," blasting the telling of a lie to save the truth. The president, caught unwillingly between two fires, resigned.

Years later another president of Fisk yielded to the widespread idea that influential Southern whites should be induced to help lead Negro college education. He cultivated white Nashville, took the Fisk Glee Club, with men and women, into the back doors of white social clubs to sing for white men, and seriously curtailed freedom and initiative among students. As my daughter was then graduating, I was to be present at Fisk and was asked to address the alumni. In a speech entitled *"Diuturni Silentiae"* [Prolonged Silence] (taken from one of Cicero's orations) I attacked the current policy, with frank and open criticism, and after a long struggle, in which I issued in New York a new *Fisk Herald*, again a president resigned.[7] This was not easy work and it brought on me much criticism from white and black, but I think I did my clear duty and gave a needed service and helped save the ideals of a great school.

CHAPTER IX

HARVARD IN THE LAST DECADES OF THE 19TH CENTURY

Harvard University in 1888 was a great institution of learning. It was 236 years old and on its governing board were Alexander Agassiz, Phillip Brooks, Henry Cabot Lodge and Charles Francis Adams; and a John Quincy Adams, but not the ex-President. Charles William Eliot, a gentleman by training and a scholar by broad study and travel, was president. Among its teachers *emeriti* were Oliver Wendell Holmes and James Russell Lowell. Among the active teachers were Francis Child, Charles Eliot Norton, Charles Dunbar, Justin Winsor and John Trowbridge; William Goodwin, Frank Taussig, Nathaniel Shaler, George Palmer, William James, Francis Peabody, Josiah Royce, Barrett Wendell, Edward Channing, and Albert Bushnell Hart. A young instructor who arrived in 1890 was George Santayana. Seldom, if ever, has any American university had such a galaxy of great men and fine teachers as Harvard in the decade between 1885 and 1895.

To make my own attitude toward the Harvard of that day clear, it must be remembered that I went to Harvard as a Negro, not simply by birth, but recognizing myself as a member of a segregated caste whose situation I accepted but was determined to work from within that caste to find my way out.

About the Harvard of which most white students conceived I knew little. Of fraternities I had not even heard of Phi Beta Kappa, and of such important social organizations as the Hasty Pudding Club, I knew nothing. I was in Harvard for education and not for high marks, except as marks would insure my staying. I did not pick out "snap" courses. I was there to enlarge my grasp of the meaning of the universe. We had for instance no chemical laboratory at Fisk. Our mathematical courses were limited; above all I wanted to study philosophy! I wanted to get hold of the basis of knowledge, and explore foundations and beginnings. I chose, therefore, Palmer's course in ethics, but he being on Sabbatical for the year, William James replaced him, and I became a devoted follower of James at the time he was developing his pragmatic philosophy.

Fortunately I did not fall into the mistake of regarding Harvard as the beginning rather than the continuing of my college training. I did not find better teachers at Harvard, but teachers better known, who had had wider facilities for gaining knowledge and had a broader atmosphere for approaching truth.

I hoped to pursue philosophy as my life career, with teaching for support. With this program I studied at Harvard from the Fall of 1888 to 1890, as undergraduate. I took a varied course in chemistry, geology, social science and philosophy. My salvation here was the type of teacher I met rather than the content of the courses. William James guided me out of the sterilities of scholastic philosophy to realist pragmatism; from Peabody's social reform with a religious tinge, I turned to Albert Bushnell Hart to study history with documentary research; and from Taussig with his reactionary British economics of the Ricardo school, I approached what was later to become sociology. Meantime Karl Marx was mentioned but only incidentally and as one whose doubtful theories had long since been refuted. Socialism as dream of philanthropy or as will-o-wisp of hotheads was dismissed as unimportant.

When I arrived at Harvard, the question of board and lodging was of first importance. Naturally, I could not afford a room in the college yard in the old and venerable buildings which housed most of the well-to-do students under the magnificent elms. Neither did I think of looking for lodgings among white families, where numbers of the ordinary students lived. I tried to find a colored home, and finally at 20 Flagg Street, I came upon the neat home of a colored woman from Nova Scotia, a descendant of those black Jamaican Maroons whom Britain deported after solemnly promising them peace if they would surrender. For a very reasonable sum, I rented the second story front room and for four years this was my home. I wrote of this abode at the time: "My room is, for a college man's abode, very ordinary indeed. It is quite pleasantly situated—second floor, front, with a bay window and one other window. The door is on the southwest corner. As you enter you will perceive the bed in the opposite corner, small and decorated with floral designs calculated to puzzle a botanist. It is a good comfortable bed, however, and my landlady keeps it neat. On the left hand is a bureau with a mirror of doubtful accuracy. In front of the bay window is a stand with three shelves of books, and on the left of the bureau is an improvised bookcase made of unpainted boards and uprights, containing most of my library of which I am growing quite proud. Over the heat register, near the door, is a mantle with a plaster of Paris pug-dog and a calendar, and the usual array of odds and ends. A sofa, commode, trunk, table and chairs complete the floor furniture. On the wall are a few quite ordinary pictures. In this commonplace den I am quite content."

Later I became a boarder at Memorial Hall, which was the great dining hall of the University, and after that a member of the Foxcraft Club, where many students of moderate means boarded.

Following the attitudes which I had adopted in the South, I sought no friendships among my white fellow students, nor even acquaintanceships. Of course I wanted friends, but I could not seek them. My class was large, with some 300 students. I doubt if I knew a dozen of them. I did not seek them, and naturally they did not seek me. I made no attempt to contribute to the college periodicals, since the editors were not interested in my major interests. Only one organization did I try to enter, and I ought to have known better than to make this attempt. But I did have a good singing voice and loved music, so I entered the competition for the Glee Club. I ought to have known that Harvard could not afford to have a Negro on its Glee Club traveling about the country. Quite naturally I was rejected.

I was happy at Harvard, but for unusual reasons. One of these circumstances was my acceptance of racial segregation. Had I gone from Great Barrington high school directly to Harvard, I would have sought companionship with my white fellows and been disappointed and embittered by a discovery of social limitations to which I had not been used. But I came by way of Fisk and the South and there I had accepted color caste and embraced eagerly the companionship of those of my own color. This was, of course, no final solution. Eventually with them and in mass assault, led by culture, we Negroes were going to break down the boundaries of race; but at present we were banded together in a great crusade and happily so. Indeed, I suspect that the prospect of ultimate full human intercourse without reservations and annoying distinctions, made me all too willing to consort now with my own and to disdain and forget as far as was possible that outer, whiter world.

In general, I asked nothing of Harvard but the tutelage of teachers and the freedom of the laboratory and library. I was quite voluntarily and willingly outside its social life. I sought only such contacts with white teachers as lay directly in the line of my work. I joined certain clubs like the Philosophical Club; I was a member of the Foxcraft dining club because it was cheap. James and one or two other teachers had me at their homes at meal and reception. I found friends, and most interesting and inspiring friends, among the colored folk of Boston and surrounding places. Naturally social intercourse with whites could not be entirely forgotten, so that now and then I joined its currents and rose or fell with them. I escorted colored girls to various gatherings, and as pretty ones as I could find to the vesper exercises, and later to the class day and commencement social functions. Naturally we attracted attention and the *Crimson* noted my girl friends; on the other part came sometimes the shadow of insult, as when at one reception a white woman seemed determined to mistake me for a waiter.

In general, I was encased in a completely colored world, self-sufficient and provincial, and ignoring just as far as possible the white world which conditioned it. This was self-protective coloration, with perhaps an inferiority complex, but with belief in the ability and future of black folk.

My friends and companions were taken mainly from the colored students of Harvard and neighboring institutions, and the colored folk of Boston and surrounding towns. With them I led a happy and inspiring life. There were among them many educated and well-to-do folk; many young people studying or planning to study; many charming young women. We met and ate, danced and argued and planned a new world.

Toward whites I was not arrogant; I was simply not obsequious, and to a white Harvard student of my day, a Negro student who did not seek recognition was trying to be more than a Negro. The same Harvard man had much the same attitude toward Jews and Irishmen.

I was, however, exceptional among Negroes in my ideas on voluntary race segregation; they for the most part saw salvation only in integration at the earliest moment and on almost any terms in white culture; I was firm in my criticism of white folk and in my dream of a Negro self-sufficient culture even in America.

This cutting off of myself from my white fellows, or being cut off, did not mean unhappiness or resentment. I was in my early manhood, unusually full of high spirits and humor. I thoroughly enjoyed life. I was conscious of understanding and power, and conceited enough still to imagine, as in high school, that they who did not know me were the losers, not I. On the other hand, I do not think that my white classmates found me personally objectionable. I was clean, not well-dressed but decently clothed. Manners I regarded as more or less superfluous, and deliberately cultivated a certain brusquerie. Personal adornment I regarded as pleasant but not important. I was in Harvard, but not of it, and realized all the irony of my singing "Fair Harvard." I sang it because I liked the music, and not from any pride in the Pilgrims.

With my colored friends I carried on lively social intercourse, but necessarily one which involved little expenditure of money. I called at their homes and ate at their tables. We danced at private parties. We went on excursions down the Bay. Once, with a group of colored students gathered from surrounding institutions, we gave Aristophanes' *The Birds* in a Boston colored church. The rendition was good, but not outstanding; not quite appreciated by the colored audience, but well worth doing. Even though it worked me near to death, I was proud of it.

Thus this group of professional men, students, white collar workers and upper servants, whose common bond was color of skin in themselves or in their fathers, together with a common history and current experience of discrimination, formed a unit which like many tens of thousands of like units across the nation had or were getting to have a common culture pattern which made them an interlocking mass; so that increasingly a colored person in Boston was more neighbor to a colored person in Chicago than to the white person across the street.

Mrs. Ruffin of Charles Street, Boston, and her daughter Birdie were often hostesses to this colored group. She was a widow of the first colored judge appointed in Massachusetts, an aristocratic lady, with olive skin and high piled masses of white hair. Once a Boston white lady said to Mrs. Ruffin ingratiatingly: "I have always been interested in your race." Mrs. Ruffin flared: "Which race?" She began a national organization of colored women and published the *Courant,* a type of small colored weekly paper which was spreading over the nation. In this I published many of my Harvard daily themes.

Naturally in this close group there grew up among the young people friendships ending in marriages. I myself, outgrowing the youthful attractions of Fisk, began serious dreams of love and marriage. There, however, were still my study plans to hold me back and there were curious other reasons. For instance, it happened that two of the girls whom I particularly liked had what was to me then the insuperable handicap of looking like whites; while they had enough black ancestry to make them "Negroes" in America. Yet these girls were intelligent and companionable. One went to Vassar College which then refused entrance to Negroes. Years later when I went there to lecture I remember disagreeing violently with a teacher who thought the girl ought not to have "deceived" the college by graduating before it knew her Negro descent! Another favorite of mine was Deenie Pindell. She was a fine forthright woman, blonde, blue-eyed and fragile. In the end I had no chance to choose her, for she married Monroe Trotter.

Trotter was the son of a well-to-do colored father and entered Harvard in my first year in the Graduate School. He was thick-set, yellow, with close-cut dark hair. He was stubborn and straight-laced and an influential member of his class. He organized the first Total Abstinence club in the Yard. I came to know him and joined the company when he and other colored students took a trip to Amherst to see George Forbes and William H. Lewis graduate in the class with Calvin Coolidge.

Lewis afterward entered the Harvard Law School and became the celebrated center of the Harvard football team. He married the beautiful Bessie Baker who had been with us on that Amherst trip. Forbes, a brilliant, cynical dark man, later joined with Trotter in publishing the *Guardian,* the first Negro paper to attack Booker T. Washington with open opposition. Washington's friends retorted by sending Trotter to jail when he dared to heckle Washington in a public Boston meeting on his political views. I was not present nor privy to this occurrence, but the unfairness of the jail sentence helped lead me eventually to form the Niagara Movement, which later became a founding part of the NAACP.

Thus I lived near to life, love and tragedy; and when I met Maud Cuney, I became doubly interested. She was a tall imperious brunette, with gold-bronze skin, brilliant eyes and coils of black hair; daughter of the Collector of Customs at Galveston, Texas. She came to study music and was a skilled performer. When the New England Conservatory of Music tried to "jim-crow" her in the dormitory, we students rushed to her defense and we won. I fell deeply in love with her, and we were engaged.

Thus it is clear how in the general social intercourse on the campus I consciously missed nothing. Some white students made themselves known to me and a few, a very few, became life-long friends. Most of my classmates, I knew neither by sight nor name. Among them many made their mark in life: Norman Hapgood, Robert Herrick, Herbert Croly, George Dorsey, Homer Folks, Augustus Hand, James Brown Scott and others. I knew none of these intimately. For the most part I do not doubt that I was voted a somewhat selfish and self-centered "grind" with a chip on my shoulder and a sharp tongue.

Something of a certain inferiority complex was possibly a cause of this. I was desperately afraid of intruding where I was not wanted; appearing without invitation; of showing a desire for the company of those who had no desire for me. I should in fact have been pleased if most of my fellow students had wanted to associate with me; if I had been popular and envied. But the absence of this made me neither unhappy nor morose. I had my "island within" and it was a fair country.

Only once or twice did I come to the surface of college life. First I found by careful calculation that I needed the cash of one of the Boylston prizes in oratory to piece out my year's expenses. I got it through winning a second oratorical prize. The occasion was noteworthy by the fact that another black student, Clement Morgan, got first prize at the same contest.

With the new increase at Harvard of students who grew up outside of New England, there arose at this time a certain resentment at the way New England students were dominating and conducting college affairs. The class marshal on commencement day was always a Saltonstall, a Cabot, a Lowell, or some such New England family. The crew and most of the other heads of athletic teams were selected from similarly limited social groups. The class poet, class orator and other commencement officials invariably were selected because of family and not for merit. It so happened that when the officials of the class of 1890 were being selected in early spring, a plot ripened. Personally, I knew nothing of it, and was not greatly interested. But in Boston and in the Harvard Yard the result of the elections was of tremendous significance; for this conspiratorial clique selected Clement Morgan as class orator. New England and indeed the whole country reverberated.

Morgan was a black man. He was working in a barber shop in St. Louis at the time when he ought to have been in school. With the encouragement and help of a colored teacher whom he later married, he came to Boston and entered the Latin School. This meant that when he finally entered Harvard, he entered as freshman in the orthodox way and was well acquainted with his classmates. He was fairly well received, considering his color. He was a pleasant unassuming person and one of the best speakers of clearly enunciated English on the campus. In his junior year, he had earned the first Boylston prize for oratory, in the same contest where I won second prize. It was, then, logical for him to become class orator and yet this was against all the traditions of America. There were editorials in the leading newspapers, and the South especially raged and sneered at the audience of "black washerwomen" who would replace Boston society at the next Harvard commencement.

At the same time, the action was contagious and that year and the next in several leading Northern colleges colored students became the class orators. Ex-President Hayes, as I shall relate later, sneered at this fact. While, as I have said, I had nothing to do with this plot, and was not even present at the election which chose Morgan, I was greatly pleased at this breaking of the color line. Morgan and I became fast friends and spent a summer giving readings along the North Shore to help our college costs.

Harvard of this day was a great opportunity for a young man and a young American Negro and I realized it. I formed habits of work rather different from those of most of the other students. I burned no midnight oil. I did my studying in the daytime and had my day parceled out almost to the minute. I spent a great deal of time in the library and did my assignments with thoroughness and with prevision of the kind of work I wanted to do later. From the beginning my relations with most of the teachers at Harvard were pleasant. They were on the whole glad to receive a serious student, to whom extra-curricular activities were not of paramount importance and one who in a general way knew what he wanted.

Harvard had in the social sciences no such leadership of thought and breadth of learning as in philosophy, literature and physical science. She was then groping and is still groping toward a scientific treatment of human action. She was facing at the end of the century a tremendous economic era. In the United States, finance was succeeding in monopolizing transportation, and raw materials like sugar, coal and oil. The power of the trust and combine was so great that the Sherman Act was passed in 1890. On the other hand, the tariff at the demand of manufacturers continued to rise in height from the McKinley to the indefensible Wilson tariff making that domination easier. The understanding between the industrial North and the New South was being perfected and in 1890 the series of disfranchising laws began to be enacted by the Southern states destined in the next 16 years to make voting by Southern Negroes practically impossible. A financial crisis shook the land in 1893 and popular discontent showed itself in the Populist movement and Coxey's Army. The whole question of the burden of taxation began to be discussed.

These things we discussed with some clearness and factual understanding at Harvard. The tendency was toward English free trade and against the American tariff policy. We reverenced Ricardo and wasted long hours on the "Wages-fund." I remember Frank Taussig's course supporting dying Ricardean economics. Wages came from what employers had left for labor after they had subtracted their own reward. Suppose that this profit was too small to attract the employer, what would the poor worker do but starve? The trusts and monopolies were viewed frankly as dangerous enemies of democracies, but at the same time as inevitable methods of industry. We were strong for the gold standard and fearful of silver. The attitude of Harvard toward labor was on the whole contemptuous and condemnatory. Strikes like the railway strikes of 1886 and the terrible Homestead strike of 1892, as well as Coxey's Army of 1894, were pictured as ignorant lawlessness, lurching against conditions largely inevitable.

Karl Marx was mentioned, only to point out how thoroughly his theses had been disproven; of his theory itself almost nothing was said. Henry George was given but tolerant notice. The anarchists of Spain, the nihilists of Russia, the British miners—all these were viewed not as part of the political development and the tremendous economic organization but as sporadic evils. This was natural. Harvard was the child of its era. The intellectual freedom and flowering of the late 18th and early 19th centuries were yielding to the deadening economic pressure which would make Harvard rich and reactionary. This defender of wealth and capital, already half ashamed of Charles Sumner and Wendell Phillips, was willing finally to replace an Eliot with a manufacturer and a nervous warmonger.[8] The social community that mobbed Garrison, easily electrocuted Sacco and Vanzetti.

It was not until I was long out of college that I realized the fundamental influence man's efforts to earn a living had upon all his other efforts. The politics which we studied in college were conventional, especially when it came to describing and elucidating the current scene in Europe. The Queen's Jubilee in June 1887, while I was still at Fisk, set the pattern of our thinking. The little old woman at Windsor became a magnificent symbol of Empire. Here was England with her flag draped around the world, ruling more black folk than white and leading the colored peoples of the earth to Christian baptism, and as we assumed, to civilization and eventual self-rule.

In 1885, Stanley, the traveling American reporter, became a hero and symbol of white world leadership in Africa. The wild, fierce fight of the Mahdi and the driving of the English out of the Sudan for 13 years did not reveal its inner truth to me. I heard only of the martyrdom of the drunken Bible-reader and freebooter, Chinese Gordon.

The Congo Free State was established and the Berlin Conference of 1885 was reported to be an act of civilization against the slave trade and liquor. French, English and Germans pushed on in Africa, but I did not question the interpretation which pictured this as the advance of civilization and the benevolent tutelage of barbarians. I read of the confirmation of the Triple Alliance in 1891. Later I saw the celebration of the renewed Triple Alliance on the Tempelhofer Feld, with the new young Emperor William II, who, fresh from his dismissal of Bismarck, led the splendid pageantry; and finally the year I left Germany, Nicholas II became Tsar of all the Russias. In all this I had not yet linked the political development of Europe with the race problem in America.

I was repeatedly a guest in the home of William James; he was my friend and guide to clear thinking; I was a member of the Philosophical Club and talked with Josiah Royce and George Palmer; I remember vividly once standing beside Mrs. Royce at a small reception. We ceased conversation for a moment and both glanced across the room. Professor Royce was opposite talking excitedly. He was an extraordinary sight: a little body; indifferently clothed; a big red-thatched head and blazing blue eyes. Mrs. Royce put my thoughts into words: "Funny-looking man, isn't he?" I nearly fainted; yet I knew how she worshipped him.

I sat in an upper room and read Kant's *Critique* with Santayana; Shaler invited a Southerner, who objected to sitting beside me, out of his class; he said he wasn't doing very well, anyway. I became one of Hart's favorite pupils and was afterwards guided by him through my graduate course and started on my work in Germany. Most of my courses of study went well. It was in English that I came nearest my Waterloo at Harvard. I had unwittingly arrived at Harvard in the midst of a violent controversy about poor English among students. A number of fastidious Englishmen like Barrett

Wendell had come to Harvard about this time; moreover New England itself was getting sensitive over Western slang and Southern drawls and general ignorance of grammar. Freshmen at this time could elect nearly all their courses except English; that was compulsory, with theses, daily themes and tough examinations.

On the other hand, I was at the point in my intellectual development when the content rather than the form of my writing was to me of prime importance. Words and ideas surged in my mind and spilled out with disregard of exact accuracy in grammar, taste in word or restraint in style. I knew the Negro problem and this was more important to me than literary form. I knew grammar fairly well, and I had a pretty wide vocabulary; but I was bitter, angry and intemperate in my first thesis. Naturally my English instructors had no idea of nor interest in the way in which Southern attacks on the Negro were scratching me on the raw flesh. Ben Tillman was raging in the Senate like a beast and literary clubs, especially rich and well-dressed women, engaged his services eagerly and listened avidly. Senator Morgan of Alabama had just published a scathing attack on "niggers" in a leading magazine, when my first Harvard thesis was due. I let go at him with no holds barred. My long and blazing effort came back marked "E"—not passed!

It was the first time in my scholastic career that I had encountered such a failure. I was aghast, but I was not a fool. I did not doubt but what my instructors were fair in judging my English technically even if they did not understand the Negro problem. I went to work at my English and by the end of that term had raised it to a "C". I realized that while style is subordinate to content, and that no real literature can be composed simply of meticulous and fastidious phrases, nevertheless that solid content with literary style carries a message further than poor grammar and muddled syntax. I elected the best course on the campus for English composition, English 12.

I have before me a theme which I wrote October 3, 1890, for Barrett Wendell, then the great pundit of Harvard

English. I wrote: "Spurred by my circumstances, I have always been given to systematically planning my future, not indeed without many mistakes and frequent alterations, but always with what I now conceive to have been a strangely early and deep appreciation of the fact that to live is a serious thing. I determined while in high school to go to college—partly because other men did, partly because I foresaw that such discipline would best fit me for life. . . . I believe, foolishly perhaps, but sincerely, that I have something to say to the world, and I have taken English 12 in order to say it well." Barrett Wendell liked that last sentence. Out of 50 essays, he picked this out to read to the class.

Commencement was approaching, when one day I found myself at midnight on one of the swaggering streetcars that used to roll out from Boston on its way to Cambridge. It was in the Spring of 1890, and quite accidentally I was sitting by a classmate who would graduate with me in June. As I dimly remember, he was a nice looking young man, almost dapper; well dressed, charming in manner. Probably he was rich or at least well-to-do, and doubtless belonged to an exclusive fraternity, although that did not interest me. Indeed I have even forgotten his name. But one thing I shall never forget and that was his rather regretful admission (which slipped out as we gossiped) that he had no idea as to what his life work would be, because, as he added, "There's nothing in which I am particularly interested!"

I was more than astonished; I was almost outraged to meet any human being of the mature age of 22 who did not have his life all planned before him—at least in general outline; and who was not supremely, if not desperately, interested in what he planned to do.

Since then, my wonder has left my classmate, and been turned in and backward upon myself: how long had I been so sure of my life-work and how had I come so confidently to survey and plan it? I now realize that most college seniors are by no means certain of what they want to do or can do with life; but stand rather upon a hesitating threshold, awaiting will, chance or opportunity. Because I had not mingled intimately or understandingly with my white Harvard classmates, I did not at the time realize this, but thought my unusual attitude was general.

In June 1890, I received my bachelor's degree from Harvard *cum laude* in philosophy. I was one of the five graduating students selected to speak at commencement. My subject was "Jefferson Davis." I chose it with deliberate intent of facing Harvard and the nation with a discussion of slavery as illustrated in the person of the president of the Confederate States of America. Naturally, my effort made a sensation. I said, among other things: "I wish to consider not the man, but the type of civilization which his life represented: its foundation is the idea of the strong man—Individualism coupled with the rule of might—and it is this idea that has made the logic of even modern history, the cool logic of the Club. It made a naturally brave and generous man, Jefferson Davis: now advancing civilization by murdering Indians, now hero of a national disgrace, called by courtesy the Mexican War; and finally as the crowning absurdity, the peculiar champion of a people fighting to be free in order that another people should not be free. Whenever this idea has for a moment escaped from the individual realm, it has found an even more secure foot-hold in the policy and philosophy of the State. The strong man and his mighty Right Arm has become the Strong Nation with its armies. Under whatever guise, however a Jefferson Davis may appear as man, as race, or as a nation, his life can only logically mean this: the advance of a part of the world at the expense of the whole; the overwhelming sense of the I, and the consequent forgetting of the Thou. It has thus happened that advance in civilization has always been handicapped by shortsighted national selfishness. The vital principle of division of labor has been stifled not only in industry, but also in civilization; so as to render it well nigh impossible for a new race to introduce a new idea into the world except by means of the cudgel. To say that a nation is in the way of civilization is a contradiction in terms and a system of human culture whose principle is the rise of one race on the ruins of another is a farce and a lie. Yet this is the type of civilization which Jefferson Davis represented; it represents a field for stalwart manhood and heroic character, and at the same time for moral obtuseness and refined brutality. These striking contradictions of character always arise when a people seemingly become convinced that the object of the world is not civilization, but Teutonic civilization."

A Harvard professor wrote to *Kate Field's Washington,* then a leading periodical: "Du Bois, the colored orator of the commencement stage, made a ten-strike. It is agreed upon by all the people I have seen that he was the star of the occasion. His paper was on 'Jefferson Davis,' and you would have been surprised to hear a colored man deal with him so generously. Such phrases as a 'great man,' a 'keen thinker,' a 'strong leader,' and others akin occurred in the address. One of the trustees of the University told me yesterday that the paper was considered masterly in every way. Du Bois is from Great Barrington, Massachusetts, and doubtless has some white blood in his veins. He, too, has been in my classes the past year. If he did not head the class, he came pretty near the head, for he is an excellent scholar in every way, and altogether the best black man that has come to Cambridge."

Bishop Potter of New York wrote in the *Boston Herald:* "When at the last commencement of Harvard University, I saw a young colored man appear . . . and heard his brilliant and eloquent address, I said to myself: 'Here is what an historic race can do if they have a clear field, a high purpose, and a resolute will.' "

The New York *Nation* commented editorially: "When the name of William Edward Du Bois was called and a slender, intellectual-looking mulatto ascended on the platform and made his bow to the President of the University, the Governor of Massachusetts, the Bishop of New York, and a hundred other notables, the applause burst out heartily as if in recognition of the strange significance of his appearance there. His theme . . . heightened this significance. Du Bois handled his difficult and hazardous subject with absolute good taste, great moderation, and almost contemptuous fairness."

Already I had now received more education than most young white men, having been almost continuously in school from the age of six to the age of 22. But I did not yet feel prepared. I felt that to cope with the new and extraordinary situations then developing in the United States and the world, I needed to go further and that as a matter of fact I had just well begun my training in knowledge of social conditions.

I revelled in the keen analysis of William James, Josiah Royce and young George Santayana. But it was James with his pragmatism and Albert Bushnell Hart with his research method, that turned me back from the lovely but sterile land of philosophic speculation, to the social sciences as the field for gathering and interpreting that body of fact which would apply to my program for the Negro. As undergraduate, I had talked frankly with William James about teaching philosophy, my major subject. He discouraged me, not by any means because of my record in his classes. He used to give me A's and even A-plus, but as he said candidly, there is "not much chance for anyone earning a living as a philosopher." He was repeating just what Chase of Fisk had said a few years previously.

I knew by this time that practically my sole chance of earning a living combined with study was to teach, and after my work with Hart in United States history, I conceived the idea of applying philosophy to an historical interpretation of race relations.

In other words, I was trying to take my first steps toward sociology as the science of human action. It goes without saying that no such field of study was then recognized at Harvard or came to be recognized for 20 years after. But I began with some research in Negro history and finally at the suggestion of Hart, I chose the suppression of the African slave trade to America as my doctor's thesis. Then came the question as to whether I could continue study in the graduate school. I had no resources in wealth or friends. I applied for a fellowship in the graduate school of Harvard and was appointed Henry Bromfield Rogers fellow for a year and later the appointment was renewed; so that from 1890 to 1892 I was a fellow at Harvard University, studying in history and political science and what would have been sociology if Harvard has yet recognized such a field.

My grandfather Du Bois died while I was at Harvard, and although the settlement of the estate was held up for lack of exact data concerning my father's death, eventually $400 was paid me during my senior year. I finished the first draft of my thesis and delivered an outline of it at the seminaries of American history and political economy December 7, 1891. I received my master's degree in the Spring. I was thereupon elected to the American Historical Society and asked to speak in Washington at their meeting in December 1892. *The New York Independent* noted this among the "three best papers presented," and continued:

"The article upon the 'enforcement of the Slave Laws' was written and read by a black man. It was thrilling when one could, for a moment, turn his thoughts from listening to think that scarcely thirty years have elapsed since the war that freed his race, and here was an audience of white men listenin to a black man—listening, moreover, to a careful, cool, philosophical history of the laws which had not prevented the enslavement of his race. The voice, the diction, the manner of the speaker were faultless. As one looked at him, one could not help saying 'Let us not worry about the future of our country in the matter of race distinctions.'"

I began with a bibliography of Nat Turner and ended with this history of the suppression of the African Slave Trade to America; neither needed to be done again at least in my day. Thus in my quest for basic knowledge with which to help guide the American Negro I came to the study of sociology, by way of philosophy and history rather than by physics and biology. After hesitating between history and economics, I chose history. On the other hand, psychology, hovering then on the threshold of experiment under Hugo Munsterberg, soon took a new orientation which I could understand from the beginning. I worked on my thesis, "The Suppression of the African Slave Trade to the United States of America," and hoped to get my doctor's degree in another two years.

Already I had made up my mind that what I needed was further training in Europe. The German universities were at the top of their reputation. Any American scholar who wanted preferment went to Germany for study. The faculties of Johns Hopkins, and the new University of Chicago, were beginning to be filled with German Ph.D's, and even Harvard had imported Munsterberg for the new experimental psychology, and Kuno Frank had long taught there. British universities did not recognize American degrees and French universities made no special effort to encourage American graduates. I wanted then to study in Germany. I was determined that any failure on my part to become a recognized American scholar must not be based on any lack of modern training.

I was confident. So far I had met no failure. I willed and lo! I was walking beneath the elms of Harvard—the name of allurement, the college of my youngest, wildest visions. I needed money; scholarships and prizes fell into my lap—not all I wanted or strove for, but all I needed to keep in school. Commencement came and standing before governor, president, and grave gowned men, I told them certain truths, waving my arms and breathing fast. They applauded with what may have seemed to many as uncalled-for fervor, but I walked home on pink clouds of glory! I asked for a fellowship and got it. I announced my plan of studying in Germany, but Harvard had no more fellowships for me. A friend, however, told me of the Slater Fund and how the board was looking for colored men worth educating.

No thought of modest hesitation occurred to me. I rushed at the chance. It was one of those tricks of fortune which always seem partly due to chance: In 1882, the Slater Fund for the education of Negroes had been established and the board in 1890 was headed by ex-President R. B. Hayes. Ex-President Hayes went down to Johns Hopkins University which admitted no Negro students and told a "darkey" joke in a frank talk about the plans of the fund. The *Boston Herald* of November 2, 1890, quoted him as saying: "If there is any young colored man in the South whom we find to have a talent for art or literature or any special aptitude for study, we are willing to give him money from the education funds to send him to Europe or give him advanced education." He added that so far they had been able to find only "orators." This seemed to me a nasty fling at my black classmate, Morgan, who had been Harvard class orator a few months earlier.

The Hayes statement was brought to my attention at a card party one evening; it not only made me good and angry but inspired me to write ex-President Hayes and ask for a scholarship. I received a pleasant reply saying that the newspaper quotation was incorrect; that his board had some such program in the past but had no present plans for such scholarships. I wrote him referring him to my teachers and to others who knew me, and intimating that his change of plan did not seem to me fair or honest. He wrote again in apologetic mood and said that he was sorry the plan had been given up; that he recognized that I was a candidate who might otherwise have been given attention. I then sat down and wrote Mr. Hayes this letter:

May 25, 1891

Your favor of the 2nd. is at hand. I thank you for your kind wishes. You will pardon me if I add a few words of explanation as to my application. The outcome of the matter is as I expected it would be. The announcement that any agency of the American people was willing to give a Negro a thoroughly liberal education and that it had been looking in vain for men to educate was to say the least rather startling. When the newspaper clipping was handed me in a company of friends, my first impulse was to make in some public way a categorical statement denying that such an offer had ever been made known to colored students. I saw this would be injudicious and fruitless, and I therefore determined on the plan of applying myself. I did so and have been refused along with a number of cases beside mine.

As to my case I personally care little. I am perfectly capable of fighting alone for an education if the trustees do not see fit to help me. On the other hand the injury you have—unwittingly I trust—

done the race I represent, and am not ashamed of, is almost irreparable. You went before a number of keenly observant men who looked upon you as an authority in the matter, and told them in substance that the Negroes of the United States either couldn't or wouldn't embrace a most liberal opportunity for advancement. That statement went all over the country. When now finally you receive three or four applications for the fulfillment of that offer, the offer is suddenly withdrawn, while the impression still remains.

If the offer was an experiment, you ought to have had at least one case before withdrawing it; if you have given aid before (and I mean here toward liberal education—not toward training plowmen) then your statement at Johns Hopkins was partial. From the above facts I think you owe an apology to the Negro people. We are ready to furnish competent men for every European scholarship furnished us off paper. But we can't educate ourselves on nothing and we can't have the moral courage to try, if in the midst of our work our friends turn public sentiment against us by making statements which injure us and which they cannot stand by.

That you have been looking for men to liberally educate in the past may be so, but it is certainly strange so few have heard it. It was never mentioned during my three years stay at Fisk University. President J. C. Price of Livingstone [then a leading Negro spokesman] has told me that he never heard of it, and students from various other Southern schools have expressed great surprise at the offer. The fact is that when I was wanting to come to Harvard, while yet in the South, I wrote to Dr. Haygood [Atticus G. Haygood, a leader of Southern white liberals] for a loan merely, and he never even answered my letter. I find men willing to help me thro' cheap theological schools, I find men willing to help me use my hands before I have got my brains in working order, I have an abundance of good wishes on hand, but I never found a man willing to help me get a Harvard Ph.D.

Hayes was stirred. He promised to take up the matter the next year with the board. Thereupon, the next year I proceeded to write the board:

"At the close of the last academic year at Harvard, I received the degree of Master of Arts, and was reappointed to my fellowship for the year 1891-92. I have spent most of the year in the preparation of my doctor's thesis on the Suppression of the Slave Trade in America. I prepared a preliminary paper on this subject and read it before the American Historical Association at its annual meeting at Washington during the Christmas holidays. . . . Properly to finish my education, careful training in a European university for at least a year is, in my mind and the minds of my professors, absolutely indispensable." I thereupon asked respectfully for "aid to study at least a year abroad under the direction of the graduate department of Harvard or other reputable auspices" and if this was not practicable, "that the board loan me a sufficient sum for this purpose." I did not of course believe that this would get me an appointment, but I did think that possibly through the influence of people who thus came to know about my work, I might somehow borrow or beg enough to get to Europe.

I rained recommendations upon Mr. Hayes. The Slater Fund Board surrendered, and I was given a fellowship of $750 to study a year abroad; with the promise that it might possibly be renewed for a second year. To salve their souls, however, this grant was made as half gift and a half repayable loan with five per cent interest. I remember rushing down to New York and talking with ex-President Hayes in the old Astor House, and emerging walking on air. I saw an especially delectable shirt in a shop window. I went in and asked about it. It cost three dollars, which was about four times as much as I had ever paid for a shirt in my life; but I bought it.

CHAPTER X

EUROPE 1892 TO 1894

When I was a young man I conceived that the foundations of world culture were laid, the way was charted, the progress toward certain great goals was undoubted and inevitable. There was room for argument concerning details and methods and possible detours in the onsweep of civilization; but the fundamental facts were clear, unquestioned and unquestionable.

Between the years 1885 and 1894 I received my education at Fisk University, Harvard College and the University of Berlin. It was difficult for me at the time to form any critical estimate of any meaning of the world which differed from the conventional unanimity about me. Apparently one consideration alone saved me from complete conformity with the thoughts and confusions of then current social trends; and that was the problem of racial and cultural contacts. Otherwise I might easily have been simply the current product of my day. Even as it was, the struggle for which I was preparing and the situations which I was trying to conceive and study, related themselves primarily to the plight of the comparatively small group of American Negroes with which I was identified, and theoretically to the larger Negro race. I did not face the general plight and conditions of all humankind. That I took for granted, and in the unanimity of thought and development of that day, as I saw it, this was scarcely to be wondered at.

It was to my mind and the minds of most of my teachers a day of Progress with a capital P. Population in all the cultured lands was increasing swiftly, doubling and more; cities everywhere were growing and expanding and making themselves the centers and almost the only centers of civilization; transportation by land and sea was drawing the nations near and making the lands of the earth increasingly accessible. Inventions and technique were a perpetual marvel and their accomplishment infinite in possibility. Commerce was madly seeking markets all around the earth; colonies were being seized and countries integrated into European civilization in Asia, Africa, South America and the islands. Of the methods of this colonial imperialism, the condition of colonial peoples and the effect of colonies on home labor, I knew little until years later.

Above all, science was becoming a religion; psychology was reducing metaphysics to experiment and a sociology of human action was planned. Fighting the vast concept of evolution, religion went into its heresy trials, its struggles with "higher criticism," its discomfort at the "revised version" of the New Testament which was published the year I entered college. Everywhere men sought wealth and especially in America there was extravagant living among the rich; everywhere the poor planned to be rich and the rich planned to be richer; everywhere wider, bigger, higher, better things were set down as inevitable.

All this, of course, dominated education; especially the economic order determined what the next generation should learn and know. On the whole, looking at the marvelous industrial expansion of America, seeing the rise of the western farmer and the wages of the eastern mechanic, all seemed well; or if not, if there were ominous protests and upheavals, these were but the friction necessary to all advance. "God's in His heaven; All's right with the world," Browning was singing—that colored Robert Browning, who died just after I received my first bachelor's degree.

Had it not been for the race problem early thrust upon me and enveloping me, I should have probably been an unquestioning worshipper at the shrine of the established social order and of the economic development into which I was born. But just that part of this order which seemed to most of my fellows nearest perfection, seemed to me most inequitable and wrong; and starting from that critique, I gradually, as the years went by, found other things to question in my environment.

At first, however, my criticism was confined to the relation of my people to the world movement. I was not questioning the world movement in itself. What the white world was doing, its goals and ideals, I had not doubted were quite right. What was wrong was that I and people like me and thousands of others who might have my ability and aspiration, were refused permission to be a part of this world. It was as though moving on a rushing express, my main thought was as to my relations with the other passengers on the express, and not to its rate of speed and its destination.

In the days of my formal education, my interest became concentrated upon the race struggle. My attention from the first was focused on democracy and democratic development; and upon the problem of the admission of my people into the freedom of democracy. This my training touched but obliquely. We studied history and politics almost exclusively from the point of view of ancient German freedom, English and New England democracy, and the development of the white United States. Here, however, I could bring criticism from what I knew and saw touching the Negro.

Europe modified profoundly my outlook on life and my thought and feeling toward it, even though I was there but two short years with my contacts limited and my friends few. But something of the possible beauty and elegance of life permeated my soul; I gained a respect for manners. I had been before, above all, in a hurry. I wanted a world, hard, smooth and swift, and had no time for rounded corners and ornament, for unhurried thought and slow contemplation. Now at times I sat still. I came to know Beethoven's symphonies and Wagner's *Ring*. I looked long at the colors of Rembrandt and Titian. I saw in arch and stone and steeple the history and striving of men and also their taste and expression. Form, color and words took new combinations and meanings.

I crossed the ocean in a trance. Always I seemed to be saying, "It is not real; I must be dreaming!" I can live it again— the little, Dutch ship—the blue waters—the smell of new-mown hay—Holland and the Rhine. I saw the Wartburg and Berlin; I made the *Hartzreise* and climbed the Brocken; I saw the Hansa towns and the cities and dorfs of South Germany; I saw the Alps at Berne, the Cathedral at Milan, Florence, Rome, Venice, Vienna, and Pest; I looked on the boundaries of Russia; and I sat in Paris and London.

On mountain and valley, in home and school, I met men and women as I had never met them before. Slowly they became, not white folks, but folks. The unity beneath all life clutched me. I was not less fanatically a Negro, but "Negro" meant a greater, broader sense of humanity and world fellowship. I felt myself standing, not against the world, but simply against American narrowness and color prejudice, with the greater, finer world at my back.

In Germany in 1892, I found myself on the outside of the American world, looking in. With me were white folk—students, acquaintances, teachers—who viewed the scene with me. They did not always pause to regard me as a curiosity, or something sub-human; I was just a man of the somewhat privileged student rank, with whom they were glad to meet and talk over the world; particularly, the part of the world whence I came.

I found to my gratification that they, with me, did not regard America as the last word in civilization. Indeed, I derived a certain satisfaction in learning that the University of Berlin did not recognize a degree even from Harvard University, no more than Harvard did from Fisk. Even I was a little startled to realize how much that I had regarded as white American, was white European and not American at all: America's music is German, the Germans said; the Americans have no art, said the Italians; and their literature, remarked the English, is mainly English. All agreed that Americans could make money and did not care how they made it. And the like. Sometimes their criticism got under even my anti-American skin, but it was refreshing on the whole to hear voiced my own attitude toward so much that America had meant to me.

I wrote in my diary: "Holland is an extremely neat and well-ordered mud-puddle, situated at the confluence of the English, French, and German languages. My memory of my first sight of it is inextricably interwoven with a smell of clover. It was after a two weeks' sea voyage—pleasant to be sure, fascinating as the changing, changeless sea ever is, but *two weeks*—then I came on deck one sunny morning to see long low green fields, sleepy little farm houses, long, prim, and decent rows of trees, stolid windmills and cows. So far as landscape is concerned, I never saw ought else in Holland and had I (God forbid!) followed my first inclinations, I should have gone away from this dear old nook with the usual uninteresting tale. I stayed a week or so, and I am very glad.

"There is to be sure a certain sameness about the homely country—a slowness which makes an American gasp and sometimes swear, and yet the very monotony of the country, the low dogged hum of its simple life, has for the loiterer a charm I can only liken to that of the backyard of my New England home. The Dutchman is in no hurry; he sees no necessary connection between the new and the good—rather the contrary; he is ponderously honest, and he is guiltless of anything savoring of personal beauty. His nation may become grasping and greedy, but the individual Dutchman is too honest to know it or to believe it when it is told.

"If Rotterdam had been any but a Dutch town, I shouldn't have seen it—I mean if Dutch business methods had not been so exasperatingly deliberate as to take six days to get a draft on Baring Bros. of London cashed, I should not have spent even a night at his interesting place. As it was, I was imprisoned for nearly a week in the town, in daily terror lest mine host should present his ruddy bill before my extremely wan purse. And I liked it: a nice place in its way. To be sure I must say I never saw a more poorly tailored town in my life. I saw very few persons whose clothes seemed to have been made with the slightest reference to their bodies, except the housemaids. In maidservants, Rotterdam has apparently reached the *ne plus ultra* [acme; furthest point]: elaborately beruffled caps, immaculate white stockings and slippers, simple gingham dresses, and healthy, honestly homely faces, made them most pleasant figures to meet on the promenade.

"Rotterdam as a city has a certain lack of individuality which is in itself characteristic. You see, it lies in the midstream of Dutch commerce with the great world and the current has changed it. It has almost forgotten its native tongue —so used is it to jabbering English, French, and German, and it has a general unconnected sort of air which would make a nervous people picturesque, but only makes the Rotterdamites a wee bit ludicrous.

"One annoyance I met here and all over Europe: the landlord would hasten to inform me beamingly that 'Fellow Americans had just arrived.' If there was one thing less desirable than white 'fellow Americans' to me, it was black 'fellow Americans' to them."

Of greatest importance was the opportunity which my *Wanderjahre* in Europe gave of looking at the world as a man and not simply from a narrow racial and provincial outlook. This was primarily the result not so much of my study, as of my human companionship, unveiled by the accident of color. From the days of my later youth in the South to my boarding a Rhine passenger steamer at Rotterdam in August 1892, I had not regarded white folk as human in quite the same way that I was. I had reached the habit of expecting color prejudice so universally, that I found it even when it was not there. So when I saw on this little steamer a Dutch lady with two grown daughters and one of 12, I proceeded to put as much space between us as the small vessel allowed. But it did not allow much, and the lady's innate breeding allowed less. Soon the little daughter came straight across the deck and placed herself squarely before me. She asked if I spoke German; before I could explain, the mother and other daughters approached and we were conversing.

Before we reached the end of our trip, we were happy companions, laughing, eating and singing together, talking English, French and German and viewing the lovely castled German towns. Once or twice when the vessel docked for change of cargo, the family strolled off to visit the town. Each time I found excuse to linger behind and visit alone later; until once at Düsseldorf, all got away before I sensed it and left me and the prettiest daughter conversing. Then seeing we had docked she suggested we follow and see the town. We did; and thereafter we continued acting like normal, well-bred human beings. I waved them all good-bye, in the solemn arched aisles of the Cologne Cathedral, with tears in my eyes.

So too in brave old Eisenach, beneath the shadow of Luther's Wartburg, I spent a happy holiday in a home where university training and German home-making left no room for American color prejudice. From this unhampered social intermingling with Europeans of education and manners, I emerged from the extremes of my racial provincialism. I became more human; learned the place in life of "Wine, Women, and Song"; I ceased to hate or suspect people simply because they belonged to one race or color; and above all I began to understand the real meaning of scientific research and the dim outline of methods of employing its technique and its results in the new social sciences for the settlement of the Negro problems in America.

In the Marbach home which took only properly introduced "paying guests" were two grown daughters, and two young women who were relatives; two young Frenchmen, an English youth and myself. *Herr Oberpfarrer* [the Rector], Doctor Marbach, and his efficient and correct wife presided. At first my German was halting and I was shy. But soon the courtesy of the elders and the ebullient spirits of the young folks evoked my good nature and keen sense of cameraderie. The very mistakes of those of us who were foreigners—mistakes in grammar and usage and etiquette—became a source of merriment and sympathy. We became a happy group closely bound to each other. We went together to church services and to concerts. We took long excursions through field and forest to places of interest, lunching in homely inns or in the open.

I remember once the contest in poetry we had in a forest glen looking out on a great mountain range; I recited in English and one of the Frenchmen in his tongue. Then Madame Marbach (who always chaperoned us) recited *Du bist wie eine Blume* [You are like a flower]. We wept openly at its beauty and I looked at Dora with her blue eyes and black hair and the lovely coloring of her skin. Dora always paired with me, first to correct my German and then by preference. Once we all went to the annual ball of the upper middle-class folk in the town. It was formal and a little stiff. The carefully gowned matrons sat around the walls of the room, knitting and gossiping and keeping watch over the demure white-gowned girls in their charge. The fathers sat at tables and drank beer. I danced with all the girls of our home; then bowing from the waist ventured to ask other young ladies to whom I had been introduced. Then came the *Damen Wahl* [Ladies' Choice], I drew back, but it was unnecessary, for my card was filled for every dance.

I was very fond of Dora Marbach and as I well knew, so was she of me. Our fellows joked about us and when I sang the folk song of *Die Lora am Thore* [Lora at the Gate], little Bertha invariably changed the name to "Dora." We confessed our love for each other and Dora said she would marry me *"gleich!"* [at once]. But I knew this would be unfair to her and fatal for my work at home, where I had neither property nor social standing for this blue-eyed stranger. She could not quite understand. Naturally I received much advice as to marriage plans. One lady told me very seriously *"Sie sollen heiraten eine hell-blonde!"* [you should marry a light blonde]. But I knew better, although there may have been some echo in my mind of the proverb:

> *Es war' so schön gewesen*
> *Es hät' nicht sollen sein!*
>
> *It was so lovely*
> *That it could not be!*

It was an American woman who sought to see to it that no entanglement between me and Dora took place. She and her husband came to board with the Marbachs for a month or so. He was a professor in Colorado, a good-natured, ill-mannered Westerner. She was a nervous gossip, astonished to see a

Negro so well received in this household. What she told Frau Marbach about American Negroes I do not know, but I can imagine. There was nothing said of the couple but all were glad when they left. I felt a little sensitive when I left. I exchanged letters with the family while I remained in Germany but I never returned to this beloved foster home.

In the Fall I went up to Berlin and registered in the university. In my study, I came in contact with several of the great leaders of the developing social sciences: in economic sociology and in social history. My horizon in the social sciences was broadened not only by teachers, but by students from France, Belgium, Russia, Italy and Poland.

For matriculation in groups of 100 we went into a large room with a high ceiling ornamented with busts of Berlin's famous professors. The year's Rector Magnificus was the widely famous Rudolf Virchow. He was a meek and calm little man, white-haired and white-bearded, with kindly face and pleasant voice. I had again at Berlin as at Harvard, unusual opportunity. Although a foreigner, I was admitted my first semester to two seminars under Gustav Schmoller and Adolf Wagner, both of them at the time the most distinguished men in their lines; I received eventually from both of them pleasant testimony on my work in economics, history and sociology. I sat under the voice of the fire-eating Pan-German, Heinrich von Treitschke; I heard Max Weber; I wrote on American agriculture for Schmoller and discussed social conditions in Europe with teachers and students. Under these teachers and in this social setting, I began to see the race problem in America, the problem of the peoples of Africa and Asia, and the political development of Europe as one. I began to unite my economics and politics; but I still assumed that in these groups of activities and forces, the political realm was dominant. Here are comments I made at the time:

"Matriculation commenced the 15th of October. I registered as number 85 of the more than 5,000 who usually matriculate here. The lectures mostly began the week following. Each professor writes a more or less legible announcement as to the time and place of the commencement of his lectures. The student then has to scurry about and examine a dozen different blackboards and hundreds of different slips of paper to find his particular professor's announcement. Poorly written English is bad enough, but when puzzling German, cloaked in execrably written German script, it is a combination fearful and wonderful to behold. Schmoller's scrawl caused me trouble, Wagner was well-nigh illegible, but Treitschke—well, I haven't deciphered his announcement yet.

"The lectures are of two sorts—private and public. The first have four hours a week, generally mornings on Tuesdays or Fridays, or on two afternoons from four to six. These lectures must be paid for at the rate of $5.00 a course for the semester. In this heaven of 'electivism' every student must take at least a one-point course. The public lectures are full, and have one or two hours a week, on Wednesday or Saturday mornings or on other evenings at six or seven.

"An American astounded a professor by asking how much work a student was expected to do. The real answer is none or all he can manage. Only two things are required: the signature of the teacher at the beginning and at the end of the course. One of the articles furnished at matriculation is an *Anmelde-Buch* in which the names of the various professors and lectures you propose to take must be written. This is taken to the Questor who receives the tuition and receipts. Then you must trot to each professor and get his signature for each set of lectures at the beginning and end of the semester.

"The students take part in the recitation-room proceeding mainly with their feet. A shuffle of feet presages disapproval, a stamping means applause. A few days ago, when Wagner mentioned Bismarck and called him the principal creator of German unity, a rub-a-dub followed from the 300 students for nearly five minutes. Shuffling is used also to express disapproval of late arrivals. Sometimes the disturbance is not generally thought great enough and the shuffling is rebuked by hissing. At other times when the tardy one is unusually noisy, there is a deafening whirr of feet which stops the lecture and never fails to abash the intruder. Commencing late, the lectures also end late. The students generally submit to remaining five minutes past but after that there comes an ominous clicking of inkstands and now and then designed and premature applause cuts off the lecturer's last words.

"To me by far the most interesting of the professors is the well-known von Treitschke, the German Machiavelli. He never comes to his lectures until very late, often commencing his ten o'clock lecture on *Politik* at 10:30—never before 10:20. He is a large man, of 'fair round belly with good capon lined,' or possibly with the more unpoetic beer; he generally dresses rather carefully in dark gray or blue cutaway with cylinder hat, gloves and the all-prevading German cane. His complexion is dark, his well-kept hair and full beard iron gray, and his features rather gross. He is stone deaf with a slight impediment in his speech, and a sort of breathless way of speaking, that makes him very difficult at first for a foreigner to understand. The task, however, is worth all pains, for his is one of the most forcible and independent minds on the faculty.

"His entrance is always the same. He comes in slowly, somewhat out of breath, with his overcoat, hat, and cane on his left arm. These he hangs on the wall and ascends to his desk where he stands as he speaks. He then takes off his right glove and putting his head a bit on one side says: '*Meine Herren,*' with a falling inflection. Then begins the lecture, which, as I overheard a puzzled and sighing American say, 'has but one period and that's at the end.' He does not speak so fast, but his articulation is bad (imagine badly articulated German!) and he has a way of catching his breath in the midst of his sentences instead of at the end, giving the ear no natural pause.

"His lectures are nevertheless intensely interesting. He is rapt in his subject, a man of intense likes and dislikes, beliefs and disbeliefs. He is the very embodiment of united monarchical, armed Germany. He has pity for France, hearty dislike for all things English—while for America, well, the

United States is his *bête noire,* which he seldom fails to excoriate. One day he startled me by suddenly declaring during a lecture on America: *'Die Mulattin sind niedrig! Sie fühlen sich niedrig.'* [Mulattoes are inferior; they feel themselves inferior.] I felt as if he were pointing me out; but I presume he was quite unaware of my presence. However my presence or absence would have made no difference to him. He was given to making extraordinary assertions out of a clear sky and evidently believing just what he said. My fellow students gave no evidence of connecting what he said with me. Yet von Treitschke was not a narrow man. His outlook is that of the born aristocrat who has something of the Carlyle contempt of levelling democracy. On the other hand he criticizes his own government and nation unsparingly when he sees fit—I have heard him characterize one of the highest officials as a *verrückte Dummkopf* [mad idiot] while the students cheered. He grows enthusiastic in his lectures, gestures considerably, and has a little half-caustic smile which always foreshadows some sharp critical sally that usually brings down the house; as for instance when he characterized some current author's work as efforts 'to widen the boundaries of human stupidity.'

"The Berlin student is not typical of his class, nor will the stranger find here so much of the purely student life. Berlin stands, I imagine, to the smaller universities something as Harvard to the Western universities. The students generally go to a local university first, then spend a semester or more in the classic glare of Berlin with its 83 full professors, 87 assistant professors, and 186 instructors; returning finally to their own universities to take their degree. The galaxy of learning here at Berlin is not so brilliant today, I imagine, as in the day of the great Theodor Mommsen.

"Yet it is sufficiently attractive. All of these professors, of course, I have not had the opportunity of seeing, much less hearing—indeed, four years at Harvard left some great names and faces unconnected in my mind. Those I have seen here are more especially connected with my department of political science; but they are celebrated enough to merit some particular notice. Wagner I have already spoken of personally —his hobby is the discovery of the golden mean between the warring extremes of his science. He comes dangerously near committing the common mistake in such cases of mistaking his extremes. He is publishing a new edition of his valuable *Lehrbuch,* and as inducement is offering various blandishments to the national apparition of socialism. The *bête noire* of the German economist is, of course, the British school founded, as Wagner says, with a jerk of his head, by 'Adahm Smiss.' Wagner, however, gives them due credit for their great work and agrees with them more fully than with the younger German radicals headed by Schmoller.

"There is evidently no intellectual love lost between Wagner and Schmoller. Schmoller is a large man about 50, with flowing beard, grown bald and prematurely gray. His complexion is dark and his eyes small and bright. He wears glasses, speaks with an accent, and is evidently a man of strong prejudices, fearless and sharp in expression of opinion, but a tireless investigator. He strikes me as more of a historian than economist. He conducts the economics seminar every other semester, alternating with Wagner. This semester Schmoller has the seminar, consisting of upward of 40 members, two of whom are American born, representing Harvard and Boston University. The papers presented so far have been indifferent, but the discussion animated and intelligent.

"The difference in general appearance between the Berlin student and his Harvard brother is very marked. The Harvard man affects a slouchy stride, jams his hands in his pockets, dresses well, and yet with a certain conscious carelessness; and would appear as a sort of devil-may-care young fellow, out of swaddling clothes but not yet in straitjacket. The Berlin student affects a strut, never uses his trouser pockets or whistles in public, dresses poorly but with a certain primness of collar, gloves, and cane; and would appear as a young man of intellect, promise, and present importance. A crowd of German students is more picturesque.

"In social life particularism is more marked here than even at Harvard. The simpleton who asks: 'Well, how about the social life of the Harvard students?' should be questioned in turn: 'Which Harvard students?' So in Berlin. Most of the students have spent their *kneipe* [carousing] years elsewhere and come here if not for more serious, at least for a different sort of play. The *Verbindungen* [student associations] do not consequently play so much of a role here as elsewhere.

"After so much has been written, most people understand the German student fraternities. They are of two sorts: the *Verbindungen* and the *Vereine*. The *Verbindungen* are in two great divisions: the *Verbindungen* with affiliate chapters in all universities; under these come the corps, to which formerly only the nobles belonged, but which now differ but little from the other divisions—the *Burschenuhaften,* the *Landsmannschaften,* which have the bulk of members. Second, the *Freie Verbindungen,* which are local societies.

"All the inter-university *Verbindungen* wear the student caps, a band of three colors across the breast; practice the sham sword duels to a considerable extent, do not wear beards, *kneipe* together, and address each other by the familiar *Du* instead of the polite *Sie*. The objects of the *Verbindungen* are purely social. They meet at stated times in their 'local,' drink beer, and sing, fight, etc. Duelling still goes on —have recently seen three or four freshly cut cheeks and heads—but not to a very great extent. I should judge that less than a tenth, possibly less than a twentieth of the members, bear scars. The custom as carried out now is entirely harmless—more so than the Harvard Dickey initiation, I should say. All the different societies parade slowly in the little square before the University in full regalia. Their number are, however, insignificant—generally not more than fifty or sixty in all.

"The *Vereine* are clubs for local social and literary purposes. They wear no caps or only colors on their fob watch chains. There are numerous *Vereine* in Berlin for all purposes, from philosophy to chess, and from converting the Jews to Alp-climbing. Outside of this, there is also an independent 'student union' of those belonging to no societies.

"The political situation is followed with keen interest by the students, though there is very little outspoken opinion. It is easy to see, that William II is not altogether popular among the young men, that many are not averse to coquetting a bit with socialism, and there is a general unrest and dissatisfaction among these future citizens.

"Naturally I am attracted to the socialist movement, but the history of the development of Marxism and of the revisionists like Lassalle, Bernstein and Bakunin was too complicated for a student like myself to understand, who had received no real teaching along this line. I was overwhelmed with rebuttals of Marxism before I understood the original doctrine. Even such great occurrences as the French Commune were minimized by the main history teaching to which I had listened in America. Until the fall of Bismarck in 1890, socialist organization or agitation were illegal in Germany, but the increase of industrial workers had led to a vast scheme of state insurance for accidents, old age relief and the like under Bismarck. In 1891, William II through his new Chancellor Caprivi tried a new social policy which allowed socialists to organize and a new Social Democratic party was beginning to grow rapidly at the time I arrived as a student. I frequently attended their meetings, but my student rank hindered me from that close personal acquaintanceship with workers which I should have had for complete understanding. I did soon realize that the Social Democratic party was the largest in the state, but kept from its rightful representation in the Reichstag by privilege and systematic gerrymandering."

The pageantry and patriotism of Germany in 1892 astonished me. In New England our patriotism was cool and intellectual. Ours was a great nation and it was our duty to preserve it. We "loved" it but with reason not passion. In the South, Negroes simply did not speak or think of patriotism for the nation which held their fathers in slavery for 250 years. On the other hand we revered rebels like Robert Dale Owen, Henry George or Edward Bellamy. When I heard my German companions sing *"Deutschland, Deutschland*

über Alles, über Alles in der Welt" I realized that they felt
something I had never felt and perhaps never would. The
march of soldiers, the saluting of magnificent uniforms, the
martial music and rhythm of movement stirred my senses.

Then there was that new, young Emperor, *"von Gottes
Gnade, deutsche Kaiser, Koenig von Preussen"* [blessed by
God, German Kaiser, King of Prussia], who led and pin-
pointed the pageantry. Ever and again he came riding ahead
of his white and golden troops on prancing chargers through
the great Brandenburg gate, up the Linden "With banners
gaily flying, with trumpet and with drum!" I thrilled at the
sight even though I knew of that shriveled left arm and of
his impossible demand for supreme power. I even trimmed
my beard and mustache to a fashion like his and still follow
it. If I a stranger was thus influenced, what about the youth
of Germany? I began to feel that dichotomy which all my
life has characterized my thought: how far can love for my
oppressed race accord with love for the oppressing country?
And when these loyalties diverge, where shall my soul find
refuge?

Germany took up my music and art where Fisk had left
me; to religious oratorio was now added opera and symphony, song and sonata. I heard cheaply and often from the
balcony seats offered students, the great music of the world:
but I heard it in reverse; I heard Wagner before Verdi; I
listened to *Tannhäuser* before *Il Trovatore*. Nevertheless
my delight in good music was signally increased.

The many vacations of the academic year I used for trips
in Germany and to other parts of Europe; but I missed after
the Summer in Eisenach, the companionship of close friends.
I kept up my older habit of traveling alone.

I had some student companionship in Germany and might
easily have had more. I was invited to join a *Gesellschaft* for
study of comparative international law; I found there some
good companions and we talked and published a set of by-
laws. To this we added a song book, to which at unanimous
request I added a translation of the then popular "Ta-ra-ra-
boom-de-ay!" Nevertheless I took my first excursion alone

and chose the Hansa cities of northwest Germany. I planned this trip for March, but before leaving there came my 25th birthday on February 23. I asked in no companions.

It was in the long, dark winter of northern Germany, and while I was comfortable, I felt a little lonesome and far away from home and boyhood friends. I arose at eight and took coffee and oranges, read letters, thought of my dead parents, and was sorry. The night before I had heard Schubert's beautiful *Unfinished Symphony,* planned my celebration and written to Grandma and Mabel and had a curious little ceremony with candles, Greek wine, oil, and song and prayer. I wandered up to the reading room, then to the art gallery, and finally had a fine dinner with Sonderhof over a bottle of Rudesheimer and cigarettes. Then we went to Potsdam for coffee and saw a pretty girl. We came back to the Seminar, took a walk, supped on cocoa, wine, oranges and cake and I came home alone. I had candles in my room on Schönburger Ufer, and a dedication of my small library to the memory of my mother; and I wrote something rather sentimental about life in general:

"Night—grand and wonderful. I am glad I am living. I rejoice as a strong man to win a race, and I am strong—is it egotism—is it assurance—or is it the silent call of the world spirit that makes me feel that I am royal and that beneath my sceptre a world of kings shall bow. The hot dark blood of a black forefather is beating at my heart, and I know that I am either a genius or a fool. O I wonder what I am—I wonder what the world is—I wonder if life is worth the *Sturm.* I do not know—perhaps I never shall know: But this I do know: be the Truth what it may I will seek it on the pure assumption that it is worth seeking—and Heaven nor Hell, God nor Devil shall turn me from my purpose till I die. I will in this second quarter century of my life, enter the dark forest of the unknown world for which I have so many years served my apprenticeship—in the chart and compass which the world furnishes me I have little faith— yet I have nothing better—I will seek till I find—and die. There is a grandeur in the very hopelessness of such a life

—Life? And is life all? If I strive, shall I live to strive again? I do not know and in spite of the wild *Sehnsucht* [yearning] for Eternity that makes my heart sick now and then—I shut my teeth and say I do not care. *Carpe Diem!* [Seize the day! —that is, enjoy the present.] What is life but life, after all? Its end is its greatest and fullest self—this end is the Good: the Beautiful is its attribute—its soul, and Truth is its being. Not three commensurable things are these, they are three dimensions of the cube. Mayhap God is the fourth, but for that very reason he will be incomprehensible. The greatest and fullest life is by definition beautiful, beautiful— beautiful as a dark passionate woman, beautiful as a golden-hearted school girl, beautiful as a grey haired hero. That is the dimension of *breadth*. Then comes Truth—what is, cold and indisputable. What is *height*. Now I will, so help my soul, multiply breadth by height, beauty by truth and then goodness, strength shall bind them together into a solid whole. Wherefore? I know not now. Perhaps infinite other dimensions do. This is a wretched figure and yet it roughly represents my attitude toward the world. I am striving to make my life all that life may be—and I am limiting that strife only in so far as that strife is incompatible with others of my brothers and sisters making their lives similar. The crucial question now is where that limit comes. I am too often puzzled to know. Paul put it as meat-eating, which was asinine. I have put it as the (perhaps) life-ruin of Amalie which is cruel. God knows I am sorely puzzled. I am firmly convinced that my own best development is not one and the same with the best development of the world and here I am willing to sacrifice. That sacrifice to the world's good becomes too soon sickly sentimentality. I therefore take the world that the Unknown lay in my hands and work for the rise of the Negro people, taking for granted that their best development means the best development of the world. . . ."

I was considerably alarmed at the end of my second semester toward the middle of the year 1893 when no word arrived as to re-appointment to my fellowship which I had confidently expected. I cabled without success. Finally this rather casual reply came from the President of Johns Hopkins, D. C. Gilman:

> The Slater Trustees have renewed your appointment with the understanding that you should give a note for one half the sum as before. You will presently hear from Mr. Strong representing the Treasurer.
>
> A telegram was received here May 8th, reading: "Was Du Bois reappointed?" without signature. I answered it and there came back a dispatch from Berlin, saying that the message was undelivered. I did not repeat the message.
>
> I shall hope to hear from you after receiving this note, and to have the semi-annual letters in the coming year as in the past.

The Christmas holidays of 1893 I spent in making a trip through south Germany. Three of us visited Weimar, Frankfort, Heidelberg and Mannheim. From Christmas Day to New Year's we stopped in a little German "Dorf" in the Rheinpfalz, where I had an excellent opportunity to study the peasant life closely and compare it with country life in the South. Three of us started out—a Scotsman, an American and myself. The American was descended from German immigrants to the United States and had relatives in the Rhineland in southwest Germany. We spent Christmas in the village of Gimmeldigen. What a lovely holiday, visiting and feasting among peasant folk who treated me like a prince! We visited perhaps 20 different families, talked, ate and drank new wine with them; listened to their gossip, attended their social assemblies, etc. The bill which my obsequious landlord presented on my departure was about one-tenth of what I expected. We stayed in Naustadt a week, with a family whose dead father had driven the first locomotive into France at the opening of the Franco-German war. The daughter was a fine, homely young woman who did everything to make us comfortable.

We then went to Strassburg, Stuttgart, Ulm, Muenchen, Nuremberg, Prague and Dresden. In those places we stayed from one to five days following our Baedekers closely and paying much attention to the Muenchen and Dresden art galleries. The whole trip cost me about $80. We parted from our American: he was a good-hearted but rather vulgar man, with an education that left no visible results. John Dollar, my British companion, and I got on famously together because we were so opposite in temperament. He was coldly and conventionally British in dress and speech. He paraded more than he walked, hated Catholic priests for no reason which he ever stated and was constitutionally afraid of women. With this went a strange simplicity and deep sympathy with human suffering. Later we decided to go down to Italy; to Genoa, Rome and Naples and then over to Venice and Vienna and Budapest. On this trip we used German instead of English because as Dollar assured me it would be much cheaper. He was quite right. We went over the vast barrier of the Alps gazing up on its heaven of snow and sky and then down on the incomparable beauty of the Italian lakes.

These were troubled days all over Europe. Switzerland was following socialism by adopting social insurance and was on the brink of buying up her railroads. Humbert I and Leo XIII were at loggerheads over papal territory in Italy. Crispi had risen, fallen and come back to power, and was now heading for the fatal Ethiopian war of 1896. We went to Genoa and Turin; to Florence, Rome and Naples. I saw for the first time some of the world's great sculpture and painting; its historical monuments; I sensed the difficulties between France and Italy when Dollar and I, mistaken for Frenchmen, were stoned by youth in the Roman Forum. We lived cheaply and fared bountifully. We saw Naples, free, lovely and dirty, in all the gay abandon of the *fin-de-siècle*. It was a great and inspiring trip. We turned back north and saw Venice with its doves and the Palace of the Doges, and then went northeast to Vienna.

This was Vienna in its glory, not at its height but still magnificent. I remember the great Opera House and the way men stood in their seats and looked the audience over; the leisurely way in which we all promenaded in the wide and long halls and lunched at will; and then the finely conducted music and acting. It was one of the world's greatest and most influential cities. Here Dollar left me. I do not think he liked Austria as much as Rome and also his engagements called him.

As for me I had further scenes to examine. While at Berlin, I found myself once explaining to a schoolmate, Stanislaus Ritter von Estreicher, the race problem in America. He was not as impressed as I thought he should be. He said: "I understand only too well; but you should see the race antagonism in my home. Come to Krakow and see the clash of German and Pole!" I promised that I would visit him when near. So now I travelled alone into Hungary, with the object of turning north through Slovenia and over the Tatra mountains into Poland. It was a journey with a hint of adventure and with a far-off likeness to my American South.

In Budapest I was struck by the hostility to German Austria. This was four years after the suicide of Crown Prince Rudolf at Meyerling. Taafe was prime minister and had sought to placate the rising Hungarian drive to greater independence by grant of manhood suffrage. But the Hungarians were asserting their desire for independence. In the post office, they pretended not to understand German even when I tried to buy stamps. It would be the very next year that Kossuth was to die in Italy and increase the demand for Hungarian independence from Austria.

I fared north over that great plain along which the Magyars came west a thousand years before. I had glimpses of Hungary as I traveled slowly by third-class railway coach, stopping to spend a night here and there. A Hungarian peasant wrote later of conditions in Hungary at the time: "Come with me in the Spring and hoe for 16 hours for 12 cents a day; eat dry bread and rotten bacon, sleep in a hole dug with his own hoe for six hours. We work even longer in summer. On the *putzas* four families, 20 to 25 people, live in one room. I have seen men collapsing on the street from starvation. Such things are not exactly calculated to make one enthusiastic about the Fatherland. Do our lords think we shall starve to death without a word?"

All this I did not actually see, but I heard its echoes; my dark face elicited none of the curiosity which it had in blonde north Germany, for there were too many dark Gypsies and other brunettes. I saw poverty and despair. I was several times mistaken for a Jew; arriving one night in a town of north Slovenia, the driver of a rickety cab whispered in my ear, *"Unter die Juden?"* [among Jews]. I stared and then said yes. I stayed in a little Jewish inn. I was a little frightened as in the gathering twilight I traversed the foothills of the dark Tatras alone and on foot. I crossed into Poland and stopped to go down into the salt mines of Wielitza.

Finally I came to Krakow and my friend. It was an interesting visit and an old tale. Tyranny in school and work; insult in home and on the street. Of course here, in contrast to America, there were the privileged Poles who escaped personal insult; there was the aristocracy who had some recognized rights. The whole mass of the oppressed were not reduced to one level; nevertheless the degradation was only too familiar. The venerable librarian of the university treated me to Polish *schnapps* which nearly choked me. The family made me most welcome. I never saw my schoolmate again, but I heard later that in the Second World War, the Germans tried to make him a Quisling for them. In 1940, von Estreicher died in a German concentration camp, after he had refused to be one of Germany's puppet rulers of Poland.

I came back to Berlin by way of Prague and Dresden and started my third and final semester. Schmoller wanted to present me for my doctorate, despite the fact that I had not finished the "triennium" required in a German university and my work at Harvard was not recognized. The faculty was willing in my case but was restrained by the professor of English who threatened to push the similar claims of several Britishers. I therefore regretfully had to forego the chance of a German doctorate and wait for the degree from Harvard.

As a farewell to Germany, I made the *Hartzreise* in the Spring of 1894. Again I went alone, but with my now familiar German and wide experience of travel, I felt at home.

I kept no diary of this trip, but started west from Berlin to Magdeburg and Halberstadt in Saxony. I passed the splendid seat of the Prince zu Steinberg-Wernigerhode. Then I climbed to the Brocken and lived Walpurgis night again; I forded streams and climbed mountains until in full darkness I came to an old inn. I ordered beer and *kalbsbratten* and dined alone. This was my perfect farewell to a Germany which no longer exists.

I stayed in Europe as long as the last penny allowed— eager for work and home and yet reluctant. My old pal Dollar wrote me from England and we planned to meet in London before I left for America.

I now turned home. If I had spent a fourth semester at Berlin, that would have not only exceeded my funds covering two years of work but also have taken me up to Christmas and made the securing of work in America for the next year unlikely. A better alternative occurred to me and that was to spend the Spring in France. The years of preparation were over and life was to begin. I computed my balance of funds carefully. I could go first class to London, spend a short time with my friend Dollar and then take first class cabin accommodation to the United States. Or by carefully husbanding my funds, riding third class on railways and returning steerage to New York I could spend a month or more in France. My earlier idea had been to spend a year in Germany and a year in France in graduate study; but I had to choose between a more complete German experience and two incomplete glimpses of both countries. So I spent nearly all my time in Germany. But here at the end was an opportunity at least to have a glimpse of France and then rough it home. Of course if I had intimated my need for further funds to Dollar he would have been willing and able to make me a loan. But here my New England frugality stopped me. I already was in debt for half of my fellowships; I had no job; and I had lived well enough in Europe to endure for a week the experience of immigrants to America. Even they on arrival might easily have a better chance for life than I in my own country.

I went to France and saw Paris; wandered wide and deep and made my French fairly understandable. I sensed the everlasting lure of Paris, three years after the suicide of Boulanger and the year of the final completion of the Franco-Russian alliance. It was also the year President Carnot was assassinated and Dreyfus condemned for treason. But these events gained only my passing attention. I was fascinated by the glory of French culture in painting, sculpture, architecture and historical monument. I saw Sarah Bernhardt; I haunted the Louvre.

In June I met my friend Dollar in London for a few days of a last farewell. Dollar, dear old boy, hadn't the slightest idea that I was going steerage and prattled finely about "selecting a cabin" and all that. We wandered about the depot, watching the crowds, edified by Dollar's explanation of the station until finally I entered the carriage, bade my good friend adieu and rattled off.

We stopped at Southampton in a sort of flurry, nobody, not even the guards seeming to know what we were to do next. As we stood helplessly on the platform the guard suddenly screamed "second cabin passengers this way" and left us steerage people alone. Finally they called us and grabbing our luggage we followed our guide who led us through the streets in one long line to a small brick shed about a mile off, where we deposited our baggage in the ante-room and entered. Within the walls were white-washed bricks, the ceiling wooden and iron and wooden columns in the center. At one end there was an alcove where several cooks were busy and distributed through the room were long wooden tables and benches on which not over-clean tablecloths were spread.

It was a most miscellaneous crowd: men, women, children, girls, husbands, wives—and as I should judge about an even mixture of honest people and rascals. Let me describe some types about me: opposite me a good-natured, honest, red-bearded Englishman, well dressed—paper collar, silver ring, etc. Tells me he's been in America before and talks sensibly. Beside me a short bull-necked candidate for states prison, drunk and sleeping with his head on the table; on the other side an ill-smelling old man with chin beard, good-natured and a bit stupid. Yonder is a tall girl—rather good looking, a bit tawdrily dressed—afraid for her future. There is a motherly old lady in black with a look of sorrow on her face—poor thing. They're eating now—grabbing things and swilling tea.

Well there we sat in this great bare room that whole afternoon: the ship would not sail till the morrow and we must of course sleep there unless, as the steward gently hinted, we went to a hotel. By careful maneuvering I secured a doorless compartment alone and an ill-smelling bunk. A rather restless night it was however—the smell, the noise of the drunken roisterers and the thoughts of the wild trip I was about to take. Two of the roisterers came staggering in about midnight, mistook my compartment for theirs, staggered about, guffawed, hiccoughed and joked and at last managed to tumble to their own bed. Then I was waked again by one of them crawling through the hall on his knees with a lighted match, seeking a penny he'd dropped—not exactly a comfort-giving exhibition in a dry, wooden hovel. Finally my troubled morning dreams were mingled with the stench of the beer which his poor stomach refused longer to hold. This was too much—I could not eat breakfast but rushed out of the fetid atmosphere of the crowded hall into the wet misty atmosphere of Southampton.

It was early Sunday morning and all shops were closed—oh what a dreary lonesome feeling that was! At last I bought an indifferent breakfast for tenpence and then returned to the "barracks" to find that we would not sail before afternoon. In despair I started off again and succeeded in finding a more interesting wandering. Southampton is in many respects a fine old town with its historic gates and old bits of town wall and I enjoyed this all thoroughly. Finally I returned to dinner—a jam and a crowd which I joined with loathing. Then came a baggage van and away we straggled to the quay amid the undisguised amusement of the inhabitants—and it was a picturesque and laughable crowd—young and old—lame and well—rags and fine clothes—Jew and gentile, Russians, English, Americans, Negroes, Poles, Germans, French, Greeks, Austrians—all running and waddling along. Ah—it was funny and yet sad—this great stream of hopes and longing, of disappointment and sorrow, of happiness and crime about to turn itself into Americans. At the quay we were hemmed in by ropes for about a half or three-quarters of an hour and a big red tag with the stamps of the U.S. Consul attached to our bags certifying that he had inspected us—which was of course a lie. Finally we showed our tickets and came on board. In a few minutes, the two tugs started with us in tow and we had embarked.

I'm not myself of the seasick getting kind but I must confess that the next morning as I felt the ship rising and fading away under my feet and rolling from side to side with something more than ordinary enthusiasm, I felt a certain settled melancholy which compelled me to confine my first breakfast to an orange and rush in rather undignified haste from the dark dungeons below onto the wet and dirty deck. I was not sicker than this, missed no meals and gave up no further offering to the sea; but it was a trying time. The sea was very choppy, even a bit stormy. Then in addition to that, the filth and nastiness of the people about me, the small amount of deck room—that was enough to cause the stoutest stomach to revolt, even on land. And the people were sick—oh so sick, it was pitiable to see them and yet at the same time so laughable. In spite of the efforts of the crew it was well nigh impossible to keep the deck clean, everywhere lay unsightly messes; as one fellow said as I told of the good dinner we'd had: "Yes, I saw a lot of it up on deck." One can hardly realize how sick it's possible to get. Some of the pale, drawn faces looked quite deathlike and the whole tone of melancholy hopelessness that pervaded the crowd was most remarkable. Some made no attempt at first to come on deck and after a few days I was continually surprised by the appearance of new faces which until then had lain low in the cabins below. Such a sort of universal sickness, however, is a strange opportunity to view human character: these 350 human beings so accidentally thrown together learned to know each other first amid pain and suffering and the little friendships made there, the little deeds good and bad, sank deeper into their souls than usual. It is perhaps this circumstance that gives a sea voyage its most peculiar flavor.

On this, our floating island, the world is much simpler than usual. First it consists of us and the trembling world of cabins, decks, masts and chimneys. Then there is a great circle of dark blue waters stretching away, away evenly in a circle until meeting with the sky in the dim and misty distance it becomes one with the sky world and its clouds and pale day moon. Our ship is a fairly large one, not very swift and a bit old—the *Chester* of the American Line with, all told, some 800 souls aboard. My first work in the morning is to get a slight bath, a thing of no ordinary difficulty for steerage passengers. I generally get up on deck a bit early. A bell rings and I hasten down two rickety pairs of steep stairs, two stories below the deck where our cabins are. This is a long room, perhaps 15 yards long and as wide as the ship. The sides are taken up with the bunks, leaving a space perhaps 15 feet in the middle through which a long narrow table of plain boards runs lengthwise. Beside this are narrow stationary seats without backs. The whole room is lighted by only a half dozen small port holes and kerosene lamps giving it a rather gloomy appearance. It is fairly well ventilated, considering its depth below the world. We range ourselves by the tables each bringing the utensils delivered to him by the steward at the beginning of the trip—a tin plate, cup and spoon, and a knife and fork. The breakfast consists of rather poor coffee (with milk and molasses already in) plenty of good bread and fair butter, and good porridge or stew: a breakfast which in spite of the noise, the broad talk and the very primitive table manners of my neighbors, I generally enjoy. The next duty is to wash your own dishes for which a can for slops and a can of hot water is provided, the dish cloth being furnished by the passenger. As usual, some omit even this bit of trouble and have apparently not washed their plates since starting.

There are five Negroes aboard. We do not go together, indeed have not all spoken together, but I think all have had a pleasant voyage with little cause to complain of any prejudice. Of course we awakened more or less curiosity with some and I fancy something of dislike in others. Yet I find us all talking to the women and one, especially from his good-heartedness, seems a general favorite; in fine, in a gradual line of individuals here the blacks would by no means stand at the bottom of the row. What I notice in all the passengers is their good-heartedness, their straightforwardness. There is not a trace of deception and desire to injure or envy others. A people with such hearts do not deserve annihilation. Society: What happens when 350 people of the lower classes are for nine days thrown together with very little outside government? The answer to this can be seen on this voyage and is most interesting. We have here of course all grades of society but a majority of what must be called lower. Yet I think that the better classes here, the better and more orderly elements though scarcely greater in numbers, have been distinctly more influential. The experience has proven in a degree what I have always thought, that the number of "estates" becomes unlimited in a sense. One can scarcely bring any sort of a crowd of people together without finding a large number of distinct classes. Then again the number of estates is quite limited, for the several classes here developed differences in no great degree different from the classes elsewhere in the world—it is the same old strife of finer souls against brutality.

We have of course strange divisions here: that of education, that of wealth, that of life object, that of nation, that of language and that of color. There is here a great number of half-educated men—men who for lack of opportunity or perseverance have but tasted the beginnings of life. They are, when not dogmatic and conceited, most interesting men and in all cases studies in human nature. They are often compounded of opposites: an intellectual acumen and desire to learn with low habits and even brutality; then again there are embryonic cranks.

After a week we began to become tired and uneasy. We wanted Life to end and begin. A new land loomed there beyond the horizon and we began searching the skies. I who was born there was also approaching something new and untried after 24 years of preparation. At last it loomed on the morning when we saw the Statue of Liberty. I know not what multitude of emotions surged in the others, but I had to recall that mischievous little French girl whose eyes twinkled as she said: "Oh yes the Statue of Liberty! With its back toward America, and its face toward France!"

CHAPTER XI

WILBERFORCE

As a student in Germany, I built great castles in Spain and lived therein. I dreamed and loved and wandered and sang; then after two long years I dropped suddenly back into "nigger"-hating America!

My Days of Disillusion which followed were not disappointing enough to discourage me. I was still upheld by that fund of infinite faith, although dimly about me I saw the shadow of disaster. I began to realize how much of what I had called Will and Ability was sheer Luck! *Suppose* my good mother had preferred a steady income from my child labor rather than bank on the precarious dividend of my higher training? *Suppose* that pompous old village judge, whose dignity we often ruffled and whose apples we stole, had had his way and sent me while a child to a "reform" school to learn a "trade." *Suppose* Principal Hosmer had been born with no faith in "darkies," and instead of sending me to college had had me taught carpentry and the making of tin pans? *Suppose* I had missed a Harvard scholarship? *Suppose* the Slater Board had then, as now, distinct ideas as to where the education of Negroes should stop? Suppose *and* suppose! As I sat down calmly on flat earth and looked at my life a certain great fear seized me. Was I the masterful captain or the pawn of laughing sprites? Who was I to fight a world of color prejudice? I raise my hat to myself when I remember that, even with these thoughts, I did not hesitate or waver; but just went doggedly to work, and therein lay whatever salvation I have achieved.

I returned to the United States at 26 years of age and after 20 years of study to look for a job and begin work. I wrote my friend Dollar in London:

"You know I landed in New York in June, 1894, with $2 plus my fare home up in Berkshire. It was not altogether a happy homecoming—it was too much of a disillusionment after months of picturesque German gutturals, days of sunny skies, and weeks of dirty mighty Romes. I felt as though the bottom of the universe was loose and might go down if after all this soaring I stepped full feet upon it. And I must step, walk, stumble and climb now; for the *lehr jahre* [learning years] were passed—I fancied—and the *meister jahre* [adult years] begun."

It was a disturbed world in which I landed; 1892 saw the high tide of lynching in the United States; Cleveland had entered his second term in 1893 and the Chicago Exposition had taken place. The Dreyfus case had opened in France with his conviction and imprisonment, and he was destined for 12 years to suffer martyrdom. The war between China and Japan broke out the year of my return. I recognized the blow democracy received when Congress repealed the Force bills in 1894, refusing longer even to try to protect the legal citizenship rights of Negroes. But on the other hand, I did not at all understand the implications of the Matabele War in 1893. I did not see how the gold and diamonds of South Africa and later the copper, ivory, cocoa, tin and vegetable oils of other parts of Africa and especially the black labor force were determining and conditioning the political action of Europe.

First came the task of earning a living. I was not exacting or hard to please. I just got down on my knees and begged for work, anything and anywhere. I began a systematic mail campaign. I wrote to no white institution—I knew there were no openings there. I wrote one colored public school in East Tennessee, not far from where I had taught school. The board hesitated, but finally indicated that I had rather too much education for their use. I applied to Howard University, Hampton Institute, Tuskegee Institute and my own Fisk. They had no openings.

So I sat down and wrote more letters: "President of so and so college; Sir: I am a Negro, 27 years of age, educated in the public schools of Massachusetts, at Fisk University, Nashville and Harvard University, where I took the degrees of A.B. and A.M. I wish to teach next year. Have you a vacancy, etc." I wrote so many that I scarcely remember where. The hot months rolled by and answers came slowly— brief no's, polite regrets, general disclaimers and one or two vague notes with dubious hopes. The editors notwithstanding, no college man expects the gates of the wide world to fly open before him "with impetuous recoil" and yet I say it wasn't too much for a colored man with a Harvard A.M. to expect a bread and butter job, was it?

At last a few offers came. The first was a telegram from Wilberforce University, a colored church school in Ohio: "Our chair of classics $800 is yours. Wire acceptance. Come next week." I immediately accepted with gratitude. Later there was Lincoln Institute, a state colored school out in Missouri, that offered $1,050 for a teacher of "classics and mathematics." I refused since I had accepted Wilberforce. I knew something about Wilberforce. It was venerable and well known. Finally, August 25, I received a telegram: "Can give mathematics if terms suit. Will you accept. Booker T. Washington." It would be interesting to speculate just what would have happened if I had received the offer of Tuskegee first, instead of that of Wilberforce.

So, late in hot August, I started for Wilberforce. Life was now begun and I was half happy. Up through the Berkshire Valley with its quiet beauty, then across New York I glided, wrapped in dreams. The lights of Buffalo bade me good-night, and half asleep, I drifted across Ohio.

The depot at Xenia was small and "busy" with a slight admixture of dirt and tobacco juice which was unpleasant. I telephoned to Wilberforce. Then I waited an hour. Finally the President entered the waiting room. I shall never forget that man. He had by long odds the prettiest smile of any man I ever saw, so quiet and charming. All I remember now of that first meeting is the vision of that smile softly entering the waiting room and remember too that it was borne on two short and rather disreputable looking bowlegs.

Wilberforce was a small colored denominational college married to a State normal school. The church was too poor to run the college; the State tolerated the normal school so as to keep Negroes out of other State schools. Consequently, there were enormous difficulties in both church and State politics. This I soon realized. I had been hired to teach "Latin and Greek." They were not my specialty and despite years spent in their study I really knew far too little to teach them. But I had assumed that I was to assist Professor William Scarborough, a well-known Negro scholar long working at Wilberforce. To my amazement I found that I was to replace him, since in a quarrel between him and the President, he had been ousted and I had been advertised as a learned professor just from Germany. This was my introduction to church politics. I did not like it but the name of Wilberforce lured me.

The breath of it had swept the water and dropped into southern Ohio, where white Southerners had once taken their cure at Tawawa Springs and where white Methodists later planted a school. Then came the little bishop, Daniel Payne, a Negro, who bought it and made it a school of the African Methodists.

Into this situation I landed with the cane and gloves of my German student days; with my rather inflated ideas of what a "university" ought to be and with a terrible bluntness of speech that was continually getting me into difficulty; as when, for instance, the student leader of a prayer meeting into which I had wandered casually to look local religion over, suddenly and without warning announced that "Professor Du Bois will lead us in prayer." I simply answered, "No, he won't," and as a result nearly lost my new job. It took a great deal of explaining to the board of bishops why a professor in Wilberforce should not be able at all times and sundry to address God in extemporaneous prayer. I was saved only by the fact that my coming to Wilberforce had been widely advertised and I was willing to do endless work when the work seemed to me worth doing.

I went to Wilberforce with high ideals. I wanted to help build a great university. I was willing to work night as well as day, and taught full time. I helped in student discipline, took part in the social life, and began to write books. But I found myself against a stone wall. Nothing stirred before my impatient pounding! Or if it stirred, it soon slept again.

The African Methodist Church was the greatest social institution of American Negroes. Wilberforce was its largest school. This school therefore became the capital of a nation-wide institution. Its large body of trustees were interested in the church organization, not in the college. The bishops and would-be bishops gathered here in force on each commencement where elders and ministers waylaid them in long conferences. The teachers also found it expedient to make powerful acquaintances at these occasions; I in my independence met no one but walked off into the woods as the hosts talked.

But I worked hard and this most students and many teachers liked. My program for the day at Wilberforce looked almost as long as a week's program now. I taught Latin, Greek, German, and English, and wanted to add sociology. I had charge of some of the most unpleasant duties of discipline and had outside work in investigation. I met and made many friends: Charles Young, a Negro soldier not long graduated from West Point, was one; he was serving as military instructor here for the Federal government. He and I both refused to attend the annual "revivals" of religion which interrupted school work every year at Christmas time. We both dreamed of a great future for this Negro school. Later Young fought in Mexico against Villa. He ranked first for a generalship in the army when the First World War opened, but was deftly shoved aside. He accepted duty later in Nigeria, West Africa, and died of black water fever. There was also at Wilberforce a student, Charles Burroughs, a gifted reader, who was in my classes; Paul Laurence Dunbar came over from Dayton and read to us. I had known his work but was astonished to find that he was a Negro. And not least, I met the slender, quiet, and dark-eyed girl Nina Gomer who became Mrs. Du Bois in 1896. Her father was chef in the leading hotel of Cedar Rapids, Iowa, and her dead mother a native of Alsace.

In May 1896, I was not only in love with a beautiful girl,

but also had carefully calculated that (a) I should marry before 30, and that (b) my salary of $800 was sufficient for two—if paid. They had an irritating way at Wilberforce in those days of not paying salaries very promptly. Indeed this nearly ruined my plans. It was May 1, I was penniless and my bride was awaiting me in Iowa. The treasurer was about to leave for General Conference where he had more weighty matters to discuss than teachers' salaries. I waylaid him and firmly persuaded him that until my salary due was paid, he was unlikely to see General Conference. He agreed and on May 12, I arrived in Cedar Rapids.

I went to a little white cottage and met a tall, heavy father, a young stepmother and a shy fat little sister. A benevolent white minister married us, and after inarticulate greetings, we rushed to the Chicago train and next day I was back at Wilberforce with a very tired young bride. There was a reception with hilarious students, critical teachers, and good town folk. I had furnished a two-room apartment in the men's dormitory: a bedroom on the west looking down on the ravine and across the hall a sitting room which I remember chiefly because of a gorgeous crimson couch cover which I had bought of Carson-Pirie in Chicago by mail order.

Probably Wilberforce was about the least likely of all Negro colleges to adopt me and my program. First of all I was cocky and self-satisfied. I doubtless strutted and I certainly knew what I wanted. My redeeming feature was infinite capacity for work and terrible earnestness, with appalling and tactless frankness. But not all was discouragement and frustration at Wilberforce. Of importance that exceeded everything, was the group of students whom I met and taught. Most of the student body was in high school grades and poorly equipped for study. But filtering into the small college department were a few men and women of first-class intelligence, able and eager to work. As working companions, we made excursions into Greek literature; I gathered a class in German which talked German from the first day; I guided the writing of English themes and did a bit of modern history. Try as I might, however, the institu-

tion would have no sociology, even though I offered to
teach it on my own time.

I tried various other lines of effort: there was for instance
a beautiful ravine where a stream of water flowing through
the campus rolled and slithered down to a wide green
meadow amid trees, vines, and boulders. On the campus
above stood Shorter Hall, named after a dead bishop whose
middle-aged son was a professor of mathematics, a good-
hearted, irascible man, combined of orthodox religion and
wrath for students who couldn't count. In the wing of
Shorter Hall, next the ravine, was the library; or rather a
few piles of old books which I had arranged to drag down
from the attic and planned in this big empty room a real
library and reading room for students and teachers. Hitherto
the only library facilities were in that upper attic where
Professor Scott might admit you with his key, if perchance
he could spare time from his chemistry. Remember the
libraries at Harvard and Berlin which I had used! And even
that at Fisk! I was determined to have a library. But there
was no money. There was never money for anything. Then
I had an idea: there were my students, boys and girls, with
talent in voice and action. There was the divine ravine:
why not give *A Midsummer Night's Dream* in that rare
bit of wood and foliage? The campus went quite wild over
the proposal. It could be given in the Spring just after Commencement. It need not cost much. The whole country
would visit it. We began to study the text, plan the scenes,
and choose the players. I began to see this play as the greatest
course in education of the whole year, of many years gone.

Then came the catastrophe: we heard that Ben Arnett had
been appointed Professor of Literature for the year beginning with Commencement. We laid down our text; we
turned our backs on the lush ravine; the waters trickled in
vain and the students wandered disconsolately. We teachers
began to fight: we wrote, we visited, we held meetings; we
stormed through the campus; we faced the bishop. And to
understand all this, one must know the bishopric of the
great African Methodist Church.

It was a hierachy of the conventional type and yet more and different. I knew a dozen of these bishops and a more varied and impressive, a more astonishing body of men I never met. Bishop Daniel Payne died the year before I arrived at Wilberforce. He was a man of tremendous character, a Man of God, if such there ever was. Tiny in figure, soft in voice, he thundered through this widespread mass of black folk like a prophet. He made them buy Wilberforce when they had nothing and knew little; he arranged the grounds, gathered the first teachers, and husbanded the pennies. He enforced discipline in the church, he traveled, he preached until his name was known from Carolina to the Rockies. Then he died, but his soul lived on.

Among his successors was Benjamin Arnett, the presiding Bishop over Wilberforce when I arrived; and what Arnett said, went. He was a thick-set man with a sharp, dark face, a blazing eye, and a rare smile and a will to do. With little literary ability, he established a sort of school of literature, bringing together and reprinting hundreds of books, pamphlets, and scraps of the writings of American Negro literature. He was a power in Ohio politics. He distributed offices in the church and settled the appointment of teachers at Wilberforce. My own appointment must have had his consent, perhaps even his advocacy, else I would not have been at Wilberforce. He lived in a lovely old home bowered by oaks and there he was handicapped by his family. His oldest son, named after him, was not a complete devil, but he certainly was not fitted to teach youth at Wilberforce. Yet at the end of my first year, the Bishop thrust him down our throats without even the courtesy of a notice; and we raised hell without stopping to consider what opposition to Bishop Arnett meant. As a body we refused to teach with Ben Arnett.

We won. Young Ben Arnett never became professor at Wilberforce. But of course the Bishop won too. He held power for life and no one stayed at Wilberforce long whom he did not like. Under my impetuous and uncurbed assault, the Bishop had to bend, but I knew well that my days at Wilberforce were numbered. The ravine with its vines and shrubbery, its singing waters and all its faerie, slept long in peace until 25 years later it was buried beneath a culvert of stone and its voice stilled forever.

As I realized that none of my dreams would be fulfilled at Wilberforce, I knew all the sadness of a spent dream. Wilberforce was near the center of the Negro population of the nation. We drew students from New Orleans and New York; from the Atlantic and the Pacific. We escaped the "jim-crow" of the slave South and the ostracism of the cold North. The college was poor and neglected and yet the church which owned it and whose prized child it was, formed a marvellous human institution. Its leaders were of every sort: selfless saints like Payne, J. R. Lee, and William Mitchell; ruthless politicians like Arnett; scoundrels like W. B. Derrick; and charging bulls like Henry M. Turner. With high ideals and brute force they rolled and jammed this mass of men and women forward and together until they became a force in the whole nation. Suppose I had had the cunning to help harness and guide this superhuman energy, what could I not have helped to turn it into? Not into a university, certainly, such as I dreamed, but perhaps into something greater. But no, I did not have ability of that sort, nor will to dream of it. And so I turned away, or, rather, I was turned toward other and different goals.

I left one curious and subtle complication spun in the subtle brain of that President Mitchell of whom I have spoken. Wilberforce, as I said, lacked funds. There was no visible source of Negro income large enough to support a college. The members of the church were fighting desperately for food and clothes. Their labor was being exploited to the last dime by every white American who had a chance or could steal it. President Mitchell found himself always in a financial hole and he eyed the coffers of the State of Ohio, as many before and since had done.

Miss Bierce carried on certain classes in teaching. She was a stern, accurate white daughter of the Western Reserve, severe and devoted to her work. When these normal classes threatened to cease because of lack of funds, the President suggested that he and Miss Bierce ask the State teaching authorities for a little help, since the State so needed teachers for its colored children. These students had a right to attend the white schools but they seldom did. The State helped. Opponents pointed out that the State had no right to support a colored State institution, but the President was ready. He and Arnett induced the Legislature to establish "a combined Normal and Industrial Department at Wilberforce University." The witchery in this wording lay in "Industrial" which lured the support of the followers of the rising Booker T. Washington; and also in that little word "at" which made this university a department not "of" Wilberforce, but "at" Wilberforce. This appropriation grew yearly until by 1900, two-thirds of the cost of Wilberforce was borne by the State. Finally, in 1942, the State set up its own college and Wilberforce again tried indifferently to stand alone.

Probably, looking back after the event, I have rationalized my life into a planned, coherent unity which was not as true to fact as it now seems; probably there were hesitancies, gropings, and half-essayed bypaths, now forgotten or unconsciously ignored. But my first quarter-century of life seems to me at this distance as singularly well-aimed at a certain goal, along a clearly planned path. I returned ready and eager to begin a life-work, leading to the emancipation of the American Negro. History and the other social sciences were to be my weapons, to be sharpened and applied by research and writing. Where and how, was the question in 1895. I became uneasy about my life program. I had published my first book, but I was doing nothing directly in the social sciences and saw no immediate prospect. Then the door of opportunity opened: just a crack, to be sure, but a distinct opening.

When a temporary appointment came from the University of Pennsylvania for one year as "assistant instructor" at $900, I accepted forthwith in the Fall of 1896; that year Abyssinia vanquished Italy; and England, suddenly seeing two black nations threatening her Cape-to-Cairo plans, threw her army back into the Sudan and recaptured Khartoum. The next

W. E. Burghardt Du Bois at 83.

The graduating class at Fisk
University in 1888; Du Bois,
seated at left, is 20 years old
in this photo.

Photo of Mrs. Du Bois (*nee*
Nina Gomer of Cedar Rapids,
Iowa) and the son, Burghardt.
This photo was carried by
Du Bois for several years. The
son, who died when in his third
year, is here 8 months old.
The photo was made in Xenia,
Ohio, locale of Wilberforce
University, where Du Bois was
then teaching.

Du Bois' daughter, Yolande, in 1928, at the time of her wedding to Countee Cullen.

The wedding of Yolande to Cullen in 1928 was held at the Salem Baptist Church in New York City, of which the groom's father was minister. Seated are, *left to right*: The Rev. Cullen, Mrs. Cullen, the Rev. George Frazier Miller, Mrs. Du Bois and Dr. Du Bois. Countee Cullen is directly behind the Rev. Miller. Directly behind Cullen is Arna Bontemps, the distinguished author and scholar, to the left of Bontemps is Langston Hughes; the tall man, *standing, second from right,* is Alphaeus Hunton.

Dr. Du Bois with the founders of the Niagara Movement in 1906; 2nd row, *second from right*, Dr. Du Bois; top row, *second from right*, Dr. Carter G. Woodson, author and historian.

Dr. Du Bois (*arrow*) leads an NAACP parade in 1919 protesting lynching and mob violence in the United States.

Dr. Du Bois at his desk at Atlanta University where he initiated and edited the famous Atlanta University Studies on Negro Americans.

Photo, taken in 1913, shows the New York State Emancipation Commission, appointed by the Governor to mark the 50th Anniversary of the Emancipation Proclamation. *Standing*: James D. Carr, Assistant Corporation Counsel, New York City; Robert N. Wood, Tammany leader; John R. Hillary, a chiropodist; *Sitting*: Rev. William A. Byrd, Presbyterian Minister; James H. Anderson, Editor, *Amsterdam News;* Dr. Du Bois; Rev. George H. Sims, Baptist Minister; J. B. Clayton, owner of an employment agency; Rev. J. Henry Taylor, A.M.E. Minister. The commission sponsored a performance of Du Bois' pageant, "Star of Ethiopia," seen by thousands in New York City.

Photo taken in Boston in 1907 in connection with the Third Annual Meeting of the Niagara Movement.

Members of the Third Pan-African Congress, meeting in Lisbon, Portugal, in May 1923. Dr. Du Bois in *center, front row.*

Board of Directors of the *Encyclopedia of the Negro*, at Howard University, Washington, D. C., May 16, 1936.

Left to right, front row, Miss Otelia Cromwell, Professor of English, Miner Teachers' College; Monroe N. Work, Director, Department of Records and Research, Tuskegee Institute; Charles H. Wesley, Professor of History, Howard University; Benjamin Brawley, Professor of English and History, Howard University; Dr. Du Bois; Eugene Kinckle Jones, Director, National Urban League; Alain Locke, Professor of Philosophy, Howard University; Waldo G. Leland, Director, American Council of Learned Societies.

Center: James Weldon Johnson, Professor of Creative Literature, Fisk University; Charles T. Loram, Sterling Professor of Education and Chairman, Department of Race Relations, Yale University.

Rear: Willis D. Weatherford, Head of Department of Religion and Humanities, Fisk University; Arthur A. Schomburg, Founder, Schomburg Collection, New York Public Library; Joel E. Spingarn, Professor of Comparative Literature, Columbia University, and President, NAACP; Clarence S. Marsh, Vice-President, American Council on Education; Anson Phelps Stokes, President, Phelps-Stokes Fund; William A. Aery, Dean of Instruction, Hampton Institute; James H. Dillard, former President, Jeanes Foundation and Slater Funds; Miss Florence Read, President of Spelman College; Mordecai W. Johnson, President of Howard University.

John Howard Lawson (*left*) joins Dr. Du Bois in greeting
Soviet author A. Fadeyev and composer Dmitri Shostakovich (1949).

Reception at Soviet Embassy, Washington, D. C. (1959). Mrs. Alice
Crawford, cousin of Dr. Du Bois, Mrs. Jocelyn Chisley, Shirley Graham
Du Bois, and the late Yolande Du Bois Williams, only daughter of Dr.
Du Bois. Dr. Du Bois received the Lenin Peace Prize at this reception.

With the great Paul Robeson.

With the late Vito Marcantonio, Congressman from New York.

Dr. Du Bois with the Very Reverend Hewlett
Johnson, Dean of Canterbury Cathedral,
November 1948.

Reunion of Harvard Class of 1890, taken in 1950
on the grounds of the University.

With John T. MacManus, Independent-Socialist candidate for Governor of New York in 1958.

Car caravan in campaign to defend Dr. Du Bois from prosecution for circulating Stockholm Peace Appeal.

With Gus Hall, General Secretary of the Communist
Party of the United States, on the occasion of Dr.
Du Bois joining the party.

At Idlewild Airport, New York, in 1961, awaiting plane to take
him to Ghana; with Dr. Du Bois is Herbert Aptheker.

With Zdenek Fierlinger, Chairman of the National Assembly of Czechoslovakia, in Prague, 1958.

At Charles University in Prague, receiving an honorary Doctorate of
Historical Sciences.

In China with Premier Chou En-lai *on the left*, Shirley Graham Du Bois *on the right*.

Dr. and Shirley Graham Du Bois celebrate New Year's Day 1959 in Peking.

President Ben Bella (*with book*) and other members of the Algerian delegation visit Dr. Du Bois in Ghana.

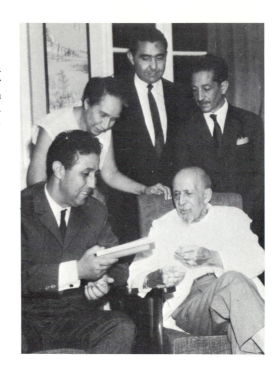

President Kwame Nkrumah of Ghana toasts Dr. Du Bois on his 95th birthday, in Accra.

Zorach's bust of Dr. Du Bois,
on exhibit at the Schomberg
Collection of the New York Public
Library.

Dr. Du Bois in his 70's.

year the free silver controversy of Bryan and McKinley flamed in America.

First, then, in 1896, I married—a slip of a girl, beautifully dark-eyed and thorough and good as her mother, a German housewife. Then I accepted a job to make a study of Negroes in Philadelphia for the University of Pennsylvania, one year at $900. How did I dare these two things? I do not know. Yet they spelled salvation. To remain at Wilberforce without doing my ideals meant spiritual death. Both my wife and I were homeless. I dared a home and a temporary job. But it was a different daring from the days of my first youth. I was ready to admit that the best of men might fail. I meant still to be captain of my soul, but I realized that even captains are not omnipotent in uncharted and angry seas.

CHAPTER XII

UNIVERSITY OF PENNSYLVANIA

In the Fall of 1896, I went to the University of Pennsylvania as "assistant instructor" in sociology. It all happened this way: Philadelphia, then and still one of the worst governed of America's badly governed cities, was having one of its periodic spasms of reform. A thorough study of causes was called for. Not but what the underlying cause was evident to most white Philadelphians: the corrupt, semi-criminal vote of the Negro Seventh Ward. Everyone agreed that here lay the cancer; but would it not be well to give scientific sanction to the known causes by an investigation, with imprimatur of the University? It certainly would, answered Samuel McCune Lindsay of the Department of Sociology. And he put his finger on me for the task.

If Lindsay had been a smaller man and had been induced to follow the usual American pattern of treating Negroes, he would have asked me to assist him as his clerk in this study. Probably I would have accepted having nothing better in sight for work in sociology. But Lindsay regarded me as a scholar in my own right and probably proposed to make me an instructor. Evidently the faculty demurred at having a colored instructor. But since I had a Harvard Ph.D., and had published a recognized work in history, the University could hardly offer me a fellowship. A compromise was hit on and I was nominated to the unusual status of "assistant" instructor. Even at that there must have been some opposition, for the invitation was not particularly cordial. I was offered a salary of $900 for a period limited to one year. I was given no real academic standing, no office at the University, no official recognition of any kind; my name was eventually omitted from the catalogue; I had no contact with students, and very little with members of the faculty, even in my own department.

I did not hesitate an instant but reported for duty with

a complete plan of work and outline of methods and aims and even proposed schedules to be filled out. My general plan was promptly accepted and I started to work, consulting Lindsay regularly but never meeting the faculty. With my bride of three months, I settled in one room in the city over a cafeteria run by a College Settlement, in the worst part of the Seventh Ward. We lived there a year, in the midst of an atmosphere of dirt, drunkenness, poverty, and crime. Murder sat on our doorsteps, police were our government, and philanthropy dropped in with periodic advice.

The world seized and whirled me. I hardly knew what was important, what negligible; somehow I remember life, curiously enough, chiefly as a succession of homes: the settlement at Philadelphia at Seventh and Lombard in the slums where kids played intriguing games like "cops and lady bums"; and where in the night when pistols popped, you didn't get up lest you find you couldn't.

I wrote of my first Christmas in Philadelphia:

"We haven't been married long enough to escape the condescending smiles of our neighbors, and yet we feel quite like old married folks. This is our first Christmas and wife thinks we owe to the public to tell just how merry it has been. It began some days ago when wife asked me cautiously how much we could afford to spend for Christmas. I sat down and figured carefully: for there was the sewing machine to pay for out of this month's salary, and doctor's bill, and one other debt—an old family friend. I finally evolved a surplus of $10.56, and told wife that we could spend five dollars apiece for the holidays. She was perfectly happy, and after some hours of calculating sallied forth to Wanamaker's.

"The next week was filled with shopping and bookkeeping; one would have thought we were spending hundreds of dollars. Wife consulted me religiously on many points; however, both of us maintained a jolly silence. Tuesday we both went down South Street to the Second Street market, and bought two wreaths, a cross, and a 15-cent Christmas tree. Wife was somewhat alarmed at first at the prospect of a Christmas tree in our snug little room, but when it was safely ensconced in a corner on the machine, with tinsel, fruit, and cotton snow, she was quite delighted.

"Christmas Eve found our little gift-packages mailed, the tree glowing and both our empty stockings hung beside it. I had secreted a dainty silk umbrella under the lounge, and I knew that other corners of the room held secrets, the question being how to get them into the stockings.

"About eight in the evening we sallied out into the crisp air and hurried down to the Mission, where the folks had a tree for the little ones. How much happiness can be packed within four walls! The children were boisterous, rude, and noisy, but so brimming over with pleasure that it did one good to see them. Once at home again and with a last look at our own little tree, we were soon snug in bed, and the thought of the hidden umbrella alone kept me awake. I had almost despaired of getting it into the stocking, when the regular breathing of my wife told me that she had fallen asleep in spite of herself. I carefully slipped from bed, listened, crawled across the floor, listened again, and at last slipped the umbrella into wife's stocking; in a minute more I had chuckled myself to sleep. I was dreaming that I held a professorship that paid $1,500 a year, when suddenly I awoke with a start. Wife hasn't forgiven me yet for awaking so inopportunely, and if I had known the situation before I awoke, I would have stayed asleep. As it was, I awoke and caught wife in her little white gown secreting bundles in and about my sock. I laughed, then kept as quiet as I could, and wife didn't say a word.

"Christmas day came with laughing over the night's adventure, the revealing of hiding places and enjoyment of the umbrella, suspenders, and neckties. At three came a cozy dinner with a little brown chicken and bills-of-fare written on old visiting cards. Finally the whole day melted away in misty happiness and to round it out, I wrote this."

The Provost of the University furnished the following credentials:

In connection with the College Settlement, the Trustees of the University of Pennsylvania have undertaken the study of the social condition of the Colored People of the Seventh Ward of Philadelphia.

The University has entered upon this work as a part of its duty and wishes to make the investigation as thorough and exact as possible. We want to know precisely how this class of people live; what occupations they follow; from what occupations they are excluded; how many of their children go to school; and to ascertain every fact which will throw light upon this social problem; and then having this information and these accurate statistics before us, to see to what extent and in what way, proper remedies may be applied. Dr. W. E. B. Du Bois is the investigator on behalf of the University, and I write to bespeak for him your cordial reception and earnest co-operation.

The two years at Wilberforce had been my uneasy apprenticeship, and with my advent into the University of Pennsylvania, I began a more clearly planned career which had an unusual measure of success, but was in the end pushed aside by forces which, if not entirely beyond my control, were yet of great weight.

The opportunity opened at the University of Pennsylvania seemed just what I wanted. I had offered to teach social science at Wilberforce outside of my overloaded program, but I was not allowed. My vision was becoming clearer. The Negro problem was in my mind a matter of systematic investigation and intelligent understanding. The world was thinking wrong about race, because it did not know. The ultimate evil was stupidity. The cure for it was knowledge based on scientific investigation. At the University of Pennsylvania I ignored the pitiful stipend. It made no difference to me that I was put down as an "assistant instructor" and even at that, that my name never actually got into the catalogue; it goes without saying that I did no instructing save once to pilot a pack of idiots through the Negro slums.

Of the theory back of the plan of this study of Negroes I neither knew nor cared. I saw only here a chance to study an historical group of black folk and to show exactly what their place was in the community. I did it despite extraordinary difficulties both within and without the group. Whites said: Why study the obvious? Blacks said: Are we animals to be dissected and by an unknown Negro at that? Yet, I made a study of the Philadelphia Negro so thorough that it has withstood the criticism of 60 years.

I counted my task here as simple and clear-cut; I proposed

to find out what was the matter with this area and why. I started with no "research methods" and I asked little advice as to procedure. The problem lay before me. Study it. I studied it personally and not by proxy. I sent out no canvassers. I went myself. Personally I visited and talked with 5,000 persons. What I could, I set down in orderly sequence on schedules which I made out and submitted to the University for criticism. Other information I stored in my memory or wrote out as memoranda. I went through the Philadelphia libraries for data, gained access in many instances to private libraries of colored folk and got individual information. I mapped the district, classifying it by conditions; I compiled two centuries of the history of the Negro in Philadelphia and in the Seventh Ward.

I essayed a thorough piece of work in Philadelphia. I labored morning, noon, and night. Few persons ever read that fat volume on *The Philadelphia Negro,* but they treat it with respect, and that consoles me. The colored people of Philadelphia received me with no open arms. They had a natural dislike to being studied like a strange species. I met again and in different guise those curious cross-currents and inner social whirlings. They set me to groping. I concluded that I did not know so much as I might about my own people.

It was a hard job, but I completed it by the Spring of 1898 and published it a year later, under the auspices of the University, as *The Philadelphia Negro;* a formidable tome of nearly a thousand pages. But the greatest import to me was the fact, that after years, I had at last learned just what I wanted to do, in this life program of mine, and how to do it. First of all I became painfully aware that merely being born in a group, does not necessarily make one possessed of complete knowledge concerning it. I had learned far more from Philadelphia Negroes than I had taught them concerning the Negro Problem.

It was as complete a scientific study and answer as could have then been given, with defective facts and statistics, one lone worker and little money. It revealed the Negro group as a symptom, not a cause; as a striving, palpitating group, and not an inert, sick body of crime; as a long historic development and not a transient occurrence.

In this appointment there was one fly which I have never mentioned; it would have been a fine thing if after this difficult, successful piece of work, the University of Pennsylvania had at least offered me a temporary instructorship in the college or in the Wharton School. Harvard had never dreamed of such a thing; a half century later one of Harvard's professors said of a gifted Negro student: "We'd give him a position if he were not a Negro!" White classmates of lower academic rank than I, became full professors at Pennsylvania and Chicago. Here in my case an academic accolade from a great American university would have given impetus to my life work which I was already determined to make in a Negro institution in the South. The thing that galled was that such an idea never even occurred to this institution whose head was a high official of the Sugar Trust. But I did not mention this rebuff. I did not let myself think of it. But then, as now, I know an insult when I see it.

Before the American Academy, affiliated with the University, I laid down in public session in 1899, a broad program of scientific attack on this problem, by systematic and continuous study; and I appealed to Harvard, Columbia and Pennsylvania, to take up the task. Needless to say, they paid not the slightest attention to this challenge and for 25 years thereafter not a single first-grade college in America undertook to give any considerable scientific attention to the American Negro. Of the methods of my research, I wrote:

The best available methods of sociological research are at present so liable to inaccuracies that the careful student discloses the results of individual research with diffidence; he knows that they are liable to error from the seemingly ineradicable faults of the statistical method; to even greater error from the methods of general observation; and, above all, he must ever tremble lest some personal bias, some moral conviction or some unconscious trend of thought due to previous training, has to a degree distorted the picture in his view. Convictions on all great matters of human interest one must have to a greater or less degree, and they will enter to some extent into the most cold-blooded scientific research as a disturbing factor.

Nevertheless, here are some social problems before us demanding careful study, questions awaiting satisfactory answers. We must study, we must investigate, we must attempt to solve; and the utmost that the world can demand is, not lack of human interest and moral conviction, but rather the heart-quality of fairness and an earnest desire for the truth despite its possible unpleasantness.

At the end of that study, I announced with a certain pride my plan of studying the complete Negro problem in the United States. I spoke at the 42nd meeting of the American Academy of Political and Social Sciences in Philadelphia, November 19, 1897, and my subject was "The Study of the Negro Problem." I began by asserting that in the development of sociological study there was at least one positive answer which years of research and speculation had been able to return, and that was: "The phenomena of society are worth the most careful and systematic study, and whether or not this study may eventually lead to a systematic body of knowledge deserving the name of science, it cannot in any case fail to give the world a mass of truth worth the knowing." I then defined and tried to follow the development of the Negro problem not as one problem, but "rather a plexus of social problems, some new, some old, some simple, some complex; and these problems have their one bond of unity in the fact that they group themselves about those Africans whom two centuries of slave-trading brought into the land."

I insisted on the necessity of carefully studying these problems and said: "The American Negro deserves study for the great end of advancing the cause of science in general. No such opportunity to watch and measure the history and development of a great race of men ever presented itself to the scholars of a modern nation. If they miss this opportunity— if they do the work in a slipshod, unsystematic manner—if they dally with the truth to humor the whims of the day, they do far more than hurt the good name of the American people; they hurt the cause of scientific truth the world over, they voluntarily decrease human knowledge of a universe of which we are ignorant enough, and they degrade the high end of truth-seeking in a day when they need more and more to dwell upon its sanctity."

Finally I tried to lay down a plan for the study, postulating only that the Negro "is a member of the human race, and as one who, in the light of history and experience is capable to a degree of improvement and culture, is entitled to have his interests considered according to his numbers in all conclusions as to the common weal."

Dividing the prospective scientific study of the Negro into two parts: the social group and his peculiar social environment, I proposed to study the social group by historical investigation, statistical measurement and sociological interpretation. Particularly with regard to anthropology, I said:

"That there are differences between the white and black races is certain, but just what those differences are is known to none with an approach to accuracy. Yet here in America is the most remarkable opportunity ever offered of studying these differences, of noting influences of climate and physical environment, and particularly of studying the effect of amalgamating two of the most diverse races in the world— another subject which rests under a cloud of ignorance."

In concluding, I said:

It is to the credit of the University of Pennsylvania that she has been the first to recognize her duty in this respect and in so far as restricted means and opportunity allowed, has attempted to study the Negro problems in a single definite locality. This work needs to be extended to other groups, and carried out with larger system; and here it would seem is the opportunity of the Southern college. We hear much of higher Negro education, and yet all candid people know there does not exist today in the center of Negro population a single first-class fully equipped institution, devoted to the higher education of Negroes; not more than three Negro institutions in the South deserve the name of "college" at all; and yet what is a Negro college but a vast college settlement for the study of a particular set of peculiarly baffling problems?

What more effective or suitable agency could be found in which to focus the scientific efforts of the great universities of North and East, than an institution situated in the very heart of these social problems, and made the center of careful historical and statistical research? Without doubt the first effective step toward the solving of the Negro question will be the endowment of a Negro college which is not merely a teaching body, but a center of sociological research, in close connection and co-operation with Harvard, Columbia, Johns Hopkins, and University of Pennsylvania.

Finally the necessity must again be emphasized of keeping clearly before students the object of all science, amid the turmoil and intense feeling that clouds the discussion of a burning social question. We live in a day when in spite of the brilliant accomplishments of a remarkable century, there is current much flippant criticism of scientific work; when the truth-seeker is too often pictured as devoid of human sympathy, and careless of human ideals. We are still prone in spite of all our culture to sneer at the heroism of the laboratory while we cheer the swagger of the street broil. At such times true lovers of humanity can only hold higher the pure ideals of science, and continue to insist that if we would solve a problem we must study it, and there is but one coward on earth and that is the coward that dare not know.

While I was making this study, I tried to interest the Federal government in making some such studies in other areas. In 1897, I wrote Carroll D. Wright, head of the Federal Bureau of Labor Statistics, and received an encouraging reply. I then wrote more in detail.

In accordance with your suggestion I have been for the last month giving considerable thought as to method of studying certain aspects of the industrial development of the Negro. It seems to me that the difficulties of studying so vast and varied a subject are so large that the first work to be done should be rather of an experimental or preliminary nature calculated to locate and define the difficulties and to indicate lines upon which a larger investigation could be carried to success. At the same time the results of a series of preliminary studies could be published and would by allaying false notions and prejudices prepare the public mind for the larger work.

Both the preliminary and the main work must of course be strictly limited in scope; great care must be taken to avoid giving offense to white or black, to raise no suspicions and at the same time to get definite accurate information. For the preliminary work I propose two plans—the first to my mind preferable, the second feasible:

PLAN A

The Industrial Development of the Negro

Preliminary Study: The economic situation of a typical town containing from 1,000–5,000 Negro inhabitants situated in Va., or the Carolinas, or Ga.

Study:	Occupations	Economic History
	Wages	Cost of Living
	Ownership of Homes	Organizations
	Hours of Labor	Crops

Study to be conducted, visits, schedules, county records, etc. To be carried out in the months of July and August 1897.

Plan B

The Industrial Development of the Negro

Preliminary Study: Condition of Negroes in the
(Barber)
(Public waiter)
(Caterer)
(Building)
(Mining)
(etc.)

In the city of Richmond or Raleigh or Charleston or Atlanta, etc.

Study:
Number	Economic History
Wages	Organization
Hours of Labor	General Condition
Cost of Living	

Other Plans

A study of domestic service in a certain city

A study of the Negro in the professions in several cities

A study of the Negro farm laborer in a typical agricultural region

A study of the Negro church as a social institution in certain cities

An "Enquote" of the graduates of Southern schools into their own economic life and the general industrial situation

A study of the attitude of organized labor toward Negroes

A study of Negro stevedores

A bibliography of the economic condition of the Negro since emancipation

Plan A could be begun immediately. I could spend the summer in some typical village of the South and have the results ready to print in the fall. This plan could be repeated from time to time until these preliminary studies conducted in various districts in various times of year and under various circumstances would give a basis of fact and experience upon which a larger survey could be planned with a great saving of time and expense. Or, after one or two experiments the whole enterprise might take the form of a series of simultaneous investigations of this sort in selected typical districts of town and country upon lines indicated by the actual experience of the preliminary studies.

Plan B could also be carried out this summer within certain limitations. The other plans are suggested and if they strike you as preferable to the first two I could work them out more carefully.

Will you kindly look over these plans and let me know which, if any, meet your ideas. We can then discuss details further.

Eventually this resulted in a series of studies for the Labor Bureau and one major effort which I shall tell of in a later chapter. The successors of Carroll Wright deliberately destroyed this piece of my best sociological work.

CHAPTER XIII

ATLANTA UNIVERSITY

From the Fall of 1894 to the Spring of 1910, for 16 years, I was a teacher and a student of social science. For two years I remained at Wilberforce; for a year and a half at the University of Pennsylvania; and for 13 years at Atlanta University in Georgia. I sought in these years to know my world and to teach youth the meaning and way of the world.

The main result of my schooling had been to emphasize science and the scientific attitude. I got some insight into the laws of the physical world at Fisk and in the chemical laboratory and class in geology at Harvard. I was interested in evolution, geology and the new psychology. I began to conceive of the world as a continuing growth rather than a finished product. In Germany I turned still further from religious dogma and began to grasp the idea of a world of human beings whose actions, like those of the physical world, were subject to law. The triumphs of the scientific world thrilled me: the X-ray and radium came during my teaching term, the airplane and the wireless. The machine increased in technical efficiency and the North and South Poles were invaded.

On the other hand the difficulties of applying scientific law and discovering cause and effect in a world of living persons was still great. Social thinkers were engaged in vague statements and were seeking to lay down the methods by which, in some not too distant future, social law analogous to physical law would be discovered. Herbert Spencer finished his ten volumes of *Synthetic Philosophy* in 1896. The biological analogy, the vast generalizations, were striking, but actual scientific accomplishment lagged. For me an opportunity seemed to present itself. I could not lull my mind to hypnosis by regarding a phrase like "consciousness of kind" as a scientific law. But turning my gaze from fruitless word-twisting and facing the facts of my own social situation and racial world, I determined to put science into sociology through a study of the conditions and problems of my own group.

I was going to study the facts, any and all facts, concerning the American Negro and his plight, and by measurement and comparison and research, work up to any valid generalizations which I could. I entered this primarily with the utilitarian object of reform and uplift; but nevertheless, I wanted to do the work with scientific accuracy. Thus, in my own sociology, because of firm belief in a changing racial group, I easily grasped the idea of a changing developing society rather than a fixed social structure.

The decade and a half in which I taught, was riotous with happenings in the world of social development; with economic expansion, with political control, with racial difficulties. Above all, it was the era of empire and while I had some equipment to deal with a scientific approach to social studies, I did not have any clear conception or grasp of the meaning of that colonial imperialism which was beginning to grip the world. My only approach to meanings and helpful study there again was through my interest in race contact.

That interest began to clear my vision and interpret the whirl of events which swept the world. Japan was rising to national status and through the Chinese War and the Russian War, despite rivalry with Germany, Russia, and Great Britain, she achieved a new status in the world, which only the United States refused to recognize.

All this, I began to realize, was but a result of the expansion of Europe into Africa where a fierce fight was precipitated for the labor, gold, and diamonds of South Africa; for domination of the Nile Valley; for the gold, cocoa, raw materials, and labor of West Africa; and for the exploitation of the Belgian Congo. Europe was determined to dominate China and all but succeeded in dividing it between the chief white nations, when Japan stopped the process. After 16 years, stirred by the triumph of the Abyssinians at Adowa, and the pushing forward of the French in North Africa, England returned to the Egyptian Sudan.

The Queen's Jubilee, I knew, was not merely a sentimental

outburst; it was a triumph of English economic aggression around the world and it aroused the cupidity and fear of Germany who proceeded to double her navy, expand into Asia, and consolidate her European position. Germany challenged France and England at Algeciras, prelude to the World War. Imperialism, despite Cleveland's opposition, spread to America, and the Hawaiian sugar fields were annexed. The Spanish war brought Cuban sugar under control and annexed Puerto Rico and the Philippines. The Panama Canal brought the Pacific nearer the Atlantic and protected capital investment in Santo Domingo and South America.

All this might have been interpreted as history and politics. Mainly I did so interpret it, but continually I was forced to consider the economic aspects of world movements as they were developing at the time. Chiefly this was because the group in which I was interested were workers, earners of wages, owners of small bits of land, servants. The labor strikes interested and puzzled me. They were for the most part strikes of workers led by organizations to which Negroes were not admitted. There was the great steel strike; the railway strikes, actual and threatened; the teamsters' strike in Chicago; the long strike in Leadville, Colorado. Only in the coal strike were Negroes involved. But there was a difference. During my school days, strikes were regarded as futile and ill-advised struggles against economic laws; and when the government intervened, it was to cow the strikers as lawbreakers. But during my teaching period, the plight of the worker began to sift through into the consciousness of the average citizen. Public opinion not only allowed but forced Theodore Roosevelt to intervene in the coal strike, and the steel strikers had widespread sympathy.

Then there were the tariff agitations, the continual raising and shifting and manipulation of tariff rates, always in the end for the purpose of subsidizing the manufacturer and making the consumer pay. The political power of the great organizations of capital in coal, oil and sugar, the extraordinary immunities of the corporations, made the President openly attack the trusts as a kind of super-government and we began to see more and more clearly the outlines of economic battle. The Supreme Court stood staunchly behind capital. It outlawed the labor boycott, it denied the right of the States to make railway rates. It declared the income tax unconstitutional.

With all that, and the memory of the Panic of 1873 not forgotten, came the Panic of 1893 and the financial upheaval of 1907. Into this economic turmoil, politics had to intrude. The older role of free, individual enterprise, with little or no government interference, had to be surrendered and the whole political agitation during these days took on a distinct economic tinge and object. The impassioned plea of Bryan in 1896 that labor be not "crucified upon a cross of gold" could not be wholly ridiculed to silence. The Populist movement which swept over the West and South, I began now to believe, was a third party movement of deep significance and it was kept from political power on the one hand by the established election frauds of the South, of which I knew, and by the fabulous election fund which made McKinley President of the United States. With this went the diversion of the Spanish war with its sordid scandals of rotten beef, cheating and stealing, fever and death from neglect. Politics and economics thus in those days of my teaching became but two aspects of a united body of action and effort.

I tried to isolate myself in the ivory tower of race. I wanted to explain the difficulties of race and the ways in which these difficulties caused political and economic troubles. It was this concentration of thought and action and effort that really, in the end, saved my scientific accuracy and search for truth. But first came a period of three years when I was casting about to find a way of applying science to the race problem. In these years I was torn with excitement of quick-moving events. Lynching, for instance, was still a continuing horror in the United States at the time of my entrance upon a teaching career. It reached a climax in 1892, when 235 persons were publicly murdered, and in the 16 years of my teaching nearly 2,000 persons were publicly killed by mobs, and not a single one of the murderers punished. The partition, domination, and exploitation of Africa gradually entered my thought as part of my problem of race. I saw in Asia and the West Indies the results of race discrimination while right here in America came the wild foray of the exasperated Negro soldiers at Brownsville and the political-economic riot at Atlanta.

One happening in America linked in my mind the race problem with the general economic development, and that was the speech of Booker T. Washington in Atlanta in 1895.[9] When many colored papers condemned the proposition of compromise with the white South, which Washington proposed, I wrote to the *New York Age* suggesting that here might be the basis of a real settlement between whites and blacks in the South, if the South opened to the Negroes the doors of economic opportunity and the Negroes cooperated with the white South in political sympathy. But this offer was frustrated by the fact that between 1895 and 1909 the whole South disfranchised its Negro voters by unfair and illegal restrictions and passed a series of "jim-crow" laws which made the Negro citizen a subordinate caste.

As a possible offset to this came the endowment of the General Education Board and the Sage Foundation; but they did not to my mind plan clearly to attack the Negro problem: the Sage Foundation ignored us, and the General Education Board in its first years gave its main attention to the education of whites and to black industrial schools.

I was approached by President Horace Bumstead of Atlanta University in 1896 and asked to come to Atlanta University and take charge of the work in sociology, and of the new conferences which they were inaugurating on the Negro problem. With this program in mind, I eagerly accepted the invitation. Dr. Bumstead later wrote:

Let me express the keen satisfaction I take in having been the one chiefly responsible, perhaps, for bringing Doctor Du Bois to Atlanta University. He has recently called his thirteen years of service there his "real life work"; and I am proud to have helped open the way for him to begin it, and to have been closely associated with his labors for more than a decade, till I ceased to be president. I cannot but smile when I think of the objections and misgivings of some of our trustees and other friends when he came. We wanted a professor of sociology with special reference to investigating conditions concerning the Negro; and I said that Dr. Du Bois was the one man, white or black, far and away best fitted for the position. I knew of his long preparation at Fisk, Harvard, and in Germany, and I had read the unstinted praise which the New York *Nation* had given to his first publication, *The Suppression of the Slave Trade,* and I knew of the confidence which Provost Harrison of the University of Pennsylvania had in him when he engaged him to spend a year or more in making a scientific study of the Philadelphia Negro.

But, said some, if you are going to give the position to a Negro, why not to a graduate of Atlanta rather than of Fisk? Because, said I, we want the *best* man, regardless of where he was graduated. But how about his religion—he's studied in Germany—perhaps if you scratch him, you'll find an agnostic. Now it is true that Atlanta University has always had a pronounced religious, though undenominational, life —a life inherited from the New England people represented by its founders; and it has always looked to its teachers, so far as possible, to help to maintain it—so I must need have some assurances on this point. But, as Doctor Du Bois will remember, they were not very easy to get. He seemed to be one of those persons who, when asked about their religion, reply that they "have none to speak of." But though reluctant to speak of his religion or to say what he would do at Atlanta, I observed that at the time of my interview with him he was living with his newly wedded bride in the center of the Negro slums of Philadelphia, doing the beneficent work to which Provost Harrison had called him, and I thought there were some indications of genuine religion in that fact. Nor was I disappointed, later, when some of the deepest and most vital expressions of the religious life came from his lips as he conducted evening devotions at the University.

So, in spite of objections and misgivings, Doctor Du Bois came to Atlanta University, and we held him there for thirteen years notwithstanding several offers to go elsewhere and get double the salary that we could afford to pay him. His work became a memorable part of the history of the Institution. Let me specify two of its most prominent and valuable features.

One was the inauguration, for the first time in any American college, of a thoroughly scientific study of the conditions of Negro life, covering all of its most important phases, and resulting in a score of annual *Atlanta University Publications,* conceded to be of the highest authority, both in this country and in Europe.

Even more important than this, was the stimulating personal influence of Doctor Du Bois upon our students. He had acquired his own education where the highest standards prevailed, and he would tolerate no lower ones in his own classrooms. Not only in study but also in conduct, he demanded of his pupils the best that was in them. He taught them the nobility and sacredness of their manhood—endowed, as they were, with all the inherent rights and possibilities of development enjoyed by humanity anywhere. To his fellow teachers, too, he brought joy, for though often looked upon in the outside world as a pessimist, he was about the jolliest member of our Faculty. The inspiration of his stimulating personality has gone out through all the South and will be felt for generations to come.

The hundred hills of Atlanta are not all crowned with factories. On one, toward the west, the setting sun throws three buildings in bold relief against the sky. The beauty of the group lies in its simple unity: a broad lawn of green rising from the red street with mingled roses and peaches; north and south, two plain and stately halls; and in the midst, half hidden in ivy, a larger building, boldly graceful, sparingly decorated, and with one low spire. It is a restful group—one never looks for more; it is all here, all intelligible. There I live, and there I hear from day to day the low hum of restful life.

In winter's twilight, when the red sun glows, I can see the dark figures pass between the halls to the music of the night-bell. In the morning, when the sun is golden, the clang of the daybell brings the hurry and laughter of 300 young hearts from hall and street, and from the busy city below—children all dark and heavy-haired—to join their clear young voices in the music of the morning sacrifice. In a half dozen classrooms they gather then, here to follow the love song of Dido, here to listen to the tale of Troy divine; there to wander among the stars, there to wander among men and nations—and elsewhere other well worn ways of knowing this queer world. Nothing new, no time-saving devices, simply old time-glorified methods of delving for Truth, and searching out the hidden beauties of life, and learning the good of living.

The riddle of existence is the college curriculum that was

laid before the Pharaohs, that was taught in the groves by Plato, that formed the *trivium* and *quadrivium** and is to-day laid before the freedmen's sons by Atlanta University. And this course of study will not change; its methods will grow more deft and effectual, its content richer by toil of scholar and sight of seer; but the true college will ever have one goal—not to earn meat, but to know the end and aim of that life which meat nourishes.

The vision of life that rises before these dark eyes has in it nothing mean or selfish. Not at Berlin nor at Leipzig, not at Harvard nor Yale is there an air of higher resolve or more unfettered striving; the determination to realize for men, both black and white, the broadest possibilities of life, to seek the better and the best, to spread with their own hands the Gospel of Sacrifice—all this is the burden of their talk and dream. Here, amid a wide desert of caste and proscription, amid the heart-hurting slights and jars and vagaries of a deep race-dislike, lies this green oasis, where hot anger cools, and the bitterness of disappointment is sweetened by the springs and breezes of Parnassus; and here men may lie and listen and learn of a future fuller than the past, and hear the voice of Time:

> *Entbehren sollst du, sollst entbehren.*
>
> *Thou shalt forego, shalt do without*

They made their mistakes, those who planted Fisk and Howard and Atlanta before the smoke of battle had lifted; they made their mistakes, but those mistakes were not the things at which we lately laughed somewhat uproariously. They were right when they sought to found a new educational system upon the university: where, forsooth, shall we ground knowledge save on the broadest and deepest knowl-

---

* *Trivium* and *quadrivium,* literally, a crossroads with three and another with four intersections; here, having reference to the elementary content in medieval education consisting of grammar, rhetoric, and dialectic and the more advanced content in that education consisting of arithmetic, geometry, astronomy and music.—*Ed.*

edge? The roots of the tree, rather than the leaves, are the sources of its life; and from the dawn of history, from Academus to Cambridge, the culture of the university has been the broad foundation-stone on which is built the kindergarten's A B C.

But these builders did make a mistake in minimizing the gravity of the problem before them; in thinking it a matter of years and decades; in therefore building quickly and laying their foundation carelessly, and lowering the standard of knowing, until they had scattered haphazard through the South some dozen poorly equipped high schools and miscalled them universities. They forgot, too, just as their successors are forgetting, the rule of inequality—that of the million black youth, some were fitted to know and some to dig; that some had the talent and capacity of university men, and some had the talent and capacity of blacksmiths; and that true training meant neither that all should be college men nor all artisans, but that the one should be made a missionary of culture to an untaught people, and the other a free workman among serfs.

My real life work was begun at Atlanta for 13 years, from my 29th to my 42nd birthday. They were years of great spiritual upturning, of the making and unmaking of ideals, of hard work and hard play. Here I found myself. I lost most of my mannerisms. I grew more broadly human, made my closest and most holy friendships, and studied human beings. I became widely acquainted with the real condition of my people. I realized the terrific odds which faced them. I saw the Atlanta riot.[10]

The main significance of my work at Atlanta University, during the years 1897 to 1910, was the development at an American institution of learning, of a program of study on the problems affecting the American Negroes, covering a progressively widening and deepening effort designed to stretch over the span of a century. This program was grafted on an attempt by George Bradford of Boston, one of the trustees, to open for Atlanta University a field of usefulness for city Negroes comparable to what Hampton and Tuskegee were doing for rural districts in agriculture and industry. At the Hampton and Tuskegee Conferences, there came together annually and in increasing numbers, workers, experts and observers to encourage by speeches and interchange of experience the Negro farmers and laborers of adjoining areas. Visitors, white and colored, from North and South, joined to advise and learn. Mr. Bradford's idea was to establish at Atlanta a similar conference, devoted especially to problems of city Negroes. The first conference, emphasizing particularly Negro health problems, was held in 1896. Immediately the University looked about for a man to teach history and political science, and take charge of future conferences. I was chosen.

When I took charge of the Atlanta Conference, I did not pause to consider how far my developed plans agreed or disagreed with the ideas of the already launched project. It made little essential difference, since only one conference had been held and a second planned. These followed the Hampton and Tuskegee model of being primarily meetings of inspiration, directed toward specific efforts at social reform and aimed at propaganda for social uplift in certain preconceived lines. This program at Atlanta, I sought to swing as on a pivot to one of scientific investigation into social conditions, primarily for scientific ends. I put no special emphasis on special reform effort, but increasing and widening emphasis on the collection of a basic body of fact concerning the social condition of American Negroes, endeavoring to reduce that condition to exact measurement whenever or wherever occasion permitted. As time passed, it happened that many uplift efforts were in fact based on our studies: the kindergarten system of the city of Atlanta, white as well as black; the Negro Business League, and various projects to better health and combat crime. We came to be, however, as I had intended, increasingly, a source of general information and a basis for further study, rather than an organ of social reform.

The proverbial visitor from Mars would have assumed as elemental a study in America of American Negroes—as physical specimens; as biological growths; as a field of investigation in economic development from slave to free labor; as a psychological laboratory in human reaction toward caste and discrimination; as a unique case of physical and cultural intermingling. These and a dozen other subjects of scientific interest, would have struck the man from Mars as eager lines of investigation for American social scientists. He would have been astounded to learn that the only institution in America in 1900 with any such program of study was Atlanta University, where on a budget of $5,000 a year, including salaries, cost of publication, investigation and annual meetings, we were essaying this pioneer work.

My program for the succession of conference studies was modified by many considerations: cost, availability of suitable data, tested methods of investigation; moreover I could not plunge too soon into such controversial subjects as politics or miscegenation. Within these limitations, I finished a ten-year cycle study as follows:

1896, *Mortality among Negroes in Cities*
1897, *Social and Physical Condition of Negroes in Cities*
1898, *Some Efforts of Negroes for Social Betterment*
1899, *The Negro in Business*
1900, *The College-Bred Negro*
1901, *The Negro Common School*
1902, *The Negro Artisan*
1903, *The Negro Church*
1904, *Notes on Negro Crime*
1905, *A Select Bibliography of the American Negro*

I then essayed for the second decade a broader program, more logical, more inclusive, and designed to bring the whole subject matter into a better integrated whole. But continued lack of funds and outside diversions (like the request of the Carnegie Institution of 1907 for a study of co-operation) kept even the second decade from the complete logic of arrangement which I desired; finally, my leaving Atlanta in 1910 and at last the severing of my connection with the conference in 1914, left the full form of my program still unfinished. I did, however, publish the following eight studies:

1906, *Health and Physique of the Negro American*
1907, *Economic Co-operation among Negro Americans*

1908, *The Negro American Family*
1909, *Efforts for Social Betterment among Negro Americans*
1910, *The College-Bred Negro American*
1911, *The Common School and the Negro American*
1912, *The Negro American Artisan*
1914, *Morals and Manners among Negro Americans*

With the publication of 1914, my connection with Atlanta ceased for 20 years. Although studies and publications were prepared by others at the university in 1915 and 1918, the war finally stopped the enterprise.

What I was laboriously but steadily approaching in this effort was a recurring cycle of ten studies in succeeding decades; with repetition of each subject or some modification of it in each decade, upon a progressively broader and more exact basis and with better method; until gradually a foundation of carefully ascertained fact would build a basis of knowledge, broad and sound enough to be called scientific in the best sense of that term.

Just what form this dream would eventually have taken, I do not know. So far as actually forecast, it had assumed in 1914, some such form as this:

1. Population: Distribution and Growth
2. Biology: Health and Physique
3. Socialization: Family, Group and Class
4. Cultural Patterns: Morals and Manners
5. Education
6. Religion and the Church
7. Crime
8. Law and Government
9. Literature and Art
10. Summary and Bibliography

I proposed as I have said, to repeat each of these every ten years, basing the studies on ever broader and more carefully gathered data. Eventually I hoped to keep all the inquiries going simultaneously, only emphasizing and reporting on one particular subject each year. This would have allowed some necessary shifting or combination of subjects as time and developments might suggest; and adjustments to new scientific advance in fields like anthropology and psychology.

The plan would have called in time for a large and well-paid staff of experts and a study of method and testing of results such as no group of Americans were engaged in at the time; beginning with a definite, circumscribed group, but ending with the human race.

The program, however, was weak on its economic side. It did not stress enough the philosophy of Marx and Engels and was of course far too soon for Lenin. The program ought to have been—and as I think would have been if I had kept on this work—the Economic Development of the American Negro Slave; on this central thread all the other subjects would have been strung. But this I had no chance to essay.

Social scientists at the time were thinking in terms of theory and vast and eternal laws, but I had a concrete group of living beings artificially set off by themselves and capable of almost laboratory experiment. I laid down an ambitious program for a hundred years of study. I proposed to take up annually in each decade the main aspects of the group life of Negroes with as thorough study and measurement as possible, and repeat the same program in the succeeding decade with additions, changes and better methods. In this way, I proposed gradually to broaden and intensify the study, sharpen the tools of investigation and perfect our methods of work, so that we would have an increasing body of scientifically ascertained fact, instead of the vague mass of the so-called Negro problems. And through this laboratory experiment I hoped to make the laws of social living clearer, surer, and more definite.

Some of this was accomplished, but of course only an approximation of the idea. For 13 years we poured forth a series of studies; limited, incomplete, only partially conclusive, and yet so much better done than any other attempt of the sort in the nation that they gained attention throughout the world. In all we published a total of 2,172 pages which formed a current encyclopedia on American Negro problems.

These studies with all their imperfections were widely distributed in the libraries of the world and used by scholars. It may be said without undue boasting that between 1896 and 1920 there was no study made of the race problem in America which did not depend in some degree upon the investigations made at Atlanta University; often they were widely quoted and commended.

I had heartening letters from persons of eminence and character. William James wrote in 1907: "I have just looked through the last installment of your studies on the American Negro. I wish the portraits might have been better printed. But it is splendid scientific work." Frank Taussig of Harvard wrote the same year: "In my judgment no better work is being done in the country, and no better opportunity is afforded for financial support on the part of those who wish to further the understanding of the Negro problem." Booker Washington, who spoke at our conference on the Negro artisan in 1911, said: "The whole country should be grateful to this institution for the painstaking and systematic manner in which it has developed from year to year a series of facts which are proving most vital and helpful to the interests of our nation." Professor E. R. A. Seligman wrote: "I take great pleasure in testifying to my very high appreciation of the studies on the Negro problem which you have been editing for the past few years. They are essentially scholarly and that means sober and temperate, and they are covering a field which is almost untilled and which is not apt to be cultivated by others." Jane Addams attended our conference in 1908 and commended our work.

Many periodicals mentioned our work:

London Spectator, 1900: "This work is being done with much intelligence, discrimination and assiduity at the instance and under the inspiration of the Atlanta University."

School Review, 1902: "The work of this conference is constructive and merits hearty support."

Outlook, 1903: "No student of the race problem, no person who would either think or speak upon it intelligently, can afford to be ignorant of the facts brought out in the Atlanta series of sociological studies of the conditions and the progress of the Negro."

Publications of the Southern History Association, 1904: "The work done under the direction of the Atlanta Conference is entitled to the respectful and thoughtful consideration of every man interested in any aspect of the life of the American Negro."

South Atlantic Quarterly, 1904: "They constitute, so far as the re-
viewer can learn, the most important body of direct evidence ever
published as to moral and religious conditions of our colored people."
N. Y. Evening Post, 1905: "The only scientific studies of the Negro
question being made today are those carried on by Atlanta University."

It must be remembered that the significance of these
studies lay not so much in what they were actually able to
accomplish, as in the fact that at the time of their publication
Atlanta University was the only institution in the world
carrying on a systematic study of the Negro and his development, and putting the result in a form available for the
scholars of the world.

In addition to the publications, we did something toward
bringing together annually at Atlanta University persons and
authorities interested in the problem of the South. Among
these were Charles William Eliot, Booker T. Washington,
Frank Sanborn, Franz Boas, and Walter Wilcox. We were
asked from time to time to cooperate in current studies. I
cooperated in the taking of the Twelfth Census and wrote
one of the monographs. I wrote magazine articles in the
World's Work and in the *Atlantic Monthly* where I joined
in a symposium and one of my fellow contributors was
Woodrow Wilson.

Also I joined with the Negro leaders of Georgia in efforts
to better local conditions; to stop discrimination in the distribution of school funds; to keep the legislature from making further discriminations in railway travel. I became a
member of the American Association for the Advancement
of Science in 1900 and was made a fellow in 1904. I went to
Europe and while abroad I sat in London with the wife of
Coleridge-Taylor and heard the first rendition of *Hiawatha's
Wedding Feast.*

In 1909 I tried to start an "Encyclopedia Africana" and
secured as members of the board of advisers the following
distinguished scholars:

Sir Harry Johnston, K.C.B., England
Prof. W. M. Flinders Petrie, D.C.L., England
William Archer, Esq., England
Miss Alice Werner, England

Dr. Francis Hoggan, England
Prof. Giuseppi Sergi, Italy
Dr. Karl Weule, Germany
Dr. J. Deniker, France
Major R. M. Daniel, Bechuanaland, Africa
Prof. A. B. Hart, L.L.D., Harvard
Prof. William James, L.L.D., Harvard
Prof. Hugo Munsterberg, L.L.D., Harvard
President G. Stanley Hall, L.L.D., Clark
Prof. A. F. Chamberlain, Ph.D., Clark
Prof. Franz Boas, Ph.D., Columbia

Sixty-two Negro scholars were on the Editorial Board, including: Kelley Miller, A.M., Howard; H. O. Tanner, France; Richard T. Greener, A.B., Harvard; Charles W. Chesnutt; John R. Lynch, U.S. Army; W. S. Scarborough, L.L.D., Oberlin, and many others. I was not able to raise funds to carry this enterprise further forward.

I testified before Congressional Commissions in Washington and appeared on the lecture platform with Walter Page, afterwards ambassador to England; I did a considerable amount of lecturing throughout the United States. I had wide correspondence with men of prominence in America and Europe: Lyman Abbott of the *Outlook;* E. D. Morel, the English expert on Africa; Max Weber of Heidelberg; Professor Wilcox of Cornell; Bliss Perry of the *Atlantic Monthly;* Horace Traubel, the great protagonist of Walt Whitman; Charles Eliot Norton and Talcott Williams. I began to be regarded by many groups and audiences as having definite information on the Negro to which they might listen with profit.

In 1900, came a significant occurrence which not until lately have I set in its proper place in my life. I had been for over nine years studying the American Negro problem. The result had been significant because of its unusual nature and not for its positive accomplishment. I wanted to set down its aim and method in some outstanding way which would bring my work to the notice of the thinking world. The great World's Fair at Paris was being planned and I thought I might put my findings into plans, charts and figures, so one might see what we were trying to accomplish. I got a couple of my best students and put a series of facts into charts: the size and growth of the Negro American group; its division by age and sex; its distribution, education and occupations; its books and periodicals. We made a most interesting set of drawings, limned on pasteboard cards about a yard square and mounted on a number of movable standards. The details of finishing these 50 or more charts, in colors, with accuracy, was terribly difficult with little money, limited time and not too much encouragement. I was threatened with nervous prostration before I was done and had little money left to buy passage to Paris, nor was there a cabin left for sale. But the exhibit would fail unless I was there. So at the last moment I bought passage in the steerage and went over and installed the work. It was an immediate success. It occupied a small room, perhaps 20 feet square but the room was always full. The American press, white and colored, was full of commendation and in the end, the exhibit received a Grand Prize, and I, as its author, a Gold Medal.

I was pleased and satisfied. I sat back quietly to hear the commendation and it came not only for this particular exhibit but for the work of the Atlanta conferences in general. I was sure that the work I had planned was certain of support and growth. But it was not. Within less than ten years it had to be abandoned because $5,000 a year could not be found in this rich land for its support. Where had I failed? There were many answers, but one was typically American, as the event proved; I did the deed but I did not advertise it. Either I myself or someone for me should have called public attention to what had been done or otherwise it would quickly be forgotten. Indeed the philosophy then current and afterward triumphant was that the Deed without Advertising was worthless and in the long run Advertising without the Deed was the only lasting value. Perhaps Americans do not realize how completely they have adopted this philosophy. But Madison Avenue does.

At the very time when my studies were most successful, there cut across this plan which I had as a scientist, a red ray which could not be ignored. I remember when it first, as it were, startled me to my feet: a poor Negro in central Georgia, Sam Hose, had killed his landlord's wife. I wrote out a careful and reasoned statement concerning the evident facts and started down to the Atlanta *Constitution* office, carrying in my pocket a letter of introduction to Joel Chandler Harris. I did not get there. On the way news met me: Sam Hose had been lynched, and they said that his knuckles were on exhibition at a grocery store farther down on Mitchell Street, along which I was walking. I turned back to the university. I began to turn aside from my work. I did not meet Joel Chandler Harris nor the editor of the *Constitution*.

Two considerations thereafter broke in upon my work and eventually disrupted it: first, one could not be a calm, cool, and detached scientist while Negroes were lynched, murdered and starved; and secondly, there was no such definite demand for scientific work of the sort that I was doing, as I had confidently assumed would be easily forthcoming. I regarded it as axiomatic that the world wanted to learn the truth and if the truth were sought with even approximate accuracy and painstaking devotion, the world would gladly support the effort. This was, of course, but a young man's idealism, not by any means false, but also never universally true. The work of the conference for 13 years including my own salary and small office force did not average $5,000 a year. Probably with some effort and sacrifice Atlanta University might have continued to raise this amount if it had not been for the controversy with Booker T. Washington that arose in 1903 and increased in intensity until 1908.

There were, of course, other considerations which made Atlanta University vulnerable to attack at this time. The University from the beginning had taken a strong and unbending attitude toward Negro prejudice and discrimination; white teachers and black students ate together in the same dining room and lived in the same dormitories. The charter of the institution opened the doors of Atlanta University to any student who applied, of any race or color; and when the State in 1887 objected to the presence of a few white students who were all children of teachers and professors, the institution gave up the small appropriation from the State rather than repudiate its principles. In fact, this appropriation represented not State funds, but the Negroes' share of the sum received from the Federal government for education.

When later there came an attempt on the part of the Southern Education Board and afterwards of the General Education Board to form a working program between educated Negroes and forward-looking whites in the South, it gradually became an understood principle of action that colored teachers should be encouraged in colored schools; that the races in the schools should be separated socially; that colored schools should be chiefly industrial; and that every effort should be made to conciliate Southern white public opinion. Schools which were successfully carrying out this program could look for further help from organized philanthropy. Other schools, and this included Atlanta University, could not.

Even this would not necessarily have excluded Atlanta University from consideration at the hands of the philanthropists. The University had done and was doing excellent and thorough work. Even industrial training in the South was often in the hands of Atlanta graduates. Tuskegee had always been largely manned by graduates of Atlanta and some of the best school systems of the South were directed by persons trained at Atlanta University. The college department was recognized as perhaps the largest and best in the South at the time among Negroes. But unfortunately, at this time, there came a controversy between myself and Booker Washington, which became more personal and bitter than I had ever dreamed and which necessarily dragged in the University.

Meantime, the task of raising money for Atlanta University and my work became increasingly difficult. In the fall of 1904 the printing of our conference report was postponed by the trustees until special funds could be secured. I did not at the time see the handwriting on the wall. I did not realize how strong the forces were back of Tuskegee and how they might interfere with my scientific study of the Negro. My continuing thought was that we must have a vehicle for both opinion and fact which would help me carry on my scientific work and at the same time be a forum less radical than the [Boston] *Guardian,* and yet more rational than the rank and file of Negro papers now so largely arrayed with Tuskegee. With this in mind, as early as 1904, I helped one of the Atlanta University graduates, who was a good printer, set up a job office in Memphis.

In 1905 I wrote to Jacob Schiff, reminding him of having met him in Bar Harbor in 1903.

"I want to lay before you a plan which I have and ask you if it is of sufficient interest to you for you to be willing to hear more of it and possibly to assist in its realization. The Negro race in America is today in a critical condition. Only united concerted effort will save us from being crushed. This union must come as a matter of education and long continued effort. To this end there is needed a high-class journal to circulate among the intelligent Negroes, tell them of the deeds of themselves and their neighbors, interpret the news of the world to them, and inspire them toward definite ideals. Now we have many small weekly papers and one or two monthlies, and none of them fill the great need I have outlined. I want to establish, therefore, for the nine million American Negroes and eventually for the whole Negro world, a monthly journal. To this end I have already in Memphis a printing establishment which has been running successfully at job work a year under a competent printer—a self-sacrificing educated young man. Together we shall have about $2,000 invested in this plant by April 15."

Mr. Schiff wrote back courteously, saying: "Your plans to establish a high-class journal to circulate among the intelligent Negroes is in itself interesting, and on its face has my sympathy. But before I could decide whether I can become of advantage in carrying your plans into effect, I would wish to advise with men whose opinion in such a matter I consider of much value." Nothing ever came of this, because, as I might have known, most of Mr. Schiff's friends were strong and sincere advocates of Tuskegee.

It was with difficulty that I came fully to realize the situation that was thus developing: first of all, I could not persuade myself that my program of solving the Negro problem by scientific investigation was wrong, or that it could possibly fail of eventual support when once it was undertaken; that it was understood in widening circles of readers and thinkers, I was convinced, because of the reception accorded the *Atlanta University Studies*. When, however, in spite of that, the revenue of the University continued to fall off, and no special support came for my particular part of its work, I tried several times by personal effort to see if funds could not be raised.

In 1906 I made two appeals: first and boldly, I outlined the work of the Atlanta Conference to Andrew Carnegie, reminding him that I had been presented to him and Carl Schurz some years before. I hoped that despite his deep friendship for Mr. Washington and the Tuskegee idea, he would see the use and value of my efforts in Atlanta. The response was indirect. At the time a white Mississippi planter, Alfred W. Stone, was popular in the North. He had grave doubts about the future of the Negro race, widely criticized black labor, and once tried to substitute Italians on his own plantations, until they became too handy with the knife. To his direction, Mr. Carnegie and others entrusted a fund for certain studies among Negroes. This is standard American procedure; if there is a job to be done and a Negro fit to do it, do not give the job or the responsibility to the Negro; give it to some white man and let the Negro work under him. Why they selected Stone and neglected an established center like Atlanta University, I cannot imagine; but at any rate, Stone turned to me and offered to give the University a thousand dollars to help finance a special study of the history of economic co-operation among Negroes. I had planned that year, 1907, to study the Negro in politics, but here support was needed and I turned aside and made the study asked for.

About the same time, I approached the United States Commissioner of Labor. For several years I had been able to do now and then certain small studies for the Bureau of Labor, which had been accepted and paid for. It began with a proposal to Carroll D. Wright in 1897 for a study of the Negro in a Virginia town in 1898, which Mr. Wright authorized me to make on my own responsibility, promising only to print it if he liked it. He did like it. This was followed by a major study of the Negro in the Black Belt in 1899 and among Negroes in Georgia in 1901, and I then approached the Bureau with a new proposal.

I asked United States Commissioner of Labor Neill, in 1906, to authorize a study of a Black Belt community. I wanted to take Lowndes County, Alabama, in a former slave state with a large majority of Negroes, and make a social and economic study from the earliest times when documents were available, down to the present; supplemented by studies of official records and a present house-to-house canvass of Negroes. I plied Commissioner Neill with plans and specifications until at last he authorized the study. Helped by Monroe Work, of Tuskegee Institute, and R. R. Wright, later a bishop of the A.M.E. Church, and a dozen or more local employees, I settled at the Calhoun School and began the study.

It was carried on with all sorts of difficulties, including financing which was finally arranged by loans from the University, and with the greeting of some of my agents with shotguns in certain parts of the county; but it was eventually finished. The difficult schedules were tabulated and I made chronological maps of the division of the land; I considered the distribution of labor; the relation of landlord and tenant; the political organization and the family life and the distribution of the population. The report was finished by hand with no copy, and rushed to Washington. I was criticized and I spent some weeks there in person, revising and perfecting it. It was finally accepted by the government, and $2,000 paid for it, most of which went back to the University in repayment of funds which they had kindly furnished me to carry on the work. But the study was not published. I knew the symptoms of this sort of treatment: in 1898, S. S. McClure had sent me to south Georgia to make a study of social situations there. He paid for the report but never published the manuscript and he afterward did the same thing in the case of Sir Harry Johnston.

I finally approached the Bureau and tried to find out when it would be published and was told that the Bureau had decided not to publish the manuscript, since it "touched on political matters." I was astonished and disappointed, but after a year I went back to them again and asked if they would allow me to have the manuscript since they were not going to use it. They told me it had been destroyed!

While I was down in Lowndes County finishing this study, there came the news of the Atlanta riot. I took the next train for Atlanta and my family. On the way, I wrote the "Litany of Atlanta."

Professor Seligman of Columbia wrote me:

"Like so many other of your well-wishers I was amazed and disgusted at the happenings in Atlanta. But perhaps I did not realize the horror of it all, until I read your beautiful poem in the *Independent*. It must indeed be a tragedy for men like you—a tragedy all the greater because of the seeming impasse. But perhaps you will learn—as I have learned after going thro' the fire of affliction—that there are really only two things worth living for in this world—the one is the love of those most nearly related to you, or thrown into close contact with you—and the other is work, the chance to express oneself in some form of activity however humble. Those things are open to every human being, and at bottom there is nothing else which is comparable with them—wealth, reputation, ambition or what not. Let us hold to the things that are eternally true, and let us seek within ourselves the compensation for the things that are withheld by an unthinking and uncivilized world."

It was of course crazy for me to dream that America, in the dawn of the 20th century with colonial imperialism, based on the suppression of colored folk, at its zenith, would encourage, much less adequately finance, such a program at a Negro college under Negro scholars. My faith in its success was based on the firm belief that race prejudice was based on widespread ignorance. My long-term remedy was Truth: carefully gathered scientific proof that neither color nor race determined the limits of a man's capacity or desert. I was not at the time sufficiently Freudian to understand how little human action is based on reason; nor did I know Karl Marx well enough to appreciate the economic foundations of human history.

I was therefore astonished and infinitely disappointed, gradually to realize that our work in the Atlanta conferences was not getting support; that, far from being able to command increased revenue for better methods of investigation and wider fields, it was with increasing difficulty that the aging and overworked President, with his deep earnestness and untiring devotion to principle, could collect enough to maintain even our normal activities. The conference had not been without a measure of success. Our reports were widely read and commented upon. On the other hand, so far as the American world of science and letters was concerned, we never "belonged"; we remained unrecognized in learned societies and academic groups. We rated merely as Negroes studying Negroes, and after all, what had Negroes to do with America or science? Gradually and with deep disappointment I began to realize, as early as 1906, that my program for studying the Negro problems must soon end, unless it received unforeseen support.

With all this came the strengthening and hardening of my own character. The billows of birth, love, and death swept over me. I saw life through all its paradox and contradiction of streaming eyes and mad merriment. I emerged into full manhood, with the ruins of some ideals about me, but with others planted above the stars; I was scarred and a bit grim, but hugging to my soul the divine gift of laughter and withal determined, even unto stubbornness, to fight the good fight.

At last, forebear and waver as I would, I faced the great decision. My life's last and greatest door stood ajar. What with all my dreaming, studying, and teaching was I going to *do* in this fierce fight? Despite all my youthful conceit and bumptiousness, I found developed beneath it all a reticence and new fear of forwardness, which sprang from searching criticisms of motive and high ideals of efficiency; but contrary to my dream of racial solidarity and notwithstanding my deep desire to serve and follow and think, rather than to lead and inspire and decide, I found myself suddenly the leader of a great wing of people fighting against another and greater wing. Nor could any effort of mine keep this fight from sinking to the personal plane. Heaven knows I tried. I finally wrote in March 1910:

"I insist on my right to think and speak; but if that freedom is made an excuse for abuse of and denial of aid to Atlanta University, then with regret I shall withdraw from Atlanta University."

For the American Negro, the last decade of the 19th and the first decade of the 20th centuries were more critical than the Reconstruction years of 1868 to 1876. Yet they have received but slight attention from historians and social students. They were usually interpreted in terms of personalities, and without regard to the great social forces that were developing. This was the age of triumph for big business, for industry, consolidated and organized on a world-wide scale, and run by white capital with colored labor. The southern United States was one of the most promising fields for this development, with a fine climate, invaluable staple crops, with a mass of cheap and potentially efficient labor, with unlimited natural power and use of unequalled technique, and with a transportation system reaching all the markets of the world.

The profit promised by the exploitation of this quasi-colonial empire was facing labor difficulties, threatening to flare into race war. The relations of the poor-white and Negro working classes were becoming increasingly embittered. In the year when I undertook the study of the Philadelphia Negro, lynching of Negroes by mobs reached a crimson climax in the United States, at the astounding figure of nearly five a week. Government throughout the former slave states was conducted by fraud and intimidation, with open violation of state and federal law. Reason seemed to have reached an impasse; white demagogues, like Ben Tillman and J. K. Vardaman, attacked Negroes with every insulting epithet and accusation that the English language could afford, and got wide hearing. On the other hand Negro colleges and others were graduating colored men and women, few in the aggregate, but of increasing influence, who demanded the full rights of American citizens; and even if their threatening surroundings compelled silence or whispers, they were none the less convinced that this attitude was their only way of salvation. Supporting Negro education were the descendants of those Northerners who founded the first Negro institutions and had since contributed to their upkeep. But these same Northerners were also investors and workers in the new industrial organization of the world. Toward them now turned the leaders of the white South, who were at once apprehensive of race war and desirous of a new, orderly industrial South.

Conferences began between whites of the North and the South, including industrialists as well as teachers, business men rather than preachers. At Capon Springs, on the Robert Ogden[11] trips to Hampton and Tuskegee, in the organization of the Southern Education Board, and finally in the founding of the General Education Board, a new racial philosophy for the South was evolved. This philosophy seemed to say that the attempt to over-educate a "child race" by furnishing chiefly college training to its promising young people, must be discouraged; the Negro must be taught to accept what the whites were willing to offer him; in a world ruled by white people and destined so to be ruled, the place of Negroes must be that of a humble, patient, hard-working group of laborers, whose ultimate destiny would be determined by their white employers. Meantime, the South must have education on a broad and increasing basis, but primarily for whites; for Negroes, education, for the present, should be confined increasingly to elementary instruction, and more especially to training in farming and industry, calculated to make the mass of Negroes laborers contented with their lot and cheap.

White and Negro labor must, so far as possible, be taken out of active competition, by segregation in work: to the whites the bulk of well-paid skilled labor and management; to the Negro, farm labor, unskilled labor in industry and domestic service. Exceptions to this general pattern would occur especially in some sorts of skills like building and repairs; but in general the "white" and "Negro" job would be kept separate and superimposed.

Finally, Northern philanthropy, especially in education, must be organized and incorporated, and its dole distributed according to this program; thus a number of inefficient and even dishonest attempts to conduct private Negro schools and low-grade colleges would be eliminated; smaller and competing institutions would be combined; above all, less and less total support would be given higher training for Negroes. This program was rigorously carried out until after the First World War.

To the support of this program, came Booker T. Washington in 1895. The white South was jubilant; public opinion was studiously organized to make Booker Washington the one nationally recognized leader of his race, and the South went quickly to work to translate the program into law. Disfranchisement laws were passed between 1890 and 1910 by all the former slave states, and quickly declared constitutional by the courts, before contests could be effectively organized: "jim-crow" legislation, for travel on railroads and streetcars, and race separation in many other walks of life, were rapidly put on the statute books.

By the second decade of the 20th century, a legal caste system based on race and color, had been openly grafted on the democratic constitution of the United States. This explains why, in 1910, I gave up my position at Atlanta University and became Director of Publications and Research for the newly formed National Association for the Advancement of Colored People, of which I was one of the incorporators in 1911.

Very early in my work in Atlanta, I began to feel, on the one hand, pressure being put upon me to modify my work; and on the other hand, an inner emotional reaction at the things taking place about me. To note the latter first: as a scientist, I sought the traditional detachment and calm of the seeker for truth. I had deliberately chosen to work in the South, although I knew that there I must face discrimination and insult. But on the other hand I was a normal human being with strong feelings and pronounced likes and dislikes, and a flair for expression; these I could not wholly suppress, nor did I try. I was on the other hand willing to endure and as my dear friend, Henry Hunt, said to me in after years, "I could keep still in seven different languages." But, if I did speak I did not intend to lie.

In one aspect of the Negro problem in America, my program had limited success; that was its relation to the white working class. The Negroes were working folk—farmers, laborers, porters and servants. They belonged in the main to the "have-nots" as over against the "haves." Yet they were not regarded as an integral part of the American workers and I as student of their plight and their efforts was continually treating them as a separate class instead of grouping them with the mass of workers. This was not because of any failure on my part to conceive of the Negroes as primarily workers whose chief interest lay in the working class. The fault lay at the door of the powerful forces in the state which had separated the working class into antagonistic groups hating and fearing each other more than they feared their exploiters. In slavery days the poor whites hated and feared the black slaves. These slaves deprived the free white workers of land and livelihood; drove them to the hills and barrens or to the slums of cities; they were largely disfranchised and managed to make a living by fawning on slaveowners, becoming slave overseers or bearing arms to keep black slaves from revolt. They protested bitterly against this condition.

To these poor whites, emancipation seemed not an opportunity for Negroes to rise to the status of free white workers, but rather the chance of white labor to climb on the backs of Negroes. The freedmen therefore were not only exploited by former slaveowners but even more by the up-struggling whites; and when white workers got the vote, blacks were disfranchised. A caste legislation put the Negro legally under the feet of the white workers, limiting his work, his wages, his dwelling place and his personal freedom. In the eyes of the Negro the white worker became his chief enemy; he led the lynch mobs, insulted him on the streets and took the food out of his mouth.

The mass of the Northern working class opposed slavery and wanted slaves emancipated. But they were largely foreign emigrants and many, like the Irish, met the competition of free Negro workers on arrival and fought for work in pitched battles. The newer emigrants were warned against cheap competing Negro labor and did not regard these dark strangers as fellow workmen. Employers threw white and black into competing groups. So that the National Labor Union representing the best of American labor, despite its brave repudiation of color discrimination, was unable in 1869 to secure admission of Negro workers into unions. Negroes, rebuffed, tried to form their own unions but had to start with the demand for political power. For this they depended on the Republican party and that party reduced them to serfdom in 1876. The Northern unions in tight craft organizations generally segregated the Negro worker or completely barred him. Some of the trades, like miners, longshoremen and cigarmakers, admitted Negroes; but many of the better paid trades, like blacksmiths, smelters, engineers, metal workers, boilermakers, electric workers, glassmakers, oil workers, textile workers and a host of similar unions, admitted in the new century few or no Negroes.

When, therefore, I essayed to study the Negro worker, I had no meeting ground with the white laboring class. I invited the secretary of the Georgia Federation of Labor to our conference and he spoke, but his hearers knew that his federation discriminated against Negroes. We studied Negro employees in Southern factories. We corresponded with all the unions in the nation but with small result. The American working class remained split by the color line. My study therefore became a study not of a working class but of a small part of one and the relations of these groups became more important than relations between worker and employer.

Of the general life in Atlanta, a word must be said. I stayed upon the campus as much as possible. My contact with the surrounding white city was limited to some necessary shopping. I did not vote since the "white primary," which was the real election, was closed to me. I did not enter parks or museums. I assumed that when the public was invited to any place or function, either the white people were meant, or, if not, attendance of Negroes meant segregated parts or times. Once I remonstrated with a colored teacher of literature for attending the "jim-crow" section of a theater in the top balcony. She answered: "Where else can I see Shakespeare? I cannot afford to go to New York."

One of the most annoying sorts of race discrimination was on the railroads. Did you ever see a "jim-crow" waiting room? There are some exceptions but usually no heat in winter and no air in summer; undisturbed loafers and white train hands and broken disreputable settees; to buy a ticket is torture: you stand and stand and wait and wait until every white person at the "Other Window" is waited on. Then the tired agent yells across (because all the tickets and change are over there): "What d'y' want? WHAT! WHERE?" He browbeats and contradicts you, hurries and confuses the ignorant; gives many the wrong change; for lack of time compels a number to purchase tickets on the train at a higher price and sends all out on the platform burning with indignation and hatred.

The "jim-crow" car is up next the baggage car and engine. The train stops out beyond the covering in the rain or sun or dust. Usually there is no step to help one climb on, and often the car is a smoker cut in two and you must pass through the white smokers and then they pass through your part with swagger and noise and stares. Your apartment is a half or a quarter or an eighth of the oldest car in service on the road. Unless it happens to be a through express, the old plush is caked with dirt, the floor is gummy and the windows dirty.

An impertinent white newsboy occupies two seats at the end and importunes you to buy cheap candy, Coca-Cola and worthless if not vulgar books. He yells and swaggers and a continued stream of white men saunters back and forth from the smoker to buy and listen. The white train crew from the baggage car uses the "jim-crow" to lounge in and perform their toilet. The conductor appropriates two seats for himself and his papers and yells gruffly for your tickets before the train has scarcely started. It is best not to ask him for information even in the gentlest tones. His information is for whites chiefly. It is difficult to get lunch or drinking water. Lunch rooms either "don't serve niggers" or serve them at some dirty and ill-attended hole in the wall. Toilet rooms are often filthy. If you have to change cars be wary of junctions which are usually without accommodation and filled with quarrelsome whites who hate a "darky dressed up." You are apt to have the company of a sheriff and a couple of meek or sullen black prisoners on part of your way and the dirty colored section hands will pour in toward night and drive you to the smallest corner. "No," said the little lady in the corner (she looked like an ivory cameo and her dress flowed on her like a caress), "We don't travel much."

CHAPTER XIV

THE NIAGARA MOVEMENT

In 1905 I was still a teacher at Atlanta University and was in my imagination a scientist, and neither a leader nor an agitator; I had much admiration for Mr. Washington and Tuskegee, and I had in 1894 applied at both Tuskegee and Hampton for work. If Mr. Washington's telegram had reached me before the Wilberforce bid, I should have doubtless gone to Tuskegee. Certainly I knew no less about mathematics than I did about Latin and Greek.

Since the controversy between me and Washington has become historic, it deserves more careful statement than it has had hitherto, both as to the matters and the motives involved. There was first of all the ideological controversy. I believed in the higher education of a Talented Tenth who through their knowledge of modern culture could guide the American Negro into a higher civilization. I knew that without this the Negro would have to accept white leadership, and that such leadership could not always be trusted to guide this group into self-realization and to its highest cultural possibilities. Mr. Washington, on the other hand, believed that the Negro as an efficient worker could gain wealth and that eventually through his ownership of capital he would be able to achieve a recognized place in American culture and could then educate his children as he might wish and develop their possibilities. For this reason he proposed to put the emphasis at present upon training in the skilled trades and encouragement in industry and common labor.

These two theories of Negro progress were not absolutely contradictory. Neither I nor Booker Washington understood the nature of capitalistic exploitation of labor, and the necessity of a direct attack on the principle of exploitation as the beginning of labor uplift. I recognized the importance of the Negro gaining a foothold in trades and his encouragement in industry and common labor. Mr. Washington was not absolutely opposed to college training and sent his own children to college. But he did minimize its importance, and discouraged the philanthropic support of higher education. He thought employers "gave" laborers work, thus opening the door to acquiring wealth. I openly and repeatedly criticized what seemed to me the poor work and small accomplishment of the Negro industrial school, but did not attack the fundamental wrong of giving the laborer less than he earned. It was characteristic of the Washington statesmanship that whatever he or anybody believed or wanted must be subordinated to dominant public opinion and that opinion deferred to and cajoled until it allowed a deviation toward better ways. It was my theory to guide and force public opinion by leadership. While my leadership was a matter of writing and teaching, the Washington leadership became a matter of organization and money. It was what I may call the Tuskegee Machine.

The years from 1899 to 1905 marked the culmination of the career of Booker T. Washington. In 1899 Mr. Washington, Paul Laurence Dunbar, and myself spoke on the same platform at the Hollis Street Theater, Boston, before a distinguished audience. Mr. Washington was not at his best and friends immediately raised a fund which sent him to Europe for a three months' rest. He was received with extraordinary honors: he had tea with the aged Queen Victoria, but two years before her death; he was entertained by two dukes and members of the aristocracy; he met James Bryce and Henry M. Stanley; he was received at the Peace Conference at The Hague and was greeted by many distinguished Americans, like ex-President Harrison, Archbishop Ireland and two justices of the Supreme Court. Only a few years before he had received an honorary A.M. from Harvard; in 1901, he received a LL.D. from Dartmouth; and that same year he dined with President Roosevelt to the consternation of the white South.

Returning to America he became during the administrations of Theodore Roosevelt and William Taft, from 1901 to 1912, the political referee in all Federal appointments or action taken with reference to the Negro and in many regarding the white South. In 1903 Andrew Carnegie made the future of Tuskegee certain by a gift of $600,000. There was no question of Booker T. Washington's undisputed leadership of the ten million Negroes in America, a leadership recognized gladly by the whites and conceded by most of the Negroes.

But there were discrepancies and paradoxes in this leadership. It did not seem fair, for instance, that on the one hand Mr. Washington should decry political activities among Negroes, and on the other hand dictate Negro political objectives from Tuskegee. At a time when Negro civil rights called for organized and aggressive defense, he broke down that defense by advising acquiescence or at least no open agitation. During the period when laws disfranchising the Negro were being passed in all the Southern states, between 1890 and 1909, and when these were being supplemented by "jim-crow" travel laws and other enactments making color caste legal, his public speeches, while they did not entirely ignore this development, tended continually to excuse it, to emphasize the shortcomings of the Negro, and were interpreted widely as putting the chief onus for his condition upon the Negro himself.

All this naturally aroused increasing opposition among Negroes and especially among the younger class of educated Negroes, who were beginning to emerge here and there, particularly from Northern institutions. This opposition began to become vocal in 1901 when two men, Monroe Trotter, Harvard 1895, and George Forbes, Amherst 1895, began the publication of the Boston *Guardian*. The *Guardian*, a weekly periodical, was bitter, satirical, and personal; but it was well edited, it was earnest, and it published facts. It attracted wide attention among colored people; it circulated among them all over the country; it was quoted and discussed. I did not wholly agree with the *Guardian*, and indeed only a few Negroes did, but nearly all read it or were influenced by it.

This beginning of organized opposition, together with other events, led to the growth at Tuskegee of what I have called the Tuskegee Machine. It arose first quite naturally. Not only did presidents of the United States consult Booker T. Washington, but governors and congressmen; philanthropists conferred with him, scholars wrote to him. Tuskegee became a vast information bureau and center of advice. It was not merely passive in these matters but, guided by Emmett Scott, a young secretary who was intelligent, suave and far-seeing, active efforts were made to concentrate influence at Tuskegee. After a time almost no Negro institution could collect funds without the recommendation or acquiescence of Mr. Washington. Few political appointments of Negroes were made anywhere in the United States without his consent. Even the careers of rising young colored men were very often determined by his advice and certainly his opposition was fatal. How much Mr. Washington knew of this work of the Tuskegee Machine and was directly responsible, one cannot say, but of its general activity and scope he must have been aware.

Moreover, it must not be forgotten that this Tuskegee Machine was not solely the idea and activity of black folk at Tuskegee. It was largely encouraged and given financial aid through certain white groups and individuals in the North. This Northern group had clear objectives. They were capitalists and employers of labor and yet in most cases sons, relatives, or friends of the Abolitionists who had sent teachers into the new Negro South after the war. These younger men believed that the Negro problem could not remain a matter of philanthropy. It must be a matter of business. These Negroes were not to be encouraged as voters in the new democracy, nor were they to be left at the mercy of the reactionary South. They were good laborers and they could be made of tremendous profit to the North. They could become a strong labor force and properly guided they would restrain the unbridled demands of white labor, born of the Northern labor unions and now spreading to the South and encouraged by European socialism.

One danger must be avoided and that was to allow the silly idealism of Negroes, half-trained in missionary "colleges," to mislead the mass of laborers and keep them stirred-up by ambitions incapable of realization. To this school of thought, the philosophy of Booker T. Washington came as a godsend and it proposed by building up his prestige and power, to control the Negro group. The control was to be drastic. The Negro intelligentsia was to be suppressed and hammered into conformity. The process involved some cruelty and disappointment, but that was inevitable. This was the real force back of the Tuskegee Machine. It had money and it had opportunity, and it found in Tuskegee tools to do its bidding.

There were some rather pitiful results in thwarted ambition and curtailed opportunity. I remember one case which always stands in my memory as typical. There was a young colored man, one of the most beautiful human beings I have ever seen, with smooth brown skin, velvet eyes of intelligence, and raven hair. He was educated and well-to-do. He proposed to use his father's Alabama farm and fortune to build a Negro town as an independent economic unit in the South. He furnished a part of the capital but soon needed more and he came North to get it. He struggled for more than a decade; philanthropists and capitalists were fascinated by his personality and story; and when, according to current custom, they appealed to Tuskegee for confirmation, there was silence. Mr. Washington would not say a word in favor of the project. He simply kept still. Will Benson struggled on with ups and downs, but always balked by a whispering galley of suspicion, because his plan was never endorsed by Tuskegee. In the midst of what seemed to us who looked on the beginnings of certain success, Benson died of overwork, worry, and a broken heart.

From facts like this, one may gauge the bitterness of the fight of young Negroes against Mr. Washington and Tuskegee. The controversy as it developed was not entirely against Mr. Washington's ideas, but became the insistence upon the right of other Negroes to have and express their ideas.

Things came to such a pass that when any Negro complained or advocated a course of action, he was silenced with the remark that Mr. Washington did not agree with this. Naturally the bumptious, irritated, young black intelligentsia of the day declared: "I don't care a damn what Booker Washington thinks. This is what I think, and *I have a right to think*."

It was this point, and not merely disagreement with Mr. Washington's plans, that brought eventually violent outbreak. It was more than opposition to a program of education. It was opposition to a system and that system was part of the economic development of the United States at that time. The fight cut deep: it went into social relations; it divided friends; it made bitter enemies. I can remember that years later, when I went to live in New York and was once invited to a social gathering among Brooklyn colored people, one of the most prominent Negroes of the city refused to be present because of my attitude toward Mr. Washington.

When the *Guardian* began to increase in influence, determined effort was made to build up a Negro press for Tuskegee. Already Tuskegee filled the horizon so far as national magazines and the great newspapers were concerned. In 1901 the *Outlook*, then the leading weekly, chose two distinguished Americans for autobiographies. Mr. Washington's *Up From Slavery* was so popular that it was soon published and circulated all over the earth. Thereafter, every magazine editor sought articles with Washington's signature and publishing houses continued to ask for books. A number of talented "ghost writers," black and white, took service under Tuskegee, and books and articles poured out of the institution. An annual letter "To My People" went out from Tuskegee to the press. Tuskegee became the capital of the Negro nation. Negro newspapers were influenced and finally the oldest and largest was bought by white friends of Tuskegee. Most of the other papers found it to their advantage certainly not to oppose Mr. Washington, even if they did not wholly agree with him,

I was greatly disturbed at this time, not because I was in absolute opposition to the things that Mr. Washington was advocating, but because I was strongly in favor of more open agitation against wrongs and above all I resented the practical buying up of the Negro press and choking off even mild and reasonable opposition to Mr. Washington in both the Negro press and the white.

Then, too, during these years there came a series of influences that were brought to bear upon me personally, which increased my discomfort and resentment. I had tried to keep in touch with Hampton and Tuskegee, for I regarded them as great institutions. I attended the conferences which for a long time were held at Hampton, and at one of them I was approached by a committee. It consisted of Walter Hines Page, editor of the *Atlantic Monthly;* William McVickar, Episcopal bishop of Rhode Island; and Dr. H. B. Frissell, principal of Hampton and brother of a leading New York banker. They asked me about the possibilities of my editing a periodical to be published at Hampton. I told them of my dreams and plans, and afterwards wrote them in detail. But one query came by mail: that was concerning the editorial direction. I replied firmly that editorial decisions were to be in my hands, if I edited the magazine. This was undiplomatic and too dogmatic; and yet, it brought to head the one real matter in controversy: would such a magazine be dominated by and subservient to the Tuskegee philosophy, or would it have freedom of thought and discussion? Perhaps if I had been more experienced, the question could have been discussed and some reasonable outcome obtained; but I doubt it. I think any such magazine launched at the time would have been seriously curtailed in its freedom of speech. At any rate, the project was dropped.

Beginning in 1902 pressure was put upon me to give up my work at Atlanta University and go to Tuskegee. There again I was not at first adverse in principle to Tuskegee, except that I wanted to continue the studies which I had begun and if my work was worth support, it was worth support at Atlanta University. I was unable to obtain assurance that my studies would be continued at Tuskegee, and that I would not sink to the level of a "ghost writer." I remember a letter came from Wallace Buttrick late in 1902, asking that I attend a private conference in New York with Felix Adler, William H. Baldwin, Jr., George Foster Peabody, and Robert Ogden. The object of the conference was ostensibly the condition of the Negro in New York City. I went to the conference and did not like it. Most of the more distinguished persons named were not present. The conference itself amounted to little, but after adjournment I was whisked over to William H. Baldwin's beautiful Long Island home and there what seemed to me to be the real object of my coming was disclosed. Mr. Baldwin was at that time president of the Long Island Railroad and slated to be president of the Southern. He was a rising industrial leader of America; also he was a prime mover on the Tuskegee board of trustees. Both he and his wife insisted that my place was at Tuskegee; that Tuskegee was not yet a good school, and needed the kind of development that I had been trained to promote.

This was followed by two interviews with Mr. Washington himself. I was elated at the opportunity and we met twice in New York City. The results to me were disappointing. Booker T. Washington was not an easy person to know. He was wary and silent. He never expressed himself frankly or clearly until he knew exactly to whom he was talking and just what their wishes and desires were. He did not know me, and I think he was suspicious. On the other hand, I was quick, fast-speaking and voluble. I had nothing to conceal. I found at the end of the first interview that I had done practically all the talking and that no clear and definite offer or explanation of my proposed work at Tuskegee had been made. In fact, Mr. Washington had said about as near nothing as was possible.

The next interview did not go so well because I myself said little. Finally, we resorted to correspondence. Even then I could get no clear understanding of just what I was going to do at Tuskegee if I went. I was given to understand that the salary and accommodations would be satisfactory. In fact, I was invited to name my price. Later in the year I went to Bar Harbor for a series of speeches in behalf of Atlanta University, and while there met Jacob Schiff, the [William J.] Schieffelins and Merriam of Webster's dictionary. I had dinner with the Schieffelins and their mother-in-law, whose father [Melville W. Fuller] was once Chief Justice of the United States. Again I was urged to go to Tuskegee.

Early in the next year I received an invitation to join Mr. Washington and certain prominent white and colored friends in a conference to be held in New York. The conference was designed to talk over a common program for the American Negro and evidently it was hoped that the growing division of opinion and opposition to Mr. Washington within the ranks of Negroes would thus be overcome. I was enthusiastic over the idea. It seemed to me just what was needed to clear the air.

There was difficulty, however, in deciding what persons ought to be invited to the conference; how far it should include Mr. Washington's extreme opponents, or how far it should be composed principally of his friends. There ensued a long delay and during this time it seemed to me that I ought to make my own position clearer than I had hitherto. I was increasingly uncomfortable under the statements of Mr. Washington's position: his depreciation of the value of the vote; his evident dislike of Negro colleges; and his general attitude which seemed to place the onus of blame for the status of Negroes upon the Negroes themselves rather than upon the whites. And above all I resented the Tuskegee Machine.

I had been asked sometime before by A. C. McClurg & Co. of Chicago if I did not have some material for a book; I planned a social study which should be perhaps a summing up of the work of the Atlanta Conference, or at any rate, a scientific investigation. They asked, however, if I did not have some essays that they might put together and issue immediately, mentioning my articles in the *Atlantic Monthly* and other places. I demurred because books of essays almost always fall so flat. Nevertheless, I got together a number of my fugitive pieces. I then added a chapter, "Of Mr. Booker T. Washington and Others," in which I sought to make a frank evaluation of Booker T. Washington. I left out the more controversial matter: the bitter resentment which young Negroes felt at the continued and increasing activity of the Tuskegee Machine. I concentrated my thought and argument on Mr. Washington's general philosophy. As I read that statement now, I am satisfied with it. I see no word that I would change. I said:

"The black men of America have a duty to perform, a duty stern and delicate—a forward movement to oppose a part of the work of their greatest leader. So far as Mr. Washington preaches Thrift, Patience, and Industrial Training for the masses, we must hold up his hands and strive with him, rejoicing in his honors and glorying in the strength of this Joshua called of God and of man to lead the headless host. But so far as Mr. Washington apologizes for injustice, North or South, does not rightly value the privilege and duty of voting, belittles the emasculating effects of caste distinctions, and opposes the higher training and ambition of our brighter minds—so far as he, the South, or the Nation, does this—we must unceasingly and firmly oppose him. By every civilized and peaceful method we must strive for the rights which the world accords to men, clinging unwaveringly to those great words which the sons of the Fathers would fain forget: 'We hold these truths to be self-evident: That all men are created equal; that they are endowed by their Creator with certain unalienable rights; that among these are life, liberty, and the pursuit of happiness.' "

Pressure came from white Northern friends, who I believed appreciated my work and on the whole wished me and my race well. But they were apprehensive; fearful because as perhaps the most conspicuously trained young Negro of my day, and, quite apart from any question of ability, my reaction toward the new understanding between North and South, and especially my attitude toward Mr. Washington, were bound to influence Negroes. As a matter of fact, at that time I was not over-critical of Booker Washington. I regarded his Atlanta speech as a statesmanlike effort to reach understanding with the white South; I hoped the South would respond with equal generosity and thus the nation could come to understanding for both races. When, however, the South responded with "jim-crow" legislation, I became uneasy. Still I believed that my program of investigation and study was just what was needed to bring understanding in the long run, based on truth. I tried to make this clear. I attended the conferences at Hampton for several years, and became increasingly critical of those Hampton opinions. In all the deliberations to which I listened, and resolutions, which were passed at Hampton, never once was the work of Atlanta University nor college work anywhere for Negroes, commended or approved. I ceased regular attendance at the conferences; but when later I was invited back I delivered a defense of higher training for Negroes and a scathing criticism of the "Hampton Idea." I was not asked to return to Hampton for 25 years.

My book settled pretty definitely any further question of my going to Tuskegee as an employee. But it also drew pretty hard and fast lines about my future career. Meantime, the matter of the conference in New York dragged on until finally in October 1903, a circular letter was sent out setting January 1904 as the date of meeting. The conference took place accordingly in Carnegie Hall, New York. About 50 persons were present, most of them colored and including many well-known persons. There was considerable plain speaking but the whole purpose of the conference seemed revealed by the invited white guests and the tone of their message. Several persons of high distinction came to speak to us, including Andrew Carnegie and Lyman Abbott. Their words were lyric, almost fulsome in praise of Mr. Washington and his work, and in support of his ideas. Even if all they said had been true, it was a wrong note to strike in a conference of conciliation. The conference ended with two speeches by Mr. Washington and myself, and the appointment of a Committee of Twelve in which we were also included.

The Committee of Twelve which was thus instituted was unable to do any effective work as a steering committee for the Negro race in America. First of all, it was financed, through Mr. Washington, probably by Mr. Carnegie. This put effective control of the committee in Mr. Washington's hands. It was organized during my absence and laid down a plan of work which seemed to me of some value but of no lasting importance and having little to do with the larger questions and issues. I therefore soon resigned so as not to be responsible for work and pronouncements over which I would have little influence. My friends and others accused me of refusing to play the game after I had assented to a program of cooperation. I still think, however, that my action was wise.

By this time I was pretty throughly disillusioned. It did not seem possible for me to occupy middle ground and try to appease the *Guardian* on the one hand and the Hampton-Tuskegee idea on the other. I began to feel the strength and implacability of the Tuskegee Machine; the Negro newspapers definitely showing their reaction and publishing jibes and innuendoes at my expense. Filled with increasing indignation, I published in the *Guardian* a statement concerning the venality of certain Negro papers which I charged had sold out to Mr. Washington. It was a charge difficult of factual proof without an expenditure of time and funds not at my disposal. I was really at last openly tilting against the Tuskegee Machine and its methods. These methods have become common enough in our day for all sorts of purposes: the distribution of advertising and favors, the sending out of special correspondence, veiled and open attacks upon recalcitrants, the narrowing of opportunities for employment and promotion. All this is a common method of procedure today, but in 1904 it seemed to me monstrous and dishonest, and I resented it. On the other hand, the public expression of this resentment greatly exercised and annoyed Mr. Washington's friends. Some knew little about these activities at Tuskegee; others knew and approved. The New York *Evening Post* challenged me to present proof of my statements and refused to regard my answer as sufficient, which was of course true.

Then came a new and surprising turn to the whole situation which in the end quite changed my life. In the early summer of 1905, Mr. Washington went to Boston and arranged to speak in a colored church to colored people—a thing which he did not often do in the North. Trotter and Forbes, editors of the *Guardian,* determined to heckle him and make him answer publicly certain questions with regard to his attitude toward voting and education. William H. Lewis, a colored lawyer whom I myself had introduced to Mr. Washington, had charge of the meeting, and the result was a disturbance magnified by the newspapers into a "riot," which resulted in the arrest of Mr. Trotter. Finally he served a term in jail.

With this incident I had no direct connection whatsoever. I did not know beforehand of the meeting in Boston, nor of the projected plan to heckle Mr. Washington. But when Trotter went to jail, my indignation overflowed. I did not always agree with Trotter then or later. But he was an honest, brilliant, unselfish man, and to treat as a crime that which was at worst mistaken judgment was an outrage. I sent out from Atlanta in June 1905 a call to a few selected persons "for organized determination and aggressive action on the part of men who believe in Negro freedom and growth." I proposed a conference during the summer "to oppose firmly present methods of strangling honest criticism; to organize intelligent and honest Negroes; and to support organs of news and public opinion."

Fifty-nine colored men from 17 different states eventually signed a call for a meeting near Buffalo, New York, during the week of July 9, 1905. I went to Buffalo and hired a little hotel on the Canadian side of the river at Fort Erie, and waited for the men to attend the meeting. If sufficient men had not come to pay for the hotel, I should certainly have been in bankruptcy and perhaps in jail; but as a matter of fact, 29 men, representing 14 states, came. The "Niagara Movement" was incorporated January 31, 1906, in the District of Columbia.

Its particular business and objects were to advocate and promote the following principles:

1. Freedom of speech and criticism.
2. An unfettered and unsubsidized press.
3. Manhood suffrage.
4. The abolition of all caste distinctions based simply on race and color.
5. The recognition of the principle of human brotherhood as a practical present creed.
6. The recognition of the highest and best human training as the monopoly of no class or race.
7. A belief in the dignity of labor.
8. United effort to realize these ideals under wise and courageous leadership.

The Niagara Movement raised a furor of the most disconcerting criticism. I was accused of acting from motives of envy of a great leader and being ashamed of the fact that I was a member of the Negro race. The leading weekly of the land, the New York *Outlook,* pilloried me with scathing articles. But the movement went on. The next year, 1906, instead of meeting in secret, we met openly at Harper's Ferry, the scene of John Brown's raid, and had in significance if not in numbers one of the greatest meetings that American Negroes ever held. We made pilgrimage at dawn bare-footed to the scene of Brown's martyrdom and we talked some of the plainest English that had been given voice to by black men in America. The resolutions which I wrote expressed with tumult of emotion my creed of 1906:

The men of the Niagara Movement, coming from the toil of the year's hard work, and pausing a moment from the earning of their daily bread, turn toward the nation and again ask in the name of ten million the privilege of a hearing. In the past year the work of the

Negro hater has flourished in the land. Step by step the defenders of the rights of American citizens have retreated. The work of stealing the black man's ballot has progressed and fifty and more representatives of stolen votes still sit in the nation's capital. Discrimination in travel and public accommodation has so spread that some of our weaker brethren are actually afraid to thunder against color discrimination as such and are simply whispering for ordinary decencies.

Against this the Niagara Movement eternally protests. We will not be satisfied to take one jot or tittle less than our full manhood rights. We claim for ourselves every single right that belongs to a freeborn American, political, civil, and social; and until we get these rights we will never cease to protest and assail the ears of America. The battle we wage is not for ourselves alone, but for all true Americans. It is a fight for ideals, lest this, our common fatherland, false to its founding, become in truth the land of the Thief and the home of the Slave —a byword and a hissing among the nations for its sounding pretensions and pitiful accomplishment.

Never before in the modern age has a great and civilized folk threatened to adopt so cowardly a creed in the treatment of its fellow-citizens, born and bred on its soil. Stripped of verbiage and subterfuge and in its naked nastiness, the new American creed says: fear to let black men even try to rise lest they become the equals of the white. And this in the land that professes to follow Jesus Christ. The blasphemy of such a course is only matched by its cowardice.

In detail our demands are clear and unequivocal. First, we would vote; with the right to vote goes everything: freedom, manhood, the honor of our wives, the chastity of our daughters, the right to work, and the chance to rise, and let no man listen to those who deny this.

We want full manhood suffrage, and we want it now, henceforth and forever.

Second. We want discrimination in public accommodation to cease. Separation in railway and street cars, based simply on race and color, is un-American, undemocratic and silly. We protest against all such discrimination.

Third. We claim the right of freemen to walk, talk and be with them who wish to be with us. No man has a right to choose another man's friends, and to attempt to do so is an impudent interference with the most fundamental human privilege.

Fourth. We want the laws enforced against rich as well as poor; against Capitalist as well as Laborer; against white as well as black. We are not more lawless than the white race, we are more often arrested, convicted and mobbed. We want justice even for criminals and outlaws. We want the Constitution of the country enforced. We want Congress to take charge of the Congressional elections. We want the Fourteenth Amendment carried out to the letter and every State disfranchised in Congress which attempts to disfranchise its rightful voters. We want the Fifteenth Amendment enforced and no State allowed to base its franchise simply on color.

The failure of the Republican Party in Congress at the session just closed to redeem its pledge of 1904 with reference to suffrage conditions in the South seems a plain, deliberate, and premeditated breach of promise, and stamps that party as guilty of obtaining votes under false pretense.

Fifth. We want our children educated. The school system in the country districts of the South is a disgrace and in few towns and cities are the Negro schools what they ought to be. We want the national government to step in and wipe out illiteracy in the South. Either the United States will destroy ignorance, or ignorance will destroy the United States.

And when we call for education, we mean real education. We believe in work. We ourselves are workers, but work is not necessarily education. Education is the development of power and ideal. We want our children trained as intelligent human beings should be and we will fight for all time against any proposal to educate black boys and girls simply as servants and underlings, or simply for the use of other people. They have a right to know, to think, to aspire.

These are some of the chief things which we want. How shall we get them? By voting where we may vote; by persistent, unceasing agitation; by hammering at the truth; by sacrifice and work.

We do not believe in violence, neither in the despised violence of the raid nor the lauded violence of the soldier, nor the barbarous violence of the mob; but we do believe in John Brown, in that incarnate spirit of justice, that hatred of a lie, that willingness to sacrifice money, reputation, and life itself on the altar of right. And here on the scene of John Brown's martyrdom, we reconsecrate ourselves, our honor, our property to the final emancipation of the race which John Brown died to make free.

Here at last I approached in my thinking the fundamental matter of the exploitation of the worker, regardless of race and color. The thought was not yet clear and the philosophy of socialism was not yet applied. But the philosophy hovered in the background.

Meantime, I refused to give up the idea that a critical periodical for the American Negro might be founded. I had started in Memphis with the help of two graduates of Atlanta University the little printing shop that I have already mentioned, and from this was published weekly a paper called *The Moon* beginning in 1906. *The Moon* was in some sort precursor of *The Crisis*. It was published for a year in

Memphis and then the printing office given up and in 1907 in conjunction with two friends in Washington there was issued a miniature monthly called *Horizon*. *Horizon* was published from 1907 to 1910, and in the fall of 1910 *The Crisis* was born.

Gradually I began to realize that the difficulty about support for my work in Atlanta University was largely personal; that on account of my attitude toward Mr. Washington I had become *persona non grata* to powerful interests, and that Atlanta University would not be able to get support for its general work or for its study of the Negro problem so long as I remained at the institution. No one ever said this to me openly, but I sensed it in the worries which encompassed the new young President Edmund Ware who had succeeded Dr. Horace Bumstead. I began to realize that I would better look out for work elsewhere.

About this time an offer came from the city of Washington. The merging of the white and colored school systems into one had thrown colored folk into uproar lest their control of their own schools be eliminated and colored children not admitted to white schools. The new and rather eccentric superintendent of schools, W. C. Chancellor, wanted an assistant superintendent to put in charge of the Negro schools. To my great surprise he offered the position to me, while I was on a chance visit to the city. I asked for time to consider it. My reaction was to refuse even though the salary was twice what I was getting; for I doubted my fitness for such a job; but when I thought the matter over further and my position at Atlanta University, I began to wonder if I should not accept.

I was not called upon to decide, for forces started moving in Washington. The Tuskegee Machine backed by white capital was definitely against me and they involved the local interests of the Negro group. A prominent colored member of the School Board took the matter straight to President Theodore Roosevelt and emphasized the "danger" of my appointment. He never forgot the "danger" of my personality as later events proved. The offer was never actually withdrawn, but it was not pressed, and I finally realized that it probably would not have gone through even if I had indicated my acceptance.

Still my eventual withdrawal from Atlanta University seemed wise. Young President Ware had received almost categorical promises that under certain circumstances increased contributions from the General Education Board and other sources might be expected, which would make the university secure, and perhaps even permit the continuance of the conference. I was sure that I was at least one of these "circumstances," and so my work in Atlanta and my dream of the settlement of the Negro problem by science faded. I began to be acutely conscious of the difficulty which my attitudes and beliefs were making for Atlanta University.

My career as a scientist was to be swallowed up in my role as master of propaganda. This was not wholly to my liking. I was no natural leader of men. I could not slap people on the back and make friends of strangers. I could not easily break down an inherited reserve; or at all times curb a biting, critical tongue. Nevertheless, having put my hand to the plow, I had to go on. The Niagara Movement with less momentum met in Boston in 1907 and in Oberlin in 1908. It began to suffer internal strain from the dynamic personality of Trotter and my own inexperience with organizations. Finally, it practically became merged with a new and enveloping organization of which I became a leading official —the National Association for the Advancement of Colored People.

CHAPTER XV

THE NAACP

The NAACP started with a lynching 100 years after the birth of Abraham Lincoln, and in the city, Springfield, Illinois, which was his long time residence. William English Walling, a white Southerner, dramatized the gruesome happening and a group of liberals formed a committee in New York, which I was invited to join. A conference was held in 1909.

This conference contained four groups: scientists who knew the race problem; philanthropists willing to help worthy causes; social workers ready to take up a new task of Abolition; and Negroes ready to join a new crusade for their emancipation. An impressive number of scientists and social workers attended; friends of wealthy philanthropists were present and many Negroes but few followers of Booker Washington. In the end Trotter, the most radical Negro leader, and Mrs. Ida Wells Barnett who was leading an anti-lynching crusade, refused to join the new organization, being distrustful of white leadership. I myself and most of the Niagara Movement group were willing to join. The National Association for the Advancement of Colored People was formed, which without formal merger absorbed practically the whole membership of the Niagara Movement. With some hesitation I was asked to join the organization as Director of Publications and Research. My research work was to go on but my activities would be so held in check that the Association would not develop as a center of attack upon Tuskegee.

Here was an opportunity to enter the lists in a desperate fight aimed straight at the real difficulty: the question as to how far educated Negro opinion in the United States was going to have the right and opportunity to guide the Negro group. Back of this lay an unasked question as to the relation of the American Negro group to the whole labor movement. This was not yet raised but several of the group were Socialists, including myself.

One may consider the personal equations and clash of ideologies possible here as a matter of the actions and thoughts of certain men, or as a development of larger social forces beyond personal control. I suppose the latter aspect is the truer. My thoughts, the thoughts of Washington, Trotter and Oswald Garrison Villard were the expression of social forces more than of our own minds. These forces or ideologies embraced more than reasoned acts. They included physical, biological and psychological habits, conventions and enactments. Opposed to these came natural reaction; the physical recoil of the victims, the unconscious and irrational urges, as well as reasoned complaints and acts. The total result was the history of our day. That history may be epitomized in one word—Empire; the domination of white Europe over black Africa and yellow Asia, through political power built on the economic control of labor, income and ideas. The echo of this industrial imperialism in America was the expulsion of black men from American democracy, their subjection to caste control and wage slavery. This ideology was triumphant in 1910.

I accepted the offer of the NAACP in 1910 to join their new organization in New York as Director of Publications and Research.

My new title showed that I had modified my program of research, but by no means abandoned it. First, I directed and edited my Atlanta study of 1912, *in absentia* with the help of my colleague, Augustus Dill, my student and successor as teacher in Atlanta. Then in our study of 1913, I secured the promise of Dr. J. H. Dillard, of the Slater Board, to join Atlanta University in keeping up the work of the conferences. The work of research was to be carried on in New York, with a conference and annual publication at Atlanta. I was jubilant at the projected survival of my work. But on advice of President Ware himself, this arrangement was not accepted by the trustees of Atlanta University. Ware was probably warned that his tie with a radical movement would hamper the university.

In August 1910, I reported at my new office and new work at 20 Vesey Street, New York. As I have said elsewhere, the NAACP "proved between 1910 and the first World War, one of the most effective organizations of the liberal spirit and the fight for social progress which America has known." It fought frankly to make Negroes "politically free from disfranchisement, legally free from caste and socially free from insult."

This new field of endeavor represented a distinct break from my previous purely scientific program. While "research" was still among my duties, there were in fact no funds for such work. My chief efforts were devoted to editing and publishing *The Crisis*, which I founded on my own responsibility, and over the protest of many of my associates. With *The Crisis*, I essayed a new role of interpreting to the world the hindrances and aspirations of American Negroes. My older program appeared only as I supported my contentions with facts from current reports and observation or historic reference. My writing was reinforced by lecturing, and my knowledge increased by travel; my thought was broadened by study of socialism.

We had on our board of directors many incongruous elements as was to be expected: philanthropists like Oswald Villard; social workers like Florence Kelley; liberal Christians like John Haynes Holmes and liberal Jews like the Spingarns; spiritual descendants of the Abolitionists like Mary Ovington and radical Negroes. Clashes now and then were inevitable.

To a white philanthropist like Villard, a Negro was quite naturally expected to be humble and thankful or certainly not assertive and aggressive; this Villard resented. I knew Villard's mother, who was Garrison's favorite child, and I liked her very much. His uncles were cordial and sympathetic. There was much that I liked in Villard himself, but one thing despite all my effort kept us far apart. He had married a wife from Georgia, a former slave State, and consequently I could never step foot in his house as a guest, nor could any other of his colored associates. Indeed I doubt if any of his Jewish co-workers were ever invited. I knew the reasons for this discrimination, but I could hardly be expected to be happy over them or to be his close friend.

My first rather bitter falling out with Villard was at a meeting of the Board of Directors. Villard presumed to tell me how to edit *The Crisis,* and suggested that with my monthly record of lynchings, I also publish a list of Negro crimes. I resented this, not only because it was logically silly, but because it was interfering with my business. It was for this reason and from similar clashes that he finally resigned the chairmanship of the board and was replaced by Joel Spingarn. Villard, however, kept his membership on the board and his interest in our work. Social workers like Florence Kelley criticized my status: I held the rather anomalous position of being both a member of the board and, as executive officer, the board's employee. This was not from any demand which I made, but was due to the inescapable fact that I knew the Negro problem better than any of the white members of the board, and at the same time I was the one colored man whom they could put their hands on to carry out the objects of the organization. My double capacity was repeatedly a matter of discussion, and sometimes dispute; but no answer was forthcoming for 24 years.

Few of us realized what an organization of this sort had to be and what changes of form it had to go through. In early years it was a conference of men and women seeking agreement for common action, and finally carrying out the work decided upon by means of a committee of one or more. It was this form that the NAACP had in mind when it was organized in 1909. It needed money, and that Villard and some of the other members of the committee proposed to raise from their wealthy friends, or from well-known philanthropists. It became increasingly necessary for the organization to have a paid executive whose chief business was to raise money.

When I was called to join the group it was expected that I would become that executive, but that was just what I refused to do, because I knew that raising money was not a job for which I was fitted. It called for a friendliness of approach and knowledge of human nature, and an adaptability which I did not have. What I had was knowledge of the Negro problem, an ability to express my thoughts clearly, and a logical method of thought. I wanted then to write and lecture; and this become my job. We needed, however, an executive secretary, and after relying a few years on untrained services, we hired a white trained social worker at $5,000 a year. It seemed to many of us a huge sum and an impossible effort, but it worked out under three secretaries; the first white, the other two colored.[12]

It was carried on in accordance with growing experiences among philanthropic organizations. The secretaries trained to raise money used approved and tried methods and expected and received cooperation from a Board of Directors whom they helped to select because of their money and their advertising value. This meant that the secretary had to have power put in his hands and the more money he raised for the objects of the organization, the more power he got. If he knew his job and had a broad conception of the purposes of his organization, things would go well. If he became more interested in money and power, and less clear as to ideal, the organization might not go as well. Changes due to these facts have occurred in the NAACP during its long and successful career.

The span of my life from 1910 to 1934 is chiefly the story of *The Crisis* under my editorship, but it had also an astonishing variety of subsidiary interests and activities.

Beginning a little before this period I continued my visits to Europe. I went in 1900 to the Paris Exposition and again by the grace of an English friend in 1906. I helped organize and took part in the great Races Congress in 1911 and went to France in December 1918, just after the Armistice. This close touch with Europe and European developments had much to do with my understanding of social problems and trends of the world. I followed the development of English imperialism and the forces in England, France, Italy and Germany which resulted in the Balkan War, the World

War and eventually the Russian Revolution. In the United States I studied the political development from the free silver controversy led by Bryan through the administrations of Theodore Roosevelt and Taft, and especially the "Bull Moose" campaign and the election of Wilson.

I kept on writing and publishing not with as much concentration of effort as I ought to have had, but with some effectiveness. In 1907 appeared *The Negro in the South*— from lectures, two by myself and two by Mr. Washington. In 1909 I published *John Brown,* one of the best written of my books, but one which aroused the unfortunate jealousy of Villard who was also writing a biography of Brown. In 1915 I published my volume on *The Negro.* To this must be added part of a bulletin in the Twelfth Census of the United States and several magazine articles.

I still clung to my idea of investigation in lines which would temper and guide my exposition of a racial philosophy; and for that reason I determined from the beginning to make my work with the Association not that of executive secretary but editor of its official organ. There was opposition to this organ from the first. First of all, organs of this sort were known to be usually costly and this organization had no money. Secondly, organs were of doubtful efficiency. My good friend, Albert E. Pillsbury, Attorney-General of Massachusetts, wrote feelingly: "If you have not decided upon a periodical, for heaven's sake don't. They are as numerous as flies"—and he meant to conclude about as useful. I came to New York to occupy a bare office; associated with a treasurer, Villard (who said frankly, "I don't know who is going to pay your salary. I have no money"), and with a generally critical if not hostile public which expected the NAACP to launch a bitter attack upon Booker T. Washington and Tuskegee.

My first job was to get *The Crisis* going; and arriving in August, I got the first copy off the press in November 1910. It came at the psychological moment and its success was phenomenal. From the 1,000 which I first ventured to publish, it went up a thousand a month until by 1918 (due, of course, to special circumstances), we published and sold over 100,000 copies.

With this organ of propaganda and defense we were able to organize one of the most effective assaults of liberalism upon reaction that the modern world has seen. The NAACP secured extraordinary helpers; great lawyers like Moorfield Storey and Louis Marshall; earnest liberals like Villard, John Milholland, John Haynes Holmes, Jane Addams, and the Spingarns; Socialists like Mary W. Ovington, Charles Edward Russell and William English Walling.

We gained a series of court victories before the highest courts of the land which perhaps never have been equaled, beginning with the recognition of the validity of the 15th Amendment and the overthrow of the vicious Grandfather Clauses in 1915; and the breaking of the legal backbone of housing segregation in 1917. Above all, we could, through *The Crisis* and our officers, our secretaries and friends, place consistently and continuously before the country a clear-cut statement of the legitimate aims of the American Negro and the facts concerning his condition. We tried to organize his political power and make it felt, and we started a campaign against lynching and mob law which was the most effective ever organized, and at long last seemed to bring the end of the evil in sight.

With these efforts came other activities. I lectured widely in nearly every state in the Union. I furnished information to people everywhere on all sorts of subjects closely and remotely connected with race problems, and carried on from time to time studies and investigations. I was held more responsible for the success of the NAACP than I cared to confess to myself, than most other people wanted to admit. I had to spread myself over a whole field of activities when I would have done great deal better work if I could have confined myself to writing and study.

The development of *The Crisis,* where most of my writing was done, was interesting and difficult. It was impaired first and last by lack of trained business management. For the most part I was my own business manager which meant the loss of much time in details. Then there was the delicate matter of policy; of how far I should express my own ideas and reactions in *The Crisis* or the studied judgment of the organization. From first to last I thought strongly, and as I still think rightly, to make the opinion expressed in *The Crisis* a personal opinion; because as I argued, no organization can express definite and clear-cut opinions; so far as this organization comes to conclusions it states them in its annual resolutions; but *The Crisis* states openly the opinion of its editor so long as that opinion is in general agreement with that of the organization.

This of course was a dangerous and delicate matter bound eventually to break down in case there was any considerable divergence of opinion between the organization and the editor. It was perhaps rather unusual that for two decades the two lines of thinking ran so largely together. If on the other hand *The Crisis* had not been in a sense a personal organ and the expression of myself, it could not possibly have attained its popularity and effectiveness. It would have been the dry kind of organ that so many societies support for purposes of reference and not for reading. It took on the part of the organization, a great deal of patience and faith to allow me the latitude that they did for so many years; and on the other hand I was enabled to lay down for the NAACP a clear, strong and distinct body of doctrine that could not have been stated by majority vote. It was probably inevitable that in the end a distinct and clear-cut difference of opinion on majority policies should lead to the dissolution of this interesting partnership.

One of the first difficulties that the Association met was the case of its attitude toward Mr. Washington. I carefully tried to avoid any exaggeration of our differences of thought; but to discuss the Negro question in 1910 was to discuss Booker T. Washington and almost before we were conscious of the inevitable trends we were challenged from Europe. Mr. Washington was in Europe in 1910 and made some speeches in England in his usual conciliatory lines. John Milholland, who had been so influential in the organization of the Association with paid employees and an office, wrote me that American Negroes must combat the idea that they were satisfied with conditions. I therefore wrote an appeal to England and Europe.

"If Mr. Booker T. Washington, or any other person, is giving the impression abroad that the Negro problem in America is in process of satisfactory solution, he is giving an impression which is not true. We say this without personal bitterness toward Mr. Washington. He is a distinguished American and has a perfect right to his opinions. But we are compelled to point out that Mr. Washington's large financial responsibilities have made him dependent on the rich charitable public and that, for this reason, he has for years been compelled to tell, not the whole truth, but that part of it which certain powerful interests in America wish to appear as the whole truth. In flat contradiction, however, to the pleasant pictures thus pointed out, let us not forget that the consensus of opinion among eminent European scholars who know the race problem in America from De Tocqueville down to Von Halle, De Laveleys, Archer and Johnston, is that it forms the gravest of American problems. We black men who live and suffer under present conditions, and who have no reason, and refuse to accept reasons, for silence, can substantiate this unanimous testimony."

In furtherance of this statement and in anticipation of the meeting of the Races Congress in 1911, Mr. Milholland arranged that I should go early to the conference and make some addresses. The plan simmered down to a proposed address before the Lyceum Club, the leading woman's group of London. There it ran against the opposition of an American woman who wrote: "I think there is serious objection to entertaining Dr. Du Bois at the Lyceum." The result was a rather acrimonious controversy, from which I tried gently to withdraw but was unable to; and finally, led by Her Highness the Ranée of Sarawak and Dr. Etta Sayre, a luncheon was held at the Lyceum Club with a bishop and two countesses, several knights and ladies and with Maurice Hewlett and Sir Harry Johnston.

The Races Congress in 1911 would have marked an epoch in the racial history of the world if it had not been for the World War. Felix Adler and I were made secretaries of the American section of the Congress in London. It was a great and inspiring occasion bringing together representatives of numerous ethnic and cultural groups and bringing new and frank conceptions of scientific bases of racial and social relations of people. I had a chance twice to address the Congress in the great hall of the University of London and to write one of the two poems which greeted the assembly.

Returning to the United States I was plunged into the "Bull Moose" campaign. I thought I saw a splendid chance for a third party movement on a broad platform of votes for Negroes and industrial democracy. Sitting in the office of *The Crisis* I wrote out a proposed plank for the Progressives to adopt at their Chicago meeting: "The Progressive party recognizes that distinctions of race or class in political life have no place in a democracy. Especially does the party realize that a group of 10,000,000 people who have in a generation changed from a slave to a free labor system, reestablished family life, accumulated $1,000,000,000 of real property, including 20,000,000 acres of land, and reduced their illiteracy from 80 to 30 percent, deserve and must have justice, opportunity and a voice in their own government. The party, therefore, demands for the American of Negro descent the repeal of unfair discriminatory laws and the right to vote on the same terms on which other citizens vote."

This was taken to Chicago by Joel V. Spingarn and advocated by two other directors of the Association, Dr. Henry Moskowitz and Jane Addams. They worked in vain for its adoption. Theodore Roosevelt would have none of it. He told Mr. Spingarn frankly that he should be "careful of that man Du Bois," who was in Roosevelt's opinion a "dangerous" person. The "Bull Moose" convention refused to seat most of the colored delegates and finally succeeded in making Woodrow Wilson President of the United States.

Bishop Alexander Walters and myself conceived the idea that Mr. Wilson might be approachable. I proposed to throw the weight of *The Crisis* against Roosevelt and Taft and for Wilson, and Bishop Walters went to see him. He secured from Woodrow Wilson a categorical expression over his signature "of his earnest wish to see justice done the colored people in every matter; and not mere grudging justice, but justice executed with liberality and cordial good feeling. I want to assure them that should I become President of the United States they may count upon me for absolute fair dealing, for everything by which I could assist in advancing the interests of their race in the United States."

In this effort to divide the Negro vote which was successful to an unusual degree, we were cruelly disappointed when the Democratic party won and the next Congress met. There was the greatest flood of discriminatory bills both in Congress and among the States that has probably ever been introduced since the Civil War. Only united and determined effort defeated bills against intermarriage and for other discriminations in eight States; and while most of the proposed legislation in Congress was kept from the statute books, the administration carried out a segregation by color in the various departments which we had to fight for years and vestiges of which remain even today.

In other respects our lines were cast in difficult places. The Socialists began to consider the color line and to discriminate against the membership of colored people in the South, lest whites should not be attracted. Mr. Villard tried to get the President to appoint a National Race Commission to be privately financed to the extent of $50,000, but nothing was done. Suddenly war and revolution struck the world: the Chinese Revolution in 1912; the Balkan War in 1912-13; and finally, in 1914, the World War.

In that very year the National Council of Social Agencies

met in Memphis without daring to discuss the color question, but Spingarn and I went down and held open meetings
advertising "for all who dared hear the truth." We had an
interesting time. This success and the death of Booker T.
Washington in 1915 led to the first Amenia conference later
that year which tried to unite the American Negro in one
program of advance.

Finally the World War touched America; with it and in
anticipation of it, came a sudden increase of lynching, including the horrible burning alive of a Negro at Dyersburg;
there came renewed efforts at segregation; the whole extraordinary difficulties of the draft and the question of Negro
officers. We offered our service to fight. What happened?
Most Americans have forgotten the extraordinary series of
events which worked the feelings of black America to fever
heat.

First was the refusal to accept Negro volunteers for the
army except in the four black regiments already established.
While the nation was combing the country for volunteers
for the regular army it would not let the American Negro
furnish even his proportionate quota of regular soldiers.
This led to some grim bantering among Negroes:

"Why do you want to volunteer?" asked many. "Why
should you fight for this country?"

Before we had a chance to reply to this there came the
army draft bill and the proposal by Senator Vardaman and
his ilk to exempt Negroes. We protested to Washington in
various ways and while we were insisting that colored men
should be drafted just as other citizens, the bill went through
with two little "jokers."

First, it provided that Negroes should be drafted but
trained in "separate" units and, secondly, it somewhat am-
biguously permitted men to be drafted for "labor."

A wave of fear and unrest spread among Negroes; and
while we were looking askance at both these provisions suddenly we received the draft registration blank. It directed
persons "of African descent" to "tear off the corner!" Prob-

ably never before in the history of the United States has a portion of the citizens been so openly and crassly discriminated against by action of the general government. It was disheartening and on top of it came the celebrated "German plots." It was alleged in various parts of the country with singular unanimity that Germans were working among the Negroes and it was further intimated that this would make the Negroes too dangerous an element to trust with guns. To us, of course, it looked as though the discovery and the proposition came from the same thinly veiled sources.

Considering carefully these series of happenings the American Negro sensed an approaching crisis and faced a puzzling dilemma. Here was evidently being prepared fertile ground for the spread of disloyalty and resentment among the black masses as they were forced to choose apparently between forced labor or a "jim-crow" draft. Manifestly when a minority group is thus segregated and forced out of the nation they can in reason do but one thing—take advantage of the disadvantage. In this case we asked for colored officers for the colored troops.

General Wood was early approached and asked to admit suitable candidates to the Plattsburg Officers Camp. He refused. We thereupon pressed the government for a "separate" camp for the training of Negro officers. Not only did the War Department hesitate at this request but strong opposition arose among the colored people themselves. They said this really was going too far. "We will obey the law but to ask for voluntary segregation is to insult ourselves." But strong, sober second thought came to rescue. We said to our protesting brothers: "We face a condition, not a theory. There is not the slightest chance of our being admitted to white camps, therefore, it is either a case of a 'jim-crow' officers training camp or no colored officers. Of the two things, no colored officers would be the greatest calamity."

Thus we gradually made up our minds. But the War Department still hesitated. It was besieged and when it presented its final argument, "We have no place for such a camp," the trustees of Howard University said: "Take our campus." Eventually 1,200 colored cadets were assembled at Fort Des Moines for training.

The city of Des Moines promptly protested but it finally changed its mind. The city never before had seen such a class of colored men. They rapidly became popular with many classes and encomiums were passed upon their conduct. Especially was the money they spent popular with merchants. Their commanding colonel pronounced their work first class and declared that they presented excellent material for officers.

Meantime, with one accord, the thought of the colored people turned toward Colonel Young, their highest officer in the regular army. Charles Young was an heroic figure. He was the typical soldier—silent, uncomplaining, brave and efficient. From his days at West Point throughout his 28 years of service he had taken whatever task was assigned him and performed it efficiently, and there is no doubt but that the army had been almost merciless in the requirements which it had put upon this splendid officer. He had been segregated, discriminated against and insulted. He came through everything with flying colors. In Haiti, Liberia, in Western camps, in the Sequoia forests of California, and finally with Pershing in Mexico—in every case he triumphed. Just at the time we were looking to the government to call him to head the colored officers training at Des Moines, he was retired from the army because of "high blood pressure!" There is no disputing army surgeons and their judgment in this case may have been justified, but coming at the time it did, every Negro in the United States believed that the "high blood pressure" that retired Colonel Young was in the prejudiced heads of the southern army oligarchy who were determined that no Negro should ever wear the star of a general.

To say that Negroes of the United States were disheartened at the retirement of Colonel Young is to put it mildly; but there was more trouble. The provision that Negro troops must be trained separately looked simple and was simple in places where there were large Negro contingents; but in the

North with solitary Negroes drafted here and there we had some extraordinary developments. Regiments appeared with one Negro and he had to be separated like a pest and put in a house or even a village by himself, while the commander frantically telegraphed to Washington. Small wonder that one poor black fellow in Ohio solved the problem by cutting his throat. The whole process of drafting Negroes had to be held up until the government could find methods and places for assembling them.

On the top of this came Houston. In a moment the nation forgot the whole record of one of the most celebrated regiments in the U.S. Army and their splendid service in the Indian Wars and in the Philippines. It was the first regiment mobilized in the Spanish American War and it was the regiment that volunteered to a man to clean up the yellow fever camps when others hesitated. It was one of the regiments to which Pershing said:

"Men, I am authorized by Congress to tell you all that our people back in the States are mighty glad and proud at the way the soldiers have conducted themselves while in Mexico, and I, General Pershing, can say with pride that a finer body of men never stood under the flag of our nation than we find here tonight."

The nation also forgot the deep resentment mixed with the pale ghost of fear which Negro soldiers call up in the breasts of the white South. It is not so much that they fear the Negro will strike if he gets a chance, but rather that they assume with curious unanimity that he has *reason* to strike; that any other person in his circumstances or treated as he is would rebel. Instead of seeking to relieve the cause of such a possible feeling, most of them strain every effort to bottle up the black man's resentment. Is it inconceivable that now and then it bursts all bounds?

So, in the midst of this mental turmoil came Houston and East St. Louis, in 1917. At Houston, black soldiers, goaded and insulted, suddenly went wild and "shot up" the town. At East St. Louis, white strikers on war work killed and mobbed Negro workingmen. And this is the result:

Houston	East St. Louis
Offense	*Offense*
17 white persons killed	125 Negroes killed
Punishment	*Punishment*
19 colored soldiers hanged	9 white men imprisoned 5-15
51 colored soldiers imprisoned	years
for life	11 white men imprisoned 1
40 colored soldiers imprisoned	year
	18 white men fined
	10 colored men imprisoned 14
	years

My career had at this time a certain sense of drama. I had never before seen Theodore Roosevelt but in November 1918 I presided at a meeting in Carnegie Hall where he made his last public speech, appearing together with Irwin Cobb and a representative of the French High Commission. I remember my introduction: "I have the honor to present Theodore Roosevelt." Then on my 50th birthday there was a public celebration and many kindly messages. *The Crisis* had reached a monthly circulation of 68,000 and during the year I had a little dinner with Glendowen Evans, Margaret DeLand and William James; and Albert Bushnell Hart wrote the words: "Out of his fifty years of life I have followed a good thirty—and have counted him always among the ablest and keenest of our teacher-scholars, an American who viewed his country broadly."

The most important work of the decade as I now look back upon it was my travel. Before 1918 I had made three trips to Europe; but now between 1918 and 1928 I made four trips of extraordinary meaning: to France directly after the close of the war and during the Congress of Versailles; to England, Belgium, France and Geneva in the earliest days of the League of Nations; to Spain, Portugal and Africa in 1923 and 1924; and to Germany, Russia, and Constantinople in 1926. I could scarcely have encompassed a more vital part of the modern world picture than in those stirring journeys. They gave me a depth of knowledge and a breadth of view which was of incalculable value for realizing and judging modern conditions, and above all the problem of race in America.

But this was only part of my work. In the United States I was still fighting the battle of liberalism against race prejudice; trying to adjust war and postwar problems to the questions of racial justice; trying to show from the injustices of war time what the new vision must encompass; fighting mobs and lynchings; encouraging Negro migration; helping woman suffrage; encouraging the new rush of young blacks to college; watching and explaining the political situation and traveling and lecturing over thousands of miles and in hundreds of centers.

In addition to this I was encouraging the writing of others and trying to help develop Negro art and literature. Besides editing *The Crisis* continuously, I published *Darkwater* in 1920; *The Gift of Black Folk* in 1924; and the essay on Georgia in *These United States* in 1924. This Georgia fought bitterly to keep from appearing. Ernest Gruening, now senator from Alaska, who edited the series, accepted it. I also wrote the concluding chapter in *The New Negro* edited by Alain Locke in 1925, besides a number of magazine articles. Most of the young writers who began what was called the renaissance of Negro literature in the 20's saw their first publication in *The Crisis* magazine.

Above all in these days I made two efforts toward which I look back with infinite satisfaction: the two-year attempt in the *Brownie's Book* to furnish a little magazine for Negro children in which my efforts were ably seconded by Augustus Dill and Jessie Fauset; and most especially my single-handed production of the pageant "The Star of Ethiopia." The pageant was an attempt to put into dramatic form for the benefit of large masses of people, a history of the Negro race. It was first attempted in the New York celebration of Emancipation in 1913; it was repeated with magnificent and breath-taking success in Washington with 1,200 participants; it was given again in Philadelphia in 1916; and in Los Angeles in 1924. Finally I attempted a little theatre movement which went far enough to secure for our little group second prize in an international competition in New York.

When President Wilson was planning to attend the Congress of Versailles, I wrote him a letter, saying:

"The International Peace Congress that is to decide whether or not peoples shall have the right to dispose of themselves will find in its midst delegates from a nation which champions the principle of the 'consent of the governed' and 'government by representation.' That nation is our own, and includes in itself more than twelve million souls whose consent to be governed is never asked. They have no members in the legislatures of states where they are in the majority, and not a single representative in the national Congress."

In 1918 I was asked rather suddenly by the NAACP to go to Europe right after the Armistice, to investigate the treatment of Negro soldiers and keep the record straight; and then at the behest of a group of American Negroes I considered that the interests of Africa ought to be represented during the peace efforts following the war. With infinite difficulty and through the cooperation of Blaise Diagne, the French Deputy from Senegal, I succeeded in gathering in February 1919, at the Grand Hotel in Paris, a Pan-African Congress of 57 delegates including 16 American Negroes, 20 West Indians and 12 Africans. France, Belgium and Portugal were represented by officials. This was to my mind but a beginning and in 1921 I returned and held a Second Pan-African Congress in London, Brussels and Paris from August 28 to September 6. There were 113 accredited delegates from 26 different groups, including 35 from the United States, 39 from Africa and the rest from the West Indies and Europe. Among the speakers were Sir Sidney, afterward Lord Olivier; Florence Kelley, Bishop Hurst, Paul Otlet, often called the father of the League of Nations; Senator La Fontaine of Belgium, Dr. Vitellian, former physician to Menelik of Abyssinia; General Sorelas, Blaise Diagne, Norman Laya, and others.

The attention which the congress evoked all over Europe

was astonishing. It was discussed in the London *Times,
Observer* and *Daily Graphic;* in the Paris *Petit Parisian,
Matin* and *Tempe;* in the *Manchester Guardian* and in practically all the daily papers of Belgium. It led to heated debate in Brussels touching the rights of these delegates to
discuss the relation of colonies, and it emphasized in the
minds of all of us the consequent importance of such discussions.

Two of us visited the League of Nations and the International Labor Office with petitions and suggestions. In
1923 a Third Pan-African Congress, less broadly representative than the second, but nevertheless of some importance,
was held in London, Paris and Lisbon; and thence I went
to Africa and for the first time saw the homeland of the
black race.

It was the time when the United States had disappointed
Liberia by not granting her a promised loan, and a gesture
of goodwill was in order. At the suggestion of William H.
Lewis, Assistant Attorney-General in Washington, I was
therefore designated by cable as special minister plenipotentiary and envoy extraordinary to represent President
Coolidge at the inauguration of President King. In the presence of the diplomatic and consular representatives of England, France, Germany, Spain, Belgium, Holland and
Panama of whom I was Dean, I had the honor to tell the
President of Liberia: "Your Excellency: . . . I am sure
that in this special mark of the President's favor, he has had
in mind the wishes and hopes of Negro Americans. He
knows how proud they are of the hundred years of independence which you have maintained by force of arms and
brawn and brain upon the edge of this mighty continent; he
knows that in the great battle against color caste in America
the ability of Negroes to rule in Africa has been and ever
will be a great and encouraging reinforcement."

At the London meeting of the Third Pan-African Congress, Harold Laski, H. G. Wells, and Sir Sidney Olivier
spoke. Ramsay MacDonald had promised to speak to us but
was hindered by the sudden opening of the campaign which

eventually made him prime minister of England. Among other efforts, at this time we held conferences with members of the Labour Party of England at which Mrs. Sidney Webb, Mr. John Robert Clynes and others were present. We emphasized the importance of labor solidarity between white and black labor in England, America and elsewhere. They were not particularly impressed. In Portugal our meeting was attended by cabinet ministers and deputies and though small was of great interest.

To return again to the fight in the United States, there arose early in this decade the case of Marcus Garvey. I heard of him first when I was in Jamaica in 1915 when he sent a letter "presenting his compliments" and giving me "a hearty welcome to Jamaica, on the part of the United Improvement and Conservation Association." Later he came to the United States. In his case, as in the case of others, I have repeatedly been accused of enmity and jealousy, which have been so far from my thought that the accusations have been a rather bitter experience.

In 1920 when his movement was beginning to grow in America I said in *The Crisis* that he was "an extraordinary leader of men" and declared that he had "with singular success capitalized and made vocal the great and long suffering grievances and spirit of protest among the West Indian peasantry." On the other hand, I noted his difficulties of temperament and training, inability to get on with his fellow workers, and denied categorically that I had ever interfered in any way with his work. Later when he began to collect money for his steamship line I characterized him as a sincere and hard-working idealist but called his methods bombastic, wasteful, illogical and almost illegal and begged his friends not to allow him foolishly to overwhelm with bankruptcy and disaster one of the most interesting spiritual movements of the modern world.

But he went ahead, wasted his money, got into trouble with the authorities and was deported. As I said at the time: "When Garvey was sent to Atlanta, no word or action of ours accomplished the result. His release and deportation were a matter of law which no deed or wish of ours influenced in the slightest degree. We have today, no enmity against Marcus Garvey. He has a great and worthy dream. We wish him well. He is free; he has a following; he still has a chance to carry on his work in his own home and among his own people and to accomplish some of his ideas. Let him do it. We will be the first to applaud any success that he may have."

I felt for a moment as the war progressed that I could be without reservation a patriotic American. The government was making sincere efforts to meet our demands. It had commissioned over 700 Negro officers; I had had a personal interview with Newton Baker, Secretary of War, and he had made categorical promises; Wilson had spoken out against lynching; and I myself had been offered a captaincy in the Intelligence Service, afterwards, to be sure, rather incontinently withdrawn as the higher command realized just who I was. Nevertheless, I tried to stand by the country and wrote the widely discussed editorial "Close Ranks" in which I said to the Negroes: "Forget your grievances for the moment and stand by your country."

I am not sure that I was right but certainly my intentions were. I did not believe in war, but I thought that in a fight with America against militarism and for democracy we would be fighting for the emancipation of the Negro race. With the Armistice came disillusion. I saw the mud and dirt of the trenches; I heard from the mouths of soldiers the kind of treatment that black men got in the American army; I was convinced and said that American white officers fought more valiantly against Negroes within our ranks than they did against the Germans. I still believe this was largely true. I collected some astonishing documents of systematic slander and attack upon Negroes and demands upon the French for insulting attitudes toward them, and when I published these documents in America the government started to interfere by refusing *The Crisis* mailing facilities; then, realizing that this was an admission of guilt, they quickly withdrew their prohibition.

I was especially upset by the mobs and lynchings during this time: by that extraordinary upheaval wherein for several hours black men fighting against a mob practically held the city of Washington in their hands; then the riot and murder in Chicago.[13] We fought back through the NAACP, the columns of *The Crisis,* through lectures and articles, with every force at hand. Mary Talbert started the Anti-Lynching Crusaders and with her help and that of our secretary, James Weldon Johnson, we raised a defense fund of $70,000 and put the Dyer Lynch Bill through the House of Representatives and on to the floor of the Senate. It was not until years after that I knew what killed that anti-lynching bill. It was a bargain between the South and the West by which lynching was permitted on condition that the Japanese were excluded.

Court cases kept pressing upon us: there were the Elaine riots and the Arkansas cases; there was the Sweet case in Detroit;[14] and equally significant to my mind but to few other Negroes the Sacco-Vanzetti case in Massachusetts. We continued winning court victories and yet somehow, despite them, we did not seem to be getting very far. We added to the Grandfather Case of 1915 and the Segregation Case of 1917, the victories in the Arkansas cases, the white primary case and another segregation case in the high courts, in addition to the eventual freeing of Dr. Sweet and his family. Still injustice prevailed. In the case of the Mississippi flood, the Red Cross allowed the Negroes to be treated as slaves and peons, and in Oklahoma, the Episcopal church refused to prosecute a white murderer on its own school grounds. Above all there came disquieting situations among Negro students: a strike at Hampton, disturbed conditions at Wilberforce, turmoil at Howard, and an uprising at Fisk.

It was thus a decade of infinite effort and discouraging turmoil. I suppose it had to be. I suppose that with the best will, it would have been impossible for me to concentrate on a few great lines of creative effort. I had to be a part of the revolution through which the world was going and to feel in my own soul the scars of its battles. Two events made a sort of finale to the decade: the Fourth Pan-African Congress held in New York in 1927 with Dantes Bellegarde, George Vylvain and other speakers; and the Congress of British West Africa which began its meetings in 1920 and forced the British government to the greatest step toward democratic method ever taken up to that time in black colonies.

Finally, to my surprise and quite against my best judgment, there was given for me upon my return from Africa at the Cafe Savarin in New York, a dinner. Among the speakers were Heywood Broun, Walter Hampden and Mrs. Mary McCleod Bethune, and tributes were sent by Witter Bynner, Zona Gale and Eugene O'Neill. It was a very beautiful and touching tribute.

CHAPTER XVI

MY CHARACTER

When I was a young man, we talked much of character. At Fisk University character was discussed and emphasized more than scholarship. I knew what was meant and agreed that the sort of person a man was would in the long run prove more important for the world than what he knew or how logically he could think. It is typical of our time that insistence on character today in the country has almost ceased. Freud and others have stressed the unconscious factors of our personality so that today we do not advise youth about their development of character; we watch and count their actions with almost helpless disassociation from thought of advice.

Nevertheless, from that older generation which formed my youth I still retain an interest in what men are rather than what they do; and at the age of 50, I began to take stock of myself and ask what I really was as a person. Of course I knew that self-examination is not a true unbiased picture; but on the other hand without it no picture is quite complete.

From childhood I tried to be honest; I did not mean to take anything which did not belong to me. I told the truth even when there was no call for the telling and when silence would have been golden. I did not usually speak in malice but often blurted out the truth when the story was incomplete and was therefore as seemed to me wrong. I had strict ideas about money and its earning. I worked and worked hard for the first 25 cents a week which I earned. I could never induce myself to gamble or take silly chances because I figured the loss vividly in fatigue and pain. Once on a French train I played the pea in a shell game and lost two dollars. Forty years later in Mexico I won two dollars on a horse race. These were my first and last games of chance.

I was careful about debt. My folk were poor but seldom

in debt. I have before me a statement of my indebtedness, September 1, 1894, when I started on my first life job. My salary was $800 a year and my living expense I calculated at: Board $100; Room $35; Clothes $65; Books $100; Debts $350; Sundries $25—Total $675; Savings $125. This proved too optimistic but still I kept out of debt. When I taught at Atlanta at a salary of $1,200 a year for 12 years, I owed nobody. I had a wife and child and each year I took them somewhere north so as to give them fresh air and civilization. It took every cent of my salary, together with small fees from lectures and writing, to pay our way and yet only once was I compelled to overdraw my salary for a month ahead.

Saving I neglected. I had had no experience in saving. My mother's family with whom I lived as a child never had a bank account nor insurance; and seldom a spare dollar. I took out a small life insurance of $1,000 when I was 27. I was cheated unmercifully by the white Pennsylvania company in the fee charged because I was colored. Later after marriage I took out $10,000 of insurance in a Negro company, the Standard Life. Eventually the company went bankrupt and I lost every cent. I was then too old to obtain more insurance on terms which I could afford.

My income has always been low. During my 23 years with the NAACP, I received for the first five years $2,500 a year. For the next 18 years, $5,000. With savings from this I bought a home and then sold it later for an apartment building in Harlem. There were five apartments, one of which my family was to occupy and the others I calculated would pay me a permanent income. But the house was overpriced; neglected orders for expensive sewer repairs were overdue. The down payment which I could afford was low and the property was overloaded with three mortgages on which I had to pay bonuses for renewal. Downtown banks began to squeeze black Harlem property holders and taxes increased. With the depression, tenants could not pay or moved.

There was one recourse: to turn the property into a rooming house for prostitution and gambling. I gave it to the owners of the mortgages and shouldered the loss of all my savings at 60 years of age. In all this I had followed the advice of a friend skilled in the handling of real estate but who assumed that I was trying to make money and not dreaming of model housing conditions. As many of my friends have since informed me, I was a fool; but I was not a thief which I count to my credit.

I returned to Atlanta University in 1934 at a salary of $4,500 a year but still out of debt. When ten years later I was retired without notice, I had no insurance and but small savings. A white classmate, grandson of a railway magnate, berated me for not wishing to give up work. He could not conceive of a man working for 50 years without saving enough to live on the rest of his days. In money matters I was surely negligent and ignorant; but that was not because I was gambling, drinking or carousing; it was because I spent my income in making myself and my family comfortable instead of "saving for a rainy day." I may have been wrong, but I am not sure of that.

On one aspect of my life, I look back upon with mixed feelings; and that is on matters of friendship and sex. I couple them designedly because I think they belong together. I have always had more friends among women than among men. This began with the close companionship I had with my mother. Friends used to praise me for my attention to my mother; we always went out together arm in arm and had our few indoor amusements together. This seemed quite normal to me; my mother was lame, why should I not guide her steps? And who knew better about my thoughts and ambitions? Later in my life among my own colored people the women began to have more education, while the men imitated an American culture which I did not share: I drank no alcoholic beverages until I went to Germany and there I drank light beer and Rhine wine. Most of the American men I knew drank whiskey and frequented saloons which from my boyhood were out of bounds.

Indeed the chief blame which I lay on my New England schooling was the inexcusable ignorance of sex which I had when I went south to Fisk at 17. I was precipitated into a region, with loose sex morals among black and white, while I actually did not know the physical difference between men and women. At first my fellows jeered in disbelief and then became sorry and made many offers to guide my abysmal ignorance. This built for me inexcusable and startling temptations. It began to turn one of the most beautiful of earth's experiences into a thing of temptation and horror. I fought and feared amid what should have been a climax of true living. I avoided women about whom anybody gossiped and as I tried to solve the contradiction of virginity and motherhood, I was inevitably faced with the other contradiction of prostitution and adultery. In my hometown sex was deliberately excluded from talk and if possible from thought. In public school there were no sexual indulgences of which I ever heard. We talked of girls, looked at their legs, and there was rare kissing of a most unsatisfactory sort. We teased about sweethearts, but quite innocently. When I went South, my fellow students being much older and reared in a region of loose sexual customs regarded me as liar or freak when I asserted my innocence. I liked girls and sought their company, but my wildest exploits were kissing them.

Then, as teacher in the rural districts of East Tennessee, I was literally raped by the unhappy wife who was my landlady. From that time through my college course at Harvard and my study in Europe, I went through a desperately recurring fight to keep the sex instinct in control. A brief trial with prostitution in Paris affronted my sense of decency. I lived more or less regularly with a shop girl in Berlin, but was ashamed. Then when I returned home to teach, I was faced with the connivance of certain fellow teachers at adultery with their wives. I was literally frightened into marriage before I was able to support a family. I married a girl whose rare beauty and excellent household training from her dead mother attracted and held me.

I married at 29 and we lived together for 53 years. It was not an absolutely ideal union, but it was happier than most, so far as I could perceive. It suffered from the fundamental drawback of modern American marriage: a difference in aim and function between its partners; my wife and children were incidents of my main life work. I was not neglectful of my family; I furnished a good home. I educated the child and planned vacations and recreation. But my main work was out in the world and not at home. That work out there my wife appreciated but was too busy to share because of cooking, marketing, sweeping and cleaning and the endless demands of children. This she did naturally without complaint until our firstborn died—died not out of neglect but because of a city's careless sewage. His death tore our lives in two. I threw myself more completely into my work, while most reason for living left the soul of my wife. Another child, a girl, came later, but my wife never forgave God for the unhealable wound.

As I wandered across the world to wider and higher goals, I sensed two complaints against the pairing of the sexes in modern life: one, that ties between human beings are usually assumed to be sexual if a man and woman are concerned; and two, that normal friendships between men and women could not exist without sex being assumed to be the main ingredient. Also, if a man and woman are friends, they must be married and their friendship may become a cloying intimacy, often lasting 24 hours a day, with few outside friends of the opposite sex on pain of gossip, scandal and even crime engulfing the family. My travel and work away from home saved us from this. One difficulty of married life we faced as many others must have. My wife's life-long training as a virgin, made it almost impossible for her ever to regard sexual intercourse as not fundamentally indecent. It took careful restraint on my part not to make her unhappy at this most beautiful of human experiences. This was no easy task for a normal and lusty young man.

Most of my friends and helpers have been women; from my mother, aunts and cousins, to my fellow teachers, students, secretaries, and dreamers toward a better world. Sex indulgence was never the cause or aim of these friendships. I do not think my women friends ever gave my wife harm or unease. I was thoughtful of her comfort and support and of her treatment in public and private. My absence from home so much helped in the household drudgery. I still make my own bed of mornings; for many years I prepared my own breakfast, especially my coffee; I always leave a bathroom cleaner than when I enter; but sewing and sweeping I neglect. I have often wondered if her limitation to a few women friends and they chiefly housekeepers; and if her lack of contact with men, because of her conventional upbringing and her surroundings—if this did not make her life unnecessarily narrow and confined. My life on the other hand threw me widely with women of brains and great effort to work on the widest scale. I am endlessly grateful for these contacts.

My first married life lasted over half a century, and its ending was normal and sad, with the loneliness which is always the price of death. To fill this great gap, and let my work go on, I married again near the end of my days. She was a woman 40 years my junior but her work and aim in life had been close to mine because her father had long believed in what I was trying to do. The faith of Shirley Graham in me was therefore inherited and received as a joy and not merely as a duty. She has made these days rich and rewarding.

In the midst of my career there burst on me a new and undreamed of aspect of sex. A young man, long my disciple and student, then my co-helper and successor to part of my work, was suddenly arrested for molesting men in public places. I had before that time no conception of homosexuality. I had never understood the tragedy of an Oscar Wilde. I dismissed my co-worker forthwith, and spent heavy days regretting my act.

I knew far too few of my contemporaries. I was on occasion incomprehensibly shy, and almost invariably loath to interrupt others in seeking to explain myself. This in the case of my fellow Negroes was balanced by our common experiences and shared knowledge of what each other had lived through; but in the case of white companions, and especially those newly met, we could not talk together, we lived in different worlds. We belonged to no social clubs, and did not visit the same people or even stand at the same liquor bars. We did not lunch together. I did not play cards, and could never get wildly enthusiastic even over baseball. Naturally we could not share stories of sex.

Thus I did not seek white acquaintances, I let them make the advances, and they therefore thought me arrogant. In a sense I was, but after all I was in fact rather desperately hanging on to my self-respect. I was not fighting to dominate others; I was fighting against my own degradation. I wanted to meet my fellows as an equal; they offered or seemed to offer only a status of inferiority and submission.

I did not for the most part meet my great contemporaries. Doubtless this was largely my own fault. I did not seek them. I deliberately refused invitations to spend weekends with Henry James and H. G. Wells. I did not follow up an offer of the wife of Havelock Ellis to meet him and Bernard Shaw. Later, when I tried to call on Shaw he was coy. Several times I could have met Presidents of the United States and did not. Great statesmen, writers and artists of America, I might have met, and in some cases, might have known intimately. I did not try to accomplish this. This was partly because of my fear that color caste would interfere with our meeting and understanding; if not with the persons themselves, certainly with their friends. But even beyond this, I was not what Americans called a "good fellow."

This too illustrates a certain lack of sympathy and understanding which I had for my students. I was for instance a good teacher. I stimulated inquiry and accuracy. I met every question honestly and never dodged an earnest doubt. I read my examination papers carefully and marked them with sedulous care. But I did not know my students as human beings; they were to me apt to be intellects and not souls. To the world in general I was nearly always the isolated outsider looking in and seldom part of that inner life. Partly that role was thrust upon me because of the color of my skin. But I was not a prig. I was a lusty man with all normal appetites. I loved "Wine, Women and Song." I worked hard and slept soundly; and if, as many said, I was hard to know, it was that with all my belligerency I was in reality unreasonably shy.

One thing I avoided, and that was envy. I tried to give the other fellow his due even when I disliked him personally and disagreed with him logically. It became to me a point of honor never to refuse appreciation to one who had earned it, no matter who he was. I loved living, physically as well as spiritually. I could not waste my time on baseball but I could appreciate a home run. My own exercise was walking, but there again I walked alone. I knew life and death. The passing of my first-born boy was an experience from which I never quite recovered. I wrote:

"The world loved him; the women kissed his curls, the men looked gravely into his wonderful eyes, and the children hovered and fluttered about him. I can see him now, changing like the sky from sparkling laughter to darkening frowns, and then to wondering thoughtfulness as he watched the world. He knew no color-line, poor dear—and the veil, though it shadowed him, had not yet darkened half his sun. He loved the white matron, he loved his black nurse; and in his little world walked souls alone, uncolored and unclothed. I—yea, all men—are larger and purer by the infinite breadth of that one little life. She who in simple clearness of vision sees beyond the stars said when he had flown—'He will be happy There; he ever loved beautiful things.' And I, far more ignorant, and blind by the web of my own weaving, sit alone winding words and muttering, 'If still he be, and he be There, and there be a There, let him be happy, O Fate!'

"Blithe was the morning of his burial, with bird and song and sweet-smelling flowers. The trees whispered to the grass, but the children sat with hushed faces. And yet it seemed a ghostly unreal day—the wraith of Life. We seemed to rumble down an unknown street behind a little white bundle of posies, with the shadow of a song in our ears. The busy city dinned about us; they did not say much, those pale-

faced hurrying men and women; they did not say much—
they only glanced and said 'Niggers.' "

My religious development has been slow and uncertain. I
grew up in a liberal Congregational Sunday School and
listened once a week to a sermon on doing good as a reasonable duty. Theology played a minor part and our teachers
had to face some searching questions. At 17 I was in a
missionary college where religious orthodoxy was stressed;
but I was more developed to meet it with argument, which I
did. My "morals" were sound, even a bit puritanic, but
when a hidebound old deacon inveighed against dancing I
rebelled. By the time of graduation I was still a "believer"
in orthodox religion, but had strong questions which were
encouraged at Harvard. In Germany I became a freethinker
and when I came to teach at an orthodox Methodist Negro
school I was soon regarded with suspicion, especially when
I refused to lead the students in public prayer. When I became head of a department at Atlanta, the engagement was
held up because again I balked at leading in prayer, but the
liberal president let me substitute the Episcopal prayer
book on most occasions. Later I improvised prayers on my
own. Finally I faced a crisis: I was using Crapsey's *Religion
and Politics* as a Sunday School text. When Crapsey was
hauled up for heresy, I refused further to teach Sunday
School. When Archdeacon Henry Phillips, my last rector,
died, I flatly refused again to join any church or sign any
church creed. From my 30th year on I have increasingly
regarded the church as an institution which defended such
evils as slavery, color caste, exploitation of labor and war.
I think the greatest gift of the Soviet Union to modern civilization was the dethronement of the clergy and the refusal
to let religion be taught in the public schools.

Religion helped and hindered my artistic sense. I know
the old English and German hymns by heart. I loved their
music but ignored their silly words with studied inattention.
Great music came at last in the religious oratorios which we
learned at Fisk University but it burst on me in Berlin with

the Ninth Symphony and its Hymn of Joy. I worshipped Cathedral and ceremony which I saw in Europe but I knew what I was looking at when in New York a Cardinal became a strike-breaker and the Church of Christ fought the Communism of Christianity.

I revered life. I have never killed a bird nor shot a rabbit. I never liked fishing and always let others kill even the chickens which I ate. Nearly all my schoolmates in the South carried pistols. I never owned one. I could never conceive myself killing a human being. But in 1906 I rushed back from Alabama to Atlanta where my wife and six-year old child were living. A mob had raged for days killing Negroes. I bought a Winchester double-barreled shotgun and two dozen rounds of shells filled with buckshot. If a white mob had stepped on the campus where I lived I would without hesitation have sprayed their guts over the grass. They did not come. They went to south Atlanta where the police let them steal and kill. My gun was fired but once and then by error into a row of *Congressional Records,* which lined the lower shelf of my library.

My attitude toward current problems arose from my long habit of keeping in touch with world affairs by repeated trips to Europe and other parts of the world. I became internationally-minded during my four years at Harvard, two in college and two in the graduate school. Since that first trip in 1892, I have made 15 trips to Europe, one of which circled the globe. I have been in most European countries and traveled in Asia, Africa and the West Indies. Travel became a habit and knowledge of current thought in modern countries was always a part of my study, since before the First World War when the best of American newspapers took but small account of what Europe was thinking.

I can remember meeting in London in 1911 a colored man who explained to me his plan of leading a black army out of Africa and across the Pyrenees. I was thrilled at his earnestness! But gradually all that disappeared, and I began building a new picture of human progress.

This picture was made more real in 1926 when it became

possible for me to take a trip to Russia. I saw on this trip not only Russia, but prostrate Germany, which I had not seen for 30 years. It was a terrible contrast.

By 1945 all these contacts with foreign peoples and foreign problems and the combination of these problems with the race problem here was forced into one line of thought by the Second World War. This strengthened my growing conviction that the first step toward settling the world's problems was Peace on Earth.

Many men have judged me, favorably and harshly. But the verdict of two I cherish. One knew me in mid-life for 50 years and was without doubt my closest friend. John Hope wrote me in 1918:

"Until the last minute I have been hoping that I would have an opportunity to be with you next Monday when you celebrate the rounding out of 50 years in this turbulent but attractive world. But now I am absolutely certain that I cannot come, so I am writing Mr. Shillady expressing my regret and shall have to content myself with telling you in this letter how glad I am that your 50th birthday is going to be such a happy one because you can look back on so much good work done. But not the good work alone. What you may look upon with greatest comfort is good intention. The fact that every step of the way you have purposed to be a man and to serve other people rather than yourself must be a tremendous comfort to you. Sometime soon if I chance to be back in New York I am going to have you take your deferred birthday dinner with *me*. You do not realize how much that hour or two which we usually spend together when I am in New York means to me."

Joel Spingarn said:

"I should like to have given public expression by my presence and by my words, not merely to the sense of personal friendship which has bound us together for 15 years, but to the gratitude which in common with all other Americans I feel we owe you for your public service. It so happens that by an accident of fate, you have been in the forefront of the great American battle, not merely for justice to a single race, but against the universal prejudice which is in danger of clouding the whole American tradition of toleration and human equality.

"I congratulate you on your public service, and I congratulate you also on the power of language by which you have made it effective. I know that some people think that an artist is a man who has nothing to say and who writes in order to prove it. The great writers of the world have not so conceived their task, and neither have you. Though your service has been for the most part the noble one of teacher and prophet (not merely to one race or nation but to the world), I challenge the artists of America to show more beautiful passages than some of those in *Darkwater* and *The Souls of Black Folk*."

Let one incident illustrate the paradox of my life.

Robert Morse Lovett was perhaps the closest white student friend I made at Harvard; when not long before his last visit to New York about 1950 he wanted to see and talk with me, he proposed the Harvard Club of which he was a member. I was not. No Negro graduate of Harvard was ever elected to membership in a Harvard club. For a while Jews were excluded, but no longer. I swallowed my pride and met Lovett at the Club. A few months later he died.

CHAPTER XVII

THE DEPRESSION

From 1910 to 1920, I had followed sociology as the path to social reform and social uplift as a result of scientific investigation; then, in practice, I had conceived an interracial culture as superseding our goal of a purely American culture. Before I had conceived a program for this path, and after throes of bitter racial strife, I had emerged with a program of Pan-Africanism, as organized protection of the Negro world led by American Negroes. But American Negroes were not interested.

Abruptly, I had a beam of new light. Karl Marx was scarcely mentioned at Harvard and entirely unknown at Fisk. At Berlin, he was a living influence, but chiefly in the modification of his theories then dominant in the Social Democratic party. I was attracted by the rise of this party and attended its meetings. I began to consider myself a Socialist. After my work in Atlanta and my advent in New York, I followed some of my white colleagues—Charles Edward Russell, Mary Ovington, and William English Walling —into the Socialist party. I resigned when I regarded a vote for Wilson better for Negroes than a vote for Theodore Roosevelt, Taft or an unknown Socialist. Then came war, the Russian Revolution and the fight of England, France and the United States against the Bolsheviks. I began to read Karl Marx. I was astounded and wondered what other areas of learning had been roped off from my mind in the days of my "broad" education. I did not, however, jump to the conclusion that the new Russia had achieved the ideal of Marx. And when I was offered a chance to visit Russia in 1926, with expenses paid, I carefully stipulated in writing that the visit would not bind me in any way to set conclusions.

My visit to Germany and the Soviet Union in 1926 and then to Turkey and Italy on return, brought change in my thought and action. The marks of war were all over Russia —of the war of France and England to turn back the clock of revolution. Wild children were in the sewers of Moscow; food was scarce, clothes were in rags, and the fear of renewed Western aggression hung like a pall. Yet Russia was and still is to my mind the most hopeful land in the modern world. Never before had I seen so many among a suppressed mass of poor, working people—people as ignorant, poor, superstitious and cowed as my own American Negroes—so lifted in hope and starry-eyed with new determination, as the peasants and workers of Russia, from Leningrad and Moscow to Gorki and from Kiev to Odessa. The art galleries were jammed, the theatres crowded, the schools opening in new places and with new programs each day; and work was beginning to be a joy. Their whole life was being renewed and filled with vigor and ideal, as Youth Day in the Red Square proclaimed.

I saw of course but little of Russia in one short month. I came to no conclusions as to whether the particular form of the Russian state was permanent or a passing phase. I met but few of their greater leaders; only Radek did I know fairly well, and he was imprisoned during the subsequent purge. I do not judge Russia in the matter of war and murder, no more than I judge France and England. But of one thing I am certain: I believe in the dictum of Karl Marx, that the economic foundation of a nation is widely decisive for its politics, its art and its culture. I saw clearly, when I left Russia, that our American Negro belief that the right to vote would give us work and decent wage; would abolish our illiteracy and decrease our sickness and crime; and that poverty was not our fault but our misfortune, the result and aim of our segregation and color caste; that the solution of letting a few of our capitalists share with whites in the exploitation of our masses, would never be a solution of our problem, but the forging of eternal chains, as India may learn to its sorrow.

I did not believe that the communism of the Russians was the program for America; least of all for a minority group like the Negroes; I saw that the program of the American Communist party was inadequate for our plight. But I did believe that a people where the differentiation in classes because of wealth had only begun, could be so guided by intelligent leaders that they would develop into a consumer-conscious people, producing for use and not primarily for profit and working into the surrounding industrial organization so as to reinforce the economic revolution bound to develop in the United States and all over Europe and Asia sooner or later. I believed that revolution in the production and distribution of wealth could be a slow, reasoned development and not necessarily a bloodbath. I believed that 13 millions of people, increasing albeit slowly in intelligence, could so concentrate their thought and action on the abolition of their poverty, as to work in conjunction with the most intelligent body of American thought; and that in the future as in the past, out of the mass of American Negroes would arise a far-seeing leadership in lines of economic reform.

The Pan-African congresses which I called in 1919, 1921, and 1923, were chiefly memorable for the excitement and opposition which they caused among the colonial imperialists. Scarcely a prominent newspaper in Europe but used them as a text of warning, and persisted in coupling them with the demagogic "Garvey Movement," then in its prime, as a warning for colonial governments to clamp down on colonial unrest. My only important action in this time, was a first trip to Africa, almost by accident, and a vaster conception of the role of black men in the future of civilization.

But here I was going too fast for the NAACP. The board was not interested in Africa. Following postwar reaction it shrank back to its narrowest program: to make Negroes American citizens, forgetting that if the white European world persisted in upholding and strengthening the color bar, America would follow in its wake.

If it had not been for the depression, I think that through *The Crisis*, the little monthly which I had founded in 1910 and carried on with almost no financial assistance for over

20 years, I could have started this program on the way to adoption by American Negroes. But the depression made the survival of *The Crisis* dependent on help from the main office of the NAACP. This changed my whole conception of *The Crisis* as an independent organ leading a liberal organization toward radical reform. It was this sting in *The Crisis* which for 23 years had made it what it was. But the Board was still mainly conservative; it represented largely capital and investment, and only to a small degree labor and socialism. If the Association had to pay for *The Crisis* it would have a right to determine its policy, not only in broad outline but in every detail. The financial relations of *The Crisis* and the NAACP were unusual. I was responsible for the cost of publishing the magazine. The NAACP at first paid all my $2,500 salary. After two years *The Crisis* paid half and after four years all the salary; but the NAACP always determined its amount. I was responsible for all the other expenses—manufacture, distribution, salaries of all the clerks and employees, and finally our share of the rent. We could incur no debts nor accumulate a backlog.

At first we had no bank account but when Walter Sachs became treasurer he let me set up a *Crisis* Fund and we drew our own checks. But we could solicit no gifts nor organize any group of *Crisis* Associates to help support us in need. The NAACP originally promised to meet any deficit we might incur up to $50 a month, but we never called on it for a cent. At times, as for instance when I went abroad for the Second Pan-African Congress, the NAACP ordered my business manager to pay $700 from the *Crisis* Fund toward my expenses.

I made no complaint on this situation. After all, the NAACP was the object of *The Crisis*. It was never a profit-making institution. We could get few advertisements because we were classed as a propaganda organ. I was helped enormously in business matters by Robert Wood, the first Negro Tammany politician, who was also a printer contractor and gave me unselfish advice in buying paper and securing printers. For 23 years we paid our way. We left no debts and made the NAACP a universally known organization. But when the depression came we had nothing to fall back on and had to hand over control to the NAACP which legally owned *The Crisis*. It was suggested to me that I claim at least part ownership and try to run it as a personal organ. This I refused to consider although I do not doubt but that a good lawyer might have made a case. But my attitude was that *The Crisis* belonged to the NAACP and that its future value depended on how the NAACP upheld its high ideals.

However, there was one circumstance which worried me and that was the change of secretaries which took place in 1931. James Weldon Johnson had resigned and Walter White had succeeded him, and was destined to head the organization for 25 years. I knew Walter White. I knew his father and mother; I taught in college his brother and sisters. When in 1917, James Weldon Johnson, our field secretary met White in Atlanta, he suggested to me that White would make a good assistant secretary. I readily concurred and urged his appointment.

White could be one of the most charming of men. He was small in stature, appealing in approach, with a ready smile and a sense of humor. Also he was an indefatigable worker, who seemed never to tire. On the other hand, he was one of the most selfish men I ever knew. He was absolutely self-centered and egotistical to the point that he was almost unconscious of it. He seemed really to believe that his personal interests and the interest of his race and organization were identical. This led to curious complications, because to attain his objects he was often absolutely unscrupulous.

As assistant to James Weldon Johnson who became secretary in 1920, White was an outstanding success. He investigated lynchings at great personal risk; and especially, he carried out the plans which Johnson laid down. It was Johnson's strong point to consult widely and decide carefully. White then took over and put the plans to work. For 12 years this team worked harmoniously and well. Then Johnson was invited to the Pacific to study race relations and given a fellowship by the Rosenwald Fund. White ran the

Association during his absence. After Johnson's return he came to me and said that White was not cooperating as usual. At the conference in Cleveland, White had simply done almost no work; Johnson intimated that he would have to resign if he lost the cooperation of his executive helper. I think that White had already concluded that he should be secretary instead of working under Johnson. Nothing more was said, but in 1931 Johnson resigned and went to Fisk University. Walter White was elected to succeed him.

White's assumption of office was to set off an explosion within a year. His attitude and actions were unbearable. The whole staff appealed to me as the senior executive officer to lead a protest to the Board of Directors. As editor of *The Crisis,* this was not in my line of duty; but on the other hand as one of the incorporators of the Association and a member of the Board of Directors, I could not shirk this appeal. I wrote a protest and all the staff signed it including the new assistant, Roy Wilkins; and all the older members, William Pickens, Robert Bagnall, and others. It was a strong and biting arraignment but all accepted it and signed it.

The Board was deeply moved and while it did not attempt to deny the charges, thought the protest was too strong and not quite fair. They asked us to withdraw our signatures and promised to investigate the situation. White abased himself before the Board and made every promise of reform. Nearly all the signers, at the urgent request of Joel Spingarn, President of the Board, withdrew their names. But I refused. I did not trust Walter White. The matter was dropped and was not heard of afterwards. But White radically changed his attitude toward the staff. He became pleasant and approachable. Above all he went to work. He worked hard and went underground to accomplish many of his aims. Any employee who opposed him soon lost his job; but White never appeared as the cause. Everyone who signed the protest except Wilkins, lost his position and Wilkins yielded to White in every request. White increased his prestige, and under his administration the Association grew in membership and influence.

It was evident by 1932 that *The Crisis* could survive only if the Association helped support it. As such, *The Crisis* would become the traditional "organ" of an organization. Moreover, White was increasingly raising the funds which helped keep the NAACP alive. This would soon impose an impossible position for me and a difficult one for White.

I think I may say without boasting that in the period from 1910 to 1930 I was a main factor in revolutionizing the attitude of the American Negro toward caste. My stinging hammer blows made Negroes aware of themselves, confident of their possibilities and determined in self-assertion. So much so that today common slogans among the Negro people are taken bodily from the words of my mouth.

But, of course, no idea is perfect and forever valid. Always to be living and apposite and timely, it must be modified and adapted to changing facts. I began to realize that the heights and fastnesses which we black folk were assailing, could not in America be gained by sheer force of assault, because of our relatively small numbers. They could only be gained as the majority of Americans were persuaded of the rightness of our cause and joined with us in demanding our recognition as full citizens. This process must deal not only with conscious rational action, but with irrational and unconscious habit, long buried in folkways and custom. Intelligent propaganda, legal enactment, and reasoned action must attack the conditioned reflexes of race hate and change them.

Slowly but surely I came to see that for many years, perhaps many generations, we could not count on any such majority; that the whole set of the white world in America, in Europe, and in the world was too determinedly against racial equality, to give power and persuasiveness to our agitation.

Therefore, I began to emphasize and restate certain implicit aspects of my former ideas. I tried to say to the American Negro: during the time of this frontal attack which you are making upon American and European prejudice, and with your unwavering statement and restatement of what is right and just, not only for us, but in the long run for all men; during this time, there are certain things you must do for your own survival and self-preservation. You must work together and in unison; you must evolve and support your own social institutions; you must transform your attack from the foray of self-assertive individuals to the massed might of an organized body. You must put behind your demands, not simply American Negroes, but West Indians and Africans, and all the colored races of the world.

These things I began to say with no lessening, or thought of lessening, of my emphasis upon the essential rightness of what we had been asking for a generation in political and civic and social equality. It was clear to me that agitation against race prejudice and a planned economy for bettering the economic condition of the American Negro were not antagonistic ideals but part of one ideal; that it did not increase segregation; the segregation was there and would remain for many years. But now I proposed that in economic lines, just as in lines of literature and religion, unified racial action should be planned and organized and carefully thought through. This plan would not establish a new segregation; it did not advocate segregation as the final solution of the race problem; exactly the contrary; but it did face the facts and faced them with thoughtfully mapped effort.

The NAACP from the beginning faced this bogey. It was not, never had been, and never could be an organization that took an absolute stand against race segregation of any sort under all circumstances. This would be a stupid stand in the face of clear and incontrovertible facts. When the NAACP was formed, the great mass of Negro children were being trained in Negro schools; the great mass of Negro church-goers were members of Negro churches; the great mass of Negro citizens lived in Negro neighborhoods; the great mass of Negro voters voted with the same political party; and the mass of Negroes joined with Negroes and cooperated with Negroes in order to fight the extension of this segregation and to move toward better conditions.

What was true in 1910 was still true in 1940 and will be true in 1970. But with this vast difference: that the segregated Negro institutions are better organized, more intelligently planned and more efficiently conducted, and today form in themselves the best and most compelling argument for the ultimate abolition of the color line.

It was a curious dilemma still unsolved for most American Negroes: the NAACP said, "No discrimination based on race and color." But it did not say nor even contemplate what path Negroes would follow when they once became Americans who suffered no discrimination. I tried to face the problem of what to do, assuming that discrimination would last through our lifetime.

The legal department of the NAACP sought to attack discrimination head on. They were beginning to win and in 1954, they won. But this posed another dilemma: the court decision was not enforced and will not be for many years. Meantime what should be our program? We must accept and fight for integrated schools which we do not have in the overwhelming portion of the South where most Negroes live. That leaves the battle to our children and lets them learn nothing in school of Negro history; do nothing for Negro culture, have no program for themselves as Americans. I wavered for years, advocating socialism first as a racial program; then as a national effort and after this trip of 1958 as a definite and direct step to join the world movement toward a socialism leading toward communism, and embracing the colored world and that part of the white world willing to give up colonialism and private capitalism. But as I say, this decision was slow in making. Meantime, I was fighting segregation but simultaneously advocating such segregation as would prepare my people for the struggle they were making.

No sooner had I come to this conclusion than I saw that I was out of touch with my organization and that the question of leaving it was only a matter of time, especially as

The Crisis was no longer self-supporting. This was not an easy decision; to give up *The Crisis* was like giving up a child; to leave the Association was leaving the friends of a quarter of a century. But on the other hand, staying meant silence, a repudiation of what I was thinking and planning. Under such circumstances, what could I do? I had seen the modern world as few of my fellow workers had; West African villages, Jamaican homes, Russian communism, German disaster, Italian fascism, Portuguese and Spanish life, France and England repeatedly, and every State in the United States. I knew something of the seething world. I could seek through my editorship of *The Crisis* slowly but certainly to change the ideology of the NAACP and of the Negro race into a racial program for economic salvation along the paths of peace and socialism.

When now I came advocating new, deliberate, and purposeful segregation for economic defense in precisely the lines of business and industry whither the NAACP was not prepared to follow, it was not an absolute difference of principle, but it was a grave difference as to further procedure. When I criticized the secretary for his unsound explanation of the historic stand of the NAACP on segregation, the Board of Directors voted May 21, 1934, "that *The Crisis* is the organ of the Association and no salaried officer of the Association shall criticize the policy, work, or officers of the Association in the pages of *The Crisis.*"

Thereupon I forthwith gave up my connection with the Association, saying:

"In 35 years of public service my contribution to the settlement of the Negro problems has been mainly candid criticism based on a careful effort to know the facts. I have not always been right, but I have been sincere, and I am unwilling at this late day to be limited in the expression of my honest opinions in the way in which the Board proposes. . . . I am, therefore, resigning . . . this resignation to take effect immediately."

The Board refused to accept this resignation and asked me to reconsider. I did so, but finally wrote, June 26, "I appreciate the good will and genuine desire to bridge an awkward break which your action indicated, and yet it is clear to me, and I think to the majority of the Board, that under the circumstances my resignation must stand." Negotiations followed but there was but one possible decision.

In finally accepting my resignation the Board was kind enough to say in part: "He founded *The Crisis* without a cent of capital, and for many years made it completely self-supporting, reaching a maximum monthly circulation at the end of the World War of 100,000. This is an unprecedented achievement in American journalism, and in itself worthy of a distinguished tribute. But the ideas which he propounded in it and in his books and essays transformed the Negro world as well as a large portion of the liberal white world, so that the whole problem of the relation of black and white races has ever since had a completely new orientation. He created, what never existed before, a Negro intelligentsia, and many who have never read a word of his writings are his spiritual disciples and descendants. Without him the Association could never have been what it was and is.

"The Board has not always seen eye to eye with him in regard to various matters, and cannot subscribe to some of his criticism of the Association and its officials. But such differences in the past have in no way interfered with his usefulness, but rather on the contrary. For he had been selected because of his independence of judgment, his fearlessness in expressing his convictions, and his acute and wide-reaching intelligence. A mere yes-man could not have attracted the attention of the world, could not even have stimulated the Board itself to further study of various important problems. We shall be the poorer for his loss, in intellectual stimulus, and in searching analysis of the vital problems of the American Negro; no one in the Association can fill his place with the same intellectual grasp. We therefore offer him our sincere thanks for the services he has rendered, and we wish him all happiness in all that he may now undertake."

I had already for some years begun to canvass the possibility of a change of work. This, of course, is not easy when a person is over 60 years of age. If he has not had the grace to die before this, he ought, in accordance with prevalent public opinion, at least be willing to stop acting and thinking. I did not agree with that. I thought of many possibilities, but at last determined to accept an offer that had been made to me quietly in 1929, and periodically repeated from time to time when John Hope of Atlanta came to town. Every American should read the story of John Hope as told by Ridgely Torrence.[15] He was "colored"—a white man with Negro blood and American Negro culture. We had been close friends since 1897. We taught together until 1910. Hope had joined the Niagara Movement and the NAACP. We met in France in 1918 while he was a YMCA secretary, and I promoting Pan-Africa. Always when he came to New York, we did a theatre and a dinner, and discussed the reformation of the world. When he became president of the newly organized Atlanta University, he invited me to join him.

About 1925, the General Education Board adopted a new program. It had become clear that the studied neglect of the Negro college was going too far; and that the Hampton-Tuskegee program was inadequate even for its own objects. A plan was adopted which envisaged, by consolidation and endowment, the establishment in the South of five centers of university education for Negroes. Atlanta had to be one of these centers, and in 1929 Atlanta University became the graduate school of an affiliated system of colleges which promised a new era in higher education for Negroes. My life-long friend, John Hope, became president, and immediately began to sound me out on returning to Atlanta to help him in his great enterprise. He promised me leisure for thought and writing, and freedom of expression, so far, of course, as Georgia would permit it.

It seemed to me that a return to Atlanta would not only have a certain poetic justification, but would relieve the NAACP from financial burden during the depression, as well as free it for greater efforts of reconsidering its essential program. I went to Atlanta in 1933 for a series of lectures and the next year became head of the Department of Sociology.

The untimely death of John Hope in 1936 marred the full fruition of our plans. These plans in my mind fell into three categories; first, with leisure to write, I wanted to fill in the background of certain historical studies concerning the Negro race; secondly, I wanted to establish at Atlanta University a scholarly journal of comment and research on world race problems; finally, I wanted to restore in some form at Atlanta, the systematic study of the Negro problem.

The first thing which hindered this program was the set opposition of Florence Read, President of Spelman College, the institution for women in the newly integrated Atlanta University. Laura Spelman was a Rockefeller and the Rockefellers had endowed this school. Miss Read was a white woman. She was not a scholar but she was a capable executive who had worked for the Rockefellers and represented the Rockefeller interests in the new organization. She believed completely in American business methods and was put in her position by those who wanted to placate the white South in every reasonable way and keep the new institution from radical influences. She was very fond personally of John Hope at a time when he needed friendship. She respected me but feared my radical thought in many directions. She was set to act as a balance wheel to Hope's plans for accommodation and my plans for social reform.

She delayed the invitation for me to join the university and when I came, delayed some of my proposals. I proposed a quarterly magazine to record the situation of the colored world and guide its course of development. Her opposition delayed the starting of *Phylon* from 1934 until 1940. She made the re-opening of the Atlanta University studies of the Negro problems much slower than I had hoped and she made my opportunity to confer and plan with Hope very difficult. Indeed I fear that the very pressure exerted on him from two of his closest friends depressed Hope very much and contributed to his untimely death. Hope was sensitive and overcareful to do no injustice. He was the perfect target for overwork at Atlanta University.

Between 1935 and 1940, I wrote and published three volumes: a study of the Negro in Reconstruction; a study of the black race in history and an autobiographical sketch of my concept of the American race problem. To these I was anxious to add an Encyclopedia of the Negro. I had planned an "Encyclopedia Africana" in 1909 but my leaving Atlanta for New York postponed this project and the World War prevented its renewal. In 1934 I was chosen to act as editor-in-chief of a new project of the Phelps-Stokes Fund to prepare and publish an Encyclopedia of the Negro. I spent nearly ten years of intermittent effort on this project and secured cooperation from many scholars, white and black, in America, Europe and Africa. But the necessary funds could not be secured. Perhaps again it was too soon to expect large aid for so ambitious a project directed by Negroes and built mainly on Negro scholarship. Nevertheless, a preliminary volume summarizing this effort was published in 1945.

John Hope died in 1936 and after a year Rufus Clement became his successor. Clement was head of a colored municipal college in Louisville and while not experienced, came of a good family and had done some work in research for his doctorate. I greatly preferred him over Miss Read who was an active candidate. On his advent I immediately began pushing for my delayed program.

At Atlanta University I celebrated quite elaborately my 70th anniversary. There was a bronze bust by Alexander Portnoff; J. E. Spingarn and James Weldon Johnson spoke; W. S. Braithwaite read a poem written for the occasion. I succeeded in getting *Phylon* published in 1940. I kept it going for the four years that I remained at the university with a subvention of only $1,000 a year from the university. We sold it for only a dollar a year. I then began to push the reestablishment of my plan of study of the Negro problems.

In this we faced the fact that in the 23 years which had

passed since their discontinuance, the scientific study of the American Negro had spread widely and efficiently. Especially in the white institutions of the South had intelligent interest been aroused. There was, however, still need of systematic, comprehensive study and measurement, bringing to bear the indispensable point of view and inner knowledge of Negroes themselves. Something of this was being done at Fisk University, but for the widest efficiency, large funds were required for a South-wide study. I made a beginning in 1941.

The story of the depression as it affected American Negroes, has not yet been adequately attempted. In many great centers of population more than a third of the Negroes went on public charity and more ought to have gone but suffered deliberate discrimination in the South. In addition to this, the greater tragedy was the loss of thousands of farms and homes, the disappearance of savings among the rising Negro middle class, the collapse of Negro business—banks, insurance, and retail businesses. The economic change deserves to be called revolutionary, because this "middle" class was the upper class in the Negro world in knowledge, training and wealth. Organizations demanded the displacement of the Negro in industry, and the Ku Klux Klan rose and flourished with new life, largely on this issue. The new organizations of "White Shirts," "Blue Shirts," and the like, spread in the South; and beyond such organized demand, was the widespread feeling in America that in the matter of reemployment and readjustment after the depression, the first duty of white Americans was toward white folk and that consideration of long service and desert and need ought not to be taken into account across the color line.

Under the New Deal the Negro came in for some attention, but the pressing question was chiefly as to how far discrimination against him should be recognized either in wages, hours of work, or employment under any circumstances. Also starting with the New Deal came a rationalization of the displacement of the Negro worker due to efforts toward raising wages. When minimum wages and standards of work have been enforced by law or made advisable by public opinion, in numberless cases poorly paid Negro workers are replaced by white workers with better wages and better hours of work. The resultant natural increase in efficiency has often been attributed to racial replacement alone. In the labor movement, the organization of the CIO gave Negroes far better recognition than the American Federation of Labor ever had. Despite all this, unemployment among Negroes reached a dangerous height.

This worked for social dislocation among Negroes. It is difficult to get figures, but certainly spread of disease must have greatly retarded the Negro population; and stealing and homicide must have been largely augmented. A general philosophy arose tinged with irritation and despair. Pressure groups demanding employment and even threatening violence appeared in Chicago, New York and Washington. Their success both encouraged and appalled.

A rough calculation of Negro incomes which I essayed in 1939 had to be largely guesswork because of lack of data; and yet it seemed to indicate that of over 2,800,000 Negro families in the United States, 1,200,000 were receiving less than $500 a year and 1,000,000 between $500 and $1,000; leaving 600,000 families with $1,000 or more a year, of whom only one-tenth received more than $2,500. This estimate is not exactly accurate, but I believe that it is not an unfair indication of the truth. Housing and youth projects have helped Negroes greatly, but only indirectly have they faced the basic problem of employment and income.

The years of the depression and of the New Deal illustrated the complicated currents which influenced me. I was, for example, born in a world which was not simply fundamentally capitalistic, but had no conception of any system except one in which capital was privately owned. Whatever was mentioned in school or in books did not fundamentally contradict that what a man made or received as gift or inheritance was his to do with as he wished. A wages contract might be entered into in which the laborer's work was balanced against the savings of the man who hired him.

I remember hearing my grandmother in sharp and angry argument with a white landowner, for whose father she had worked. She was insisting that the wages paid had not been fair, and he was retorting that the fact that they had been received without complaint at the time, settled the matter. The truth concerning the wages contract remained largely hidden from me, because I had so little actual contact with artisans and workers. I never saw the inside of the cotton mills in our town. I knew little of the actual work of carpenters and plumbers. My relatives had moved from farming to house service, or to work in hotels, and not in factories.

In high school and college, socialism meant to me some amelioration of the wages contract, more human relations between employer and employee, but it involved no fundamental study of Marxism. What I wanted was the same economic opportunities that white Americans had. Beyond this I was not thinking, and did not realize what wretched exploitation white Americans and white workers of all sorts faced and had faced in the past, and would face in years to come. Although a student of social progress, I did not know the labor development in the United States. I was bitter at lynching, but not moved by the treatment of white miners in Colorado or Montana. I never sang the songs of Joe Hill, and the terrible strike at Lawrence, Massachusetts, did not stir me, because I knew that factory strikers like these would not let a Negro work beside them or live in the same town. It was hard for me to outgrow this mental isolation, and to see that the plight of the white workers was fundamentally the same as that of the black, even if the white worker helped enslave the black.

When now the depression came and thousands of workers, black and white, were starving in the 30's, I began to awake and to see in the socialism of the New Deal, emancipation for all workers, and the labor problem, which included the Negro problem. I knew that Hitler and Mussolini were fighting communism, and using race prejudice to make some white people rich and all colored peoples poor. But it was not until later that I realized that the colonialism of Great

Britain and France had exactly the same object and methods as the fascists and the Nazis were trying clearly to use.

While going through this transformation, I found myself fighting for such projects as the Tennessee Valley Authority, and also opposing Roosevelt because in his industrial organization he deliberately provided lower wages for Southern Negro workers. I even brought myself to sympathize with Roosevelt when he strove to use American wealth to save the British Empire, not realizing that the British Empire had been built on the same exploitation of land and labor and race hate which Hitler and Mussolini were planning to establish, so that they could rule the world. I blamed the Communists when I thought that their agitation made the ignorant Scottsboro boys suffer for the sins of others, and failed to give those same Communists credit for making the Scottsboro case known to the civilized world. It was not until I saw the miracle of modern China that I realized how splendidly and surely the world could be led by the working class; even if at times they wavered and made vast mistakes.

The advent of the Second World War found the Negro fighting desperately for a place in the new defense industry and accomplishing something; but in the long run that is a passing and minor matter as compared with the general economic future when the world is again sane and at peace, and when the world's whole pattern of income, work, and wage will be found radically altered.

There loomed, then, before colored men of education and vision the question as to what can be done by thought and planning for the future of Negro economy, for solving the question as to how the Negro is going to earn a decent living and be in position to take a normal part in the future world. If economic planning for nations presents great difficulties, similar planning for national minorities is unusually hazardous. It faces all the difficulties of racial segregation, of artificial loyalties and increased animosities; so that among Negroes today there is serious difference of opinion, first as to whether any such economic planning is possible; and secondly, whether it is in any way advisable. Can a group within a group plan for its work and wage except as a part of a larger group and in accordance with the will of the majority? And even if it can, is not this a direct and dangerous way of increasing racial friction?

Whatever the answer to this question was, manifestly it was a time for careful conference and thought. Several such conferences had been held, notably at Hampton Institute, Fisk University, and elsewhere. But they had been primarily concerned with the integration of the Negro in the defense program. It seemed to me at Atlanta University that a further movement was necessary—that is, a series of conferences looking toward a long-time program of Negro economic stabilization after the war.

CHAPTER XVIII

NEW DEAL FOR NEGROES

John Hope and I set out to build in the lower South a university equal to if not superior to anything which this former seat of Negro slavery ever saw. As in my previous service at Atlanta University, half my time was to be devoted to teaching graduate students. I laid out two or three courses, one of which was on communism. My text was *The Communist Manifesto* and I gathered a good classroom library on socialism and communism, probably at the time the best in the South. I had no thought of propaganda. I was not and never had been a member of the Communist party. But I saw the growth of socialism and believed in the possibility of communism. I was convinced that no course of education could ignore this great world movement. I was reading and learning with the class. I had a dozen or more excellent students, and with lectures, conferences and reports we had a fine course of study. Many of my students in this course received master's degrees and afterward in several cases became teachers in colored and white universities, here and abroad; others became successful social workers. I never heard of any criticism of this course, but it is quite possible that the course eventually stirred up opposition against me.

In 1934 Hope and I set out to revive the old Atlanta University conferences and studies of the Negro problems. Hope sought unsuccessfully to obtain funds for this enterprise. After his death I tried to see if some cooperative plan might supply funds. Frederick Koppell of the Carnegie Foundation gave us money for preliminary work in 1940 and 1941. I called the First Phylon Conference in April 1941. A good cross-section of Negro leaders in education attended. Reports were made from each State on the economic conditions of Negroes. I tried to sum up the current conditions in this statement:

I. a. If 13 million people starve to death, it is because they are stupid.

   b. Many American Negroes today are virtually starving.

II. a. There is no such thing as lack of useful, needed work.

   b. There is wide and dangerous lack of adequate wage and income for certain individuals.

III. a. Facing these paradoxes the world is changing its economic organization today to meet them and is planning further change.

   b. We as a minority group must plan also, not in opposition but in intelligent accord with this general world planning.

IV. a. We must especially beware of propaganda and distortion as to the present economic conditions and changes in the world.

     1. We must not assume that business enterprise and economic welfare are synonymous terms nor assume that because a business is profitable it is for that reason beneficial to the race or nation.

     2. We must not assume that because racial organization cannot hire 13 million Negroes, it cannot and should not hire 13 thousand or more.

     3. Because, as a minority group, we must in the main conform to the national economic patterns, is no proof that we cannot by intelligent action influence these patterns to our advantage.

V. a. Finally, we must get at the facts by the latest scientific technique.

   b. We must gather, study, test, and interpret these facts.

   c. Within limits of law and order we must experiment with and test remedies.

   d. We must remember that the starvation of Negroes in the United States benefits nobody; that full employment at a living wage for all Negroes as well as all whites is at once the greatest patriotism and the greatest defense against war and evil.

Atlanta University did not have funds to undertake any movement for investigation and publication, so I visited Negro institutions from Virginia to Texas in order to see what cooperation I could start.

I became convinced of several things: first, the role of the government-supported land-grant colleges in the development of Negro education was going to be large and progressively increasing. Second, these land-grant colleges needed a program for social science studies which was quite undeveloped. Third, rapid changes were taking place in the Negro ethnic group and even more momentous ones impended. The war had upset conventional economy, exacerbated racial consciousness and already led to bitter clashes. The developments after the war were bound to add to these difficulties. There is one and only one fundamental and definitive way to meet this situation and that is to begin a systematic study of the essential facts of the present condition of the Negro race and to establish a way of continuing and making more complete and effective such a study. Then in the event the nation can turn its attention and energies to remedial measures, it will not be necessary to waste time in belated efforts to get at the essential truth.

Careful and exact knowledge of conditions and changes then are imperative and had to be gathered in order to be available during and after the war. Fourth, this should not be the conventional type of "social study"—an instantaneous photograph of a sample group; but should be planned so as eventually to approach the stature of a total study of a complete situation, continuously photographed, and rephotographed, measured and remeasured; so that our knowledge of the vast and momentous social experiment in race relations now making in the United States, would attain a completeness and authority that would be unquestioned and unquestionable and available in the postwar world which will surely need this sort of information. I believed that here was a chance not only to serve the Negro race and America, but also to serve the world and social science in a unique way.

Fifth, the Negro land-grant colleges, distributed usually one to a State and manned by presidents chosen by boards of Southern whites, would in many respects be ideal centers of social studies in each State, on matters touching the condition in each State of the people for whom the school exists and for whose advancement the school was established. Each of these schools has proclaimed its aim to be the promotion of industry and lifting the social status of Negroes. Any such program needs exact knowledge of facts for its foundation.

Sixth, such studies to be effective must be well done and in accord with the latest scientific technique. They must not sink to mere propaganda or white-washing. Most of the land-grant colleges are not at present equipped with personnel or funds for this work; a few are. All need expert advice and guidance, to integrate, synchronize and direct this work and help in the proper interpretation of its results. Seventh, here is where the Negro private institution of higher learning could well cooperate with the states and call to aid the advice of other universities, North and South.

Three Negro universities seemed best fitted for this work of guidance and integration: Howard, which holds to the Federal government a position analogous to that of the land-grant colleges to the States; Fisk, which has among Negroes the best equipped department of social sciences in the South; Atlanta, where the first attempt was made in America to carry on a scientific study of the Negro problems.

My first step toward realizing this project was to seek to sell the idea to the Negro land-grant colleges. I talked the plan over with President Banks of Prairie View, Texas, who was a former student of mine, who, as I knew, had long had some such collaboration in mind, and who had the best social science department among Negro land-grant colleges. He was enthusiastically in favor. I then secured permission to present the scheme to the annual conference of the presidents of Negro land-grant colleges at Chicago in 1941.

In 1935, the Federal government was giving $18 million annually to land-grant colleges in Southern States which had colleges separated by race. Negroes forming over a fifth of the population of these States received only about five per cent of this money. For some time the Negro colleges had been pressing for a larger share, but the reply had been that such work as research in agriculture or chemistry was being carried on in the white colleges and that it was not necessary to duplicate this work in Negro institutions. It occurred to me that a careful program of race studies planned for the Negro colleges might be the basis for a demand for a much larger Negro share of Federal funds. I therefore addressed the organization of Negro land-grant college presidents. I said:

With a comparatively small group like that of the American Negro, in a country of great economic efficiency like America, and spurred by every high incentive, there is no real reason why cultivated brains among us may not guide the great mass of our folk to desired economic and cultural ends. This, of course, depends on the extent to which these potential leaders have the will to sacrifice their talent to this end; and also on the actual knowledge which they possess to guide the mass toward real progress and not back to out-worn reaction.

The problem before us is this: to put 14 million people to work so that they may receive an income which will insure a civilized standard of living; to make it possible for them to preserve their health; to keep crime down to a minimum and to educate their children; with the eventual object of giving this group sufficient leisure to advance by means of talented persons among them in science and art and cultural patterns. And with the further idea that insofar as these objects are successful, the group will become nearer to actual equality with their fellow Americans and to civilized people the world over, and will thus remove from color prejudice a very real reason for its perpetuation.

How can the college help the community earn a living? First, it can train students for existent needs, for which the community now pays. Sometimes educational philosophers talk as though this were the one end of the college; and a situation could be easily imagined where that might be pretty nearly true; where you have settled normal culture and an arrangement of work which is suitable for that culture; and relatively stable economic organization. Under these circumstances if a college trained men efficiently for these jobs and at the same time supplied a broad cultural outlook toward the future it would come near doing its main work.

The college today, however, must do more—far more—than prepare men for jobs at present in demand and socially needful. The college must anticipate the future needs of the community and prepare education to meet them.

Unless the college goes further than training for current jobs and goes out to meet and cooperate with the community in such a way that the man waiting and prepared to do a necessary future work for the community can be employed now according to his capacity; unless this is done, the college program is fatally handicapped and the community expansion is crippled. The same thing applies to work which although needed is not now available for Negroes and may not be during the present generation. In that case a careful survey of the possibilities among 14 million people might give an opportunity to create such jobs within our own group or by cooperating with others. This even more than the other case, involves a broad study of the economic conditions among Negroes and possibilities of their organizations. It would call not simply for the efforts of one college with its immediate community or its State, but the cooperative efforts of the Negro educational institutions of the South.

This leads us to the fact that if the college is to make real and advantageous approach to its community, either its local or its general community, it must be helped by a careful, broad and continuous study of the social and economic set-up of that community; that is, we must know as we do not know today, the existing occupations of Negroes; not in the vague and general and necessarily inaccurate report of the decennial census, but by minute and complete survey and study of counties, towns and cities, where the Negro population is resident. We must take such a beginning as Charles Johnson's regional study of Southern counties, extend the data to 1940 and then complete it and carry it on continuously from year to year. We must have a group to group and person to person knowledge of the condition of the laboring masses, of their opportunities and hindrances. And this kind of study ought to be made in accordance with the latest scientific techniques and on a national basis. There is no reason why a study like that of Allison Davis' *Deep South* (1941) should not be made over the whole South so that we could paint with descriptions, facts and figures, the real social condition of the American Negro. The interpretation of this knowledge and its interaction with past history and current trends must be the continuously and critically examined conclusions of the best trained students of the social sciences. We must not depend on the narrow experience and conventional standards of business men; we must not resort to untried panaceas or emotional utopias. This study must be increasingly a matter of science, carried out to its inexorable and tested conclusions.

We need in sociology, a race regionalism which will narrow and concentrate on our Negroes the general regional studies of the South. Instead of the occasional snapshot of social conditions which was the social study of yesterday, we must aim at a continuous moving picture of ever increasing range and accuracy.

A national planning institute must annually gather up and compare and interpret this great body of facts. There must be provided for this work, sufficient research funds and sufficient time for research. And finally through a central office, there must be wide and carefully edited publication of results.

It is not only illogical but it is an indictment of the Negro college that the chief studies of the Negro's condition today are not being done by Negroes and Negro colleges. The center of gravity as well as the truth of investigation should be brought back to the control of an association of Negro colleges; and this not for the purpose of creating a Negro science or purely racial facts; but in order to make sure that the whole undistorted picture is there and that the complete interpretation is made by those most competent to do it, through their own lives and training.

Under the leadership of these same colleges, the communities must proceed to act, explore, experiment and build. They must organize their spending power to the last dollar, realizing that a carefully and intelligently spent dollar is a more powerful ballot than a vote for a coroner. Advantage must be taken of decentralized cheap power like the TVA to push a new era of home manufactures and producers' cooperation. The churches can branch into real social work; they might organize free legal defense for every accused Negro; the secret orders can further transform their regalias, rituals and parades into orphanages and student aid. We can have cooperative medicine and dentistry and field hospitals to replace private practice. We have an enormously fertile field for economic experiment, here on the threshold of a new industrial era. All it needs is scientific study, personal character and coordinated intelligence guided by the colleges. It is for the inception and carrying out of this program that I am appealing to you today.

I proposed that this body agree to the following general plan:

1. A continuous and intensive study of the Negroes of each Southern State by each of the Negro land-grant colleges.

2. Preparation for ability to do this scientifically by strengthening the division of social sciences in each institution (history, political science, psychology, anthropology, sociology, economics) and provision of time and funds for study and research.

3. Inauguration of a general program of subjects and methods of research, with annual conferences, at which experts and representatives of other colleges should be present. Periodical integration, interpretation and publication of results.

I suggested the following detailed program for each land-grant college:

1. A division of the "Social Sciences," teaching history, anthropology, sociology, economics, psychology, political sciences.

2. The integration of this teaching into one closely articulated study of:

A. History
   History of Europe
   History of Asia
   History of Africa
   History of America

    History of the United States
    History of the Negro People in:
      Africa
      South and Central America
      United States
      In each State

B. SOCIAL SCIENCES
    Social Institutions (Modern world)
    Anthropology (United States)
    Economic Organization (among Americans)
    Government (among Negroes)
    Psychological Reactions (among Negroes in this State)

3. A study of the facts concerning the Negroes of the State by counties, subdivisions of counties, villages, towns, cities, wards, blocks and households. The study to be carried on by professors, instructors, fellows, social workers, volunteers and affiliated organizations.

The study to include: Number of individuals, family groups, character of homes, location of homes; occupation of persons, incomes, expenditures, age, marital relations, education, property and recreation.

4. The scope of this study will include the observation and measurement of all facts and situations which have to do with the status of the Negro population in the State; becoming, as funds and facilities increase, more and more intensive and comprehensive, until at last it virtually means a checking of every Negro family in the State including their activities, institutions and organizations.

5. The study will use all available data as the basis of its work, including the Federal census of 1940, all State censuses, all reports of the State, the county and its subdivisions, concerning education, occupation, dependency and delinquency.

SPECIAL STUDIES

6. All organizations of Negroes or working with or for Negroes: details of work, including churches, lodges, cemeteries, clubs, etc.; their property and budgets.

7. All business conducted by Negroes and among Negroes; character, amount, approximate money value.

8. Commercialized recreations, movies, billiard rooms, gambling, prostitution, etc.

9. Public recreation: parks, playgrounds, etc., number, upkeep.

10. The participation of Negroes in government as voters and officials; taxpayers, property-holders; officials and administrative methods.

METHODS, INTERPRETATION AND PUBLICATION

11. The methods and scope of these studies to be outlined by an annual conference, with each college represented and outside experts.

12. The resulting studies to be collected, interpreted and made public for an annual state meeting and for a public museum and laboratory of the social sciences with maps, charts, models.

13. All the college reports to be brought together, studied, tabulated, analyzed and interpreted and integrated into an annual joint report.

The Northern Negro

14. Arrangements to be entered into with private Negro institutions to join with departments of the social sciences in Northern colleges to make similar studies of Northern Negroes.

Resultant Body of Knowledge

15. This body of knowledge, continuously added to, checked and reviewed; improved in method and object; tabulated, interpreted, and integrated, to be used as the basis of raising the standard of living and cultural pattern of American Negroes through education, work, law and social action.

Resultant Work for Social Uplift

16. For every social problem, institutional failure, or individual maladjustment made evident, located and measured, organizations will then attempt to discover or promote in the locality and State, remedies in:

Education: special kinds and specific methods; private, industrial, group, State and national efforts.

Social Uplift Work: by hiring thoroughly trained social workers by group effort; by voluntary effort.

Health: by physicians and dentists; by group medical care; by hospitalization; by special campaigns against tuberculosis, cancer, heart diseases, syphilis; by childbirth and child welfare efforts.

Recreation: music, a folk theatre, playgrounds, library facilities, sports.

17. But of all these efforts, the college and community should concentrate their first and chief attention upon the problems of earning a living among Negroes, since these are fundamental to practically all other efforts. Attention should be paid especially to work now available, to openings for earning a living which may be made available, and for general economic reorganization, such as is involved in consumers' and producers' cooperation; whereby not only intelligent saving can be made in the expenditure of income, but that new occupations, especially in home industries and small manufacturers, can be established among Negroes.

18. Every attempt should be made to use existing institutions and organizations among Negroes, for undertaking efforts at social reform as outlined above: churches, fraternal lodges, women's clubs, schools,

and in many cases, private businesses, can be used for increasing employment, finding new employment, furnishing legal defense, furnishing direct relief, improving health, organizing recreation, furnishing student aid and promoting consumers, and producers, cooperation.

19. An immediate attempt on the part of the college in each State to reorganize their budgets so as to provide a gradually increasing minimum of funds for this program:

A. For teaching the social sciences.
B. For giving trained teachers, time and funds for investigation.
C. For providing, at the earliest moment, for the employment of social workers and fellows for investigation and social uplift.
D. For a publication fund.
E. For laying down a present program with plans for future expansion.

20. Minimum requirements for initiating the program:

1. One or two teachers of history.
2. One or two teachers of anthropology and sociology.
3. One teacher of economics.
4. One teacher of psychology, with laboratory.
5. A teaching fellow with some time and funds for field work.
6. A social worker with whole time for investigation and advice.

The presidents of the Negro land-grant colleges received this proposal with favor and adopted this general plan, June 12, 1942:

To initiate a series of cooperative studies of the social condition of the American Negro and more especially of his economic situation during and after this war.

For this purpose they propose to use in their institutions the division of the Social Sciences including, history, anthropology, sociology, economics, political science, psychology, and other cognate subjects so as to give their students unified knowledge of social conditions and modern trends.

In addition to this they propose to recommend the use of one or more of their qualified instructors, with sufficient time and funds for a series of social studies, whose subject, methods and scope shall be determined after conferences with executives and investigators in other institutions, and with outside experts in the social sciences, including students of conditions among the white population. This proposal is subject to the approval of the governing boards in the various states.

The ultimate object of such conferences and studies shall be to accommodate a body of knowledge, intensively pursued according to the best scientific methods, continuously added to, checked and reviewed; improved in method and object; tabulated, interpreted and integrated to be used as the basis of raising the standard of living and cultural pattern of American Negroes through education, work, law, and social action.

We propose that the results of these studies by each college in its own state or section of state, shall be brought together, periodically compared, edited and published annually in some convenient form for the use of students, legislators and social reformers.

For these purposes of conference, investigation and publication we propose to set aside in our annual budget such sums as may be approved by the various state authorities.

This was signed by the presidents of 20 Negro land-grant colleges and eventually by the presidents of Atlanta, Fisk and Howard. Representatives of War Production Board, the American Council of Education, the North Carolina Institute for Research in Social Science commended the plan as did *School and Society* and the *Journal of Higher Education*.

The *Journal of Negro Education* said in an article:

"Briefly, Dr. W. E. B. Du Bois' proposal, agreed upon by the Presidents of the Land-Grant Colleges, assumes first a core of social studies in each of our Negro colleges and graduate schools. It assumes that by internal administrative and staff effort these may be internally unified and coordinated for a joint, continuous attack upon the problem of the study of the Negro population in the area surrounding each college. It assumes that, pouring into a central headquarters, yet to be designated, for review and analysis by a central board, yet to be chosen, there would be a continuous flow of raw data and completed studies. It assumes central coordination, synthesis and report of these studies. It assumes that by this great increase in knowledge, sound and rich and full, we would have materials wholly convincing as to the needs of local, regional, and national Negro populations. It assumes that with this knowledge we could so increase our wisdom as to be able both to make Negro higher education very much better than it is in all aspects and we would have the facts at last on which to base valid requests for support from foundations, individuals, and local, state, and national governments. By knowing what the problems are we could know also how to arrange them in priorities and further, much better than we know now, how to attack them each in turn with some expectation of success.

The plan was finally implemented by this vote of the Conference of Negro Land-Grant College Presidents on October 28, 1942:

1. That Dr. W. E. B. Du Bois be designated the official coordinator of the proposed sociological studies to be instituted by the various land-grant colleges.

2. That each President appoint from his faculty a liaison officer to serve as the agent for continued implementation of the project. This officer to report progress and seek further cooperation from the administration and faculty; preferably, though not necessarily, he should be a social scientist.

3. That each President agree to try to find funds in the college budget to permit attendance of liaison officer at a methodological conference to be called by Dr. Du Bois at a convenient time and place, after appropriate correspondence should have further clarified various issues.

4. That the Executive Committee at this meeting address itself to possible ways and means of further financing said study, conference, or other aspects of the program.

The 26th Atlanta University Conference met at Robert Hall, Morehouse College, Atlanta, April 19 and 20, 1943. It became the first conference of the Negro land-grant colleges, for coordinating a program of cooperative social studies. Among those present were: E. Franklin Frazier, Library of Congress; Charles S. Johnson, Fisk University; Howard W. Odum, University of North Carolina; E. B. Reuter, University of Iowa; T. Lynn Smith, Louisiana State University; Edgar T. Thompson, Duke University; Donald Young, Social Service Research Council. Thirty-four persons attended, representing 30 institutions. The sessions lasted two days and consisted of exhibits, reports, addresses and conferences.

By special invitation, there were present at the conference eight well-known sociologists, from leading American institutions. These persons, after observation and consultation, have written the following opinions on the possibilities of this movement. The names are arranged in order of academic seniority.

HOWARD WASHINGTON ODUM, *Kenan Professor of Sociology, and Director of the Institute for Research in Social Science, University of North Carolina:* "It seems to me that in two or three ways a strong, integrated program for research in the land-grant colleges would constitute an important step forward. In the first place, the area in which they work is still virgin and important, and their laboratories are adequate for genuine research and experimentation. They have a fine opportunity to combine the social studies with the physical sciences and to implement them in practical programs."

EDWARD BYRON REUTER, *Professor of Sociology and Chairman of the Department, College of Commerce, University of Iowa:* "The plan for cooperative studies to be carried on by the Negro land-grant colleges seems to me to be a very wise development and one that may lead to increasingly important results. It will make possible a pooling of resources—of time, staff, and funds—to discover and make known information that now gets too little public notice."

EDWARD FRANKLIN FRAZIER, *Professor of Sociology and Head of Department, Howard University; Consultant in Negro Bibliography, Library of Congress:* "To my mind, the Conference was significant because it represented the broadening and deepening of the stream of a great tradition which owes much to you. Moreover, the Conference was a distinct success in that it brought together and stimulated men and women who have generally been forced to work in isolation. Even if no other conferences were held, I am sure that many of those who attended this one would return to their work with a feeling that they were engaged in a worthwhile endeavor and that they had the support and appreciation of their fellow workers."

CHARLES SPURGEON JOHNSON, *Director of the Department of Social Science, Fisk University; Trustee of the Julius Rosenwald Fund; Chairman of the Race Relations Committee of the American Missionary Association:* "The fact that so large a number of persons were present without direct financial aid from an outside source pointed to a reserve of interest that might be counted on to carry along a coordinated movement among the colleges. Not to be overlooked, however, is the prestige of an established and admired scholar in this field who has served as an effective catalysing agent."

DONALD RAMSEY YOUNG, *Research Secretary of the Social Science Research Council:* "I have no doubt whatever concerning the value of your objective. There is need for the encouragement and guidance of social and economic research at the land-grant colleges, both in terms of the benefits which should be derived therefrom by the institutions and their faculties and also in terms of the practical social utility of the anticipated results."

EDGAR TRISTRAM THOMPSON, *Associate Professor of Sociology, Duke University:* "I feel that you have a good idea and that you deserve support in your efforts to carry it out. I appreciate your including me among the invited sociologists and I feel that my efforts to contribute to the conference have taught me something."

WILLIAM EARLE COLE, *Professor of Sociology and Head of the De-*

partment, University of Tennessee; Acting Chairman of the Commission on Interracial Cooperation: "I think you are starting something which is very fundamental and which should go a long way in improving not only the Negroes of the South but other peoples as well. I was greatly impressed with what the Negro colleges have been doing and the prospects for the future."

THOMAS LYNN SMITH, *Professor of Sociology and Head of the Department, University of Louisiana:* "I think well of your plan for promoting research work on the part of the social science personnel at the land-grant colleges for Negroes. The advice of sociologists at institutions for whites should be sought from time to time as the work goes along; but not to the extent that there is any tendency at any institution for the white man to determine, even by suggestion, what shall be done by the Negro."

A second Conference was planned for the Spring of 1944, and I wrote in July 1943:

"This whole plan will come up for discussion and modification in the Second Land-Grant College Conference in the Spring of 1944. The main consideration is this: The economic situation of the Negro during and after the present war is a matter of critical and vital importance. There is going to be increased race friction and finally want and unemployment in the midst of violent social change. At such time we want accurate and carefully made social measurements, tested techniques and the machinery for further investigation. There will be neither time nor disposition during times of turmoil to initiate new and calm investigation. If now we begin this nation-wide study of economic and social conditions, it can be continuously pursued through storm and stress and after the post-war calm and form a priceless guide to social survival and lasting peace."

Many other commendations came from across the nation, from white and black. Especially was the new cooperation among Negro institutions noted, with Atlanta University as the acknowledged head and center of work.

Then at the moment of triumph of this carefully thought-out and carefully planned scheme, came catastrophe. Without notice to me of any kind, I was retired from my professorship and headship of the Department of Sociology at Atlanta University. This was not merely a personal disaster.

It was removing from leadership the one person who because of age and long experience, because of works published and a wide acquaintanceship based on the relation of teacher and student, happened to be the person to whom the presidents of Negro land-grant colleges and other Negroes of influence were willing to entrust this cooperative venture. President Clement of Atlanta University had quarreled with the land-grant colleges a few years past. Thus, many of their leaders did not like him personally. Most of the others did not know him but they did know Atlanta University and they knew me. They were willing to put this plan into these hands but they would not consent to cooperate with President Clement. There were doubtless at other Negro institutions persons capable of doing this job, but they were not as well-known and in any case my selection gained unusual agreement and Atlanta University unprecedented prestige as the center of this venture.

My sudden retirement then savored of a deliberate plot, although this cannot be proven. The retirement age at Atlanta University was 65. But I was 65 when President Hope called me to the University. Nothing was said between us about the conditions of eventual retirement—due to my usual neglect of financial considerations and because my good health gave me no thought of stopping work at any near time. Hope must have mentioned the matter to Florence Read, treasurer, but they reached no decision that I knew of. Later I opposed Miss Read's election as president to succeed Hope; and the new plan gained me wide acclaim. Even the General Education Board which handled Rockefeller funds favored my plan. President Clement while supporting the plan was not enthusiastic. As a new young unknown president, perhaps he saw my reputation overshadowing him. Letters came to me; visitors asked for me and no doubt Miss Read encouraged his jealousy. I was conscious that this might occur and tried to be careful. On all my plans I consulted him. All invitations went out in his name. His delays and small objections seemed petty and

I said so. Perhaps I was too brusque and not diplomatic enough in this and did not take into account his inexperience and lack of understanding. Doubtless too he had no desire to stop the development of the plan, but had no idea that I was at least for the time being so necessary for its firm establishment.

Neither Miss Read nor President Clement said a word to me about retirement; but at the meeting of the Board of Trustees in 1944, Miss Read proposed that I be retired. President Clement seconded the motion and apparently with little or no objection the Board passed the vote. Presumably most of the members assumed that the matter had been discussed with me and had my agreement. No pension was mentioned.

The result of this action was disastrous; not merely to me but to the American Negro. Up until this time the Negro himself had led in the study and interpretation of the condition of his race in the United States. Beginning with 1944, with accelerated speed the study of the Negro passed into the hands of whites and increasingly Southern whites. There were colored sociologists and historians but they worked without coordinated plan, without adequate funds or under superiors who were not interested. Finally, many Negro writers found it profitable to write what business and the government demanded and not the whole truth; until in the decade 1949 to 1959 with increasing unanimity, the thesis has been defended in a thousand books and papers that the Civil War was not a struggle to preserve and spread the slavery of black workers, but a holy crusade to maintain the superior civilization of white folk, and today current historians can treat American history and take no account of American Negroes and their activities in the 20th century.

At any rate, without a word of warning I found myself at the age of 76 without employment and with less than $5,000 of savings. Not only was a great plan of scientific work killed at birth, but my own life was thrown into confusion. I felt the world tottering beneath my feet and I fought back in despair. Finally the trustees gave me a year's full salary in lieu of my never having been given notice of retirement. Also after offering me a pension of $100 a month, they finally granted me $1,800 a year for five years and $1,200 a year thereafter.

A word from the poet Sara Teasdale expressed my mood:

> *When I can look life in the eyes,*
> *Grown calm and very coldly wise,*
> *Life will have given me the Truth*
> *And taken in exchange—my youth.*

My youth? I laughed grimly. It was not my youth that I was losing; it was my old age; and old age was worthless in the United States.

There were some earnest attempts to carry the proposed program on. It was transferred to Howard University, with E. Franklin Frazier in charge. An excellent conference was held in 1945. But Frazier was not given funds for continuing the project and the land-grant colleges gradually ceased to cooperate. The whole scheme died within a year or two. It has never been revived.

There was another loss in the giving up of this plan, which I have never mentioned. Here was an unprecedented chance for an experiment in sociology; for measuring and classifying human action, on a scale never before attempted; it would be reasonably sure of adequate funds and the best of trained cooperation and nationwide if not worldwide criticism. On such a base a real science of sociology could have been built. The opportunity was surrendered and the whole science of sociology has suffered. I even had projected a path of scientific approach: I was going to plot out beside the world of physical law, a science of sociology which measured "the limits of chance in human action." If this field proved narrow or non-existent, world law was proven. If not, the resultant "chance" was what men had always regarded as "free will." Meantime, as students of human action hesitated and waited, psychology measured nervous reaction; physics merging with chemistry rose to enormous accomplishment and helped by vast provision of mathematics, recast our whole conception of the universe. Finally biology revealed new realms of what we now can name as nothing but chance beyond the area of conscious mind. Sociology has been bypassed, and reduced to social work.

CHAPTER XIX

I RETURN TO THE NAACP

Howard University, Fisk University and North Carolina College for Negroes offered me work after my retirement. For the most part it was for lectures and part-time employment. Then came an unexpected offer for me to return to the employment of the NAACP which I had helped found and from which I had resigned in 1934. I had had at various times requests to cooperate with the NAACP—to attend mass meetings, to take part in Spingarn Medal installations, to serve on committees, etc. I had steadfastly refused in order to avoid seeming to interfere in any way with an organization from which I had parted; and especially because I never had come to trust the secretary, Walter White. But now I was without employment to support me and my family, and two men whom I regarded as close friends urged me to give serious heed to this invitation, Arthur Spingarn and Louis Wright. Spingarn's brother was one of my closest friends before his untimely death. I believed that Arthur was also a friend, although we had not been thrown as closely together. Louis Wright I had known from his youth. His stepfather was my family physician and since I had come to New York, Louis, also a physican, had willingly taken care of me and my family without charge.

These two friends assured me that a real welcome awaited me at the NAACP. They said that Walter White was the chief mover in this offer and urged my acceptance. I wrote them in detail and at last came to New York to consult Arthur Spingarn, Louis Wright, Walter White and Hubert Delany. I asked a salary of $5,000; two offices, one for myself and library and one for my secretary; I wanted leisure to write and assured them that I expected no role in the executive department of the organization; that I would be glad to revive the Pan-African movement and give general attention to the foreign aspects of the race problem. The com-

mittee assented to everything, willingly, although nothing
was reduced to writing except in my letters.

As events soon proved, in my invitation to return to the
NAACP, there were three conflicting ideas as to what my
status would be. My own thought was that I was to have no
power or place in the regular organization except to give
such advice as I was asked for. I was to have freedom to
write and express my opinions, avoiding of course anything
that would hurt the organization. I was to continue the long
interrupted interest of the NAACP in Africa, by calling
Pan-African Congresses and consulting with them. The
NAACP might be able to help finance such Congresses, and
perhaps other methods of assisting the Africans, but that
naturally would be at the direction of the main organization
under the secretary, Walter White. I naturally expected to
work and to have an area of work which was mine. That I
would continue to think and express and publish my
thoughts; that in fine I would continue to be myself, working in cooperation but not in complete subordination to
anybody. It did not occur to me that anyone would expect
or ask that.

On the other hand, as his actions later developed, Walter
White expected me to help him by writing such documents
as he needed; by appearing for him on such public occasions
as he wished; and in general to act as ghost writer and representative. It was for this reason that he did not want me to
occupy separate offices, or to take any action which he did
not initiate.

The third theory of my new status was a theory of my two
friends, my former physician, Louis Wright, who was chairman of the Board of Directors, and the brother of one of my
closest friends, Arthur Spingarn, who was president of the
Association. They assumed with some others that at 75 my
life work was done; that what I wanted was leisure and
comfort and for that I would willingly act as window dressing, say a proper word now and then and give the Association
and its secretary moral support. This theory did not occur
to me. I had no thought of doing nothing or of subordinat-

ing myself entirely to anybody in thought or deed. I was determined not to try to run the Association and I wanted to cooperate with Walter White in every possible way.

Since the donations from philanthropists never became large, the NAACP depended more and more on membership dues. The three first secretaries, Shillady, Johnson and White increased this source of support, until mainly Negroes themselves were paying the cost of their emancipation. Especially under White, the income increased rapidly, and with it his power and independence. The Board of Directors became chiefly window dressing, and real power of the organization lay in the hands of an executive committee, most of whom were selected by White from among his subordinate appointees.

I returned to the NAACP after an absence of ten years during which I had not followed closely its development. The results astonished me. The income had quadrupled, the membership approached a half-million; the staff had tripled or more. It had become a big business, smoothly run and extraordinarily influential. The newspapers vied for its releases, courts listened to its attorneys, and men of prominence readily accepted places on its Board of Directors.

One thing, however, filled me with foreboding; almost every vestige of democratic method and control had disappeared from the organization. This change slapped me in the face within three months. I had hesitated in accepting this work; repeatedly during my sojourn at Atlanta I had refused invitations from Mr. White to attend NAACP meetings and to cooperate in other ways. Invariably I had refused because I did not like Mr. White's methods nor did I trust his personal attitude toward me.

No sooner had I reached New York than ominous things occurred which I tried to ignore. I was expected to join the NAACP in August; but the United States government invited me to join their organization in Haiti and lecture before the teachers at a Summer conference. I thought this an ideal start of my work, but White objected. When I pressed the necessity of acceptance, White declared that my salary could not be paid while I was in Haiti. However, Spingarn and Wright intervened and in the end all was amicably adjusted.

However, when in September I reported for my duties at the NAACP, I found that despite the rush for my presence, my promised office space was not ready for me, and indeed for the four years that I remained I was never furnished the offices promised. I was jammed—books, desk and secretary —in one office about five by ten feet, where the voices of the whole organization were plainly audible. Most of my books and office paraphernalia had to be stored. No one but a writer can realize what lack of office facilities means to an author. I had had beautiful and commodious offices in Atlanta. My first request on considering coming back to the NAACP was office accommodations. I remembered my offices which I occupied from 1910 to 1933 and while I did not insist on similar accommodations I did want comfort, space and quiet. I asked this clearly and there was no whisper of objection. It proved, however, that this was the one thing to which White objected. He wanted me visibly at his elbow so that at no point could my subordination to him be doubted. I did not dream of this reaction of his and could not understand why in all New York he could not find me office space. I asked and protested about adequate quarters but got no results until the secretary took a trip to the military front in Asia and loaned me his own office during his absence.

This was in 1945 and the meeting of the UNO in San Francisco was projected. The NAACP was asked to send a consultant and the Board of Directors selected me. I corresponded with interested persons, especially Negroes, and was making ready to start to San Francisco when White without notice appeared on the scene and took back his offices. Also when final authorization came from Washington, White was set down as consultant and I as assistant. The NAACP Board was not consulted. I made no complaint since as secretary he undoubtedly would have been so designated had he been in the country. Yet it was his maneuvering in Washington which enabled him without notice to me or the Board to change my designation. I went with him and rendered every service I could. I wrote statements and appeals; wrote a daily column in the San Francisco *Chronicle* and consulted men like John Foster Dulles. Yet White was the official representative of the NAACP and was consulted in many cases where I was not invited.

When I returned to New York, no offices were yet ready. I protested to Spingarn and Wright and to the Board of Directors, but got no results. This seemed to me wretchedly unfair. However, it was true that the NAACP offices were crowded and that the organization was moving into a new building which was being purchased on 40th Street. I hoped to have the space promised. Finally I hired offices for myself on Sixth Avenue and 42nd Street in the suite of a friend. I paid $476 for these out of my own pocket. I laid my plight before Mr. Spingarn in person, with plans based on the new building.

By this time after much delay I had finally arranged for attending the Fifth Pan-African Congress in England. In the four years in which I remained with the NAACP I attended the Fifth Pan-African Congress in England, wrote two books on colonies and Africa, edited two others and wrote many articles, pamphlets and newspaper columns. I attended several conferences and traveled 20,000 miles to deliver 150 lectures on subjects connected with my work for the NAACP as I conceived it. I was instructor for two semesters at the New School for Social Research in New York and I was guest speaker at Vassar, Yale and Princeton.

I was, however, taken aback when I saw how the organization was being conducted. At first I attended meetings of the Board of which I was not a member. Few directors usually attended. Their work was to accept the report of the Committee on Administration which consisted of the secretary, his five assistants whom he appointed, and nine members of the Board, only two or three of whom usually attended. Unfinished business of the Board was referred to this committee. There was little discussion at Board meetings and the chief work was to accept the report of the Committee of Administration after brief discussion.

Once the secretary summoned a staff conference for general criticism. I was included in the invitation and thought my opinion was desired. It was elaborately conducted at a suburban resort. I wrote a general criticism pointing out that the executive was trying to do too many things and not giving his helpers enough initiative and authority. The statement won wide assent, but it was given no executive attention and no further conferences were called.

The result of this close dictatorship was soon apparent in my work. I tried to confine myself to my department of relations of the organization to Africa, other colored people and colonies. But try as I did I could get no action or direction as to this work.

Walter White soon undoubtedly set out to get rid of me. In 1946, he accused me before the Board of Directors of appearing before a Congressional Committee without his consent. This was Senator Connally's committee on assent to the Charter of the United Nations. They invited me as an individual and not as representative of the NAACP. My first words in testifying were that I spoke for no organization and only for myself. Walter White was also invited but he did not go.

Next he accused me of interfering with a court case on school segregation being tried by the NAACP in Dayton, Ohio. This was my answer to one of dozens of letters asking my opinion on many subjects. In this case I was asked my present interpretation of a passage in my *Dusk of Dawn*. My answer expressed my personal opinion. Finally White demanded the right to open and read my mail for the reason that many persons wrote me as an officer of the NAACP rather than as an individual. I assured the secretary that I would turn over to him immediately any letter which came to me but belonged in his hands; but that under no circumstances could he open mail addressed to me. I saw the handwriting on the wall, but I was sure that my two sponsoring friends would see the attack being made on me and stand by me.

In 1946 I was asked to visit Columbia, S.C., and speak to a meeting of the Southern Negro Youth Congress, whose leaders, James Jackson and Louis Burnham, I knew and admired for their hard work and sacrifice. They had called a "Southern Youth Legislature" in the former center of secession with white and Negro members. I went and said in part:

"The future of American Negroes is in the South. Here 327 years ago, they began to enter what is now the United States of America; here they have made their greatest contribution to American culture; and here they have suffered the damnation of slavery, the frustration of reconstruction and the lynching of emancipation. I trust then that an organization like yours is going to regard the South as the battleground of a great crusade. Here is the magnificent climate; here is the fruitful earth under the beauty of the Southern sun; and here if anywhere on earth, is the need of the thinker, the worker and the dreamer. This is the firing line not simply for the emancipation of the American Negro but for the emancipation of the African Negro and the Negroes of the West Indies; for the emancipation of the colored races; and for the emancipation of the white slaves of modern capitalistic monopoly.

"There could be no more splendid vocation beckoning to the youth of the 20th century, after the flat failures of white civilization, after the flamboyant establishment of an industrial system which creates poverty and the children of poverty which are ignorance and disease and crime; after the crazy boasting of a white culture that finally ended in wars which ruined civilization in the whole world; in the midst of allied peoples who have yelled about democracy and never practiced it either in the British Empire or in the American Commonwealth or in South Carolina."

In 1946 I had planned an appeal to the Commission on Human Rights of the UN, in behalf of American Negroes and their disabilities. I had proposed a pamphlet which I would edit and to which a group of experts would contribute articles. The Directors assented. I secured the cooperation of Earl Dickerson, Milton Konvitz, William R. Ming, Jr., Leslie S. Perry and Rayford Logan. To this appeal of 80 pages I wrote an introduction.

When the appeal was ready for the press, the secretary, without consulting me as editor, held it up for weeks because he wanted to add an introduction by himself. I pointed out that for a pamphlet of less than 100 pages there was no call for two introductions and that my introduction of 14 pages was an integral part of the plan. After further and unnecessary delay the appeal was issued. At first the Human Rights Commission refused to receive it except for filing. At last, however, the appeal was received formally by an undersecretary and at a public meeting. Walter White made the speech of presentation.

One other development of the NAACP gradually dawned on me. The organization had divided into two parts: A Legal Department under Arthur Spingarn as chairman and Thurgood Marshall as legal director, occupied separate offices and was supported by a separate fund. Although still a department of the NAACP, they were largely independent of the executive secretary and their work was decided by a few men. They achieved unexpected and extraordinary success in a series of court decisions which culminated in the decision of the Supreme Court in 1954, outlawing race segregation in the schools and other public facilities.

To me this success was beyond anything I had dreamed. But it proved two things which the public did not realize: (1) No such decision would have been possible without the world pressure of communism led by the Soviet Union. It was simply impossible for the United States to continue to lead a "Free World" with race segregation kept legal over a third of its territory. (2) Legal enactment and decision in the United States is necessary but it does not ensure action. The South is rebelling against the Supreme Court decision and for many years will have its way; not forever but long enough to ruin the education of millions of black and white children.

Within this context is to be seen the political campaign of
1948. I had never belonged to an active political organization, but I had expressed my views on candidates since the
election of 1912. I early donned a Wallace button and let it
be known that I was going to support him. A poll in the
NAACP office showed that 70 per cent of the staff favored
Wallace. I was then warned by the secretary not to take
part in "politics." I replied that I certainly would be careful
not to appear to speak for the NAACP nor to take the time
for active political work; but I assumed that I had the right
to vote and tell my choice; that this was what the NAACP
had stood for during 30 years. The secretary merely reiterated that the Board insisted that no salaried employee
should take part in politics. When later at a non-political
meeting in Philadelphia, I advised the audience to vote for
Wallace, I was careful to preface my remarks by saying that
I did not officially speak for the NAACP or any official. I
was rebuked by the secretary for this, while at the same time
he was making a nationwide drive for Truman, by letter,
newspaper articles, telegrams and public speech.

In 1947 the Human Rights Commission of the UN sched-
uled a meeting in Paris at which our Appeal would be considered. Walter White decided himself to attend. Naturally
I regarded White's trip at this point as interfering in a
matter which was in my domain, but I said nothing. He
asked for a memoranda from me which I furnished. Then he
asked for a second memorandum from me which I refused to
write until the Board of Directors took some action on the
matter of just what my area of work was. Here again I quite
misconceived the attitude of the Board toward me and my
work. I was to have no area of work which was mine. I was
to be completely at the direction of the secretary. He could
direct or interfere as he chose and he was the judge as to
what was the proper procedure. In a tight modern business
corporation this had become standard procedure. But I could
not conceive being asked to function in such a capacity.
Surely in my nearly 50 years of work for the American Negro
I had earned the right to some small niche where I could

think and act with reasonable freedom. The Board paid not the slightest attention to my request. Indeed, since I sent it in care of the secretary, it is quite possible that the Board never received it at all. White prepared to sail before the next meeting of the Board.

At Geneva nothing important took place. The Soviet delegate tried to take up our appeal and another appeal from women. But Mrs. Roosevelt and Jonathan Daniels objected. Mr. White not being a member of the Commission did not even have the right to attend the meeting.

I then took a decisive step. I sent a memorandum to each member of the Board protesting against the handling of this case which lay in my department. And I protested also against the political activity of the secretary and his representation of his appointment as consultant to the UNO as reason for supporting Truman. I pointed out that the Annual Meeting of the NAACP to which I was not invited, was turned into a Truman rally. I sent copies of this protest to the Board, and the office staff. I did not send any copy of this protest to any newspaper nor did I speak to any newspaper reporter.

The Board promptly dismissed me from my position effective December 31. They did not discuss at all the facts, but dismissed me for refusing "to cooperate" with the secretary and for distributing my memorandum before the meeting of the Board.

A considerable number of persons now urged me to lead a fight protesting my treatment and planning a reorganization of the NAACP. I refused. I was too old for such a task which was the duty of younger persons. Moreover White was not wholly responsible for what had happened. Much of the blame lay on the shoulders of my two friends at whose insistence I had returned to the NAACP. I now realized that between Spingarn and Wright, on the one hand, and the secretary on the other, there had been an understanding that at any time White could not get along with me, I was to go. They assumed that my days of work were over and they wanted to furnish me leisure and dignity before death.

White, on the other hand, wanted me for window dressing, as one who would boost his prestige with reports which he would use and speeches made at his direction. On the other hand, I myself had not even at the age of 80 felt any serious diminution of my power to work or to follow my ideals. I could not work as long or reason so quickly; but in joining the NAACP I had no thought of sitting down and doing nothing; and it never occurred to me that I would be expected to act as showpiece or figurehead for someone else.

I started in to do a job and I was succeeding when White decided that my work interfered with his and he asked Spingarn and Wright to redeem their promise. They hesitated. They asked me once when I had appealed to them about office space, "Why do you work so hard? Why not take it more leisurely?" I did not understand. I merely smiled and proceeded to point out that in the newly purchased headquarters I had been allotted a small office of some 10 by 12 feet for myself and secretary, 2,500 books, ten file cases and office furniture. They pointed out that the new offices were already too small and that the growing legal department was seriously cramped and needed even the space that I was occupying.

Finally, I was not dismissed because of my radical thought —this was never discussed; nor for disobeying the secretary or the rules of the organization. I was dismissed on the technical charge of sending to the newspapers facts about a difference of opinion between the secretary and myself over furnishing him more data for his trip to the Human Relations Conference in Paris. This in fact I had not done and told this to the Board. But I added that if the newspapers had asked me about this difference I would have stated the facts. For this the Board dismissed me.

The NAACP has a noble record of which all Negroes and all Americans should be proud. All the more reason that its future path be guided by wisdom and by use of that vast reservoir of human knowledge and experience which can be called into use by democracy. It is difficult to guide a mass of people. Continually we are tempted to use our own

limited knowledge and experience to push through decisions
and compel action, instead of trusting the slower, muddled
and hesitating development of mass action. Yet without this
action we land in tyranny and fatal mistake. The hundred
thousands of members of the NAACP are not people of the
highest education or widest experience. But that is no excuse for turning their most effective organ of protest and
progress into a rigid dictatorship, virtually under the control
of one man. We see too much of this attitude already in current America, in the broad areas of business and industry;
in the organized church; in social reform and uplift of every
sort; in politics and government. It is the growing custom to
narrow control, concentrate power, disregard and disfranchise the public; and assuming that certain persons by divine
right of money-raising or by sheer assumption, have the
power to do as they think best without consulting the wisdom of mankind.

It is the tragedy of the day that the democracy of which
we prate so glibly is being murdered in the house of its
friends, and in everyday life far more than in broad governmental decisions. The nation which cannot conduct its
philanthropy in a democratic manner, will not in the end
convince the world that it knows more of good government
abroad than it does at home. The present condition of the
NAACP illustrates what I have said. The NAACP is today
divided in two parts, with separate offices, officials and funds.
The legal department is under the control of two lawyers;
one a conservative white man, honest and careful, trained
as an expert in conserving the private funds of the rich and
well-to-do. He has had broad human contacts, but he has no
sympathy with radical thought or experiment. The other
lawyer is a talented colored man, trained in the strict field
of current law and with narrow cultural background. These
men have collected a fund which they administer, and pursued a line of legal attack on color caste with extraordinary
success, culminating with the epoch-making decision of the
Supreme Court against segregation by race in the public
schools. They have drawn around them a number of able

young helpers and are supported by the strong public opinion of the nation, black and white. Walter White tried several times in vain to interfere with their work but never succeeded.

The remaining field of the NAACP has to do with social uplift of all sorts: education, housing, occupations, race relations, literature and art, history, science and social progress. Here rests the whole theory of the future of the Negro race in America and its relation to the Negroes of Africa and the West Indies, and the colored peoples of the world. It matters not how many may think that these relations may be ignored, the fact is that they must be considered.

Moreover and beyond this, the relations of American Negroes to the working people of America and to the socialist and communist movements of the world have got to be matters of grave and present consideration. The whole world is confronting these problems, while the NAACP, the greatest organization among 20 million of the most advanced group of Negroes in the world, has no program or leadership; no experts, no commentators or leaders but can only answer each problem with the parrot-like call, "No Discrimination." This was the slogan of the last generation. It is desperately inadequate today. Given no race discrimination, Negro citizens still face modern problems and for a long time face them as a group working together because of blood relationship and cultural ties. For this they must organize, plan and work; how can they plan to live with friends and acquaintances; how shall the history of Negroes be taught; what occupations shall their children be prepared to follow; what shall their attitude be toward socialism and communism, and especially toward the Soviet Union and China who above all nations fight the very color bar which we try to get rid of. All these matters call for trained knowledge and expert advice and wide experience.

This the main office of the NAACP today lacks. Its secretary [Roy Wilkins] has been trained as a newspaper reporter; he is intelligent and good-willed but lacks all training in social science, has traveled little and has no broad background of education. He has a staff of excellent clerks but few if any professional social workers, artists, writers or research specialists. The branches and their officials have no scientifically planned program except to raise money and defend cases of injustice or discrimination in courts. The organization fears the processes of democracy and avoids discussion. All meetings and programs are "fixed." When a North Carolina official voices what every Negro at sometime has thought—namely retaliation for attack and injustice— there is no discussion, but he is buried by a prepared vote. What is demanded is wide planning, thoughtful cooperation, organized social work and the selection of men and women of genius and training to solve one of the most difficult of modern problems of race relations.

Above all the American Negro needs to be taught to read and to support a school of art and literature which will preserve his history and culture and add to the great treasure of human accomplishment; rather than let the unique and marvelous life and experience of the black race in America be distorted or even lost to memory as it threatens to be today.

PART THREE

PART THREE

CHAPTER XX

WORK FOR PEACE

I am not sure just when I began to feel an interest in Africa. Some folks seem to assume that just as Irish Americans have a sentimental regard for Ireland, and German Americans and Americans of Scandinavian descent look back to their mother countries, either through their own experience or that of their parents, so in similar ways Negro Americans should regard Africa.

This was true in the 17th and early 18th centuries, when there actually were, in the United States, Negroes who either remembered Africa or inherited memories from their fathers or grandfathers. Among Negroes of my generation there was not only little direct acquaintance or consciously inherited knowledge of Africa, but much distaste and recoil because of what the white world taught them about the Dark Continent. There arose resentment that a group like ours, born and bred in the United States for centuries, should be regarded as Africans at all. They were, as most of them began gradually to assert, Americans. My father's father was particularly bitter about this. He would not accept an invitation to a "Negro" picnic. He would not segregate himself in any way.

Notwithstanding all this, I became interested in Africa by a sort of logical deduction. I was tired of finding in newspapers, textbooks and history, fulsome lauding of white folk, and either no mention of dark peoples, or mention in disparaging and apologetic phrase. I made up my mind that it must be true that Africa had a history and destiny, and that one of my jobs was to disinter this unknown past, and help make certain a splendid future. Along this line I did, over a stretch of years, a great deal of reading, writing, research, and planning.

When I returned to New York from Atlanta in 1944 to become Director of Special Research for the NAACP, it was in my mind specifically for the purpose of concentrating on study of colonial peoples and people of Negro descent throughout the world, and to revive the Pan-African Congresses. From this plan came the Fifth Pan-African Congress in England, 1945; and my book, *The World and Africa,* in 1947. I should have liked to join the Council on African Affairs, and expected to be invited, but the secretary, Max Yergan, did not seem to want my cooperation.

Nothing illustrates more clearly the hysteria of our times than the career of the Council on African Affairs. It had been the dream of idealists in earlier days that the stain of American slavery would eventually be wiped out by the service which American descendants of African slaves would render Africa. Most of those American Negroes who gained their freedom in the 18th century looked forward to a return to Africa as their logical end. They often named their clubs and churches, their chief social institutions, "African." But the Cotton Kingdom and colonial imperialism gradually drove this dream entirely from their minds until the Negroes of the post-Civil War era regarded Africa as renewal of color caste and slavery. They regarded the colonization and "back to Africa" movements of Lincoln and Bishop Turner with lackluster eye; and when in 1918 I tried to found a social and spiritual Pan-African movement, my American Negro following was small.

The Council on African Affairs was planned in London in 1939, when Max Yergan, a colored YMCA secretary, returning from long and trying service in South Africa, met Paul Robeson returning from a visit to West Africa. They set up an organization in New York. In 1943 they were joined by Alphaeus Hunton, son of the greatest Negro secretary the American YMCA ever had; himself a doctor of philosophy in English, and a professor for 17 years at Howard University.

With the cooperation of Frederick V. Field, a fine African library and collection of African art, along with offices for the new organization, were secured. A monthly fact sheet devoted to developments in new Africa was issued. Money was raised for starving people in South Africa and striking miners in West Africa. African visitors were welcomed, and lectures delivered.

Then came the witch-hunting scare, and the Council was put on the Attorney-General's list of "subversive" organizations. Immediately, without consulting his board, Yergan as secretary, issued a newspaper release attacking "Communists." Robeson protested. His position was that the Council was not a Communist organization even if some of the supporters were Communists. It was doing a specific and needed work; that the political or religious opinions of its members or officials were their own business, so long as the actions of the organization as such were legal.

A division immediately arose within the ranks of the Council and many of the members of the board resigned. At this time, on invitation of Robeson, I was asked to join the Council, which I did. I joined on account of my faith in his sincerity, and my belief in the necessary function of the Council on African Affairs. Since Yergan now was at odds with the board, he was dismissed from his office. Legal complications followed, due to Yergan's claims to property which the Council and Mr. Field considered theirs. When settlement was finally made, the Council resumed work, hampered by its proscription by the Attorney-General.

When I was dismissed by the NAACP as Director of Special Research in 1948, I was offered the honorary position of Vice-Chairman of the Council on African Affairs, without salary but with an office rent-free, and the services of a secretary to be furnished by the Council. I accepted for two reasons: first, because of my belief in the work which the Council should do for Africa; and secondly, because of my belief that no man or organization should be denied the right to a career because of political or religious beliefs.

The Council was, however, on shaky foundations so far as funds were concerned. Membership fell, and money-raising efforts were not very successful. One promising effort presented itself in May 1950. We had received from South Africa a moving appeal for assistance from a native musician,

Michael Moerane. We turned to the brilliant, black orchestra leader, Dean Dixon, and asked him to arrange a concert of symphonic music by Negro composers of all lands, including Moerane. The concert was successful. We gave it at Town Hall. A thousand persons paid to listen. Critics applauded.

But alas for our dream! The concert cost $4,617, and our receipts were $3,236, leaving a loss of $1,381. This was not bad in itself; but since we had very limited funds and a dwindling income this result made any plans for repeating the concert annually, as Dixon so ardently desired, impossible. Yet the Voice of America broadcast news of this concert as proof of the encouragement of Negro culture by the United States! It failed to add that this was done by an organization listed by the United States as "subversive."

The ability of the Council to finance even my rent and clerical help decreased, and by 1950 it seemed my duty to relieve them of this obligation. However, the officers came to me and asked me earnestly not to do this, and disclosed a plan which they had considered; and that was that I would consent to a celebration of my 83rd birthday in February 1951, for the declared purpose of raising a publication fund; that this fund would go to maintaining my office and my connection with the Council on African Affairs, and also for re-publication of some of my works long out of print, and for new publications of certain unprinted manuscripts. They were sure that such a proposition would be welcomed by a large number of people, and would mean not only forwarding my work, but the renewed activity of the Council on African Affairs, at a time when its services were greatly needed.

It was a particularly difficult situation because the increased costs called for a high charge a plate, and other expenses meant a great outlay of money. Yet I did not feel free to refuse. I consented. A committee was organized, and the dinner planned. Publicity sent out by Dr. E. Franklin Frazier of Howard University, past president of the American Sociological Association and chairman of the sponsoring group, said:

"More than 200 prominent individuals from all sections of the United States, among them Dr. Albert Einstein, Mrs. Mary McLeod Bethune, Dr. Kirtley F. Mather, Langston Hughes, Lion Feuchtwanger, and Hon. J. Finley Wilson, have joined in sponsoring a testimonial dinner honoring W. E. B. Du Bois on the occasion of his eighty-third birthday this month.

"Honorary chairmen of the sponsoring group for the dinner include Dr. Mordecai W. Johnson, President of Howard University; Rabbi Abba Hillel Silver of Cleveland; Thomas Mann, noted author; Mrs. Mary Church Terrell of Washington; Miss Mary White Ovington, a founder of the NAACP; Dr. Alain Locke; Dr. William H. Jernagin; Carey McWilliams; and Bishop William J. Walls.

"At the peak of his unparalleled experience, learning, and skill, we have the rare opportunity of paying tribute to him in a tangible way by assuring continuing facilities for his research, writings, and publications. His priceless library must be kept intact and preserved. His unique collection of scores of thousands of letters and manuscripts must be edited and published. Most important of all, his basic works now out of print must be made available through the publishing of The Collected Works of Dr. W. E. B. Du Bois."

Then suddenly came news of my indictment. I was indicted as a criminal by a grand jury in Washington, on February 9, 1951, for not registering as an agent of a foreign power in the peace movement!

My connection with the peace movement had been long. Even in my college days I had vowed never to take up arms. I wrote in *The Crisis* in 1913 concerning the meeting of the peace societies at St. Louis:[16]

"Peace today, if it means anything, means the stopping of the slaughter of the weaker by the stronger in the name of Christianity and culture. The modern lust for land and slaves in Africa, Asia, and the South Seas is the greatest and almost the only cause of war between the so-called civilized peoples. For such 'colonial' aggression and 'imperial' expansion, England, France, Germany, Russia, and Austria are straining every nerve to arm themselves; against such policies Japan and China are arming desperately. And yet the American peace movement thinks it bad policy to take up this problem of machine guns, natives, and rubber, and wants 'constructive' work in 'arbitration treaties and international law.' For our part we think that a little less dignity and dollars and a little more humanity would make the peace movement in America a great democratic philanthropy instead of an aristocratic refuge."

At the Congress of Versailles in 1919, my contribution was the Pan-African Congresses, and appeals to the Mandate Commission and the International Labor Organization. In 1945, as consultant to the American delegation to the UNO in San Francisco, I tried to stress the colonial question. I wrote May 16, 1945:

"The attempt to write an International Bill of Rights into the San Francisco Conference without any specific mention of the people living in colonies seems to me a most unfortunate procedure. If it were clearly understood that freedom of speech, freedom from want and freedom from fear, which the nations are asked to guarantee, would without question be extended to the 750 million people who live in colonial areas, this would be a great and fateful step. But the very fact that these people, forming the most depressed peoples in the world, with 90 per cent illiteracy, extreme poverty and a prey to disease, who hitherto for the most part have been considered as sources of profit and not included in the democratic development of the world; and whose exploitation for three centuries has been a prime cause of war, turmoil, and suffering—the omission of specific reference to these peoples is almost advertisement of their tacit exclusion as not citizens of free states, and that their welfare and freedom would be considered only at the will of the countries owning them and not at the demand of enlightened world public opinion."

On February 5, 1949, O. John Rogge, formerly U.S. Assistant Attorney-General, wrote me:

"The recent development in American-Soviet relations places a new emphasis on the need for a meeting such as our Cultural and Scientific Conference for World Peace. Certainly intellectuals today are faced with no greater challenge than to give the best of their talent, skills, and special knowledge to the problem of how we achieve a real peace.

"We are most eager to make this Conference a real contribution to the solution of the problems that now block the way to peace. For that reason we are asking you and a small group of key individuals among our sponsors to meet with us to help in the preparation of the subject matter and program as well as speakers for this Conference. . . ."

The conference took place in March 1949, at the Waldorf-Astoria Hotel, New York, and marked an era in the cultural history of the United States. It was sponsored by 550 of the outstanding leaders of American cultural and liberal thought. It succeeded in bringing together an extraordinary representation of the leaders of modern culture, and especially cultural leaders of the Soviet Union.

So rabid was its reception by the American press, that a concerted and directed movement against peace and in favor of war against the Soviet Union was made clear. Distinguished cultural figures like Picasso were refused visas to attend. The meeting became a matter of bitter recrimination; the sessions were picketed, and the distortion of the whole enterprise in the press was unprecedented.

Thus a conference called by persons of the highest standing in science, literature and art, and conceived with the best motives, became as the *New York Times* said, one of "the most controversial meetings in recent New York history"; and a signal expression of the witch-hunting and calumny in this nation which drove free speech and the right to inquire and reason into almost total eclipse.

At the final meeting in Madison Square Garden I said in introducing the Chairman, Harlow Shapley:

"We know and the saner nations know that we are not

traitors nor conspirators; and far from plotting force and violence it is precisely force and violence that we bitterly oppose. This conference was not called to defend communism nor socialism nor the American way of life. It was called to promote peace! It was called to say and say again that no matter how right or wrong differing systems of beliefs in religion, industry, or government may be, war is not the method by which their differences can successfully be settled for the good of mankind."

The next month I was urged by O. John Rogge, Albert E. Kahn, and others to attend a world peace meeting in Paris. The American committee offered to pay a part of my expense, and I paid the rest. I went to what seems to me to have been the greatest demonstration for peace in modern times. For four days witnesses from nearly every country in the world set forth the horrors of war and the necessity of peace if civilization was to survive. On the concluding Sunday, 500,000 pilgrims from all parts of France, coming on foot, by automobiles, by train and plane, filed through the vast Buffalo Stadium crying, "Peace, no more war!" At this Conference I emphasized colonialism and said:

"Let us not be misled. The real cause of the differences which threaten world war is not the spread of socialism or even of the complete socialism which communism envisages. Socialism is spreading all over the world and even in the United States. . . . Against this spread of socialism, one modern institution is working desperately and that is colonialism, and colonialism has been and is and ever will be one of the chief causes of war. . . . Leading this new colonial imperialism comes my own native land, built by my father's toil and blood, the United States. The United States is a great nation; rich by grace of God and prosperous by the hard work of its humblest citizens. . . . Drunk with power we are leading the world to hell in a new colonialism with the same old human slavery which once ruined us; and to a Third World War which will ruin the world."

On Monday, April 25th, during the last session of the Congress, a Peace Manifesto was adopted. This historic doc-

ument whose preamble declared it was drawn up by representatives of the people of 72 countries, "men and women
of every creed, philosophy, color, and type of civilization,"
solemnly proclaimed that "the defense of Peace is henceforth the concern of all peoples." In the name of the 600
million represented, the Congress sent out this message:
"We are ready and resolved to win the battle for Peace,
which means to win the battle for Life."

The Congress adjourned and the delegates returned to
their 72 countries.

In July 1949, I joined with Linus Pauling, John Clark,
Uta Hagen and O. John Rogge to call an "American Con-
tinental Congress for World Peace" to be held in Mexico
City in September.

Again in August 1949, 25 prominent Americans were
asked to attend an all-Soviet peace conference in Moscow.
For reasons which arose directly from the violent reception
given the peace congress in March, I was the only one
who accepted the invitation. I addressed the 1,000 persons
present:

I represent millions of citizens of the United States who are just as
opposed to war as you are. But it is not easy for American citizens
either to know the truth about the world or to express it. This is true
despite the intelligence and wealth and energy of the United States.
Perhaps I can best perform my duty to my country and to the cause
of world peace by taking a short time to explain the historic reasons
for the part which the United States is playing in the world today.
I can do this the more appropriately because I represent that large
group of 15 million Americans, one tenth of the nation, who in a sense
explain America's pressing problems.

The two great advantages of the United States have been vast natural
resources and effective labor force. The first effective labor force were
slaves, at first both white and black; but increasingly as time went on
black Africans brought in by an intense effort made by the English
especially in the 18th century. That succeeded in landing 15 million
black laborers in all the Americas from 1500 to 1800, at a cost of
100 million souls to Africa, disrupting its culture and ruining its economy. This labor gave the world tobacco, cotton, sugar, and numbers of
other crops and opened America to the world. There followed an
increasing migration of millions of workers chiefly from Europe who
became energetic laborers with initiative and skill encouraged by the

large and immediate returns from their efforts. With free land, favorable climate and freedom of trade, the individual laborer could make a living and often become rich without the necessity of any wide social control for the common good. Plenty for most workers, without socialism, marked America from 1800 to 1900.

But this was possible not only because of vast resources but also because of the slavery of the blacks. So long as a depressed class of slaves with no political nor social rights supplied a rich mass of basic materials and a whole area of personal service the share of white capital and white labor was abnormally large. Even when the expanding mass of white labor tried to build a democratic form of government, inspired by the thinkers of the late 18th century, they faced the uncomfortable fact of slavery in the land of liberty. Some wanted to abolish Negro slavery forthwith; but slaves represented too much invested property and income for this to be easy. In 1787, the United States, beginning work on the drafting of a Constitution, and having previously declared that "All men are created equal" faced the problem of slavery and the slave trade. The phrase "All men are created equal" was not complete hypocrisy. Most persons believed that Negro slavery could not continue without a slave trade so they arranged to suppress this African slave trade in 20 years and thus gradually they hoped the slave labor would disappear.

This did not happen, because slave labor in the United States even with a curtailed slave trade began to raise so valuable a cotton crop that this crop by use of newly invented machinery became one of the most profitable investments of the modern world. The spindles for spinning cotton cloth in Europe increased from five million in 1800 to 150 million in 1900 and black labor furnished the raw material. This was the Cotton Kingdom and it represented vast capital and the income of millions of people. Slavery therefore in the United States by 1820, had so firm an economic foundation that emancipation became impossible without cataclysm.

This pressure for social upheaval naturally did not come from the organizers of industry, nor from property owners, nor even at first from white workers, who had been taught that their high wages depended on the slavery of Negroes. The pressure came primarily from the Negroes; first by their sheer physical expansion from 750,000 in 1790 to 3 million in 1840, of whom nearly 400,000 had gained their freedom by purchase, escape, or philanthropy. They organized systematic escapes from the territory where the slave system prevailed; they joined with white men in an abolition movement; and their kin in Haiti and other West Indian Islands shook the world with bloody revolt.

But the struggle of the black slave for freedom did not gain the sympathy of the majority of citizens of the United States. This was because a persistent propaganda campaign had been spread as slave labor began to increase in value, to prove by science and religion that black men were not real men; that they were a sub-species fit only for slavery. Consequently the fight for democracy and especially the struggle for a broader social control of wealth and of individual effort was hindered and turned aside by widespread contempt for the lowest class of labor and the consequent undue emphasis put on unhampered freedom of individual effort, even at the cost of social loss and degradation. Therefore at the time when socialism and broad social control for the common good should have spread in the United States as it was spreading in Europe, there grew on the contrary exaltation of industrial anarchy, tightening of the slave system and belief in individual or group success even at the expense of national welfare.

The catastrophe was precipitated as the workers gradually discovered that slavery of their black fellows was not to their advantage if slave labor spread to the free soil of the West. The nation went to Civil War therefore not to abolish slavery, but to limit it to the cotton states. The South was determined to spread slavery in the North and if not there, into the Caribbean and South America. This would cut Northern capital off from its most valuable market, and the North fought to preserve this market. But the North could not win without the cooperation of the slaves themselves, since the slaves were raising food for the Southern armies. Gradually by a general strike the Negroes began to desert to the Northern armies as laborers, servants, and spies, until at last 200,000 of them became armed soldiers while a million more stood ready to fight. Thus American Negroes gained their freedom.

Now came the problem as to what to do with them. They were ignorant, poverty-stricken, sick. The Northerners wanted to let them drift. The freedmen desperately wanted land and education. A plan of socialistic control with schools and land distribution was worked out by philanthropists, but industry rejected it as too costly and as alien to American individualism. Then came a hitch; unless the slaves were given the right to vote, their numerical voting strength would go to their white former masters, who would vote to lower the tariff on which war industry flourished and to scale the war debt owned by Northern banks. Suddenly industry gave the black freedmen the vote, expecting them to fail but meantime to break the power of the planters. The Negroes did not fail; they enfranchised their fellow workers, establishing public schools for all and began a modern socialistic legislation for hospitals, prisons, and land distribution. Immediately the former slave owners made a deal with Northern industrial leaders for the disfranchisement of the freedmen. The South would support the tariff and the debt. The freedmen lost the right to vote but retained their schools, poorly supported as they were by their own meager wages and Northern philanthropy.

The history of the United States in the last 75 years has been one of the great series of events in human history. With marvellous technique based on scientific knowledge, with organized expert management, vast natural resources, and world wide commerce, this country has built the greatest industrial machine in history—still capable of wide expansion. This organization is socialistic in its planning and coordination and methods but it is not under democratic control, nor are its objects those of the welfare state.

Our industry is today controlled, as George Seldes tells us, by 1,000 individuals and is conducted primarily for their profit and power. This does not exclude a great deal which is for the progress of America and the world, but human progress is not its main object nor its sole result. The American philosophy brought over from pioneer days was that individual success was necessarily social uplift, and today large numbers of Americans firmly believe that the success of monopolized industry controlled by an oligarchy is the success of this nation. It is not; and the high standard of living in the United States and its productive capacity is not due to monopoly and private profit, but has come in spite of this and indicates clearly how much higher standards of living might have been reached not only in America but throughout the world, if the bounty of the United States and its industrial planning had been administered for the progress of the masses instead of the power and luxury of the few.

The power of private corporate wealth in the United States has throttled democracy and this was made possible by the color caste which followed Reconstruction after the Civil War. When the Negro was disfranchised in the South, the white South was and is owned increasingly by the industrial North. Thus, caste which deprived the mass of Negroes of political and civil rights and compelled them to accept the lowest wage, lay underneath the vast industrial profit of the years 1890 to 1900 when the greatest combinations of capital took place.

The fight of Negroes for democracy in these years was the main movement of the kind in the United States. They began to gain the sympathy and cooperation of those liberal whites who succeeded the Abolitionists and who now realized that physical emancipation of a working class must be followed by political and economic emancipation or means nothing. For more than half a century this battle of a group of black and white Americans for the abolition of color caste has gone on and made striking progress: The American Negro is beginning to vote, to be admitted to labor unions and to be granted many civil rights. But the mischief and long neglect of democracy has already spread throughout the nation. A large percentage of eligible voters do not get to the polls. Democracy has no part in industry, save through the violence or threatened violence of the strike. No great American industry admits that it could or should be controlled by those who do its work. But unless democratic methods enter industry, democracy fails to function in other parts of life. Our political life is admittedly under the control of organized wealth and while the socialized organization of all our work proceeds, its management remains under oligarchical control and its objects are what that oligarchy decide. They may be beneficial decisions, they may be detrimental, but in no case are they arrived at by democratic methods.

The claim of the United States that it represents democracy in contrast to fascism or communism is patently false. Fascism is oligarchy in control of a socialized state which is run for the benefit of the oligarchs and their friends. Communism is a socialized state conducted by a group of workers for the benefit of the mass of the people. There may be little difference in the nature of the controls exercised in the United States, Fascist Germany, and the Soviet republics. There is a world of difference in the objects of that control. In the United States today the object is to center and increase the power of those who control organized wealth and they seek to prove to Americans that no other system is so successful in human progress. But instead of leaving proof of this to the free investigation of science, the reports of a free press, and the discussion of the public platform, today in the United States, organized wealth owns the press and chief news gathering organs and is exercising increased control over the schools and making public discussion and even free thinking difficult and often impossible.

The cure for this and the way to change the socially planned United States into a welfare state is for the American people to take over the control of the nation in industry as well as government. This is proceeding gradually. Many Americans are not aware of this, but it is true: we conduct the post office; we are in the express and banking business; we have built the great Tennessee Valley river control system; we exercise control in varying degrees over railroads, radio, city planning, air and water traffic; in a thousand other ways, social control for general welfare is growing and must grow in our country. But knowledge of this, of its success and of its prevalence in other lands, does not reach the mass of people. They are being carried away by almost hysterical propaganda that the freedoms which they have and such individual initiative as remains are being threatened and that a third world war is the only remedy.

Not all America has succumbed to this indefensible belief. The Progressive Party . . . has challenged this program, the voters in 1948 declared wide agreement but were induced by fear to vote for a man who has not carried out his promises; the Council of Arts, Sciences and Professions assembled a vast protest against war last year and the religious sect of Quakers have just issued a fine balanced statement in the same line. There are millions of other Americans who agree with these leaders of the peace movement. I bring you their greetings.

My trip to the Soviet Union made it impossible for me to get to the Congress in Mexico City, but I watched with interest other peace conferences: in Cuba in August; in Australia in April 1950; the delegations to the Parliaments of the world, projected by the Defenders of Peace in Paris in February 1950. I joined a group to welcome persons selected to come here, including the Dean of Canterbury, and the great painter, Picasso. They were refused visas. A Mid-Century Conference for Peace was called by the Committee for Peaceful Alternatives in May 1950, in which I was asked to conduct a panel; but a previous engagement kept me away. I was asked to attend the meeting of the Executive Committee of the Paris Defenders of Peace in Prague in August 1951, and accepted. This meeting was to call a Second World Congress and make a new plea for disarmament.

But before this meeting, we had succeeded in forming in the United States an organization to work for peace. This was the Peace Information Center. There were about 60 Americans who attended the World Congress of the Defenders of Peace in Paris in April 1950. We were all tremendously impressed and discussed many times the question as to what we could do when we returned to America. We did nothing for nearly a year, because in the state of hysteria and war-mongering which we found in the United States, it was not at all clear as to what could be done legally.

Finally I received this telegram from O. John Rogge:

"Strongly urge your participation meeting my house 400 East 52 Street at 8 o'clock Wednesday evening March 1st. Purpose is to discuss certain vital problems relating to current activities for promotion of world peace."

I went to the meeting and found that the 30 or 40 persons attending had already in previous meetings been exploring methods of organizing for peace in the United States. The first idea seemed to have been a federation of the various peace movements in the United States already in existence. That had fallen through. Then a committee to welcome the prominent advocates of peace who proposed to visit the United States proved useless when they were refused visas. We appointed a committee to explore possibilities.

A number of the participants in this initial meeting went to Europe to attend a meeting of the Bureau of the Defenders of Peace in Stockholm, and also to visit Russia under the plan of approaching Parliaments in the interests of peace. Our committee adopted a plan which seemed to us all unusually apt and legal, and that was, as we decided at a later meeting in a private home, to form a Peace Information Center, the object of which should be simply to tell the people of the United States what other nations were doing and thinking about war.

Johannes Steele suggested that we publish what he called a "Peacegram" at intervals, and in that way we could collect information and send it over the United States. The proposal to organize was made by the chairman of the committee, Elizabeth Moos, and we proceeded to locate offices and start organized work. In July, Mrs. Moos, on account of ill health, resigned with regret after having put the organization on its feet.

Abbott Simon, a young veteran interested in work among youth, was her obvious successor and became our executive secretary from July to our dissolution. Kyrle Elkin was a young businessman, educated at Harvard, and engaged in small manufacturing. He had never been especially active in social work, but was attracted by our program, and in his quiet way helped us by accepting the duties of treasurer.

We all worked together smoothly and effectively. We issued the "Peacegrams," and then reprinted and circulated the "Stockholm Appeal" to abolish the atom bomb. We distributed this over the nation, and collected in all 2,500,000 signatures. We printed and distributed other demands and arguments for peace, like the Red Cross Appeal, the statement of the Friends, and many others.

The half-billion persons in the world who signed the Stockholm Appeal and the billion who would have signed if given the chance, were moved not by the thought of defending the Soviet Union so much as by the desire to prevent modern culture from relapsing into primitive barbarism.

The first direct public attack on the Peace Information Center came in a broadside from the United States Secretary of State, Dean Acheson, released July 12 (*New York Times*, July 13, 1950):

"I am sure that the American people will not be fooled by the so-called 'world peace appeal' or 'Stockholm resolution' now being circulated in this country for signatures. It should be recognized for what it is—a propaganda trick in the spurious 'peace offensive' of the Soviet Union. . . ."

I replied immediately on July 14, saying in a release to the press:

"The main burden of your opposition to this Appeal and to our efforts lies in the charge that we are part of a 'spurious peace offensive' of the Soviet Union. Is it our strategy that when the Soviet Union asks for peace, we insist on war? Must any proposals for averting atomic catastrophe be sanctified by Soviet opposition? Have we come to the tragic pass where, by declaration of our own Secretary of State, there is no possibility of mediating our differences with the Soviet Union? Does it not occur to you, Sir, that there are honest Americans who, regardless of their differences on other questions, hate and fear war and are determined to do something to avert it? . . . .

"We have got to live in the world with Russia and China. If we worked together with the Soviet Union against the menace of Hitler, can we not work with them again at a time when only faith can save us from utter atomic disaster? Certainly hundreds of millions of colonial peoples in Asia, Africa, Latin America and elsewhere, conscious of our support of Chiang Kai-shek, Bao Dai and the colonial system, and mindful of the oppressive discrimination against the Negro people in the United States, would feel that our intentions also must be accepted on faith.

"Today in this country it is becoming standard reaction to call anything 'communist' and therefore subversive and unpatriotic, which anybody for any reason dislikes. We feel strongly that this tactic has already gone too far; that it is not sufficient today to trace a proposal to a communist source in order to dismiss it with contempt.

"We are a group of Americans, who upon reading this Peace Appeal, regard it as a true, fair statement of what we ourselves and many countless other Americans believed. Regardless of our other beliefs and affiliations, we united in this organization for the one and only purpose of informing the American people on the issues of peace."

The Peace Information Center continued its work. The evidence of the desire for peace came in from all parts of the United States, and especially from those regions where the newspapers were suppressing information. Surprising interest and support came to us especially from the West and South.

In August, I had a cablegram from Paris inviting me to attend as a guest the meeting of the Bureau of the World Congress of the Defenders of Peace in Prague. They were meeting for two main purposes: to broaden the Stockholm Appeal by asking for disarmament; and to arrange a Second World Peace Congress. I regarded this as important and applied for extension of my passport.

It took ten days of deliberation in Washington and two telephone calls before permission came. Even then it was carefully limited to 60 days in Czechoslovakia and "necessary lands" en route, and "was not to be validated for additional countries without the express authorization of the Department of State." I felt like a prisoner on parole.

When asked at Prague to speak, I said:

"For 50 years I have been in touch with social currents in the United States. Never before has organized reaction wielded the power it does today: by ownership of press and radio, by curtailment of free speech, by imprisonment of liberal thinkers and writers. It has become almost impossible today in my country even to hold a public rally for peace. This has been accomplished by inducing Americans to believe that America is in imminent danger of aggression from communism, socialism and liberalism, and that the peace movement cloaks this threat . . . .

"Manifestly, to meet this hysteria, it is not so much a question of the concept of war under any circumstances, as the far deeper problem of getting the truth to the masses of the citizens of the United States who still in overwhelming majority hate murder, crippling destruction and insanity, as a means of progress. By personal contact, by honest appeal, by knowing the truth ourselves, we can yet win the peace in America. But it is going to take guts and the willingness to jeopardize jobs and respectability. . . ."

After this meeting in Prague where the Bureau of the Defenders of Peace finally voted to broaden the "Stockholm Appeal" so as to ask disarmament and condemn aggression and armed intervention, I started home; but on my way I received two messages in Paris, which led to a political campaign and a criminal indictment.

CHAPTER XXI

AN INDICTED CRIMINAL

As I started home in August 1950, I received two cabled messages from the United States. One was from John Abt of the American Labor Party, asking if I would run for United States Senator from New York in the current campaign. The other was from Abbott Simon, executive secretary of the Peace Information Center, informing me that the Department of Justice had demanded our registration as "agents of a foreign principal."

I proceeded to remind Abt of my age and political inexperience, and my unwillingness to run for public office. But Abt said a number of things, of which two sunk in: (1) That this campaign would afford a chance for me to speak for peace which could be voiced in no other way; (2) my candidacy would help the campaign of Vito Marcantonio.

Of all members of Congress, Vito Marcantonio had acted with courage, intelligence and steadfast integrity in the face of ridicule, mud-slinging and cheating. If I could do anything for Marcantonio, I decided to try. On August 31, I wired, "Accept. Du Bois."

My experience in practical politics had been small. First of all I had been reared in the New England tradition of regarding politics as no fit career for a man of serious aims, and particularly unsuitable for a college-bred man. Respectable participation in political life as voter, thinker, writer, and, on rare occasions as speaker, was my ideal. This preoccupation was strengthened by the fact that for Negroes entrance into political life was especially difficult. Spending as I did the 13 years of my early, active life in Georgia, I was disfranchised from the "White Primary" on account of my race, and confined my political work to advice to my students and to writing.

I went into the campaign for Senator knowing well from the first that I did not have a ghost of a chance for election, and that my efforts would bring me ridicule at best and jail at worst. On the other hand, I did have a message which was worth attention and which in the long run could not fail to have influence. The leaders of the American Labor Party and my colleagues on the ticket were more than kind and solicitous; they reduced my participation to a minimum, themselves bore an unfair part of the work, and gave me every help to keep my efforts within my strength and ability.

I delivered, in all, ten speeches and made seven broadcasts. I began with a press conference in Harlem, to which the *Times* and *Herald-Tribune* sent reporters, and the Associated Press; but only one Negro paper was represented. I addressed mass meetings in Harlem, Queens, Brooklyn and the Bronx, each attended by 1,000 to 2,500 persons, who gave me careful attention and generous applause. My last speech in the city of New York was at that marvelous gathering of 17,000 persons at Madison Square Garden on October 24, news of which was nearly blacked out by the press.

On an upstate tour from Buffalo to Albany beginning October 15, I spoke four times to audiences of a few hundred persons in small and rather obscure halls. There was a distinct air of fear and repression. I heard many stories of how the industries of Rochester and Syracuse threatened their workers. In Albany political pressure was tense. While the press was courteous, we evidently were permitted just to touch the edges of real publicity. My main thesis was thus summed up:

"The most sinister evil of this day is the widespread conviction that war is inevitable and that there is no time left for discussion. It is doubtful if the mass of Americans who accept this judgment realize just what its implications are. War is physical force exercised by men and machines on other men so as to compel submission to the will of the victors. Unquestionably in primitive times there were repeated occasions when such recourse to force was the only path to social progress. But as civilization has progressed and included larger and larger masses of men and portions of the earth, two things have become increasingly clear; one, that the costs of war have become too great for any nation to pay, no matter what the alternative; and two, that in war as now carried on, there can be no victorious party. In modern world war all contestants lose and not only lose the immediate causes of strife, but cripple the fundamental bases of human culture."

Above all, I was amazed and exasperated by the overwhelming use and influence of money in politics. Millionaires and corporations, not record and logic, defeated Marcantonio. Dewey could afford to spend $35,000 for one day on radio; when friends of mine the nation over sent $600 to further my campaign, it represented more honesty and guts than all the millions spent on Lehman and Hanley. Small wonder the result of this election throughout the land sounded like a "tale told by an idiot."

Five million persons voted in this election; of these, four per cent voted for me (15 per cent in Harlem), which was far more than I expected. More than a million of the voters stayed away from the polls. As for myself, having not expected anything but defeat, I would not have been surprised if no more than 10,000 persons had voted for me. I was astonished by a vote of 205,729, a vote from men and women of courage, without the prejudice against color which I always expect and usually experience. This meant that these faced poverty and jail to stand and be counted for peace and civil rights. For this I was happy.

The first letter from the Department of Justice to the Peace Information Center was received August 1950. It read:

"The Peace Information Center is engaged in activities within the United States which require registration with the Department under the terms of the Foreign Agents Registration Act of 1938, as amended . . . .

"In view of the length and time that has elapsed since the Peace Information Center has been acting as an agent of a foreign principal without having filed its registration statement as required by law, it is expected that the registration statement will be submitted forthwith."

The executive secretary, Abbott Simon, replied:

"The Peace Information Center is American in its conception and formation. Its activities were intended to and do relate only to the people of the United States. It acts and is responsible only to itself and to the people of this country. It has never agreed, either by contract or otherwise, to act as a 'publicity agent' for a 'foreign principal' as defined in the Act, nor does it purport or assume to act as one."

At the same time Mr. Simon sent our attorney, Gloria Agrin, to Washington, and she verbally and in writing, reiterated the position of the Peace Information Center:

"The inference which you and the Department have made seems to be founded only on the fact that there are people throughout the world who may have, and be expressing, ideas and concepts similar to those expressed by the Peace Information Center. In fact, it might even be surprising to find that this were not so. The minds and desires of men have always transcended national barriers. This is so in every field of endeavor, whether it be art, music, literature, science, or politics. Respect for an Einstein, a Mann, a Picasso, a Pasteur, or a Disraeli, has never been diminished by the fact that they were not American aborigines, nor has esteem for their ideas lessened. It would seem, therefore, to be a startlingly new pattern of reasoning that any idea or activity which is not indigenous to, and confined to, the United States, will subject the holder to the inference that he acts for some person abroad. Concomitantly, such a concept would limit the thought processes of American citizens to the four corners of the United States boundaries."

On September 19, Mr. Foley of the Department of Justice wrote us that the Center's registration "should be submitted without further delay" and added, "Again, let me stress the point that registration under the act is in no way intended to interfere with the operation of the Peace Information Center in its present program." We need not stop our work but must lie as to why we were doing it.

Finally, on February 8, 1951, we were notified that the Grand Jury in Washington had indicted the Peace Information Center and its officers for "failure to register as agent of a foreign principal."

The indictment said in part:

"Continuously during the period from April 3, 1950 to and including the date of the return of this indictment, Peace Information Center has been an agent of a foreign principal, because within the United States (1) it has acted as, and has held itself out to be a publicity center for; (2) it has reported information to; and (3) it has acted at the request of, the Committee of the World Congress of the Defenders of Peace and its successor the World Peace Council . . . ."

The Bill of Particulars added:

"During the period mentioned in the indictment, the officers, directors, and representatives of the Peace Information Center, at the request of its said foreign principal, published and disseminated in the United States the 'Stockholm Peace Appeal' and related information pertaining primarily to prohibition of the use of atomic weapons as instruments of war . . . ."

To this indictment the Peace Information Center replied in a release to the public, setting forth the truth about the organization:

"The defendants deny that peace is a foreign idea; but they gladly admit that they gathered and publicized ideas and news of action for peace from everywhere they could obtain them. They assert that any attempt to curtail such free interchange of thought, opinion, and knowledge of fact the world over is clearly an interference with the constitutional rights of American citizens. The function of this Center was to give to the citizens of this country those facts concerning the worldwide efforts for peace which the American press for the most part was ignoring or suppressing. It did this with the same object that other Americans have spread information of medical advance, efforts for labor uplift, scientific discoveries, plans for housing, suppression of crime and education of youth. The United States has as yet laid no embargo on the importation of ideas, or knowledge of international effort for social uplift; and surely there can be today no greater need for information than in the peace movement and the effort to remove the horrible threat of a Third World War."

Our board of advisers, however, had voted on October 12 to dissolve the Center. We had no intention of running counter to the government, but only wished to make it clear that we did not believe we should register under the law. But closing the office of such a movement takes time. Letters kept pouring in asking for petitions, asking about further peace congresses, asking what anyone could do to help. We answered the letters and used our remaining stock of stationery for this correspondence. We tried to break our lease on the office, but could not do this immediately. Above all we tried to turn all public interest in peace into other channels: into local peace organizations and especially toward a second world peace congress to be held in England. A special committee was organized for this end, and they opened a separate office. But all this closing activity was held against us eventually by the government as evidence of our deliberate flouting of orders. The Department of Justice thus assumed that our real crime was peace and not foreign agency. It was reiterated that the Peace Information Center continued to exist until the indictment was handed down in February 1951. This was technically true.

The Peace Information Center was in existence from April 3, 1951, to October 12 of that year, when it formally disbanded. After that, the closing down of our activities, answering continued correspondence, paying our bills, and ending our lease, kept our office partially in existence until the end of the year. During the seven months of active work, we took in a total of $25,000 from small donations, public and house meetings, and sale of literature for which there was a large demand. We printed and distributed 750,000 pieces, of which 485,000 were petitions for signatures to the Stockholm Appeal. These sold for a cent and cost us a half cent. We also issued a hundred thousand stickers, and thousands of pamphlets for children, Negroes, Jews, Catholics,

Spanish and Italian-speaking minorities whom we tried to interest in peace. In addition came the regular "Peace-gram" with its news of the world peace movement. Our largest two items of expense were about $9,000 for printing and $8,000 for rent and salaries. We had, finally, a mailing list of 6,000 persons in all parts of the nation especially interested in peace.

In 1950 the month of February had for me special meaning. I was a widower. The wife of 53 years lay buried in the New England hills beside her first-born boy. I was lonesome because so many boyhood friends had died, and because a certain illogical reticence on my part had never brought me many intimate friends. But there was a young woman, a minister's daughter, to whom I had been a sort of father confessor in literary affairs and difficulties of life for many years, especially after her father's death 15 years before. I knew her hardships and I had rejoiced in her successes. Shirley Graham, with her beautiful martyr complex, finally persuaded herself that I needed her help and companionship, as I certainly did; so we decided to get married a few days after my next birthday, when I would be 83 years old.

Preparations for a birthday dinner to be held at the Essex House, New York City, were being made at the request of the Council on African Affairs of which I had become vice-chairman after leaving the NAACP. The list of sponsors was imposing and growing daily. Before the indictment about 300 people had made reservations and paid over $2,000.

Then came a strange series of events: on February 8 I was indicted for an alleged crime; on February 14, I was married secretly to Shirley, lest if I were found guilty she might have no right to visit me in jail; February 16 I was arraigned in Washington and on February 19, four days before the dinner, the hotel at which the dinner was planned cancelled our contract by telegram saying:

"Pursuant to our rules and regulations and for other sufficient reasons we hereby advise you that reservations of our facilities for Friday evening, February 23 for the W. E. B.

Du Bois testimonial dinner is cancelled. Deposit is being returned. Vincent J. Coyle, Vice-President and Managing Director, Essex House Hotel, Inc."

We had five days before the dinner to find a place to entertain our 300 guests. In addition to this, three of our speakers, Charlotte Hawkins Brown, Mordecai Johnson and Rabbi Hillel Silver, hastily declined to appear. Some of the sponsors withdrew, but I do not know how many of the original list remained.

I can stand a good deal, and have done so during my life; but this experience was rather more than I felt like bearing, especially as the blows continued to fall. I had meantime been finger-printed, handcuffed, bailed and remanded for trial. I was more than ready to drop all thought of the birthday dinner.

But my remaining friends said No! I could do no less than stand beside them, although without Shirley's faith and strength I probably would not have allowed the dinner to take place. Franklin Frazier, the chairman, stood firm. He said the dinner must and would go on.

There ensued a period of wild search for a place of meeting; of securing other speakers and of notifying participants. Subtly the whole picture changed; instead of a polite, friendly social gesture, this dinner became a fight for civil rights, and into the seats of timid and withdrawing guests slipped a new set of firmer men and women who were willing to face even the United States government in my defense and for the preservation of American freedom. They carried on the battle while I sat uneasily in the background.

The program was hastily rearranged. No white downtown hotel would harbor us, and turning to Harlem we found Small's Paradise, well-known to the cabaret world, much too small but with a proprietor willing and eager even to lose money by the venture. At the dinner Belford Lawson, head of the Alpha Phi Alpha fraternity, volunteered and made a fighting speech; Paul Robeson spoke courageously and feelingly. A strong letter from Judge Hubert Delany was read. Franklin Frazier presided and spoke. The room was crowded to suffocation, and many could not get to their seats. But the spirit was what the Germans call *feierlich* [festive]! Finally, amid cheers, birthday cakes and flowers, I made my speech. There were about 700 persons present who paid $6,557 in dinner fees and donations.

In this indictment of the Peace Information Center, I received a severe jolt, because in fact I found myself being punished before I was tried. In the first place, the Department of Justice allowed the impression to spread that my colleagues and I had in some way betrayed our country. Although the charge was not treason, it was widely understood and said that the Peace Information Center had been discovered to be an agent of the Soviet Union.

When we were arraigned in Washington February 16, the proceedings were brusque and unsympathetic. We were not treated as innocent people whose guilt was to be inquired into, but distinctly as criminals whose innocence was to be proven, which was assumed to be doubtful.

The white commercial press treated our case either with silence or violent condemnation. The New York *Herald-Tribune* had this editorial, February 11:

"The Du Bois outfit was set up to promote a tricky appeal of Soviet origin, poisonous in its surface innocence, which made it appear that a signature against the use of atomic weapons would forthwith insure world peace. It was, in short, an attempt to disarm America and yet ignore every form of Communist aggression. A lot of 'men and women of good will through the world,' to quote the petition's bland phrasing, were snared into signing without quite realizing that this thing came straight out of the Cominform."

So far as the nation was concerned, Alice Barrows secured 220 leaders of the arts, sciences, clergy and other professions in 33 states, including 35 universities, to sign "A Statement to the American People," released June 27, calling for the withdrawal of the prosecution. The statement, initiated by the National Council of the Arts, Sciences and Professions, described the indictment as "but one of numerous recent actions against individuals and organizations that advocate peaceful solutions to the world's crisis. In this time of hysteria, the attempted labeling of 'foreign agent' on a distinguished scholar and leader of a peace movement can fairly be interpreted as an effort to intimidate and silence all advocates of peace."

The response of Negroes in general was slow. At first many Negroes were puzzled. They did not understand the indictment and assumed that I had let myself be drawn into some treasonable acts or movements in retaliation for continued discrimination in this land, which I had long fought. They understood this and forgave it, but thought my action ill-advised. The Norfolk *Journal and Guide* expressed this clearly. The *Chicago Defender* said:

"Dr. Du Bois has earned many honors and it is a supreme tragedy that he should have become embroiled in activities that have been exposed as subversive in the twilight of his years." But on the other hand, editors like Percival Prattis of the *Pittsburgh Courier,* Carl Murphy of the *Afro-American,* and columnists like Marjorie McKenzie, J. A. Rogers, and others, showed a courage and real intellectual leadership which was lacking elsewhere. The reaction of Negroes revealed a distinct cleavage not hitherto clear in American Negro opinion. The intelligentsia, the "Talented Tenth," the successful business and professional men, were not, for the most part, outspoken in my defense. There were many and notable exceptions, but as a group this class was either silent or actually antagonistic. The reasons were clear; many believed that the government had actual proof of subversive activities on our part; until the very end they awaited their disclosure.

Other Negroes of intelligence and prosperity had become American in their acceptance of exploitation as defensible, and in their imitation of American "conspicuous expenditure." They proposed to make money and spend it as pleased them. They had beautiful homes, large and expensive cars and fur coats. They hated "communism" and "socialism" as much as any white American. Their reaction toward Paul

Robeson was typical; they simply could not understand his surrendering a thousand dollars a night for a moral conviction.

This dichotomy in the Negro group, this development of class structure, was to be expected, and will be more manifest in the future, as discrimination against Negroes as such decreases. There will gradually arise among American Negroes a separation according to their attitudes toward labor, wealth and work. It is still my hope that the Negro's experience in the past will, in the end, lead the majority of his intelligentsia into the ranks of those advocating social control of wealth, abolition of exploitation of labor, and equality of opportunity for all.

I have belonged to a Negro graduate fraternity for 45 years—indeed helped its first formation. Today it contains in its membership a large number of leading business and professional Negroes in the United States. Yet of its 30 or more chapters covering the nation, only one expressed any sympathy with me, and none offered aid. It is probable that individual members of the fraternity gave my cause support, but no official action was taken save in one case. In my own New York chapter I was bitterly criticized.

Another of our projects was to secure the names of a dozen nationally prominent Negroes to this statement:

". . . We are not here concerned with the political or social beliefs of Dr. Du Bois. Many of us do not agree with him on these and other matters. But we are concerned with the right of a man to say within the law what he thinks without being subject to threat and intimidation. Especially we are concerned with Dr. Du Bois as a leader of the Negro American for 50 years. In that time until now his integrity and absolute sincerity has never been questioned. . . ."

We did not, however, succeed in getting enough such signatures to this statement to warrant its circulation. I recognized the fear in the Negro group, especially among the educated and well-to-do. One said to me sadly, "I have a son in government employ; he has a well-paid position and is in line for promotion. He has worked long for this start and has had many disappointments. I am sorry but I dare not sign this."

I served the NAACP for 28 years in all. When this case came up, although I was no longer officially connected with the organization, branches and members all over the nation wanted to help me and urged the main office to join in. The president of the Board of Directors said frankly to Shirley Graham that undoubtedly the Peace Information Center was supported by funds from the Soviet Union. He admitted that it was possible that I did not know this. At a meeting, March 12, of the Board of Directors, it was urged that the Board take a position on the indictment, and as one branch said, "give active, tangible aid to Dr. Du Bois in his present plight." However, the secretary, Walter White, reported that he had talked with Peyton Ford, assistant to the Attorney-General in Washington, and was told that there was definite evidence of guilt in the hands of the Department of Justice and that the four associates of Dr. Du Bois could not be prosecuted without prosecuting Dr. Du Bois.

A white member of the Board had offered to take up the matter of asking the legal department of the NAACP to join in our defense. After this member heard our "certain guilt" stated he made no further effort.

The Board finally passed this resolution:

"Without passing on the merits of the recent indictment of Dr. Du Bois, the board of directors of the NAACP expresses the opinion that this action against one of the great champions of civil rights lends color to the charge that efforts are being made to silence spokesmen for full equality of Negroes. The board also reaffirms its determination to continue its aggressive fight for full citizenship rights for all Americans."

Even this resolution was not given much publicity, and the main office advised the branches strongly "not to touch" this case. Some branches vigorously complained, and despite the attitude of the New York office, many branches of the NAACP supported our campaign.

Our appeal to the officials of the World Defenders of

Peace resulted in wide publicity for our case all over the world. Messages began to pour in to us from Europe, Asia and Africa; from the West Indies and South America. We received letters from England, Scotland, and France; from Belgium, Holland, Luxembourg, and Scandinavia; from Germany, the Union of Socialist Soviet Republics, Austria, Czechoslovakia, Poland, Rumania, Albania, Hungary, Trieste, and Switzerland; from Canada, Cuba, Martinique, Jamaica, British Guiana and Brazil; from West Africa, South Africa, Southeast Asia, China, Viet Nam, Indonesia, India and Australia. International bodies sent their support, including the International Union of Students, the World Federation of Teachers' Unions, the International Federation of Women, the World Federation of Scientific Workers, and others.

An "International Committee in Defense of Dr. W. E. B. Du Bois and his Colleagues" was formed. The original signers included a university professor from Holland; two professors from Switzerland; a judge of the Court of Appeals and a federal judge in Brazil; two magistrates from Colombia and Iran; an Italian senator; and the president of the French Court of Cassation; together with ten Americans, eight white and two Negro. Eventually this committee grew to 200 with 33 Frenchmen, 30 Poles, 12 Belgiums, 11 Germans, seven Englishmen, six Italians, five Brazilians, four each from Switzerland, the Soviet Union, Hungary and China; one to three each from Rumania, Bulgaria, Iran, Lebanon, Martinique, Holland, Austria; and 59 from the United States, of whom six were colored. Isabelle Blume of Belgium was chairman.

Articles were published in Austria, India, the Soviet Union, the Shanghai *China News* and *Edinburgh Review* in Scotland. The story was told in at least a dozen different languages. From the West Indies came letters, from the professors of the University of Havana and outstanding Cubans like Dr. Fernando Ortiz, Latin America's most famous sociologist; Dr. Domingo Villamil, eminent Catholic jurist; and Juan Marinello, senator and poet.

The International Union of Students wrote to the Department of Justice:

"On behalf of over 5,000,000 students in 71 countries, the International Union of Students expresses indignation at the prosecution of Dr. Du Bois and associates. Du Bois is an internationally known scholar and spokesman for peace. His work for peace is in best traditions of the American people. Prosecution is an attack upon peace supporters, upon Negro people and upon right of professors and students to act for peace. We join with peace-loving people throughout the world in demanding that you dismiss Du Bois' indictment and end persecution of United States peace supporters."

Despite the difficulty of securing meeting places in New York where we could defend our cause, we succeeded late in September in organizing a meeting in Town Hall. The National Council of the Arts, Sciences and Professions put on an interesting program, with Professor Henry Pratt Fairchild presiding. Here Bishop Wright, Corliss Lamont and Lawrence D. Reddick, former curator of the Schomburg Collection and then Librarian of Atlanta University, spoke. Dr. Reddick said in part:

"I have just come from a part of our country where the flag of the Confederacy is more popular than the flag of the United States of America; where Robert E. Lee is not only more of a hero than Ulysses S. Grant but also more than George Washington; and where the Governor threatens to close down the State's entire system of education if the courts should compel the public, tax-supported institutions that are presently maintained for whites only to admit a single Negro."

I wrote this statement for the defendants:

"This case is a blow at civilization: by instituting thought control; by seeking to stop the circulation of ideas; by seeking to shut off the free flow of culture around the world and reducing all American culture to the level of Mississippi and Nevada; by making it a crime to think as others think, if your thought is against the prejudices or graft or barbarism of some backwoods partisan; by making it treason to brand the hoary lie that War is the path to Peace; by crucifying fathers and mothers who do not want their sons raised to murder men, women and children . . .

"The Government can put into absolute control of our thinking, feeling and culture any set of half-educated fanatics from Southern rotten boroughs or western mining camps or Missouri gang politics in order to: curtail and misdirect education in America; limit thought and twist ambition; send school children hiding under desks instead of learning to read and write; make saints of spies, informers and professional liars; make a prisoned nation call Freedom that which is slavery and to change a Democracy into a police state!

"Wake up, America. Your liberties are being stolen before your very eyes. What Washington, Jefferson and Lincoln fought for, Truman, Acheson, and McGrath are striving desperately to nullify. Wake up, Americans, and dare to think and say and do. Dare to cry: No More War!"

This brought forward the whole question of costs. It had not occurred to us how costly justice in the United States is. It is not enough to be innocent in order to escape punishment. You must have money and a lot of it. In the end it cost us $35,150 to prosecute this case to a successful end, not counting the fee refused by the Chief Counsel. If, as we had confidently expected, the case had gone to higher courts to determine the constitutionality of this foreign agents Act, it might have cost us $100,000. Before this prospect of sheer cost, we stood for many weeks appalled and discouraged. We realized more than ever that this trial was not going to be simply a legal process, but a political persecution, the outcome of which would depend on public opinion; and that to raise the funds necessary for our defense, we would need the contributions of large numbers of poor people and need have no hope for gifts from the rich.

There followed an appeal to the people of the United States, by lecture trips undertaken by myself and my wife, Shirley Graham. We wished to meet the blackout in the press by explaining our case; and to collect funds for our legal expenses. But before we started West, a central committee was formed in New York. Former Minnesota Governor Elmer Benson and artist Paul Robeson were elected co-chairmen. First came all the difficulties of setting up an office, enhanced by the nature of our particular case and the usual problems of race. After two or three volunteer workers, we secured Alice Citron as secretary. She was one of the public school teachers of New York City who had been a victim of the witch-hunt.

Alice Citron taught colored children 18 years in Harlem. She was regarded widely as "the best of the best teachers in our system." On May 3, 1950, Superintendent Jansen of the New York City schools suspended her without pay because she had not answered the question: "Are you or were you ever a member of the Communist Party?" He said that he knew nothing of her record in the classroom or in the community. He might have added that he cared less. Miss Citron was dismissed. She took charge of our defense office. She became out executive secretary and threw herself into the work with unfaltering sacrifice and at a nominal salary.

We started out in the Spring, in June. Our plan was for Shirley to speak first and explain the case. Shirley spoke easily and interestingly, without notes and with an intense vigor which set the audiences on the edges of their seats. Then came the collection directed by some local person of standing. Then I spoke:

> The world is astonished at recent developments in the United States. Our actions and attitudes are discussed with puzzled wonder on the streets of every city in the world. Reluctantly the world is coming to believe that we actually want war; that we must have war; that in no other way can we keep our workers employed and maintain huge profits save by spending 70 thousand million dollars a year for war preparations and adding to the vast debt of 218 thousand millions which we already owe chiefly for war in the past. . . .
>
> If tomorrow Russia disappeared from the face of the earth, the basic problem facing the modern world would remain; and that is: Why is it, with the earth's abundance and our mastery of natural forces, and miraculous technique; with our commerce belting the earth; and goods and services pouring from our stores, factories, ships and warehouses; why is it that nevertheless most human beings are starving to death, dying of preventable disease, and too ignorant to

know what is the matter, while a small minority are so rich that they cannot spend their income?

That is the problem which faces the world, and Russia was not the first to pose it, nor will she be the last to ask and demand answer. . . .

It does not answer this worldwide demand to say that we of America have these things in greater abundance than the rest of the world, if our prosperity is based on or seeks to base itself on, the exploitation and degradation of the rest of mankind. Remember, it is American money that owns more and more of South African mines worked by slave labor; it is American enterprise that fattens off Central African copper; it is American investors that seek to dominate China, India, Korea, and Burma, and who are throttling the starved workers of the Near East, the Caribbean and South America. . . .

I have never thought I would live to see the day that free speech and freedom of opinion would be so throttled in the United States as it is today, when students in our colleges may not hear or discuss the truth. Today, in this free country, no man can be sure of earning a living, of escaping slander and personal violence, or even of keeping out of jail—unless publicly and repeatedly he proclaims that:

He hates Russia.

He opposes socialism and communism.

He supports wholeheartedly the war in Korea.

He is ready to spend any amount for further war, anywhere or anytime.

He is ready to fight the Soviet Union, China and any other country, or all countries together.

He believes in the use of the atom bomb or any other weapon of mass destruction, and regards anyone opposed as a traitor.

To that great audience of 15,000 people in the Coliseum of Chicago my address had a clear thesis. I wanted to dispel in the minds of the government and of the public any lingering doubt as to my determination to think and speak freely on the economic foundation of the wars and the frustration of the 20th century. I think even the sponsors of this meeting shrank at my outspoken analysis. I am sure the government gave up all hope that I would succumb to fear and sink to acquiescence and silence. I said in part:

Big business in the United States is forcing this nation into war, transforming our administration into a military dictatorship, paralyzing all democratic controls and depriving us of knowledge we need. The United States is ruled today by great industrial corporations controlling vast aggregations of capital and wealth. The acts and aims of this unprecedented integration of power, employing some of the best brain and ability of the land, are not and never have been under democratic control. Its dictatorship has varied from absolute monarchy to oligarchy, limited by organized labor and by often ineffective public opinion, trying repeatedly and desperately to express itself through free elections.

If sincere dislike of this state of affairs is communism, then by the living God, no force of arms, nor power of wealth, nor smartness of intellect will ever stop it. Denial of this right to think will manufacture Communists faster than you can jail or kill them. Nothing will stop such communism but something better than communism. If our present policies are examples of free enterprise and individual initiative, they feed crime and initiate suffering, as well as make wealth; if this is the American way of life, God save America.

There is no way in the world for us to preserve the ideals of a democratic America, save by drastically curbing the present power of concentrated wealth; by assuming ownership of some natural resources, by administering many of our key industries, and by socializing our services for public welfare. This need not mean the adoption of the communism of the Soviet Union, nor the socialism of Britain, nor even of the near-socialism of France, Italy, or Scandinavia; but either in some way or to some degree we socialize our economy, restore the New Deal, and inaugurate the welfare state, or we descend into military fascism which will kill all dreams of democracy; of the abolition of poverty, disease and ignorance; or of peace instead of war.

There must come vast social change in the United States; a change not violent, but by the will of the people certain and inexorable, carried out "with malice toward none but charity for all"; with meticulous justice to the rich and thrifty, and complete sympathy for the poor, the sick and the ignorant; with Freedom and Democracy for America, and on earth, Peace, Goodwill toward men.

The government not only went to trouble and large expense, risked its own reputation, but also forced us to extraordinary and worldwide effort, to escape punishment. Personally, I had no funds for such a case. I was retired from work, with a pension too small for normal expenses of living. My wife's work and income were seriously curtailed by her complete immersion in this case. We had no rich friends. None of the defendants were able personally to finance this case. Had it not been for the almost miraculous rise of American friends, we would have gone to jail by default. Not a cent of money for the trial came from abroad. Even had this been possible, it would have been used to convict us. But in this nation by popular appeal to poor and middle-class folk, Negroes and white, trade unions and other groups, we raised funds for these purposes:

Legal fees, $18,400; publicity, $5,600; office, $5,250; salaries, $3,600; travel, $2,365.

To this should be added additional legal fees of at least $13,000; $3,000 paid to an attorney hired by one of the defendants and not paid for by the Committee, and at least $10,000 which Marcantonio earned but would not accept. This amounts to a total of $40,215. To this should be added at least $2,000 in travel expenses paid by localities. How much the case cost the government we cannot know, but it could not have been less than $100,000 and it might have been much more.

I have faced during my life many unpleasant experiences; the growl of a mob; the personal threat of murder; the scowling distaste of an audience. But nothing has so cowed me as that day, November 8, 1951, when I took my seat in a Washington courtroom as an indicted criminal. I was not a criminal. I had broken no law, consciously or unwittingly. Yet I sat with four other American citizens of unblemished character, never before accused even of misdemeanor, in the seats often occupied by murderers, forgers and thieves; accused of a felony and liable to be sentenced before leaving this court to five years of imprisonment, a fine of $10,000 and loss of my civil and political rights as a citizen, representing five generations of Americans.

CHAPTER XXII

THE TRIAL

In strictly legal aspect, remember what this trial was: it was not a question of our opinions and beliefs; it involved no question as to whether we were Communists, Socialists, Jehovah's Witnesses or Nudists; it involved no imputation of moral turpitude except in so far as it is a statutory crime to say what foreigners are saying at the command of those foreigners. The judge said:

"The point in this case is whether or not this organization acted as an agent or in a capacity similar to that for a foreign organization or foreign political power, whether advocating peace, advocating this, or advocating that. They can advocate the distribution of wealth; they can advocate that all red-headed men be shot. It doesn't make any difference what they advocate."

In our case there came another angle, the colored juror. In many parts of the nation, Negroes seldom or never serve on juries. But in the District of Columbia, lately, continually there are many Negro jurors drawn, so much so that there has been a distinct movement to curb their choice. Something of this was heard by the lawyers in our case, and they were prepared to fight it. But on the other hand, we sensed another and more hurtful method of opposition. There is a considerable proportion of Negroes in government employ: in the post office, as teachers in the public schools, as civil servants in dozens of branches. All such employees in Washington, white as well as black, are in fear of attack by witch-hunts and loyalty tests.

It was not even fully admitted until the third week of the trial that the government did not allege that the Soviet Union was the "foreign principal" accused in the indictment. It was never alleged that we had no right to advocate peace. It was only the question: were we "agents" of a foreign principal? Yet and despite all this, the public was de-

liberately given to understand by spokesmen of government
and by the press that we were accused of lying, spying, and
treason in the pay of the Soviet Union. As one of the atten-
dants said in the ante-room of the court, scowling at us: "If
the damned Communists don't like this country, why don't
they go back to Russia?"

The chief dependence of the prosecution was on O. John
Rogge. Rogge the witness was a caricature of Rogge the
crusader for peace and reform. In place of the erect self-
confident if not arrogant leader, came a worn man, whose
clothes hung loosely on him, and who in a courtroom where
he had conducted many cases, had difficulty locating me in
the defendant's chair. I voluntarily stood up to help him
out.

He admitted his membership in the Peace Information
Center. He admitted his attendance at the World Peace Congress; but declared that its actual objective was not peace,
but that it was an agency for the foreign policy of the Soviet
Union. The Court asked the prosecution:

"Do you expect to show that the World Council for Peace
was in fact an agent of another principal, namely the Soviet
Union?"

Mr. Maddrix answered: "We do not intend to show that
the Committee of the Congress of the World Defenders of
Peace was an agent of the Soviet Union."

As a result of this admission the Court said:

"I thought I ought to be advised at this juncture just
exactly what the Government expected to show with reference to the Soviet Union being the principal of the Peace
Information Center."

The prosecution then again admitted: "We do not charge
in our indictment that the foreign principal in any way involves an element of agency as I understand this case, between the foreign principal, the Committee of the World
Congress, and the Soviet Union."

The Court then asked Mr. Maddrix if he considered Mr.
Rogge an expert. He said no, but that no one was in a better
position than Mr. Rogge to know what was going on and to

answer this particular question. He was a member of the policy-making group and had attended its meetings. The Court then said:

"I am not trying any propaganda lines. I am not trying any foreign policy questions involving any country, including our own. You have a very simple case here. You charged this Peace Information Center and these individuals, as officers and directors, as being agent of a foreign principal, and disseminating propaganda in the United States. You have got to show a tie-up between the principal so-called and the so-called agent. If you don't do that, you are out of court."

Thereupon, when the jury had returned, the judge addressed them saying that when Rogge was on the stand he was asked what the purpose of the World Council for Peace was, and he answered. The judge went on:

"You are now instructed by the Court, as emphatically as I can make words that lend emphasis to what I say, that you are to disregard Mr. Rogge's opinion of what he thought the purpose of the Stockholm Peace Appeal was. It is a very simple rule of evidence that excludes that type of opinion, because opinion is excluded, and the only opinion that is permitted to be introduced in a court of law, in certain circumstances, is the opinion of an expert. So, therefore, you will disregard entirely the characterization of the witness Rogge with reference to what he thought the World Council for Peace had in view."

Although we did not at the time realize it, and still watched narrowly for trumped-up testimony, it was right here that we won our case. The prosecution had rested its whole case on Rogge's testimony that we were representing the Soviet Union through the Defenders of Peace organization in Paris. They had naturally not an iota of real proof of this, but they planned to depend on public opinion. But Rogge's own testimony convicted him. He was a member of the Peace Information Center; he was a member of the policy-making bureau of the Defenders of Peace. He had visited the Soviet Union and spoken as a representative of the Defenders of Peace and the Peace Information Center.

He had sworn on oath when he himself became an agent of Yugoslavia that he was not a member of any other foreign agency.

The prosecutor tried now to say that the Peace Information Center acted and held itself out to be a publicity agent, "that the proof of that does not require the showing of any nexus or any direct connection between the Peace Information Center and the foreign principal."

The Court: "Let's stop right there. Why doesn't the statute require that?" Mr. Cunningham tried to refer to the legislative history of the bill, but this the Court refused to allow, and said: "You have got to show nexus and you have got to show nexus either by direct or circumstantial evidence."

Armistice Day, November 11, had interrupted the trial and given a three day recess. I took the occasion to fill a conditional promise to speak at the Community Church in Boston, where for some years I have made annual addresses. Mr. [Donald G.] Lothrop, the minister, in introducing me, reminded the congregation that a spiritual founder of this church, Theodore Parker, had once also been an indicted criminal. I said in part:

> The real cause of World War will persist and threaten so long as peoples of Europe and America are determined to control the wealth of most of the world by means of cheap labor and monopolies. Against this a resurgence of the revolt of the poor will raise a new Russia from the dead if we kill this one, and birth a new theory of communism so long as Africa, Asia and South America see the impossibility of otherwise escaping poverty, ignorance and disease. . . .
>
> We who have known a better America find the present scene almost unbelievable. A great silence has fallen on the real soul of the nation. We are smearing loyal citizens on the paid testimony of self-confessed liars, traitors and spies. We are making the voice of America the babble of cowards paid to travel. . . .
>
> My words are not a counsel of despair. Rather they are a call to new courage and determination to know the truth. Four times this nation has faced disaster and recovered: Once at the end of the 18th century when we hesitated between separate independent colonies and a disciplined federal state; again when in the age of Jackson, the uncouth, democratic west overbore the oligarchical well-mannered east;

once more in the 19th century when human slavery cut the heart of the nation in two and we had to cement it with blood; finally, when in 1929 our boasted industries fell in vast ruin and begged on their knees for government aid, until Roosevelt rescued them with socialist planning and gave his life to rebuilding our economy. What we have done, we can do again. But not by silence—not by refusing to face the ugly facts.

When the trial resumed Marcantonio insisted that the basic definition of "agency" in the law of 1938 was not changed by the law of 1942, and that (1) the government must establish that the Peace Information Center was subject to control of the Paris Defenders of Peace; (2) that the Peace Information Center was subject to control of the Defenders of Peace; (3) that the Defenders of Peace had consented to the fact that the Peace Information Center should act on its behalf; (4) that the Peace Information Center consented to act for the Defenders of Peace; and (5) that there was a consent on the part of the Peace Information Center to be subject to the control of the Defenders of Peace. "All these are musts; if any one of these fails, the case fails."

The argument went over into the afternoon. The judge intervened with the following analogy, directed to Mr. Maddrix of the prosecution. He said: "Suppose you were living in Vienna and published a pamphlet in New York at my expense. The Government asks me to register as your agent. I refuse. I maintain that while I agree with your thought I am not your agent and therefore will not register. Is that not right?"

Mr. Maddrix replied that the Government insisted that the agency was implied by the similarity of ideas. Here Mr. Cunningham of the prosecution, a lank Texan with a perpetually anxious scowl, came up with the extraordinary plea that no connection need be proven. He maintained that a publicity agent as defined by the law of 1942 was not an agency in the sense of the law of 1938:

"You have to go further and show, as your Honor points out, that one was doing it for the other, not necessarily by contract, and not necessarily by any agreement at all. The foreign principal may never have heard of the person here, as I have said before. We have to show it was the subjective intent of these people here to disseminate information in the United States, propaganda for and on behalf of, and further the propaganda objectives of the European organization."

The judge leaned forward and asked how a person disseminating propaganda of the type that the statute prohibits could be found guilty of acting for a foreign principal, "if the principal never heard of the disseminator and disseminator never heard of the principal?" The judge continued, "Your contention is this: that if there is an argument about salt and pepper, Congress, by virtue of its power, said, 'pepper could be salt and salt could be pepper.' "

Mr. Cunningham answered, "Yes sir. That is exactly what is confusing the issue here."

Here the arguments ended. The jury had not yet been summoned. Without giving us any chance to offer our testimony or the sworn depositions of the Defenders of Peace; without waiting for the character witnesses, Judge McGuire, sitting at his high rostrum, rendered his verdict. We still were waiting for that overwhelming proof of guilt which for nine months the Department of Justice had promised. It never came. The judge said:

"The Government has alleged that 'Peace Information Center' was the agent of a foreign principal. They proved the existence, in my judgment, of the Peace Information Center. They certainly proved the existence of the World Council for Peace . . . . There may have been, and I take it as proven, there were individuals who were officers of both; but, applying the test, as laid down here, in a case which, presumably, is the law of the land (because an appeal to the Supreme Court of the United States *certiorari* was denied in the case)—in this case the Government has failed to support, on the evidence adduced, the allegations laid down in the indictment. So, therefore, the motion, under the circumstances, for a judgment of acquittal will be granted."

For a moment a wave of surprised excitement passed over

the audience, which had been listening breathlessly. Applause seemed on the edge of bursting out. Behind me, as I afterwards learned, my wife fainted. I, myself, felt slightly numb. Someone on my left kissed my cheek. But the judge, changing his position slightly, but with no change of tone, quickly warned against any demonstration, and continued to speak. I thought that perhaps I had misunderstood him, and that some modification of his words was coming. The judge proceeded:

"The judge's function is exhausted when he determines that the evidence does or does not permit the conclusion of guilt beyond reasonable doubt within a fair operation of a reasonable mind. So, therefore, if the case should go to the jury, I would be permitting the jury to conjecture in a field of conjecture, and, in addition to that, if they could resolve the evidence in the case with any reasonable hypothesis looking toward the defendants, then, under the circumstances, they are obliged to do so, and then, as a consequence, they would have to be so instructed.

"So the case goes off, in my view, on a conception of law. The government maintains one point of view and defense maintains another. I think that the position of the defense is maintained and supported by the opinion mentioned and that opinion is conclusive in my mind; and that is my ruling."

The jury was then brought in, the ruling of the Court explained to them, and they were discharged. We were free for the first time in nine months.

We left Washington as quickly as possible. I was, frankly, bewildered. Of all the results of this fantastic and utterly unfair indictment, this was quite the last which I had awaited. At first I had confidently expected that after conference and explanation, the indictment would be quashed. Then, when it was relentlessly pushed, and the case set for trial, I had expected that after a series of delays and postponements, the actual trial would never take place. This would have been unsatisfactory, and left us long in unease, but it would have been better than a criminal procedure. Then, when the indictment was pushed and the trial opened, our best hope was for a failure to agree on the part of the jury where Negroes outnumbered whites two to one. This would have left a bad taste and brought the charge that narrow race loyalty had defeated justice—an argument for excluding Negro jurors hereafter. With the acceptance of the jury there could be but one conclusion, and that was that the government thought it had absolute proof to convict us.

Indeed, there is evidence that this is what the highest authorities said, and allowed the public to believe. But we knew that even if the government thought it had such proof, it was either mistaken or the alleged proof was based on a deliberate lie. We had never asked or been offered opportunity to act as agent of any foreign person, organization or government; our organization had never received a cent of money from abroad or from representatives of foreigners for its work, so far as we knew or believed. Indeed, the total amount of our funds was far too modest, and its expenditure too easily proven to indicate any foreign aid. It would have been possible to prove the source of every penny, if we had been pushed to divulge each contributor. But this would have been a betrayal of trust, and grossly unfair to donors, who were often so afraid of the FBI as to refuse to give anything to any cause. But the facts were clear enough without this resort. We had received no large sums, never more than single gifts of a hundred dollars, and very seldom as much as that. We had books and testimony to show receipts and every dollar of expenses.

Of course, there were many who continually intimated that while I or even most of my colleagues knew nothing of treachery and bribery, nevertheless someone in the organization might have been a spy or foreign agent. Anybody can sometimes be deceived, but to those of us who knew this group, such accusation or suspicion was simply silly.

Why, then had the Department of Justice been so arrogant, determined, and certain? Why did it so impudently brush off my offer to explain our whole work? If, after explanation, the Department had indicated any way in which we had transgressed the law, I was quite ready to change our methods or give up the whole project. But one thing we could not do, and that was to say under oath that we had been and were "agents of a foreign principal." This was a lie that no government could compel us to tell no matter what the penalty.

But of course this unjustified effort to make five persons register as the source of foreign propaganda for peace and patricularly to scare 15 million Negroes from complaint, was not the real object of this long and relentless persecution. The real object was to prevent American citizens of any sort from daring to think or talk against the determination of big business to reduce Asia to colonial subserviency to American industry; to reweld the chains on Africa; to consolidate United States control of the Caribbean and South America; and above all to crush socialism in the Soviet Union and China. That was the object of this case.

This object every intelligent American knew. Our leading thinkers and educators were perfectly aware of this assault on the basis of the democratic process in America. Even if some thought peace at present dangerous and did not believe in socialism, they knew that if democracy was to survive in modern culture and in this vaunted "Land of the Free" and leader of "free nations," the right to think and to speak; the right to know what others were thinking; particularly to know opinion in that Europe which, despite our provincial and vulgar boasting and Golgotha of world wars, is still our main source of science and culture—that this democratic right of freedom of thought and speech must be preserved from Truman and McGrath; McCarran and Smith; from McCarthy and little Georgia's Joseph Wood leading the reactionary slave South—or America was dead.

Despite this, most Americans of education and stature did not say a word or move a hand. This is the most astonishing and frightening result of this trial. We five are free but America is not. The absence of moral courage and intellectual integrity which our prosecution revealed still stands to frighten our own nation and the better world. It is clear still today, that freedom of speech and of thinking can be attacked in the United States without the intellectual and moral leaders of this land raising a hand or saying a word in protest or defense, except in the case of the Saving Few. Their ranks did not include the heads of the great universities, the leaders of religion, or most of the great names in science. Than this fateful silence there is on earth no greater menace to present civilization.

It was the State Department which started this prosecution to quell Communists, and retard the peace movement which was beginning to annoy the Pentagon. The inclusion of myself, a Negro, in the dragnet, was probably at first fortuitous, but quickly backed by the military as a needed warning to complaining Negroes. When rising public opinion fastened on me as the key figure, the determination of the government to convict me increased, especially when I refused to plead *nolo contendere* and my contumacious speeches continued. The continued appeals to Truman and McGrath must have had effect, but were ignored at the insistence of the State Department, until the volume of protest abroad compelled attention, centered emphasis on the Negro question in America, and made even the Catholic church aware that the growing extent of its proselytizing among Negroes might suffer from the fact that the Attorney-General was a Catholic.

The Department of Justice evidently put its main faith in Rogge's testimony to secure a conviction. But when the judge excluded testimony about the foreign policy of the Soviet Union, and testimony about the aims and acts of the World Defenders of Peace, demanding first that evidence of our agency of the Defenders of Peace be introduced, the value of Rogge's testimony was very small and more damning against him than us. Hearing this, the Department of Justice had made a frantic last minute search of all possible sources of information for possible discovery of spies and stoolpigeons. Practically every person who had attended any meetings of the Peace Information Center or been connected in any way was visited by FBI agents, often two or three times, and many of them subpoenaed. So little was discovered, however, that at the last moment most of these witnesses were never summoned.

As public opinion against this prosecution belted the earth and threatened to erupt into the Assembly of the United Nations, and when, despite free trips abroad for prominent Negroes and threats against Negro professionals, civil servants and businessmen, the volume of Negro protest increased rather than stopped, Truman and the National Democratic Committee began to listen to the warning of the highest placed Negro Democrats, and the pressure for conviction lessened.

There was some indication that an attack on colored jurors might be tried, but that seemed too risky. All Jews on the panel were barred, but Negroes, most of them office-holders and subject to intimidation, were accepted. But any verdict of conviction with a jury of eight Negroes and four whites was hardly probable. A devout Catholic judge, who once faced trouble for refusing to grant any divorces, was assigned to the case.

What turns me cold in all this experience is the certainty that thousands of innocent victims are in jail today because they had neither money, experience nor friends to help them. The eyes of the world were on our trial despite the desperate effort of press and radio to suppress the facts and cloud the real issues; the courage and money of friends and of strangers who dared stand for a principle freed me; but God only knows how many who were as innocent as I and my colleagues are today in hell. They daily stagger out of prison doors embittered, vengeful, hopeless, ruined. And of this army of the wronged, the proportion of Negroes is frightful. We protect and defend sensational cases where Negroes are involved. But the great mass of arrested or accused black folk have no defense. There is desperate need of nationwide organizations to oppose this national racket of railroading to jails and chain gangs the poor, friendless and black.

Only a minority of the business and professional Negroes

of Harlem attended my birthday dinner after the indictment was known. Of the 50 presidents of Negro colleges,
every one of which I had known and visited—and often
many times as speaker and advisor—of these only one,
Charles Johnson of Fisk University, publicly professed belief in my integrity before the trial; and only one congratu-
lated me after the acquittal.

The Negro churches varied: the Baptists of Philadelphia
strongly supported me, but the National Baptist Convention
took no action; several bishops of the A.M.E. and Zion
Church connections expressed sympathy, and my undergraduate Negro fraternity, the Alpha Phi Alpha, was divided in opinion. The colored Elks supported me through
their chief official, but none of the other colored secret
orders did.

Colored public school teachers sat in almost complete
silence. All this shows not necessarily lack of sympathy for
me in my persecution, but the wide fear and intimidation
of the Negro people of America, afraid for jobs, appointments, business opportunities, and even of personal safety.

In contrast to all this lethargy and fright, the mass support
which I gained from the Negroes of the nation began to
increase slowly as soon as they could understand the facts,
and then swelled in astonishing volume as the trial neared.
From the beginning of the trial the courtroom was continuously crowded, and largely by out-of-town colored people
and white, some of whom came from long distances. The
coverage by Negro newspapers attested to the nationwide demand for news and sympathy for the accused. The FBI and
the Departments of State and Justice had observers seeking
information from Negroes present. Republican and Democratic National Committees kept in touch. There is no doubt
that increasing apprehension of repercussions of the possible
results of this trial on the Negro vote played a great part in
its result.

We must admit that the majority of the American Negro
intelligentsia, together with much of the West Indian and
West African leadership, shows symptoms of following in

the footsteps of western acquisitive society, with its exploitation of labor, monopoly of land and its resources, and with private profit for the smart and unscrupulous in a world of poverty, disease, and ignorance, as the natural end of human culture. I have long noted and fought this all too evident tendency, and built my faith in its ultimate change on an inner Negro cultural ideal. I thought this ideal would be built on ancient African communism, supported and developed by memory of slavery and experience of caste, which would drive the Negro group into a spiritual unity precluding the development of economic classes and inner class struggle. This was once possible, but it is now improbable. I strove hard to accomplish this while I was yet editor of *The Crisis,* and afterward in my teaching at Atlanta University.

The Supreme Court decision on segregation in schools called for a distinct modification of my attitude toward segregation which I expressed in 1934. I assumed that legal discrimination along the color line would last much longer than it may. It is to the credit of Spingarn and Marshall that they fought so valiantly and intelligently in the courts at a time when I had little faith in substantial victory. Nevertheless the battle is not won. Unfortunately in the United States there is a long habit of ignoring and breaking the law. Especially in the South, lawlessness is common and has been for a century. The movement toward the abolition of the color line has begun and will continue, strengthened as it is by the mighty uprising of the colored peoples backed by the Soviet Union. But meantime what will happen to us? During the 25 or 50 years while the southern South refuses to obey the law, what will happen to Negro children? Widespread effort for their protection and education should be undertaken by the Negroes themselves in inner cooperative effort. We must not make the error of the German Jews. They assumed that if the German nation received some of them as intellectual and social equals, the whole group would be safe. It only took a psychopathic criminal like Hitler to show them their tragic mistake. American Negroes may yet face a similar tragedy. They should prepare for such an eventuality.

If once this line of thought and action had become established, my guidance of the young Negro intelligentsia might have been increased and implemented, and the science of sociology might have immeasurably benefited by a laboratory test of extraordinary breadth and opportunity. This as I fondly hoped, might have revived my Atlanta University studies of the late 19th century, which white "philanthropy" starved to untimely death. All this, petty envy killed, just as it was reborn.

The very loosening of outer racial discriminatory pressures had not, as I had once believed, left Negroes free to become a group cemented into a new cultural unity, capable of absorbing socialism, tolerance, and democracy, and helping to lead America into a new heaven and new earth. But rather, partial emancipation is freeing some of them to ape the worst of American and Anglo-Saxon chauvinism, luxury, showing-off, and "social climbing."

I find, curiously enough then, that my experience in this fantastic accusation and criminal process is tending to free me from that racial provincialism which I always recognized but which I was sure would eventually land me in an upper realm of cultural unity, led by "My People." I have discovered that a large and powerful portion of the educated and well-to-do Negroes are refusing to forge forward in social leadership of anyone, even their own people, but are eager to fight social medicine for sick whites or sicker Negroes; are opposing trade unionism not only for white labor but for the far more helpless black worker; are willing to get "rich quick" not simply by shady business enterprise, but even by organized gambling and the "dope" racket.

The American Negro must realize that the attack on me for socialism is but the cloaked effort of Southern whites to deprive Negroes of leadership in my and other cases. I was just as much hated by the white South before the Russian Revolution as now; and feared too by those of the educated and progressive elements who were and are determined to keep the dark world in submission. They have seized on the charge of "Communism" to silence me just as they once charged "Abolition" to shut the mouths of Northerners. And just as today the thrifty are cowed by the threat of revolution.

As I have related, there came the indictment and trial and after long struggle the acquittal. But that was not the end. The publication of my story of this persecution in my book *In Battle for Peace;* the collaboration of Shirley Graham; my open thanks to the Communists of the world for their help in my defense; and my clear stand in favor of the Soviet Union intensified the enmity of those who rule. My defense of the Rosenbergs in speech and writing and my denunciation of the hounding and imprisonment of the Communists as unjust and barbarous did the same.

All this made my enemies and the Federal government take a determined stand to insure my destruction. The secret police swarmed in my neighborhood asking about my visitors; whether I entertained and whom. When we entertained a Soviet diplomat, his wife and daughter, and Paul Robeson, the whole borough of Brooklyn was declared "out of bounds" for Soviet diplomats. My manuscripts and those of Shirley Graham were refused publication by reputable commercial publishers. My mail was tampered with or withheld. Negro newspapers were warned not to carry my writings nor mention prominently my name. Colleges ceased to invite my lectures and Negro colleges no longer asked for my lectures or my presence at Commencement exercises. From being a person whom every Negro in the nation knew by name at least and hastened always to entertain or praise, churches and Negro conferences refused to mention my past or present existence. The white world which had never liked me but was forced in the past to respect me, now ignored me or deliberately distorted my work. A whispering campaign continually intimated that some hidden treason or bribery could be laid at my door if the government had not been lenient. The central office of the NAACP refused to let local branches invite me or sponsor any lectures. I was refused the right to speak on the University of California campus, because of NAACP protest. In fine I was rejected of men, refused the right to travel abroad and classed as "controversial figure" even after being acquitted of guilt by a Federal court of law.

It was a bitter experience and I bowed before the storm. But I did not break. I continued to speak and write when and where I could. I faced my lowered income and lived within it. I found new friends and lived in a wider world than ever before—a world with no color line. I lost my leadership of my race. It was a dilemma for the mass of Negroes; either they joined the current beliefs and actions of most whites or they could not make a living or hope for preferment. Preferment was possible. The color line was beginning to break. Negroes were getting recognition as never before. Was not the sacrifice of one man, small payment for this? Even those who disagreed with this judgment at least kept quiet. The colored children ceased to hear my name.

CHAPTER XXIII

MY TENTH DECADE

My 90th birthday was a surprising occasion. Friends wanted to celebrate it, but I recoiled. Who would sponsor such an event? There had, I admitted, been some pleasant occurrences. I had a successful television interview over the Dumont Broadcasting system; my bust by Zorach had been accepted by the New York Public Library and installed in the Schomburg Collection at the 135th Street branch. At the dedication Franklin Frazier, Judge Jane Bolin and Van Wyck Brooks took part. *Tablet,* the official organ of the Brooklyn diocese of the Roman Catholic church, naturally added one sour note, writing the library: "This corporation writes to enquire whether you would accept a bust of Benedict Arnold, which we would be happy to present to you."

I spoke at Paul Robeson's 60th birthday:

The persecution of Paul Robeson by the government and people of the United States during the last nine years has been one of the most contemptible happenings in modern history. Robeson has done nothing to hurt or defame this nation. He is, as all know, one of the most charming, charitable and loving of men. There is no person on earth who ever heard Robeson slander or even attack the land of his birth. Yet he had reason to despise America. He was a black man; the son of black folk whom Americans had stolen and enslaved. Even after his people's hard won and justly earned freedom, America made their lot as near a hell on earth as was possible. They discouraged, starved and insulted them. They sneered at helpless black children. Someone once said that the best punishment for Hitler would be to paint him black and send him to the United States. This was no joke. To struggle up as a black boy in America; to meet jeers and blows; to meet insult with silence and discrimination with a smile; to sit with fellow students who hated you and work and play for the honor of a college that disowned you—all this was America for Paul Robeson. Yet he fought the good fight; he was despised and rejected of men; a man of sorrows and acquainted with grief and we hid as it were our faces from him; he was despised and we esteemed him not.

Why? Why? Not because he attacked this country. Search Britain and France, the Soviet Union and Scandinavia for a word of his against America. What then was his crime? It was that while he did not rail at America he did praise the Soviet Union; and he did that because it treated him like a man and not like a dog; because he and his family for the first time in life were welcomed like human beings and he was honored as a great man. The children of Russia clung to him, the women kissed him; the workers greeted him; the state named mountains after him. He loved their homage. His eyes were filled with tears and his heart with thanks. Never before had he received such treatment. In America he was a "nigger"; in Britain he was tolerated; in France he was cheered; in the Soviet Union he was loved for the great artist that he is. He loved the Soviet Union in turn. He believed that every black man with blood in his veins would with him love the nation which first outlawed the color line.

I saw him when he voiced this. It was in Paris in 1949 at the greatest rally for world peace this world ever witnessed. Thousands of persons from all the world filled the Salle Playel from floor to rafters. Robeson hurried in, magnificent in height and breadth, weary from circling Europe with song. The audience rose to a man and the walls thundered. Robeson said that his people wanted Peace and "would never fight the Soviet Union." I joined with the thousands in wild acclaim.

This, for America, was his crime. He might hate anybody. He might join in murder around the world. But for him to declare that he loved the Soviet Union and would not join in war against it—that was the highest crime that the United States recognized. For that, they slandered Robeson; they tried to kill him at Peekskill; they prevented him from hiring halls in which to sing; they prevented him from travel and refused him a passport. His college, Rutgers, lied about him and dishonored him. And above all, his own people, American Negroes, joined in hounding one of their greatest artists—not all, but even men like Langston Hughes, who wrote of Negro musicians and deliberately omitted Robeson's name—Robeson who more than any living man has spread the pure Negro folk song over the civilized world. Yet has Paul Robeson kept his soul and stood his ground. Still he loves and honors the Soviet Union. Still he has hope for America. Still he asserts his faith in God. But we—what can we say or do; nothing but hang our heads in endless shame.

On my 90th birthday, my friends invited my well-wishers to a party at the Roosevelt Hotel. No body of sponsors could be found, but Angus Cameron acted as chairman, and Eslanda Robeson as treasurer. Two thousand persons were present including my own great-grandson, who behaved with exemplary decorum. I addressed my remarks to him. I quote from the *National Guardian:*

The most distinguished guest of this festive occasion is none other than my great-grandson, Arthur Edward McFarlane II, who was born this last Christmas Day. He had kindly consented to permit me to read to you a bit of advice which, as he remarked with a sigh of resignation, great-grandparents are supposed usually to inflict on the helpless young. This then is my word of advice.

As men go, I have had a reasonably happy and successful life, I have had enough to eat and drink, have been suitably clothed and, as you see, have had many friends. But the thing which has been the secret of whatever I have done is the fact that I have been able to earn a living by doing the work which I wanted to do and work that the world needed done.

I want to stress this. You will soon learn, my dear young man, that most human beings spend their lives doing work which they hate and work which the world does not need. It is therefore of prime importance that you early learn what you want to do; how you are fit to do it and whether or not the world needs this service. Here, in the next 20 years, your parents can be of use to you. You will soon begin to wonder just what parents are for besides interfering with your natural wishes. Let me therefore tell you: parents and their parents are inflicted upon you in order to show what kind of person you are; what sort of world you live in and what the persons who dwell here need for their happiness and well-being.

Right here, my esteemed great-grandson, may I ask you to stick a pin. You will find it the fashion in the America where eventually you will live and work to judge that life's work by the amount of money it brings you. This is a grave mistake. The return from your work must be the satisfaction which that work brings you and the world's need of that work. With this, life is heaven, or as near heaven as you can get. Without this—with work which you despise, which bores you and which the world does not need—this life is hell. And believe me, many a $25,000-a-year executive is living in just such a hell today.

Income is not greenbacks, it is satisfaction; it is creation; it is beauty. It is the supreme sense of a world of men going forward, lurch and stagger though it may, but slowly, inevitably going forward, and you, you yourself with your hand on the wheels. Make this choice, then, my son. Never hesitate, never falter.

And now comes the word of warning: the satisfaction with your work even at best will never be complete, since nothing on earth can be perfect. The forward pace of the world which you are pushing will be painfully slow. But what of that: the difference between a hundred and a thousand years is less than you now think. But doing what must be done, that is eternal even when it walks with poverty.

And I care not to garner while others
Know only to harvest and reap
For mine is the reaping of sowing
Till the spirit of rest gives me sleep.

A purse of $7,500 was given me. Later in Chicago, Truman Gibson and Margaret Burroughs arranged another birthday celebration and gave me $1,700 more. After talks in California, I was able to take a trip to the West Indies and see the beginnings of the new British West Indian Federation.

I was invited to attend the All-African Conference at Accra. At the Fifth Pan-African Congress at Manchester, England in 1945, a Sixth Congress on the continent of Africa had been projected. When Ghana gained her independence it was planned. I was not allowed to attend the inauguration. If I had been present undoubtedly the matter would have been further discussed. Meantime George Padmore, secretary of the Pan-African Congress, was called to Ghana as chief adviser to the Prime Minister, and he published a book called *Pan-Africanism or Communism* in which he said:

"In our struggle for national freedom, human dignity and social redemption Pan-Africanism offers an ideological alternative to Communism on one side and Tribalism on the other. It rejects both white racialism and black chauvinism. It stands for racial co-existence on the basis of absolute equality and respect for human personality."

I ventured to advise Nkrumah:

I have your kind invitation of January 22, 1957. In behalf of myself and of my wife, Shirley Graham, I thank you for it and want to say how great was our desire to accept it. But since the United States government refused to issue us passports, we must with deep regret inform you of our inability to accept. I have recently also, and for the same reason, been compelled to my sorrow to decline a trip to China for lectures and participation in the celebration of the 250th anniversary of the birth of Benjamin Franklin. However, because of the fact that I am now entering the 90th year of my life and because of my acquaintanceship with you during the last 12 years, which cover the years of your imprisonment, vindication, and political triumph, I trust you will allow me a few words of advice for the future of Ghana and Africa.

Today, when Ghana arises from the dead and faces this modern world, it must no longer be merely a part of the British Commonwealth or a representative of the world of West Europe, Canada, and the United States. Ghana must on the contrary be the representative of Africa.

The consequent Pan-Africa, working together through its independent units, should seek to develop a new African economy and cultural center standing between Europe and Asia, taking from and contributing to both. It should stress peace and join no military alliance and refuse to fight for settling European quarrels. It should avoid subjection to and ownership by foreign capitalists who seek to get rich on African labor and raw material, and should try to build a socialism founded on old African communal life, rejecting the exaggerated private initiative of the West, and seeking to ally itself with the social program of the Progressive nations; with British and Scandinavian Socialism, with the progress toward the Welfare State in India, Germany, France and the United States; and with the Communist States like the Soviet Union and China, in peaceful cooperation and without presuming to dictate as to how Socialism must or can be attained at particular times and places.

Pan-African Socialism seeks the Welfare State in Africa. It will refuse to be exploited by people of other continents for their own benefit and not for the benefit of the peoples of Africa. It will no longer consent to permitting the African majority of any African country to be governed against its will by a minority of invaders who claim racial superiority or the right to get rich at African expense. It will seek not only to raise but to process the raw material and to trade it freely with all the world on just and equal terms and prices.

Pan-Africa will seek to preserve its own past history, and write the present account, erasing from literature the lies and distortions about black folks which have disgraced the last centuries of European and American literature; above all, the new Pan-Africa will seek the education of all its youth on the broadest possible basis without religious dogma and in all hospitable lands as well as in Africa for the end of making Africans not simply profitable workers for industry nor stool-pigeons for propaganda, but for making them modern, intelligent, responsible men of vision and character.

I pray you, my dear Mr. Nkrumah, to use all your power to put a Pan-Africa along these lines into working order at the earliest possible date. Seek to save the great cultural past of the Ashanti and Fanti peoples, not by inner division but by outer cultural and economic expansion toward the outmost bounds of the great African peoples, so that they may be free to live, grow, and expand; and to teach mankind what Non-Violence and Courtesy, Literature and Art, Music and Dancing can do for this greedy, selfish, and war-stricken world.

Meantime big business in America, surprised by the success of the Ghana revolution set itself to influence Nkrumah. Nkrumah was invited to the United States in 1958, and treated as never a Negro had been treated by the government. Hershey, a great manufacturer of chocolate, sent a special plane to take him to his factories; and the New York Cocoa Board of Trade dined him at the Waldorf-Astoria. I saw Mr. Nkrumah briefly. He was most cordial and I expected soon to be invited to the Sixth Pan-African Congress in Accra. No invitation came, but I received my passport and sailed for Europe. While I was in Tashkent an invitation arrived but not from Nkrumah nor for a Pan-African Congress. It was from a new "All-African" body for an African conference in December and it said nothing about my expenses. I sensed immediately that opposition had arisen in Africa over American Negro leadership of the African peoples. This had happened in 1920, when the West African Congress acknowledged no tie with the First Pan-African Congress in Paris which sparked it. American Negroes had too often assumed that their leadership in Africa was natural. With the rise of an educated group of Africans, this was increasingly unlikely. I realized how natural this was and knew that neither Nkrumah nor Padmore were calling a Sixth "Pan-African Congress" but that this "All-Africa Conference" was taking its place. However, later Padmore sent me a cordial note emphasizing the invitation and offering to pay expenses.

By this time, however, my long travel was beginning to tell on me and I was in a Soviet sanitarium near Moscow. I prepared to leave for Africa, but the council of physicians advised against the trip as too taxing. I had prepared three messages for Africa. One I delivered at Tashkent, one I sent by my wife Shirley, who attended the conference at Accra, and the last I broadcast later from Peking on my 91st birthday.

At Tashkent, before my invitation to Accra had come, I warned Africa about borrowing capital from the West.

"Boycott the export of big capital from the exploiting world, led by America. Refuse to buy machines, skills and comforts with cocoa, coffee, palm oil and fruit sold at ridiculously low prices in exchange for imported food, liquor, refrigerators and automobiles sold at exorbitant prices. Live simply. Refuse to buy big capital from nations that cheat and overcharge. Buy of the Soviet Union and China as they grow able to sell at low prices. Save thus your own capital and drive the imperialists into bankruptcy or into Socialism."

Shirley, my wife, took my speech to Accra. She was shown rare courtesy and was the only non-African allowed to address the Assembly. She read my words:

My only role in this meeting is one of advice from one who has lived long, who has studied Africa and has seen the modern world. I had hoped to deliver this word in person, but this was not possible. I have therefore asked my wife, Shirley Graham, to read it to you. It is simple and direct. In this great crisis of the world's history, when standing on the highest peaks of human accomplishment we look forward to Peace and backward to War; when we look up to Heaven and down to Hell, let us mince no words. We face triumph or tragedy without alternative. Africa, ancient Africa has been called by the world and has lifted up her hands! Which way shall Africa go? First, I would emphasize the fact that today Africa has no choice between private Capitalism and Socialism. The whole world, including Capitalist countries, is moving toward Socialism, inevitably, inexorably. You can choose between blocs of military alliance, you can choose between groups of political union, you cannot choose between Socialism and Private Capitalism, because Private ownership of capital is doomed.

But what is Socialism? It is disciplined economy and political organization in which the first duty of a citizen is to serve the state; and the state is not a selected aristocracy, or a group of self-seeking oligarchs who have seized wealth and power. No! The mass of workers with hand and brain are the ones whose collective destiny is the chief object of all effort. Gradually, every state is coming to this concept of its aim. The great Communist states like the Soviet Union and China have surrendered completely to this idea. The Scandinavian states have yielded partially; Britain has yielded in some respects, France in part and even the United States adopted the New Deal which was largely socialistic, even though today further American Socialism is held at bay by 60 great groups of corporations who control individual capitalists and the trade-union leaders.

On the other hand, the African tribe, whence all of you sprung, was communistic in its very beginnings. No tribesman was free. All were servants of the tribe of whom the chief was father and voice. Read of the West Coast trade as described by [J. E.] Casely-Hayford: There is small trace of private enterprise or individual initiative. It was the tribe which carried on trade through individuals, and the chief was mouthpiece of the common will.

Here then, my Brothers, you face your great decision: Will you for temporary advantage—for automobiles, refrigerators and Paris gowns—spend your income in paying interest on borrowed funds, or will you sacrifice present comfort and the chance to shine before your neighbors in order to educate your children, develop such industry as best serves the great mass of people and makes your country strong in ability, self-support and self-defense? Such union of effort for strength calls for sacrifice and self-denial, while the capital offered you at high price by the colonial powers like France, Britain, Holland, Belgium and the United States, will prolong fatal colonial imperialism, from which you have suffered slavery, serfdom and colonialism. You are not helpless. You are the buyers of capital goods, and to continue existence as sellers of capital, the great nations, former owners of the world, must sell or face bankruptcy. You are not compelled to buy all they offer now. You can wait. You can starve a while longer rather than sell your great heritage for a mess of western capitalistic pottage.

You cannot only beat down the price of capital as offered by the united and monopolized western private capitalists, but at last today you can compare their offers with those of socialist countries like the Soviet Union and China, which with infinite sacrifice and pouring out of blood and tears, are at last able to offer weak nations needed capital on better terms than the West. The supply which socialist nations can at present spare is small as compared with that of the bloated monopolies of the West, but it is large and rapidly growing. Its acceptance involves no bonds which a free Africa may not safely assume. It certainly does not involve slavery and colonial control which is the price which the West has demanded, and still demands. Today she offers a compromise, but one of which you must beware: She offers to let some of your smarter and less scrupulous leaders become fellow capitalists with the white exploiters, if in turn they induce the nation's masses to pay the awful cost. This has happened in the West Indies and in South America. This may yet happen in the Middle East and Eastern Asia. Strive against it with every fibre of your bodies and souls. A body of local private capitalists, even if they are black, can never free Africa; they will simply sell it into new slavery to old masters overseas.

As I have said, this is a call for sacrifice. Great Goethe sang, *"Ent-behren sollst du, sollst entbehren"*—"Thou shalt forego, shalt do without." If Africa unites it will be because each part, each nation, each tribe gives up a part of its heritage for the good of the whole. That is what union means; that is what Pan-Africa means: When the child is born into the tribe the price of his growing up is to give over a part of his freedom to the tribe. This he soon learns or dies. When the tribe becomes a union of tribes, the individual tribe surrenders some part of its freedom to the paramount tribe.

When the nation arises, the constituent tribes, clans and groups must each yield power and much freedom to the demands of the nation or the nation dies before it is born. Your local tribal, much-loved languages must yield to the few world tongues which serve the largest numbers of people and promote understanding and world literature.

This is the great dilemma which faces Africa today; faces one and all: Give up individual rights for the needs of the nation; give up tribal independence for the needs of Mother Africa. Forget nothing but set everything in its rightful place: the Glory of the six Ashanti Wars against Britain; the wisdom of the Fanti Confederation; the unity of Nigeria; the song of the Songhay and Hausa; the rebellion of the Mahdi and the hands of Ethiopia; the greatness of the Basuto and the fighting of Chaka; the revenge of Mutesa, and many other happenings and men; but above all—Africa, Mother of Men. Your nearest friends and neighbors are the colored people of China and India, the rest of Asia, the Middle East and the sea isles, once close bound to the heart of Africa and now long severed by the greed of Europe. Your bond is no mere color of skin but the deeper experience of wage slavery and contempt.

So too, your bond with the white world is closest to those like the Union of Soviet Socialist Republics, who support and defend China and help the slaves of Tibet and India, and not those who exploit the Middle East, the West Indies, and South America.

Awake, awake, put on thy strength, O Zion; reject the meekness of missionaries who teach neither love nor brotherhood, but emphasize the virtues of private profit from capital, stolen from your land and labor. Africa awake, put on the beautiful robes of Pan-African Socialism.

You have nothing to lose but your Chains!

You have a continent to regain!

You have freedom and human dignity to attain!

The address was greeted with applause. Later Shirley and Mrs. Robeson with the help of Tom Mboya, the chairman, secured the removal of Chiang Kai-shek's Formosa flag from the assembly hall at the beginning of the conference.

When in Peking, my 91st birthday was given national celebration. I pled for unity of China and Africa and my speech was broadcast to the world:

By courtesy of the government of the 600 million people of the Chinese Republic, I am permitted on my 91st birthday to speak to the people of China and Africa and through them to the world. Hail, then, and farewell, dwelling places of the yellow and black races. Hail human kind!

I speak with no authority; no assumption of age nor rank; I hold no position, I have no wealth. One thing alone I own and that is my own soul. Ownership of that I have even while in my own country for near a century I have been nothing but a "nigger." On this basis and this alone I dare speak, I dare advise.

China after long centuries has arisen to her feet and leapt forward. Africa, arise, and stand straight, speak and think! Act! Turn from the West and your slavery and humiliation for the last 500 years and face the rising sun.

Behold a people, the most populous nation on this ancient earth, which has burst its shackles, not by boasting and strutting, not by lying about its history and its conquests, but by patience and long suffering, by blind struggle, moved up and on toward the crimson sky. She aims to "make men holy; to make men free."

But what men? Not simply the mandarins but including mandarins; not simply the rich, but not excluding the rich. Not simply the learned, but led by knowledge to the end that no man shall be poor, nor sick, nor ignorant; but that the humblest worker as well as the sons of emperors shall be fed and taught and healed and that there emerge on earth a single unified people, free, well and educated.

You have been told, my Africa: My Africa in Africa and all your children's children overseas; you have been told and the telling so beaten into you by rods and whips, that you believe it yourselves, that this is impossible; that mankind can rise only by walking on men; by cheating them and killing them; that only on a doormat of the despised and dying, the dead and rotten, can a British aristocracy, a French cultural elite or an American millionaire be nurtured and grown.

This is a lie. It is an ancient lie spread by church and state, spread by priest and historian, and believed in by fools and cowards, as well as by the downtrodden and the children of despair.

Speak, China, and tell your truth to Africa and the world. What people have been despised as you have? Who more than you have been rejected of men? Recall when lordly Britishers threw the rickshaw money on the ground to avoid touching a filthy hand. Forget not the time when in Shanghai no Chinese man dare set foot in a park which he paid for. Tell this to Africa, for today Africa stands on new feet, with new eyesight, with new brains and asks: Where am I and why?

The Western sirens answer: Britain wheedles; France cajoles; while America, my America, where my ancestors and descendants for eight generations have lived and toiled; America loudest of all, yells and promises freedom. If only Africa allows American investment!

Beware Africa, America bargains for your soul. America would have you believe that they freed your grandchildren; that Afro-Americans are full American citizens, treated like equals, paid fair wages as workers, promoted for desert and free to learn and travel across the world.

This is not true. Some are near freedom; some approach equality with whites; some have achieved education; but the price for this has too often been slavery of mind, distortion of truth and oppression of our own people.

Of 18 million Afro-Americans, 12 million are still second-class citizens of the United States, serfs in farming, low-paid laborers in industry, and repressed members of union labor. Most American Negroes do not vote. Even the rising six million are liable to insult and discrimination at any time.

But this, Africa, relates to your descendants, not to you. Once I thought of you Africans as children, whom we educated Afro-Americans would lead to liberty. I was wrong. We could not even lead ourselves, much less you. Today I see you rising under your own leadership, guided by your own brains.

Africa does not ask alms from China nor from the Soviet Union nor from France, Britain, nor the United States. It asks friendship and sympathy and no nation better than China can offer this to the Dark Continent. Let it be freely given and generously. Let Chinese visit Africa, send their scientists there and their artists and writers. Let Africa send its students to China and its seekers after knowledge. It will not find on earth a richer goal, a more promising mine of information.

On the other hand, watch the West. The new British West Indian Federation is not a form of democratic progress but a cunning attempt to reduce these islands to the control of British and American investors. Haiti is dying under rich Haitian investors who with American money are enslaving the peasantry. Cuba is showing what the West Indies, Central and South America are suffering under American big business.

The American worker himself does not always realize this. He has high wages and many comforts. Rather than lose these, he keeps in office by his vote the servants of industrial exploitation so long as they maintain his wage. His labor leaders represent exploitation and not the fight against the exploitation of labor by private capital. These two sets of exploiters fall out only when one demands too large a share of the loot.

This China knows. This Africa must learn. This the American Negro has failed so far to learn. I am frightened by the so-called friends who are flocking to Africa. Negro Americans trying to make money from your toil, white Americans who seek by investment and high interest to bind you in serfdom to business as the Near East is bound and as South America is struggling with. For this America is tempting your leaders, bribing your young scholars, and arming your soldiers. What shall you do?

First, understand! Realize that the great mass of mankind is freeing itself from wage slavery, while private capital in Britain, France, and now in America, is still trying to maintain civilization and comfort for a few on the toil, disease and ignorance of the mass of men. Understand this, and understanding comes from direct knowledge. You know America and France, and Britain to your sorrow. Now know the Soviet Union, but particularly know China.

China is flesh of your flesh, and blood of your blood. China is colored and knows to what a colored skin in this modern world subjects its owner. But China knows more, much more than this: she knows what to do about it. She can take the insults of the United States and still hold her head high. She can make her own machines, when America refuses to sell her American manufactures, even though it hurts American industry, and throws her workers out of jobs. China does not need American nor British missionaries to teach her religion and scare her with tales of hell. China has been in hell too long, not to believe in a heaven of her own making. This she is doing.

Come to China, Africa, and look around. Invite Africa to come, China, and see what you can teach by just pointing. Yonder old woman is working on the street. But she is happy. She has no fear. Her children are in school and a good school. If she is ill, there is a hospital where she is cared for free of charge. She has a vacation with pay each year. She can die and be buried without taxing her family to make some undertaker rich.

Africa can answer: but some of this we have done; our tribes undertake public service like this. Very well, let your tribes continue and expand this work. What Africa must realize is what China knows; that it is worse than stupid to allow a people's education to be under the control of those who seek not the progress of the people but their use as means of making themselves rich and powerful. It is wrong for the University of London to control the University of Ghana. It is wrong for the Catholic church to direct the education of the black Congolese. It was wrong for Protestant churches supported by British and American wealth to control higher education in China.

The Soviet Union is surpassing the world in popular and higher education, because from the beginning it started its own complete educational system. The essence of the revolution in the Soviet Union and China and in all the "iron curtain" nations, is not the violence that accompanied the change; no more than starvation at Valley Forge was the essence of the American revolution against Britain. The real revolution is the acceptance on the part of the nation of the fact that hereafter the main object of the nation is the welfare of the mass of the people and not of the lucky few.

Government is for the people's progress and not for the comfort of an aristocracy. The object of industry is the welfare of the workers and not the wealth of the owners. The object of civilization is the cultural progress of the mass of workers and not merely of an intellectual elite. And in return for all this, communist lands believe that the cultivation of the mass of people will discover more talent and genius to serve the state than any closed aristocracy ever furnished. This belief the current history of the Soviet Union and China is proving true each day. Therefore don't let the West invest when you can avoid it. Don't buy capital from Britain, France and the United States if you can get it on reasonable terms from the Soviet Union and China. This is not politics; it is common sense. It is learning from experience. It is trusting your friends and watching your enemies. Refuse to be cajoled or to change your way of life, so as to make a few of your fellows rich at the expense of a mass of workers growing poor and sick and remaining without schools so that a few black men can have automobiles.

Africa, here is a real danger which you must avoid or return to the slavery from which you are emerging. All I ask from you is the courage to know; to look about you and see what is happening in this old and tired world; to realize the extent and depth of its rebirth and the promise which glows on your hills.

Visit the Soviet Union and visit China. Let your youth learn the Russian and Chinese languages. Stand together in this new world and let the old world perish in its greed or be born again in new hope and promise. Listen to the Hebrew prophet of communism:

Ho! every one that thirsteth; come ye to the waters; come, buy and eat, without money and price!

Again, China and Africa, hail and farewell!

POSTLUDE

Returning to America in 1959 after my great journey, I was welcomed home; not simply by my friends but by my government. In Sweden it was feared I might not as a member of the World Peace Council be allowed to land in England. But Pritt and Belfrage took hold and I received every courtesy. I had tea on the terrace of the House of Lords with a viscount, an earl, and two ladies; also on the terrace of the House of Commons, I had tea where I had last been entertained by Kier Hardie. I met several members of Parliament, and spent many Sunday afternoons with Donald Ogden Stewart and Ella Winter. There I met James Aldrich and Katharine Hepburn. I saw Paul Robeson and his splendid production of *Othello*. Lawrence Bradshaw, sculptor of the great head of Karl Marx, did my head.

The cabin on the *Liberté* as we returned was large and airy, and the voyage smooth and pleasant. But how would the United States receive us? We had openly spent ten weeks in China, and spoken widely and broadcast. There was some hasty last minute telephoning from the boat, I am sure, but all went well. Our passports were not seized, and the chief inspector of Customs passed our bags quickly and welcomed us home. Our relatives and friends swarmed to greet us. I was unable to understand why Scott Nearing and Waldo Frank should be forbidden to do what as yet I have been unrebuked for doing openly and proudly. However, three months later when the Supreme Court agreed to consider the cases of Waldo Frank and William Worthy,[17] the State Department demanded our passports. We asked delay until the Supreme Court made its verdict. This was granted.

I am a little puzzled now about the ordering of my life. Several times in the past I find that I have prepared for death and death has not come. Always on my desk lies a calendar of my own devising with daily and hourly tasks; with plans for the week and next week, the month and

409

months ahead and the sentinel of my main task for the year. This year-part is now getting uncertain. Even months are no longer absolutely mine, yet I am reasonably content and although my strength warns me not to try to work as many hours as once I did, yet I work and work regularly and with some efficiency, from day to day.

As I recall, I have long faced the inevitability of death and not tried to dodge the thought. In early manhood I wrote:

"I saw a mother, black and seared and iron-haired, who had watched her boy through college, for men to jeer at and discourage and tempt until he sought women and whiskey and died. She crept on a winter's Sunday into a Cathedral of St. John The Divine and crouched there where a comfortable red and yellow angel sat sunning her ample limbs 'To Keep the Memory of Obadiah James Green'—a stock-gambler. And there she rested while the organ warbled the overture to *Der Feischutz*, and the choir asserted 'My Jesus! As Thou wilt.' The priest intoned: 'Come unto Me all ye that labor and are heavy laden and I will give you rest! For my yoke is easy and my burden light.' And the window-angel moved a fat wing and murmured: 'except niggers!'

"In that dark day when all friends gathered round shall sigh: as he goes to that full dreadful home where earth shall move away and these dim eyes shall strain to scenes all glorious, shall they see on that morning round the wide, white throne a glorified Negro Problem? If so, Father of Mercies, send me to Hell."

At 50, after a serious operation I wrote:

"Last year I looked death in the face and found its lineaments not unkind. But it was not my time. Yet in nature some time soon and in the fullness of days I shall die, quietly, I trust, with my face turned South and eastward; and, dreaming or dreamless I shall, I am sure, enjoy death as I have enjoyed life."

At 60 years of age I wrote again:

"For long years we of the world gone wild, have looked

into the face of death and smiled. Through all our bitter tears we knew how beautiful it was to die for that which our souls called sufficient. Like all true beauty this thing of dying was so simple, so matter-of-fact. The boy clothed in his splendid youth stood before us and laughed in his own jolly way—went and was gone. Suddenly the world was full of the fragrance of sacrifice. We left our digging and burden-bearing; we turned from our scraping and twisting of things and words; we paused from our hurrying hither and thither and walking up and down, and asked in half whisper: 'Death—is this life? And is its beauty real or false?'

"Here, then, is beauty and ugliness, a wide vision of world-sacrifice, a fierce gleam of world-hate. Which is life and what is death and how shall we face so tantalizing a contradiction? Any explanation must necessarily be subtle and involved. No pert and easy word of encouragement, no merely dark despair, can lay hold of the roots of these things. And first and before all, we cannot forget that this world is beautiful. Grant all its ugliness and sin—the petty, horrible snarl of its putrid threads, which few have seen more near or more often than I—notwithstanding all this, the beauty of the world is not to be denied.

"And then—the Veil, the Veil of color. It drops as drops the night on southern seas—vast, sudden, unanswering. There is Hate behind it, and Cruelty and Tears. As one peers through its intricate, unfathomable pattern of ancient, old, old design, one sees blood and guilt and misunderstanding. And yet it hangs there, this Veil, between then and now, between Pale and Colored and Black and White—between You and Me. Surely it is but a thought-thing, tenuous, intangible; yet just as surely is it true and terrible and not in our little day may you and I lift it. We may feverishly unravel its edges and even climb slow with giant shears to where its ringed and gilded top nestles close to the throne of Eternity. But as we work and climb we shall see through streaming eyes and hear with aching ears, lynching and murder, cheating and despising, degrading and lying, so flashed and flashed through this vast hanging darkness that the Doer never sees the Deed and the Victim knows not the Victor and Each hate All in wild and bitter ignorance. Listen, O Isles, to those voices from within the Veil, for they portray the most human hurt of the Twentieth Cycle of that poor Jesus who was called the Christ!

"At last to us all comes happiness, there in the Court of Peace, where the dead lie so still and calm and good. If we were not dead we would lie and listen to the flowers grow. We would hear the birds sing and see how the rain rises and blushes and burns and pales and dies in beauty. We would see spring, summer, and the red riot of autumn, and then in winter, beneath the soft white snow, sleep and dream of dreams. But we know that being dead, our Happiness is a fine and finished thing and that ten, a hundred, and a thousand years, we shall lie at rest, unhurt in the Court of Peace."

From then until now the wraith of Death has followed me, slept with me and awakened me and accompanied my day. Only now it is more commonplace and reasonable. It is the end and without ends there can be no beginnings. Its finality we must not falsify. It is our great debt to the Soviet Union that it alone of nations dared stop that lying to children which so long disgraced our schools. We filled little minds with fairy tales of religious dogma which we ourselves never believed. We filled their thoughts with pictures of barbarous revenge called God which contradicted all their inner sense of decency. We repeated folk tales of children without fathers, of death which was life, of sacrifice which was shrewd investment and ridiculous pictures of an endless future. The Soviets have stopped this. They allow a child to grow up without religious lies and with mature mind make his own decision about the world without scaring him into Hell or rewarding him with a silly Heaven.

We know that Death is the End of Life. Even when we profess to deny this we know that this hope is mere wishful thinking, pretense broidered with abject and cowardly

Fear. Our endless egotism cannot conceive a world without Us and yet we know that this will happen and the world be happier for it.

I have lived a good and full life. I have finished my course. I do not want to live this life again. I have tasted its delights and pleasures; I have known its pain, suffering and despair. I am tired, I am through. For the souls who follow me; for that little boy born Christmas day before last, my great-grandson and his compeers, I bequeath all that waits to be done, and Holy Time what a task, forever!

I have seen miracles in my life. As a boy we did not have the possibility of miracles emphasized in our schools. In the weekly Sunday School, we studied the bible with its tales of the impossible but I remember distinctly that I questioned the validity of some of them, like that story of Jonah. In other words I was brought up in the shadow of modern science where all that happens had a cause and there were many things unlikely to happen. For instance, then flying by man was not to be thought of and we talked of flying as impossible and joked at man's attempts. Yet I read of the first successful flights; and myself in 1921 flew from Paris to London. I have flown tens of thousands of miles since, over land and sea. I visited the Paris World's Fair in 1900, and was astonished to see automobiles on the streets; not many but perhaps a dozen in a day. I lived to see the jokes about the possibility of these motors displacing the horse fade away and automobiles fill the streets and cover the nations.

I remember when first, in an American city, seeing the streets lighted by electricity; the lights blinked and sputtered but in a few years electric bulbs supplanted the gas lights of my boyhood. Then came the gas-filled balloons rising in the sky and men crossed the Atlantic in Zeppelins. Soon came the horror of Hiroshima and I began to feel the vast possibilities of man's brain and his coming conquest of the air. But the most startling miracle of my time before the year 1958, was Sputnik. This went beyond the internal combustion engine, the airplane and balloon; beyond the electric light and the bursting atom. This was beyond mere utility into the realm of Knowledge and the triumph of Reason. It taught the United States the superiority of Communist thought and calculation. It stopped our sneers at Soviet education.

Then this year came the climax; the triumph of thought over power and space that was the greatest miracle of which I ever dreamed. Not yet have I been able to comprehend its meaning, or to realize that it is today actually possible to send a human being to the stars. A Frenchman once said: "I know but two beautiful things on earth: the stars above us and the feeling of duty within us." Now that we have pierced the heavens, we are more sure of making Mankind willing and eager to do right.

I have lived to an age of life which is increasingly distasteful to this nation. Unless by 60 a man has gained possession of enough of money to support himself, he faces the distinct possibility of starvation. He is liable to lose his job and to refusal if he seeks another. At 70 he is frowned upon by the church and if he is foolish enough to survive until 90, he is often regarded as a freak. This is because in the face of human experience the United States has discovered that Youth knows more than Age. When a man of 35 becomes president of a great institution of learning or United States Senator or head of a multi-million dollar corporation, a cry of triumph rings in the land. Why? To pretend that 15 years bring of themselves more wisdom and understanding than 50 is a contradiction in terms. Given a born fool, a hundred years will not make him wise; but given an idiot, he will not be wise at 20. Youth is more courageous than age because it knows less. Age is wiser than youth because it knows more. This all mankind has affirmed from Egypt and China five thousand years ago, to Britain and Germany today. Only the United States knows better. I would have been hailed with approval if I had died at 50. At 75 my death was practically requested. If living does not give value, wisdom and meaning to life, then there is no sense in living at all. If immature and inexperienced men rule the earth, then the earth deserves what it gets: the repetition of age-old mistakes, and wild welcome for what men knew a thousand years ago was disaster.

I do not apologize for living long. High on the ramparts of this blistering hell of life, as it must appear to most men, I sit and see the Truth. I look it full in the face, and I will not lie about it, neither to myself nor to the world. I see my country as what Cedric Belfrage aptly characterizes as a "Frightened Giant" afraid of the Truth, afraid of Peace. I see a land which is degenerating and faces decadence unless it has sense enough to turn about and start back. It is no sin to fail. It is the habit of men. It is disaster to go on when you know you are going wrong. I judge this land not merely by statistics or reading lies agreed upon by historians. I judge by what I have seen, heard, and lived through for near a century.

There was a day when the world rightly called Americans honest even if crude; earning their living by hard work; telling the truth no matter whom it hurt; and going to war only in what they believed a just cause after nothing else seemed possible. Today we are lying, stealing, and killing. We call all this by finer names: Advertising, Free Enterprise, and National Defense. But names in the end deceive no one; today we use science to help us deceive our fellows; we take wealth that we never earned and we are devoting all our energies to kill, maim and drive insane, men, women, and children who dare refuse to do what we want done. No nation threatens us. We threaten the world.

Our President says that Foster Dulles was the wisest man he knew. If Dulles was wise, God help our fools—the fools who rule us and are today running wild in order to shoot a football into the sky where Sputnik rolls in peace around the earth. And they know why we fail, these military masters of men: we haven't taught our children mathematics and physics. No, it is because we have not taught our children to read and write or to behave like human beings and not like hoodlums. Every child on my street is whooping it up with toy guns and big boys with real pistols. When Elvis Presley goes through the motions of copulation on the public stage it takes the city police force to hold back teen-age children from hysteria. The highest ambition of an American boy today is to be a millionaire. The highest ambition of an American girl is to be a movie star. Of the ethical actions which lie back of these ideals, little is said or learned. What are we doing about it? Half the Christian churches of New York are trying to ruin the free public schools in order to install religious dogma in them; and the other half are too interested in Venezuelan oil to prevent the best center in Brooklyn from fighting youthful delinquency, or prevent a bishop from kicking William Howard Melish into the street and closing his church. Which of the hundreds of churches sitting half empty protests about this? They hire Billy Graham to replace the circus in Madison Square Garden.

Howard Melish is one of the few Christian clergymen for whom I have the highest respect. Honest and conscientious, believing sincerely in much of the Christian dogma, which I reject, but working honestly and without hypocrisy, for the guidance of the young, for the uplift of the poor and ignorant, and for the betterment of his city and his country, he has been driven from his work and his career ruined by a vindictive bishop of his church, with no effective protest from most of the Christian ministry and membership or of the people of the United States. The Melish case is perhaps at once the most typical and frightening illustration of present American religion and my reaction. Here is a young man of ideal character, of impeccable morals; a hard worker, especially among the poor and unfortunate, with fine family relations. His father had helped build one of the most popular Episcopal churches in the better part of Brooklyn. He himself had married a well-educated woman, and had three sons in school. The community about it was changing from well-to-do people of English and Dutch descent, to white-collar and laboring folk of Italian, Negro and Puerto Rican extraction. Trinity church, under the Melishes, adapted itself to changing needs, and invited neighborhood membership. It was not a large church, but it was doing the best work among the young and foreign-born of any institution in Brooklyn.

The young rector took one step for which the bishop, most of his fellow clergymen and the well-to-do community, with its business interests, pilloried him. He joined and became an official of the National Council of American-Soviet Friendship. He was accused immediately of favoring communism, and to appease criticism he gave up his official position in this organization, but refused to resign his membership. Allegedly for this reason the bishop, most of the clergy and the well-to-do community proceeded to force him out of the church. The real reason behind their fight was anger because a rich, white, "respectable" church was being surrendered to workers and Negroes. It became a renewed battle between Episcopal authority and democratic rule. That his parish wanted to retain Melish as rector was unquestionable. Through the use of technicalities in the canon law and in accord with the decision of Catholic judges who believed in Episcopal power, Howard Melish lost his church, had his life work ruined, the church itself closed, and its local influence ended. There was vigorous protest against this by a few devoted colleagues, many of them Jews and liberals. But the great mass of the Episcopal church membership was silent and did nothing.

All this must not be mentioned even if you know it and see it. America must never be criticized even by honest and sincere men. America must always be praised and extravagantly praised, or you lose your job or are ostracized or land in jail. Criticism is treason, and treason or the hint of treason testified to by hired liars may be punished by shameful death. I saw Ethel Rosenberg lying beautiful in her coffin beside her mate. I tried to stammer futile words above her grave. But not over graves should we shout this failure of justice, but from the housetops of the world.

Honest men may and must criticize America. Describe how she has ruined her democracy, sold out her jury system, and led her seats of justice astray. The only question that may arise is whether this criticism is based on truth, not whether it has been openly expressed.

What is truth? What can it be when the President of the United States, guiding the nation, stands up in public and says: "*The world also thinks of us as a land which has never enslaved anyone.*" Everyone who heard this knew it was not true. Yet here stands the successor of George Washington who bought, owned, and sold slaves; the successor of Abraham Lincoln who freed four million slaves after they had helped him win victory over the slaveholding South. And so far as I have seen, not a single periodical, not even a Negro weekly, has dared challenge or even criticize that falsehood.

Perhaps the most extraordinary characteristic of current America is the attempt to reduce life to buying and selling. Life is not love unless love is sex and bought and sold. Life is not knowledge save knowledge of technique, of science for destruction. Life is not beauty except beauty for sale. Life is not art unless its price is high and it is sold for profit. All life is production for profit, and for what is profit but for buying and selling again?

Even today the contradictions of American civilization are tremendous. Freedom of political discussion is difficult; elections are not free and fair. Democracy is for us to a large extent unworkable. In business there is a tremendous amount of cheating and stealing; gambling in card games, on television and on the stock exchange is widely practiced. It is common custom for distinguished persons to sign books, articles, and speeches that they did not write; for men of brains to compose and sell opinions which they do not believe. Ghost writing is a profession. The greatest power in the land is not thought or ethics, but wealth, and the persons who exercise the power of wealth are not necessarily its owners, but those who direct its use, and the truth about this direction is so far as possible kept a secret. We do not know who owns our vast property and resources, so that most of our argument concerning wealth and its use must be based on guesswork. Those responsible for the misuse of wealth escape responsibility, and even the owners of capital often do not know for what it is being used and how. The criterion of industry and trade is the profit that it accrues, not the good which it does either its owners or the public. Present profit is valued higher than future need. We waste materials. We refuse to make repairs. We cheat and deceive in manufacturing goods. We have succumbed to an increased use of lying and misrepresentation. In the last ten years at least a thousand books have been published to prove that the fight to preserve Negro slavery in America was a great and noble cause, led by worthy men of eminence.

I know the United States. It is my country and the land of my fathers. It is still a land of magnificent possibilities. It is still the home of noble souls and generous people. But it is selling its birthright. It is betraying its mighty destiny. I was born on its soil and educated in its schools. I have served my country to the best of my ability. I have never knowingly broken its laws or unjustly attacked its reputation. At the same time I have pointed out its injustices and crimes and blamed it, rightly as I believe, for its mistakes. It has given me education and some of its honors, for which I am thankful.

Today the United States is the leading nation in the world, which apparently believes that war is the only way to settle present disputes and difficulties. For this reason it is spending fantastic sums of money, and wasting wealth and energy on the preparation for war, which is nothing less than criminal. Yet the United States dare not stop spending money for war. If she did her whole economy, which is today based on preparation for war, might collapse. Therefore, we prepare for a Third World War; we spread our soldiers and arms over the earth and we bribe every nation we can to become our allies. We are taxing our citizens into poverty, crime and unemployment, and systematically distorting the truth about socialism. We have used the horror of germ warfare. Some of our leaders are ready to use it again.

The use of history for distortion and not for education has led to another of our greatest present evils; and that is to make fear of socialism and communism so great that we have withdrawn our efforts toward the education of children, the war on disease, and the raising of the standards of living. We encourage the increase of debt to finance present enjoyment; and above all we use newsgathering and opinion, radio and television, magazines and books, to make most Americans believe that the threat of war, especially on the part of the Soviet Union against the United States, justifies heavy taxation and tremendous expenditure for war preparation.

This propaganda began when our tremendous profits from the First World War encouraged American business to believe that the United States was about to replace Great Britain as ruler of most of mankind. The rise and spread of socialism contradicted this ambition, and made the projected American century quail in fright before the century of communism. We determined therefore to overthrow communism by brute force. Gradually we discovered the impossibility of this, unless we risked suicide. We saw communism increasing education, science and productivity. We now face the possibility of co-existence with the communist world, and competition between the methods of capitalism and the methods of socialism. It is at this crisis that I had the opportunity to live seven months in a world of socialism, which is striving toward communism as an ideal.

This is what I call decadence. It could not have happened 50 years ago. In the day of our fiercest controversy we have not dared thus publicly to silence opinion. I have lived through disagreement, vilification, and war and war again. But in all that time, I have never seen the right of human beings to think so challenged and denied as today.

The day after I was born, Andrew Johnson was impeached. He deserved punishment as a traitor to the poor Southern whites and poorer freedmen. Yet during his life, no one denied him the right to defend himself. A quarter of a century ago, I tried to state and carry into realization unpopular ideas against a powerful opposition—in the white South, in the reactionary North, and even among my own people. I found my thought being misconstrued and I planned an organ of propaganda, *The Crisis*, where I would be free to say what I believed. This was no easy sailing. My magazine reached but a fraction of the nation. It was bitterly attacked and once the government suppressed it. But in the end I maintained a platform of radical thinking on the Negro question which influenced many minds. War and depression ended my independence of thought and forced me to return to teaching, but with the certainty that I had at least started a new line of belief and action. Then they stopped my teaching.

As a result of my work and that of others, the Supreme Court began to restore democracy in the South and finally outlawed discrimination in public services based on color. This caused rebellion in the South which the nation is afraid to meet. The Negro stands bewildered and attempt is made by appointments to unimportant offices and trips abroad to bribe him into silence. His art and literature cease to function. Only the children like those at Little Rock stand and fight.

The Yale sophomore who replaced a periodical of brains by a book of pictures concealed in advertisements, proposed that America rule the world. This failed because we could not rule ourselves. But Texas to the rescue, as Johnson proposes that America take over outer space. Somewhere beyond the Moon there must be sentient creatures rolling in inextinguishable laughter at the antics of our Earth.

We tax ourselves into poverty and crime so as to make the rich richer and the poor poorer and more evil. We know the cause of this: it is to permit our rich business interests to stop socialism and to prevent the ideals of communism from ever triumphing on earth. The aim is impossible. Socialism progresses and will progress. All we can do is to silence and jail its promoters and make world war on communism. I believe in socialism. I seek a world where the ideals of communism will triumph—to each according to his need, from each according to his ability. For this I will work as long as I live. And I still live.

I just live. I plan my work, but plan less for shorter periods. I live from year to year and day to day. I expect snatches of pain and discomfort to come and go. And then reaching back to my archives, I whisper to the great Majority: To the Almighty Dead, into whose pale approaching faces, I stand and stare; you whose thoughts, deeds and dreams have made men wise with all wisdom and stupid with utter evil. In every name of God, bend out and down, you who are the infinite majority of all mankind and with your thoughts, deeds, dreams and memories, overwhelm, outvote, and coerce this remnant of human life which lingers on, imagining themselves wisest of all who have lived just because they still survive. Whither with wide revelation will they go with their stinking pride and empty boasting, whose ever recurring lies only you the Dead have known all too well? Teach living man to jeer at this last civilization which seeks to build heaven on Want and Ill of most men and vainly builds on color and hair rather than on decency of hand and heart. Let your memories teach these wilful fools all which you have forgotten and ruined and done to death.

You are not and yet you are: your thoughts, your deeds, above all your dreams still live. So too, your deeds and what you forgot—these lived as your bodies died. With these we also live and die, realize and kill. Our dreams seek Heaven, our deeds plumb Hell. Hell lies about us in our Age: blithely we push into its stench and flame. Suffer us not, Eternal Dead to stew in this Evil—the Evil of South Africa, the Evil of Mississippi; the Evil of Evils which is what we hope to hold in Asia and Africa, in the southern Americas and islands of the Seven Seas. Reveal, Ancient of Days, the Present in the Past and prophesy the End in the Beginning. For this is a beautiful world; this is a wonderful America, which the founding fathers dreamed until their sons drowned it in the blood of slavery and devoured it in greed. Our children must rebuild it. Let then the Dreams

of the Dead rebuke the Blind who think that what is will
be forever and teach them that what was worth living for
must live again and that which merited death must stay
dead. Teach us, Forever Dead, there is no Dream but Deed,
there is no Deed but Memory.

APPENDICES

REFERENCE NOTES

1. John Hope (1868-1936), born the same year as Dr. Du Bois, until his death was one of the Doctor's dearest friends. He was born in Georgia and was extremely fair of complexion; he, however, identified himself with the Negro people. He was President of Atlanta University during Du Bois' second service there; when Du Bois resigned from the NAACP, John Hope invited him back and put him at the head of the University's Department of Sociology. There is an excellent biography, *The Story of John Hope* by Ridgely Torrence (N.Y., Macmillan, 1948); this reprints Du Bois' appreciation of Hope published soon after his death in *The Pittsburgh Courier*, March 28, 1936.

2. Isabelle Blume of Belgium was and is a leader in the worldwide peace movement that developed after World War II; as an officer of the World Peace Council she played a decisive role in organizing worldwide protests against the effort by the U.S. government to jail Dr. Du Bois in 1950.

3. Father Gregory S. Petrov was one of 14 priests elected to the first Duma in 1905 in Russia. He was a fiery orator, an able publicist and a liberal in politics, verging—especially for a priest in Tsarist Russia—upon radicalism. In 1906 he was sent into exile by the Tsar and efforts to free him became a celebrated case throughout the world. *See,* John S. Curtiss, *Church and State in Russia* (N.Y., Columbia Univ. Press, 1940; reprinted, 1965, Octagon Press).

4. A delegation representing the British Trades Union Congress visited the USSR for one month commencing on November 11, 1924; it consisted of ten very prominent men in trade union, government and academic life, including Alan Findlay, Harold Grenfell, A. A. Purcell and Ben Tillett. Its "Final Report" affirmed that the USSR was a "strong and stable State" possessing the support of most of the people and one which was worthy of careful study by all. The full text makes up a volume of over 250 pages: *Russia Today: The Official Report of the British Trade Union Delegation* (N.Y., International Publishers, 1925).

5. In fact, Dr. Du Bois was buried after a State funeral, in Accra, Ghana, at the beach perhaps 100 yards from the Atlantic Ocean.

6. By "the great Mark Hopkins" Du Bois refers to the educator (1802-1887) who was President of Williams College from 1836 to 1872; from 1857 to his death, he was President of the American Board of Commissioners for Foreign Missions. President Garfield once remarked that his idea of a good college was a student at one end of a log and Mark Hopkins at the other. His nephew, Mark Hopkins, became a railroad tycoon of notoriety in connection with scandals in that industry on the West Coast.

7. The *Fisk Herald* was a paper put out in New York City in 1924-

25 largely through the efforts of Du Bois. This was part of the student rebellion at Fisk University against the administration of the white supremacist President, Fayette McKenzie; Du Bois was central in the successful effort to smash the racist President and Board of Trustees. *See* Du Bois' writings in *The Crisis,* October, 1924, and April and June, 1925, and in *The Nation,* March 3, 1926. Other rebellions among Negro students—as at Hampton in 1927—are a neglected but very important aspect of post-World War I Negro history.

8. The successor to Charles W. Eliot as President of Harvard was Abbott L. Lowell (1856-1943). Mr. Lowell assumed the Presidency in 1909 and held this office until 1933. Generally a liberal in policy and politics, he was remembered for his bitter hostility toward efforts to save Sacco and Vanzetti.

9. In September, 1895, Booker T. Washington, head of Tuskegee Institute, spoke at the Atlanta Cotton Exposition; here he projected his strategy of acquiescence in second-class citizenship on the part of the Negro people in return for white support of vocational education and assurance of more or less menial employment. The full text is in H. Aptheker, *A Documentary History of the Negro People in the U.S.* (N.Y., Citadel Press, 1951, pp. 753-57).

10. The so-called Atlanta Riot—pogrom would be more accurate—occurred in September, 1906. It was the single most outrageous instance of organized violence against the Negro to occur that decade. A local political campaign, with Negro disfranchisement as an issue, was used as the occasion, especially by the press, for whipping up fanatical chauvinism. The pogrom commenced on the evening of September 22; when, on the 24th, Negroes turned to effective self-defense, the police actively joined the mobs. Even the aged President of Atlanta University's Gammon Theological Seminary, Dr. J. E. Bowen, was beaten about the head by a uniformed sadist. Casualties came to at least two whites and ten Negroes (including two women) killed, and ten whites and 60 Negroes seriously injured. The militant Negro publication, *Voice of the Negro,* was forced to close and its editor and Du Bois' friend, J. Max Barber, forced to flee for his life to Chicago. Du Bois, then in Alabama, hastened home to his family at Atlanta; while returning he wrote his great "Litany at Atlanta."

11. Robert C. Ogden (1836-1913) was a partner in the Wanamaker stores; he devoted much of his time, however, to educational work, especially in the South. He headed the Southern Education Board and the General Education Board, was President of the Hampton Board of Trustees and a Trustee of Tuskegee. His efforts gave birth to what was called, early in the 20th century, the "Ogden movement" for Southern education.

12. The Secretaries of the NAACP were as follows: Frances Blascoer (1910-1911); Mary White Ovington (1911-1912); May Childs Nerney

(1912-1916); Mary White Ovington (January 1916 to February 1916); Royal Freeman Nash (1916-1917); James Weldon Johnson (1917 to January 1, 1918); John R. Shillady (1918-1920); James Weldon Johnson (1920-January, 1931); thereafter Walter White (until his death in 1955) and presently Roy Wilkins.

13. In the summer of 1919 white mobs, with large contingents of soldiers and sailors, attacked the Negro communities in Washington and in Chicago. Dozens were killed and scores seriously injured; in both cases, after the original assault, Negroes formed self-defense units and fought back with great effectiveness. Many other pogroms occurred in what became known as the "Red Summer" of 1919; one of these is discussed in the note that follows.

14. Negro farmers and sharecroppers in and around Elaine, Arkansas, in 1919 formed an organization for the purpose of bargaining collectively with the plantation owners; they intended to obtain wages and improvements approaching conditions suitable for human beings and also a termination of peonage. A sheriff's posse attacked their meeting; in the resistance, one deputy was shot and killed. Terror followed for three days throughout Phillips County and about 250 Negroes were killed. In a "trial"—it lasted about 45 minutes—12 Negroes were sentenced to die and 67 were given long prison sentences. In *Moore v. Dempsey* (1923), brought by the NAACP, these convictions were reversed. Du Bois wrote of this case several times; notably in *The Crisis*, February, 1920, XIX, 169*ff*.

The Sweet case refers to the attack by a mob in Detroit in 1925 upon the home of a Negro physician, Dr. O. H. Sweet, recently purchased in a "white" neighborhood. Armed resistance from the house resulted in the killing of one of the attacking mob. Dr. Sweet, his brother and some of his friends were brought to trial. The NAACP led the defense; their attorneys were Clarence Darrow and Arthur Garfield Hays, and all were finally acquitted. Du Bois' comments on the event and the trial are in *The Crisis*, January and July, 1926, XXX, 60f., XXXI, 114.

15. The biography of John Hope is mentioned in note 1, above.

16. The 4th Annual Meeting of the American Peace Congress met in St. Louis in May, 1913; it was a "correct" and respectable society and as such drew criticism at the time from Du Bois—see *The Crisis*, May, 1913, Vol. VI, p. 26; republished in his *ABC of Color*, pp. 59-60. Booker T. Washington addressed this Peace Congress; his speech may be found in, E. Davidson Washington, ed., *Selected Speeches of Booker T. Washington* (Garden City, Doubleday, Doran, 1932), pp. 213-217.

17. Late in 1958 Waldo Frank sued the State Department for validation of his passport for travel to China, where he had been invited, by the University of Peking, to deliver lectures on Walt Whitman. At about the same time, William Worthy, Jr., a correspondent for the *Afro-American* newspaper chain, also sued demand-

ing the right to visit China in his capacity as a newspaperman. Both cases went to the U.S. Supreme Court; that Court, in December, 1959, ruled against Frank and Worthy and in effect upheld the State Department's right in applying the ban.

A SELECTED BIBLIOGRAPHY OF THE PUBLISHED WRITINGS OF W. E. B. DU BOIS

This bibliography lists all books written by W. E. B. Du Bois as well as all other publications by him mentioned in this autobiography; in addition, certain other significant writings of his are included. A complete bibliography of Du Bois' published writings would cover scores of pages; but most of his more important productions will be found here.

A. BOOKS

1. *The Suppression of the African Slave Trade to the United States of America, 1638-1870* (Harvard Historical Series, No. 1), N.Y., 1896, Longmans, Green 335p. N.Y., 1965, Russell.
2. *The Philadelphia Negro: A Social Study. Together with a special report on domestic service,* by Isabel Eaton (Publications of the University of Pennsylvania. Series in Political Economy and Public Law, XLV), Phila., 1899, Published for the Univ. of Pa., 520p.
3. *The Souls of Black Folk: Essays And Sketches,* Chicago, 1903, A. C. McClurg, 264p. N.Y., 1964, Fawcett.
4. *John Brown* (American Crisis Biographies), Phila., 1909, George W. Jacobs, 406p. Revised edition, with new preface and conclusion by author, N.Y., 1962, International Publishers, 414p.
5. *The Quest of the Silver Fleece,* Chicago, 1911, A. C. McClurg, 434p.
6. *The Negro* (Home University Library of Modern Knowledge, XCI), N.Y., 1915, Henry Holt, 254p.
7. *Darkwater: Voices from within the Veil,* N.Y., 1920, Harcourt, Brace, 276p.
8. *The Gift of Black Folk: Negroes in the Making of America,* Boston, 1924, Stratford Co., 349p.
9. *Dark Princess: A Romance,* N.Y., 1928, Harcourt, Brace, 311p.
10. *Africa: Its Geography, People and Products* (63p.) and *Africa, Its Place in History* (63p.) both published as separate booklets, Girard, Kansas, 1930, Haldeman-Julius ("Blue Books").
11. *Black Reconstruction in America, 1860-1880,* N.Y., 1935, Harcourt, Brace, 746p. Cleveland, 1962, Meridian.
12. *Black Folk, Then and Now: An Essay in the History and Sociology of the Negro Race,* N.Y., 1939, Henry Holt, 401p.
13. *Dusk of Dawn: An Essay toward an Autobiography of a Race Concept,* N.Y., 1940, Harcourt, Brace, 334p.
14. *Encyclopedia of the Negro: Preparatory Volume with Reference*

* Books so marked are now (1967) in print.

Lists and Reports (with Guy B. Johnson), N.Y., 1945, Phelps-Stokes Fund, 208p.

15. *Color and Democracy: Colonies and Peace,* N.Y., 1945, Harcourt, Brace, 143p.

16. **The World and Africa: An Inquiry into the part which Africa has played in world history,* N.Y., 1947, Viking, 276p. Enlarged edition, with new writings by the author, 1955-1961, N.Y., 1965, International Publishers, 364p.

17. *In Battle for Peace: The Story of My 83rd Birthday* (with comment by Shirley Graham), N.Y., 1952, Masses & Mainstream, 192p.

18. *The Ordeal of Mansart* (Volume one of *The Black Flame*), N.Y., 1957, Mainstream, 316p.

19. *Mansart Builds a School* (Volume two of *The Black Flame*), N.Y., 1959, Mainstream, 367p.

20. *Worlds of Color* (Volume three of *The Black Flame*), N.Y., 1961, Mainstream, 349p.

21. *An ABC of Color: Selections from over a Half Century of the Writings of W. E. B. Du Bois,* Berlin, 1963, Seven Seas, 214p. (The selection was made by Du Bois; the book appeared shortly before his death.)

B. Volumes Edited by Du Bois

The following volumes all were published in Atlanta, Georgia, by the Atlanta University Press; they constituted the Proceedings of the Annual Conferences on the Negro Problem organized by Du Bois and held at the University:

1. *Social and Physical Condition of Negroes in Cities,* 1897, 86p.

2. *Some Efforts of American Negroes for Their Own Social Betterment,* 1898, 66p.

3. *The Negro in Business,* 1899, 77p.

4. *The College-Bred Negro,* 1900, 115p. (New and revised editions were issued in 1902 and 1911.)

5. *The Negro Common School,* 1901, 120p.

6. *The Negro Artisan,* 1902, 192p.

7. *The Negro Church,* 1903, 212p.

8. *Some Notes on Negro Crime, Particularly in Georgia,* 1904, 68p.

9. *The Health and Physique of the Negro American,* 1906, 112p.

10. *Economic Cooperation among Negro Americans,* 1907, 184p.

11. *The Negro American Family,* 1908, 156p.

12. *Efforts for Social Betterment among Negro Americans,* 1910, 136p. (See the volume issued in 1898, above.)

13. *The Common School and the Negro American,* 1912, 140p. (See the volume issued in 1901, above.)

* Books so marked are now (1967) in print.

14. *The Negro American Artisan,* 1913, 144p. (See the volume issued in 1902, above.)

15. *Morals and Manners among Negro Americans,* 1915, 136p.

C. Pamphlets, Essays, Articles

Selected with an eye to biographical consequence, historical signifi-cance and reference in this volume.

1. "The Enforcement of the Slave-Trade Laws," *Annual Report of the American Historical Association for the Year 1891* (Senate Misc. Doc., 173, 52nd Cong., 1st Sess., Washington, 1892), pp. 161-74.

2. "The Study of Negro Problems," *Annals of the American Academy of Political and Social Science* (Publications # 219), 1898, XI, 1-23.

3. "A Negro Schoolmaster in the New South," *Atlantic Monthly,* January, 1899, 83: 99-104.

4. "The Negro in the Black Belt: Some Social Sketches," *Bulletin of the [U.S.] Department of Labor,* May, 1899, 4: 401-417.

5. "The Suffrage Fight in Georgia," *Independent,* November 30, 1899, 51: 3226-28.

6. "The Freedmen's Bureau," *Atlantic Monthly,* March, 1901, 87: 354-65.

7. "The Storm and Stress in the Black World," *Dial,* April 16, 1901, 30: 262-64.

8. "Results of Ten Tuskegee Conferences," *Harper's Weekly,* June 22, 1901, 45: 641-45.

9. "The Relation of the Negroes to the Whites in the South," *Annals of the American Academy of Political and Social Science,* July, 1901, 18: 121-140.

10. "The Negro Landholder of Georgia," *Bulletin of the [U.S.] Department of Labor,* July, 1901, 6: 647-777.

11. "The Black North" (a series of five articles dealing with New York City, two articles; Philadelphia and Boston, one article each; and a final article, "Some Conclusions"), *New York Times Magazine Supplement,* November 17, 24, December 1, 8, 15, 1901.

12. "The Opening of the Library," *Independent,* April 3, 1902, 54: 809-10.

13. "Of the Training of Black Men," *Atlantic Monthly,* September, 1902, 90: 289-97.

14. "Possibilities of the Negro: The Advance Guard of the Race," *Booklover's Magazine,* July, 1903, 2: 2-15.

15. "The Laboratory in Sociology at Atlanta," *Annals of the American Academy of Political and Social Science,* May, 1903, 21: 160-63.

16. "The Talented Tenth," in Booker T. Washington, *et al., The Negro Problem,* N.Y., 1903, James Pott Co., pp. 31-75.

17. "The Training of Negroes for Social Power," *Outlook,* Oct. 17, 1903, 75: 409-14.

18. "The Negro Problem from the Negro Point of View: The Part ing of the Ways," *World Today*, April, 1904, 6: 521-23.

19. "The Development of a People," *International Journal of Ethics*, April, 1904, 14: 291-311.

20. "Credo," *Independent*, October 6, 1904, 57: 787. (Next only to *Souls of Black Folk*, this one-page essay was more widely read and reprinted than any other single piece of writing by Du Bois.)

21. "The Negro Farmer," *Negroes in the United States (Bulletin, No. 8, Department of Commerce and Labor, Bureau of the Census),* Washington, 1904, 69-98.

22. "The Southerner's Problem," *Dial*, May 1, 1905, 38: 315-19.

23. "The Niagara Movement," *Voice of the Negro,* September, 1905, 2: 619-22.

24. "The Economic Future of the Negro," *Publications of the American Economic Association,* February, 1906, 7 (3rd ser.): 219-42.

25. "A Litany at Atlanta," *Independent*, October 11, 1906, 61: 856-58. (Du Bois' best-known poem, widely anthologized; written after the massacre that year in that city.)

26. "The Color Line Belts the World," *Collier's*, October 20, 1906, 28:30.

27. "The Negro Farmer," U.S. 12th Census, *Special Reports: Supplementary Analysis and Derivative Tables,* Washington, 1906, 511-79.

28. *"Die Negerfrage in den Vereinigten Staaten," Archiv für Sozialwissenschaft und Sozialpolitik* (Tubingen), 1906, 22: 31-79. (This article on "The Negro Question in the U.S." was written at the request of the journal's editor, the renowned Max Weber, who had met Du Bois upon his visit to the United States in 1904.)

29. "Negro and Socialism," *Horizon*, February, 1907, 1: 7-8.

30. "The Economic Revolution in the South," and "Religion in the South," in *The Negro in the South: His Economic Progress in Relation to His Moral and Religious Development,* Philadelphia, 1907, pp. 79-122; 125-91.

31. "Race Friction Between Black and White," *American Journal of Sociology,* May, 1908, 13: 834-38.

32. "National Committee on the Negro," *Survey*, June 12, 1909, 22: 407-09. (Describes the organizational meeting resulting in the NAACP.)

33. "The Economic Aspects of Race Prejudice," *Editorial Review,* May, 1910, 2: 488-93. (This essay was given as an address at the New York City Republican Club, March 5, 1910, and was printed in pamphlet form that year by that Club.)

34. "The Negro Race in the United States," in G. Spiller, ed., *Papers on Inter-Racial Problems,* London & Boston, 1911 (published by P. S. King, and by World's Peace Foundation), pp. 348-64. (This is the paper delivered by Du Bois at the Universal Races Congress held in London in July, 1911.)

35. *Disfranchisement*, N.Y., 1912, National Woman Suffrage Association, 11p. (Du Bois argues for women suffrage.)

36. "Socialism and the Negro Problem," *New Review*, February 1, 1913, 1: 138-41.

37. "The Negro in Literature and Art," *Annals of the American Academy of Political and Social Science*, September, 1913, 49: 233-37.

38. "Booker T. Washington," *Crisis*, December, 1915, 11: 82. (An estimate written immediately after Washington's death.)

39. "Of the Culture of White Folk," *Journal of Race Development*, April, 1917, 7: 434-47.

40. "The Black Man and the Unions," *Crisis*, March, 1918, 15: 216-17.

41. "Close Ranks," *Crisis*, July, 1918, 16: 111. (Du Bois' enunciation of tactics and struggle during the War—and after.)

42. "The Pan-African Congress," *Crisis*, April, 1919, 17: 271-74.

43. "Documents of the War," *Crisis*, May, 1919, 18: 16-21 (Du Bois' sensational exposure of army racism.)

44. "An Essay Toward a History of the Black Man in the Great War," *Crisis*, June, 1919, 18: 63-87. (One of the few projects Du Bois undertook and never completed was a full history of the Negro's participation in the First World War; this essay is the fullest of his publications on this subject.)

45. "On Being Black," *New Republic*, February 18, 1920, 21: 338-41.

46. "The Republicans and the Black Voter," *Nation*, June 5, 1920, 110: 757-58.

47. "Marcus Garvey," *Crisis*, December, 1920, 21: 58-60.

48. "Socialism and the Negro," *Crisis*, October, 1921, 22: 245-47.

49. "Gandhi and India," *Crisis*, March, 1922, 23: 203-07.

50. "The South and a Third Party," *New Republic*, January 3, 1923, 33: 138-41.

51. "To the American Federation of Labor," *Crisis*, August, 1924, 28: 153-54.

52. "The Dilemma of the Negro," *American Mercury*, October, 1924, 3: 179-85.

53. "Georgia: Invisible Empire," in Ernest Gruening, ed., *These United States*, N.Y., 1924 (2 vols.), II, pp. 322-45. (Reprinted in *Nation*, January 21, 1925.)

54. "What Is Civilization? Africa's Answer," *Forum*, February, 1925, 73: 178-88.

55. "Worlds of Color," *Foreign Affairs*, April, 1925, 3: 423-44.

56. "The Negro Mind Reaches Out," in Alain Locke, ed., *The New Negro: An Interpretation*, N.Y., 1925, pp. 383-414.

57. "The Shape of Fear," *North American Review*, June, 1926, 228: 291-304.

58. "Judging Russia," *Crisis*, February, 1927, 33: 189-90.

59. "The Hampton Strike," *Nation*, November 2, 1927, 125: 471-72.

60. "The Name 'Negro'," *Crisis*, March, 1928, 35: 96-97.

61. "Race Relations in the U.S.," *Annals of the American Academy of Political and Social Science*, November, 1928, 140: 6-10.

62. "The Defeat of Judge Parker," *Crisis*, July, 1930, 37: 225-27, 248.

63. "Communists and the Color Line," *Crisis*, September, 1931, 38: 315.

64. "The Depression," *Crisis*, December, 1931, 38: 431-32.

65. "Will the Church Remove the Color Line?" *Christian Century*, December 9, 1931, 48: 1554-56.

66. "Education and Work," *Howard University Bulletin*, January, 1931, 9: 17-20. (Commencement Address at Howard University, June 6, 1931.)

67. "Karl Marx and the Negro," *Crisis*, March, 1933, 40: 55-56.

68. "Marxism and the Negro Problem," *Crisis*, May, 1933, 40: 103-04, 118.

69. "A Negro Nation Within the Nation," *Current History*, June, 1935, 42: 265-70.

70. "Inter-Racial Implications of the Ethiopian Crisis," *Foreign Affairs*, October, 1935, 14: 82-92.

71. "Social Planning for the Negro: Past and Present," *Journal of Negro Education*, January, 1936, 5: 110-25.

72. "The Revelation of St. Orgne the Damned," *Fisk News*, November-December, 1938, 12: 3-9.

73. "Black Africa Tomorrow," *Foreign Affairs*, October, 1938, 17: 100-10.

74. "The Position of the Negro in the American Social Order: Where Do We Go From Here?" *Journal of Negro Education*, July, 1939, 8: 351-70.

75. "A Program for Negro Land Grant Colleges," *Proceedings, 19th Annual Conference, Presidents of Negro Land Grant Colleges*, November, 1941, Chicago, 1941, 42-57.

76. "Chronicle of Race Relations," *Phylon*, 1942, 3: 105-15.

77. "The Realities in Africa," *Foreign Affairs*, July, 1943, 21: 721-32.

78. "Reconstruction: Seventy-Five Years After," *Phylon*, 1943, 4: 205-12.

79. "Prospects of a World Without Race Conflict," *American Journal of Sociology*, March, 1944, 49: 450-56.

80. "Jacob and Esau," *Talladegan*, November, 1944, 42: 1-6. (Text of Commencement Address, Talledega College, June 5, 1944.)

81. "What He Meant to the Negro," *New Masses*, April 24, 1945, 55:9. (An estimate of President Roosevelt.)

82. "Colonies and Moral Responsibility," *Journal of Negro Education*, Summer, 1946, 15: 311-18.

83. "Common Objectives," *Soviet Russia Today*, August, 1946, 15: 13, 32-33.

84. "A Crisis at Fisk," *Nation,* September 7, 1946, 143: 269-70.

85. "Behold the Land," *New Masses,* January 14, 1947, 62: 18-20. (Text of an address delivered at meeting of Southern Negro Youth Congress held in 1946 in Columbia, S.C.)

86. "Can the Negro Expect Freedom by 1965?" *Negro Digest,* April, 1947, 5: 4-9.

87. "The Pan-African Movement," in George Padmore, ed., *Colonial and Coloured Unity, a Program of Action: History of the Pan-African Congress,* Manchester (England), 1947, Panaf Services, pp. 13-26.

88. "The Most Hopeful State in the World," *Soviet Russia Today,* November, 1947, 16:24.

89. *Appeal to the World,* N.Y., 1947, NAACP, 94p. (This is the petition from the National Association for the Advancement of Colored People presented to the United Nations protesting against jim-crow in the United States.)

90. "From McKinley to Wallace: My Fifty Years as a Political Independent," *Masses & Mainstream,* August, 1948, 1: 3-13.

91. "Race Relations in the U.S., 1917-1947," *Phylon,* 1948, 9: 234-47.

92. "The Negro Since 1900: A Progress Report," *New York Times Magazine,* November 21, 1948, 24, 54-57.

93. "Negroes and the Crisis of Capitalism in the U.S.," *Monthly Review,* April, 1950, 4: 178-85.

94. "American Negroes and Africa," *National Guardian,* February 14, 1955.

95. "Pan-Africa: A Mission in My Life," *United Asia,* April, 1955, 7: 65-70.

96. "Colonialism and the Russian Revolution," *New World Review,* November, 1956, 24: 18-22.

97. "The Negro and Socialism," in Helen Alfred, ed., *Toward a Socialist America,* N.Y., 1958, Peace Publications, 178-91.

98. "China and Africa," *New World Review,* April, 1959, 27: 28-31.

99. "The Negro People and the United States," *Freedomways,* Spring, 1961, 1: 11-19.

A CALENDAR OF THE PUBLIC LIFE
OF W. E. B. DU BOIS

1868 (February 23): Birth at Great Barrington, Mass.

1883-1885: Western Massachusetts correspondent for *New York Age, New York Globe* and *Freeman*; and Great Barrington correspondent for *Springfield Republican*.

1884: Graduates from High School in Great Barrington; valedictorian speaker, subject: "Wendell Phillips."

1885-1888: Attends Fisk University, Nashville, Tenn., receiving B.A. in 1888; teaches in country schools during summers.

1887-1888: Chief editor of the *Fisk Herald*.

1888: Enters Harvard as a junior.

1890: Graduates, B.A., *cum laude* in a Harvard class of 300; is one of six Commencement speakers, subject: "Jefferson Davis: Representative of Civilization"; attracts national attention.

1892: Awarded, after considerable effort, a Slater Fund Fellowship for Graduate Study abroad.

1892-1894: Graduate student, mostly history and economics, at University of Berlin; also considerable travel in Europe.

1894-1896: Professor of Greek and Latin, Wilberforce University, Ohio.

1896: Ph.D. degree from Harvard University.

1896-1897: Assistant Instructor in Sociology, University of Pennsylvania.

1897-1910: Professor of Economics and History, Atlanta University.

1897-1911: Organizer of the annual Atlanta University Studies of the Negro Problem; editor of their Annual Publications.

1900: Secretary, First Pan-African Conference in England.

1905-1909: Founder and General Secretary of The Niagara Movement.

1906: Founder and editor of *The Moon,* published in Tennessee.

1907-1910: Chief founder and an editor of *The Horizon,* published in Washington, D.C.

1909: Among original founders and incorporators of The National Association for the Advancement of Colored People (NAACP).

1910-1934: Director of Publicity and Research, Member, Board of Directors, NAACP.

1910: Founder and editor of *The Crisis* (until 1934); joins Socialist Party.

1911: Participates in First Universal Races Congress in England.

1912: Supports Woodrow Wilson in Presidential campaign; helps organize first significant Negro breakaway from Republican Party; resigns from Socialist Party.

1913: Joins Editorial Board of *The New Review,* a radical, socialist-oriented magazine published in New York City.

1917-1918: Supports U.S. entry into World War; fights maltreatment of Negro troops; leads in efforts to enroll Negro officers; leads massive Silent Protest Parade (1917) down Fifth Avenue, New York City, against lynching and jim-crow.

1919: Investigates, for NAACP, racist treatment of Negro troops in Europe; exposure creates international sensation. Chief organizer of Modern Pan-African Movement, with First Conference held in Paris.

1920: Leader in exposing role of U.S. in Haiti.

1920-1921: Founder and editor of *The Brownies' Book,* a magazine for children.

1921: Second Pan-African Congress, London, Brussels and Paris.

1923: Spingarn Medalist; Special Minister Plenipotentiary and Envoy Extraordinary Representing the United States at Inauguration of President of Liberia; Third Pan-African Congress in London, Paris and Lisbon.

1926: First and extensive visit to the Soviet Union.

1927: Leader in so-called "Negro Renaissance" Movement; founds the Negro Theatre in Harlem called the "Krigwa Players"; Fourth Pan-African Congress in New York.

1933: Leading force in undertaking to produce an *Encyclopedia of the Negro.*

1934: Resigns from *The Crisis* and Board of NAACP.

1934-1944: Chairman, Department of Sociology, Atlanta University.

1936: Trip around the world.

1940: Founder and editor (to 1944) of *Phylon* Magazine, Atlanta.

1943: Organizer, First Conference of Negro Land-Grant Colleges.

1944: Extended visits to Haiti and Cuba.

1944: Returns to NAACP as Director of Special Research; holds this position to 1948.

1945: With Walter White, accredited from the NAACP as Consultant to Founding Convention of United Nations; seeks firm anti-colonial commitment on part of the United States; presides at 5th Pan-African Congress in Manchester, England.

1947: Edits, on behalf of NAACP, and presents to the UN, "An Appeal to the World," protesting jim-crow in the United States.

1948: Co-Chairman, Council on African Affairs.

1949: Helps organize, Cultural and Scientific Conference for World Peace, New York City; attends Paris Peace Congress; attends Moscow Peace Congress.

1950: Chairman, Peace Information Center; candidate in New York for U.S. Senator, Progressive Party.

1950-1951: Indictment, trial and acquittal on charge of "unregistered foreign agent" in connection with leadership of Peace Information Center.

1958-1959: Extensive journeys, especially to USSR and China.

1961: Joins the Communist Party of the United States.

1961: At invitation of President Nkrumah, takes up residence in Ghana as Director of *Encyclopaedia Africana* project.

1963: Becomes a citizen of Ghana.

1963: Dies (August 27); given a State funeral; lies buried in Accra.

ADDITIONAL NOTE

Calendar arrangement necessarily omits whole areas of Dr. Du Bois' public life. Thus, he performed economic and sociological studies for the U.S. Census Bureau and the U.S. Department of Agriculture; he wrote weekly columns for many years in various newspapers including the *Chicago Defender,* the *Pittsburgh Courier,* the *New York Amsterdam News* and the *San Francisco Chronicle.* Dr. Du Bois delivered thousands of lectures in colleges, churches, halls, schools in every State in the United States and in many countries of the world, as Great Britain, France, China, Japan, Cuba, Haiti, Hungary, the Soviet Union, Czechoslovakia, etc. He wrote poetry that is in many anthologies; his dramatic pageants were performed before thousands in New York, Philadelphia, Washington and Los Angeles. He helped inspire hundreds of novelists, poets, playwrights, sculptors, musicians and scientists not only by his work and example, but by direct assistance. And always he was a fighter and organizer against racism, colonialism, imperialism, illiteracy, poverty and war. One of his earliest significant essays—written while an undergraduate at Fisk in 1887—was entitled "An Open Letter to the Southern People," and was an appeal for civilized conduct and an attack upon jim-crow; among his last acts was to inspire a protest march upon the U.S. Embassy in Accra, in August, 1963 (the month of his death), in solidarity with the historic "March for Jobs and Freedom" to Washington that month.

Du Bois' honors were many: Fellow and Life Member, American Association for the Advancement of Science; Member, National Institute of Arts and Letters; Knight Commander of the Liberian Order of African Redemption; International Peace Prize; Lenin Peace Prize; and Honorary Degrees from: Fisk University, Howard University, Atlanta University, Wilberforce University, Morgan State College, University of Berlin, Charles University (Prague) and University of Ghana.

INDEX